3-18-467-97dt

17.95

MANAGING FEDERALISM:

Evolution and Development
of the
Grant-in-Aid System

MANAGING FEDERALISM:
Evolution and Development
of the
Grant-in-Aid System

by
Raymond A. Shapek

Foreword by
Wayne F. Anderson

Published by

CHARLOTTESVILLE,
VIRGINIA

1981

MANAGING FEDERALISM:
Evolution and Development
of the
Grant-in-Aid System

By Raymond A. Shapek

Foreword by Wayne F. Anderson

Published by Community Collaborators
P.O. Box 5429
Charlottesville, VA 22905

Library of Congress Catalog Card Number: 80-65751
International Standard Book Number: 0-930388-05-4

First Edition 1981

Contents

Chapter III: The Administrative Impacts of New Federalism

Chapter IV: Management Capacity Development: Administrative Adjustment Following the Era of New Federalism

Chapter V: General Revenue Sharing

Chapter VI: Grant Consolidation: History and Perspectives

Chapter VII: Managing Federalism

List of Tables and Figures

Foreword

By Wayne F. Anderson, Executive Director
U.S. Advisory Commission on Intergovernmental Relations

When Dr. Shapek invited me to write this introduction, he must have known he would get ACIR's hard-earned point of view and bias on the federal grant-in-aid system. I, however, can present our wares in good conscience because I believe our Commission's conclusions appropriately place his book in context and illuminate its value.

The well-known story of the billowing entangled growth of the federal grant system has unfolded largely since 1960. From about 130 programs costing $7 billion per year then, the system had burgeoned to 498 programs costing $83 billion by 1979. General Revenue Sharing and five block grants, which offer broader discretion to the state and local government recipients, have been created, but the 492 categorical programs, most of them for quite narrow purposes, still typify the system, represent over three-quarters of the money, and are the principal target of critics. Federal aid regulations, particularly the national policy requirements, have expanded even faster than the system and have been the major means of centralizing decision-making in Washington and requiring uniformity in so many fields across the nation.

ACIR, between 1974 and 1978, devoted a large part of its resources to probing the federal grant system, which dominates and pervades all corners of our intergovernmental relations world. Our initial foremost motive was to illuminate how grants could be designed better so as to improve the chances that their objectives would be achieved. This 14-volume federal aid tour de force has been followed by two years of work on "The Federal Role in the Federal System." Here, we first concentrated on gaining a better understanding of the forces accounting for the rapid expansion in federal functions and programs. Then, we moved on to identifying means by which present federal functions, where advantageous, might be converted to direct federal servicing operations or devolved to state and local governments or the private sector. Thus, our federal role study is, basically, an extension of our work on federal grants.

Concerns As We Now See Them

While we rightfully concentrate on the federal grant system's problems and desirable reforms, the accomplishments of the system should not be denied or minimized. Actions addressing numerous human and societal problems have been generated by these federal programs, many of which were and are well conceived and skillfully administered. However, ACIR's conclusions and current concerns pertain less to individual programs and more to the effects of the overall system. In the aggregate, ineffectiveness, waste, underfunding and overpromising, increasing local government dependency, and endless stories about the ridiculous results that occur when a national mold does not fit local circumstances are prime signs of the federal grant system's growing dysfunctionality.

ACIR's central finding is that the almost 500 federal grant programs have overloaded and over-intergovernmentalized our federal system. Critically-positioned parties to our democratic process have been swamped. No system can perform well under the conditions of information over-load and administrative complexity that we have faced since the federal government has moved into nearly all the domestic service fields. As is richly documented, Congress often cannot give more than superficial consideration to a $100 million program anymore. The federal government has taken on wholly new functions with little awareness or without debate of the federalism issues that marked our pre-1960 history. Presidents, in the words of one historian, have come to act like mayors, and there is grave concern about the decline of the Presidency, with overload as one cause. States and local governments, to varying degrees depending on how many federal programs they are involved in, also have suffered overload consequences. In the words of John Gardner, the national government tends "to export its own chaos on down the line." Governors, mayor, legislators, and generalist administrators, if they try at all, have a hard time wresting the field from functional specialists. Every major function of government is delivered now by a combination of federal, state, and local action. Think of the maze of often invisible relationships that require building, tending, and overseeing.

It may be, however, that the overload consequences are most grave in the citizen action realm. If members of Congress and the Executive Branch cannot cope with the flood of matters which come before them, how many of their constituents can have more than the vaguest idea of the multifarious business conducted in their name? How many can comprehend enough of the complexity to function effectively as citizens? Is it any wonder that they despair of influencing government program-by-program and resort to overall clamp-downs on taxing and spending?

Strategy For Improving the System

On the basis of its diagnosis of the problem, our Commission fashioned a five-point strategy for improving the federal grant system. Specifically, the Commission recommended that the Congress and the President give full attention to:

1. A joint effort to simplify and standardize the procedures and requirements of federal assistance programs. They stressed that progress is absolutely dependent upon joint Congressional and Executive Branch action and that without a joint approach to federal grants management, there is no effective approach.

2. The merger of the almost 500 grant programs into a much smaller number of block grants and broader categorical programs.

3. Careful assessment, both before and after their enactment, of the impact of generally applicable grant regulations and procedures, including the federal capacity to enforce them fairly and uniformly, and of the costs as well as the benefits.

4. Ongoing evaluation of the achievements, shortcomings, and impacts of federal grant programs, and the related need to exercise greater care in the design of grant instruments.

5. Reexamination of the functional responsibilities of the federal, state, and local levels, including assessment of the desirabilities of fully nationalizing some functions while reducing, eliminating, or forestalling federal involvement in others, including consideration of the possible use of instruments other than grants-in-aid to realize national objectives.

How This Book Relates To The Strategy

As ACIR's strategy implies, we concluded that it is absolutely necessary that the nation progress along all five tracks. We are convinced that the aid system is overloaded, and we try to demolish any lingering thought that one can deal with this tangle by just traveling the familiar administrative simplification and standardization route. It can't be done. The system itself, not just its administration, must be simplified.

While strongly believing that administrative simplification and standardization is only one of the approaches to be pursued, we believe it is a very important, very large, and never ending pursuit. This book pertains more to the administrative simplification and standardization strategy than to the other four, but it relates to all five in substantial ways. Dr. Shapek's title for this book is *Managing Federalism: Evolution and Development of the Grant-In-Aid System.* "Managing," however, as he uses the term, is much broader than the Executive Branch administrative activities. Managing also encompasses activities involved in consolidating programs, bringing order to regulations, evaluating and designing better programs, and reexamining what functions should be federal responsibilities. The content of this book, therefore, is of roughly equal interest and utility to administrators, Congressional participants, state and local recipients, interest groups, and other participants and educators.

This book, I found, is a rich offering, bringing within two covers the history of the grant-in-aid system, through the "cooperative federalism," "new federalism," and subsequent periods; the sagas leading to the embattled General Revenue Sharing program and the five block grants, which lend abundant testimony to the scope and complexity of efforts to improve administration; and finally some ponderings about the current condition of American federalism. Running through the book is the implication with much evidence that the central management of the system is and always has been weak, and that it would be good business for the nation to spend enough dollars and political chips to achieve strong central management of this $83 billion system. Given all of the acronyms and circulars that must dot any book on the federal grant system, which for many people are guaranteed soporifics, perhaps the most remarkable attribute of this book is that it is so readable. I recommend the reading of the following chapters to anyone who is associated with the federal aid system in any capacity and to anyone who thinks he/she might be.

Preface

Managing Federalism is the culmination of five years of research on the evolution and development of the federal grant-in-aid system. It is an attempt to describe and explain the workings of a complex system that is not readily understood. Many texts have been written on segments of the intergovernmental system. Most federal program managers are extremely knowledgeable about their own programs and often those of their agencies, but few are knowledgeable and *understand* the workings of the entire federal assistance system: its origins, interrelationships, and components. One reason for this disparity is the fragmented nature of the system itself, which results in a complex interplay between the Congress, the Executive Branch, and state and local governments. Another reason is the nature of virtually any public assistance system — the vertical relationships between the funding and recipient agencies; the political pressures exerted by public interest and recipient groups; external forces such as inflation, resource scarcity, and the pressures of a changing society. All of these forces and factors dictate the course of program development, resource distribution, allocation, and purpose.

The grant-in-aid system has been changing at an increasing pace, especially over the past five years. To understand its present condition, it is necessary to look at the origins of the assistance system and how its components came into being which this text does through a mixture of explanation and analysis. The flow of the narrative is interrupted from time to time in order to explain more fully a special program, part of the system, or a relationship that is especially significant. Because of this stylistic choice, this book reads differently than most college-level texts. *Managing Federalism* presents the material in a manner suited to a practitioner-oriented workshop as well as a classroom.

The primary purpose of *Managing Federalism* is to discuss and bring into context the administrative and management features of the intergovernmental grant-in-aid system from a federal or national perspective. The state and local components are also important but deliberatively have not been emphasized, partly because they are covered adequately elsewhere,* and partly to allow the reader to focus on the problems of change from a national perspective. Politics, in the traditional sense, also are not emphasized except where they have affected the shape of the system. Thus, presidential prerogatives, Congressional concerns, and especially Office of Management and Budet interagency actions, many of which are basically political in nature, have been included. A stress on state and local political considerations, impact assessments, and a concentration on fiscal effects at these levels has been excluded. Including these important considerations would have increased significantly the size of the text and would have hindered the primary purpose of explaining the workings of the system.

* For example, see Deil S. Wright, *Understanding Intergovernmental Relations* (North Scituate, Mass.: Duxbury press, 1978); and Peter Passell and Leonard Ross, *State Politics and Federal Programs* (New York: Praeger Pub., 1978).

It is clear that the intergovernmental grant-in-aid system is undergoing a metamorphosis; it has evolved from the era of "New Federalism" in the early 1970's to new and different relationships between the system's primary actors — the federal, state, and local governments. This change began with the "Great Society" programs of the Johnson Administration, was given a management thrust under Presidents Nixon, Ford, and Carter and now is in a period of adjustment, reassessment, and expected reform. The Congress, the Administration, and the general public are ready for reform. We have entered an era where wholesale reform of the system is being demanded. The past 20 years have witnessed a multitude of special studies, Presidential commissions, and Congressional and Administration proposals for change, but none have been comprehensive in scope nor seriously considered. Piecemeal changes and adjustments have occurred. Federal Assistance Review (FAR), development of the OMB Circular system, passage of the Intergovernmental Cooperation Act of 1968, general revenue sharing and block grants all have represented adjustments. The more recent changes resulting from the Federal Grant and Cooperative Agreement Act of 1977 are too new to evaluate at this time.

Today, good management is viewed as a general response to inefficiency, better productivity, and increased operational effectiveness at all levels of industry and government. The federal government has embraced enthusiastically program budgeting, systems analysis, management by objectives, organizational development, planning, and zero-base budgeting as means of controlling the growth and development of federal programs and solving inherent systemic management problems. On the horizon, however, is a new reform effort that has captured the attention of all serious students of the system.

This new reform mode is evident in the gradual shaping of omnibus legislation and in a Congressional authorization to OMB to conduct a comprehensive study of the federal assistance system as a basis for developing a legislative reform package that will be acceptable to all participants in the intergovernmental system. This directive was contained in the Federal Grant and Cooperative Agreement Act of 1977 (P.L. 95-224).

Intergovernmental relations as a descriptor of Congressional, federal-state-local, regional, and public-and-private-sector interactions does not capture the thrust or complexity of the intergovernmental system today. Nor does the concept of "federalism" mean, in practice, what was described, in theory, in the *Federalist Papers*. What is clear is that these relationships have evolved and that a reinterpretation of the partnership between the various actors comprising the system is required.

We have entered a new era of intergovernmental complexity, both vertically (between levels of government) and horizontally (between competing jurisdictions). Both internal forces (programmatic growth) and external forces (world and domestic events) have led to actions by the national, state, and local governments which are impossible to predict or control. After years of study, observation, and participation, students of the system have concluded that no action by the federal government, alone, can correct the problems of the grant-in-aid system; however, as the primary and most important actor, the actions of the federal government can exert the most influence toward meaningful reform.

We have entered a new era of federalism characterized by federal, state, and local governmental management initiatives. These administrative alterations represent an attempt by all levels of government to gain understanding and a measure of control of the almost $83 billion in federal grant-in-aid being funneled to state and local governments through over 1,000 federal programs. The federal government has become vitally concerned with how these resources are being utilized. One effort to measure state and local assistance needs was the assessment performed by the OMB/NSF Study Committee on Policy Management Assistance, which represents the fourth chapter of this text. The other chapters discuss where we are today and how we entered an era of intergovernmental administration and management initiatives.

Use of The Text

This book is primarily intended for use as a text in advanced undergraduate and graduate courses in state and local government. There is an increasing number of university political science, sociology, and public administration programs offering grant-in-aid or intergovernmental "relations" courses where this text will be useful in exploring the development of policy in its formative stages and the little-understood area of administration associated with the grant-in-aid system.

Chapter Explanation

Chapter I outlines the history of American federalism as it relates to the grant-in-aid system. The mechanics and operational machinery are discussed.

Chapter II focuses on the intergovernmental coordination mechanisms that have emerged in an effort to control or manage the system.

Chapter III discusses the origins, thrusts, and administrative impacts of the New Federalism and how the current problems and solutions are related to these precedents.

Chapter IV presents the federal attempts to deal with the residual impacts of the devolution/decentralization thrusts of the New Federalism era. It includes a detailed examination of the work of the OMB/NSF Study Committee on Policy Management Assistance and federal efforts to measure the management capabilities of user governments.

Chapter V covers the history, development, and implementation of General Revenue Sharing. The material is presented as a case study in federal program development and implementation.

Chapter VI includes a description of categorical grants, focusing on four major block-grant programs: Partnership for Health, Omnibus Crime Control and Safe Streets, Comprehensive Employment and Training, and Housing and Community Development.

The final chapter explores the current situation. Chapter VII includes discussions of the administrative and management initiatives of the Carter Administration's domestic policy; the national Urban Plan; and a series of studies currently being conducted by Congress, the White House, and OMB to develop a framework for control of the grant-in-aid system.

Acknowledgements

I wish to acknowledge three people who have proved especially helpful in the development of this text and in providing me with an opportunity to become a part of the intergovernmental system. I owe many thanks to Mr. Joe Robertson, currently Executive Director of the National Association of Schools of Public Affairs and Administration. As Director of the Bureau of Intergovernmental Personnel Programs, U.S. Civil Service Commission, Joe provided me with my first experiences with federal intergovernmental program management.

I also wish to recognize Dr. M. Frank Hersman who, as Director of the Intergovernmental Science and Utilization Program of the National Science Foundation, thrust me into the system by making me a staff member of the OMB/NSF Study Committee on Policy Management Assistance. What I learned in one year of practical experience far exceeded what I took from three years of graduate school courses.

Finally, I must note the opportunity provided by Alexander J. Greene who, as Director of the Grants Administration Division, Environmental Protection Agency, brought me back to Washington, D.C., and permitted me to reappraise how the grant-in-aid system had changed and where it stands today.

These three people have been important to both my professional and personal life. I owe them debts that I can never repay, but ones that I shall never forget.

I would be remiss in not acknowledging the contributions of my wife, Laurie, who encouraged me and spent many hours of her free time typing the manuscript, being patient, and assisting me in every way.

I also owe special thanks to Dan Sloan, Phil Rutledge, Ann Macaluso, Joe Julianelle, Tom Hadd, Vincent Puritano, Dave Richtmann, Bob Crawford, Jay Stein, Bob Joyce, Alan Heuerman, Linda Jones, Edi Stugart, Pat Conklin, Len Burchman, Juanita Blankenship, Quiniten Buechner, Ross Clayton, Norm Paulhaus, Ken Tharp, Dave Beam, Dennis Tirpak, Steve Gage, Dick Marland, and Arthur Richards who all encouraged or assisted me and affected my life in one way or another.

Raymond A. Shapek

About the Author

Dr. Raymond A. Shapek received his MPA and Ph.D. degrees from the University of Colorado in Boulder. His dissertation was an assessment of welfare program administration in Colorado and introduced him to the world of federal assistance. Upon obtaining his degree his first academic position was with Southwest Texas State University, where he helped develop a fledgling MPA and urban studies program and was awarded and managed his first research grants. From Texas, Dr. Shapek was selected for a National Association of Schools of Public Affairs and Administration (NASPAA) Fellowship. He came to Washington, D.C. in 1974-75 as a member of the Bureau of Intergovernmental Programs, U.S. Civil Service Commission. During this assignment, he also served as a member and staff of the OMB/NSF Study Committee on Policy Management Assistance. He returned to academia as Chairman of the Department of Public Administration, Kent State University. From there he went to the College of the Virgin Islands as Professor of Public Administration and Director of the MBA/MPA Program. He also had administrative and policy responsibility for the College's federal grant activities. In the spring of 1979, he returned to Washington, D.C. on a leave of absence from the College of the Virgin Islands under the mobility provisions of the Intergovernmental Personnel Act and was assigned to the Grants Administration Division, Environmental Protection Agency. He currently is serving as a Special Assistant to EPA's Assistant Administrator for Research and Development.

Dr. Shapek has published frequently on the topic of federal assistance and is an active participant in the activities of the American Society for Public Administration (ASPA). He was a founder of the ASPA Section on Intergovernmental Administration and Management. He is a consultant to the National Science Foundation and has been a consultant to a number of other federal, state, and local agencies. He has conducted numerous workshops and graduate-level classes on grant-in-aid writing and has been a speaker on that topic. He also is an adjunct professor teaching in the Washington graduate program of the University of Southern California.

Chapter One
Evolution of the
Intergovernmental System

Federalism - old style - is dead. Yet Federalism - new style is alive and well and living in the United States. Its name is 'intergovernmental relations.' [1]

Michael D. Reagan
1972

Introduction

This chapter briefly traces the concept of American federalism in its legal sense, from its inception in the U.S. Constitution to an era known as New Federalism or the presidency of Richard M. Nixon. Federalism is characterized as fluid and dynamic, a relationship between the national and state governments that has grown to include local governments and other significant actors as well. Because of the complexity of interactions between levels of government, eras of federalism can no longer be discussed in terms of legal relationships. A more realistic descriptor of these relationships today is Intergovernmental Relations (IGR).

This chapter attempts to clarify the distinction between eras of federalism and the more prevalent concept of IGR. Nation-centered, state-centered, dual, cooperative, and creative federalism are the precedents of New Federalism. They form the penumbra for the more comprehensive exploration of the development of the intergovernmental grant-in-aid system which is viewed as the primary force for change.

Traditional American Federalism

Federalism, in a literal sense, is a concept in which units of government join and agree to subordinate governmental powers to a superior government authority. The nature of this agreement - which powers are to be exercised by individual members and which are to be surrendered to a central authority–is what constitutes the federal relationship. There can be varying forms of federalism; the Swiss Cantons pose one example, and the City of Toronto, Canada, and its member governments constitute another. The United States, however, presents a unique example of federalism because it has been fluid and changing, evolving to meet the needs of the times and its constituent units, the member states. Federalism in the United States has changed since this relationship first was expressed formally in our Constitution in 1789 and explained in the *Federalist Papers.* These changes reflect the shifting role of the states in their partnership with the national government and provide an interesting view of the evolution of government in the United States.

American federalism was and remains a unique and bold experiment in government. It was developed, in part, because of our experience under the Articles of Confederation, which went into effect in 1781. An instrument of liberty and a proclamation of freedom and independence, the Articles established a very limited relationship between the thirteen former colonies. Each party to this agreement retained its sovereignty, with little regard for cohesion, much as the member nations now retain independence under the treaty establishing the United Nations. The Articles provided for little more than an opportunity to meet together and debate. Since each state acted independently and only in its own interests, it soon became obvious that this loose union was approaching a crisis. These concerns led to the Annapolis Convention of 1786 and the Philadelphia Convention in 1787. The resulting deliberations produced much of our present Constitution and a unique redefinition of national and state roles.

Most scholars of American federalism have been concerned with the legal relationship between the national (central) and state (constituent) governments. In the Constitution the powers of these two levels of government are specified, with some reserved specifically to each and some shared. These specified and reserved powers have been addressed on an issue-by-issue basis through rulings of the U.S. Supreme Court, and these rulings have produced a reasonably clear picture of the legal status of each actor. This picture, however, requires continual clarification because of the complexity of the issues that emerge in our evolving society. Thus, from a Constitutional (or legal) perspective, the federal-state relationship is constantly redefined. This legal relationship is complicated further by jurisdictional questions that may alter the roles of these two levels of government. For example, the Constitution does not specify the status or place in this partnership for local governments. Nor is there any reference to private, corporate, or regional government interfaces, and yet actions involving these sectors constitute a significant portion of the federal system.

The *precise meaning* of federalism in the United States is not now, nor has it ever been, completely clear. The U.S. Constitution sought to place limitations on the powers of government, both national and state, but it failed to specify relationships beyond those which appear in Articles 1 and IV and the 10th Amendment to the Constitution. Article 1 specifies the scope of national powers while Section 10 places certain restrictions on the powers of the states. Article IV, Section 1, guarantees "Full Faith and Credit" to each state, and the 10th Amendment reserves to the States (or the people) "powers not delegated to the United States by the Constitution, nor prohibited by it to the States." Thus, to argue the appropriateness of a particular or static relationship between the national government and the states by using the Constitution would be illogical.

Complicating attempts to define the nature of federalism is the growing importance of local governments. In terms of numbers alone local governments constitute a significant place in the intergovernmental arena. Today we have over 80,000 units of general purpose and special purpose local government, each with specific responsibilities (Table 1). According to the U.S. Bureau of Census, the average number of governmental units per state in 1977 was 1,603, with a high of 6,643 units in Illinois and a low of 20 in Hawaii. Each of these units has a voice in determining the nature of the federal relationship, and each may exercise a force in placing demands on this system.

Table 1

Governmental Units 1967-1977

TYPE OF GOVERNMENT	1977	1972	1967	1957
State Governments	50	50	50	48
Counties	3,042	3,044	3,049	3,047
Municipalities	18,856	18,517	18,048	17,183
Townships	16,822	16,991	17,105	17,198
School Districts	15,260	15,781	21,782	50,446
Other Special Districts*	26,140	23,885	21,264	14,405
Total	80,170	78,268	81,298	102,327

Sources: U.S. Bureau of the Census, Governments in the United States, Vol. 1, NO. 1, 1957; Census of Government: 1972, Vol. 1, Government Organization; Census of Government: 1977, Vol. 1. (Washington, D.C.: GPO).

*Includes districts with responsibilities for such functions as hospital service, water supply, fire protection, recreation.

Our founding fathers could not have been unaware of the potential impact of these governments. The first census, taken in 1790, is very incomplete and inaccurate. Only 292 counties and 5 cities (Boston, New York, Philadelphia, Baltimore and Charleston) with a population of over 8,000 were recorded. The only other category referred to included "minor civil divisions." Under this heading were towns, settlements, parishes, or townships, depending upon what individual states chose to report. It was not until the 1830 census that schools were reported, and, even then, school or special districts were not mentioned. By 1840, the census included counties, towns, and schools, but, again, there was no mention of special districts, of which school districts would constitute one type. Although the Northwest Ordinance of 1787 specifically mentioned townships and early legislation supported public works projects in cities, it appears that "local governments" were not especially significant in the framing of our Constitution, nor were they visible for some time to follow.

The situation today is, of course, very different from colonial days. Increases in the number of local governmental units, their population, their political power, and their responsibilities in federal assistance programs have made local-federal relations a complicated and integral part of the system. Further, combined jurisdictions within or between states, as well as groupings of states represented by regional commonalities or shared interests, have eroded the old concern about a two-part (national-state) view of federalism to one encompassing much more.

The intertwined nature of this relationship has been characterized best by the late Morton Grodzins as a "marble cake in which all levels of government interact in implementing public policy."[2] Today governments at all levels must deal with this increasing complexity as they work concurrently and sometimes cooperatively to solve major problems.[3]

Eras of Federalism

Our federal system began with a strong, dominant national (central) government. The early battles over the nature of federalism were almost entirely between the national government and the states. This is an era that has been labeled by some scholars as "nation-centered" federalism or the Federalist era. At approximately the time of the presidency of Thomas Jefferson, this centralist posture succumbed to demands by the states and the people for both greater representation in the decision-making process and greater autonomy. Following this period and the landmark decisions of Supreme Court Chief Justice John Marshall, which solidified a strong role for the national government, the states' desires for a greater role in this partnership began to predominate. The nation-centered view of federalism gave way to a state-centered perspective articulated in the Virginia and Kentucky resolutions of 1798. These resolutions later formed the basis for rationalizing sectional differences within the nation, particularly those of the South. Such leaders as Thomas Jefferson and John C. Calhoun argued that it was the states and state initative that led to the Constitution and, therefore, the seat of power in the nation (or sovereignty) resides in the states and not in the central government. Also, proponents of states' rights argued that the states are protected by conditional limitations restricting the power of the national government as expressed in Article 1, Section 8. This section includes a specific listing of the powers that may be exercised by the Congress. This is followed in Section 9 by a listing of prohibitions or restrictions on what Congress may not do. Things that states may not do, such as enter into treaties, etc., are contained in Section 10 of the same article. Finally, the states also are protected by the broad grant of power contained in the "reserved" phraseology of the 10th Amendment.

Using this interpretation of the Constitution, federalism became state-centered for a period running roughly from 1840 to 1861. To some extent the argument concerning the division of power between the national government and the states, especially in regard to the states' arguments over their right to secession in the period 1860-61, led to the Civil War. The Civil War, in turn, led to a period of redefined perspectives. What emerged following the Civil War was an era of "live and let live" at both levels of government. This new period has been labeled as "dual federalism."[4]

"Dual federalism" was based on the assumption that the national and state governments were two separate and autonomous entities linked only by the Constitution. This relationship was clearly articulated by the U.S. Supreme Court:

> *There are within the territorial limits of each state two govern-*
> *ments, restricted in their sphere of action, but independent of*
> *each other, and supreme within their respective spheres. Each*
> *has its separate departments, each has its distinct laws, and*
> *each has its own tribunals for their enforcement. Neither govern-*
> *ment can intrude within the jurisdiction of the other or authorize*
> *any interference therein by its judicial officers with the action of*
> *the other. (Tarbel's Case, 13 Wall, 397 (1872)).*

This separated-authority model existed for several decades as the U.S. Supreme Court attempted to arbitrate national-state relationships. It appeared that the U.S. and state courts were to impose a rigid separation long after the realities of interdependence became apparent. However by the 1930's, the depression and a reevaluation of the growing complexity of national-state and private sector interactions necessitated a reappraisal of these relationships and federalism entered a new era.

The independent spheres of authority or "dual federalism" view is discredited by some scholars today, such as Morton Grodzins and Daniel Elazar, as characterizing social and political conditions that had changed prior to the 1860's. Thus, the court decisions of the period 1860-1930 were inconsistent with the times. Before totally discarding this theory, however, one must consider the implications of a recent Supreme Court decision: on June 24, 1976 in National League of Cities v. Usery, the Court ruled that Congress did not have the authority to require that either the states or their local units of government observe minimum-wage and maximum-hour laws. A 1974 federal law extending wage and hour requirements to state and city employers was held to be unconstitutional as a violation of state sovereignty:

> *Congress has sought to wield its power in a fashion that*
> *would impair the states' ability to function effectively with the*
> *federal system....We hold that insofar as the challenged amend-*
> *ments operate to directly displace the states' freedom to struc-*
> *ture integral operations in areas of traditional governmental*
> *functions, they are not within the authority granted*
> *Congress....(44 U.S. Lawyers Weekly)*

The Court's opinion, then, was that in at least one area, the power of Congress to regulate commerce, "state sovereignty" prevents the national government from enacting laws that intrude in an area traditionally within the domain of the states. In this limited instance, the "dual federalism" concept still has some validity.

Attempts to preserve the distinction between the spheres of influence of the two levels of government prevailed until the late 1920's and the economic upheavals of the Great Depression. The subsequent national response to this crisis was a strong sense of social consciousness which was manifested in a series of social welfare programs. Washington launched a series of programs and began pouring funds into the states which ushered in a new era of federa-state relationships. These relationships were no longer logically identified as legal interactions between two distinct levels, but rather, as Professor Michael Reagen, a scholar of federalism, notes as "...the active interdependence and sharing of functions between

Washington and the states, and focusing on the national leverage that each level is able to exert on the other."[5] The concept of autonomous levels working independently gave way to assessments of shared interrelationships and cooperation.

At this point, federalism, or the relationship between the national and state governments, became influenced by the federal assistance system that burgeoned during this period. Of course, World War II had a great effect in promoting federal-state cooperation on many fronts but also signaled a trend of growing centralization of power in Washington. This era, roughly 1830 to 1962, has been called a period of "cooperative federalism." More realistically it may be considered a time when the states became administrative units for the promulgation of national policies. While the states benefited from the flow of funds and programs originated by the national government, they traded autonomy for a continued share of the federal "pie," and turned their attention from national concerns to internal housekeeping concerns. Because of world events in a period of roughly 25 years, this fourth era of identifiable federalism slipped by largely unnoticed into a new period that began in the early 1960's. This new period in federal-state relationships, spanning the Kennedy and Johnson presidencies or the period 1962-1968, has been called "creative federalism."

"Creative federalism" was a description of federal-state relations that included substantial and simultaneous interaction between the national, state, and local governments, as well as private industry. The era is characterized by creativity or the imaginative establishment of new relationships. The national government offered assistance programs to the states and localities in return for their agreement to implement and carry out programs in a variety of activities deemed important to national interests. Private industry was encouraged to participate in the regulatory process and to assume functions that also could be performed by governments. However, the "creative" model is not as viable or distinctly identifiable except for the recognition of the growing significance and impact of federal aid and the steady erosion of state prerogatives to Washington. In this sense, from the 1930's to today, except for "New Federalism" which is discussed in subsequent chapters, the eras of federalism became increasingly difficult to identify, separate, or accurately characterize.

Federalism and Intergovernmental Relations

Federalism must be viewed as a dynamic concept, which is becoming increasingly complex because of the intergovernmental effects of public policy problems associated with such issues as energy, environmental protection, water shortages, and urban blight. The modern-day study of federalism is characterized more accurately as the assessment of interactions and relationships between levels of governments, or what has been termed by some as intergovernmental relations. For the purposes of this text, the term "intergovernmental" is used loosely to mean relationships or interactions between various governmental units of different levels. The concept of intergovernmental relations (IGR) is not intended to replace that of federalism, but federalism is more accurately descriptive of federal-state linkages than of the broadened panoply of fiscal, political, and administrative relationships that are inclusive of IGR. Federalism also connotes legal relationships subject to definition by the courts. To date, over 30 descriptor terms of federalism have emerged, thus making the delineation of eras increasingly difficult. These terms, such as "national federalism" (Sundquist), "mature and emergent federalism" (Macmahon), and "centralized and peripheralized federalism" (Riker), have become value-laden and subjective, obscuring a term with historical validity and significance. Therefore, IGR as a newer and more generic concept also may be more appropriate to an era that is not clearly identifiable (also see Chapter VII).

This broadened perspective of federalism as intergovernmental relationships is well characterized by Professor Deil Wright, a leading scholar in the rapidly growing arena of IGR. Wright's interpretation of this concept includes several distinct features. First, IGR involves all levels and types of government, from school or special districts to the federal government. Second, intergovernmental relations involves the informal interaction of persons - administrators and elected officials, their beliefs, and perceptions. Third, the focus of this interaction is on working relationships in a day-to-day context. Fourth, the range of participants is all inclusive - interactors may be judges, legislators, executives, and elected or appointed administrators. Finally, IGR has a policy component involving an intermix of financial and political decisions.[6]

The complex and interactive nature of IGR has evolved through phases (Table 2). The changes in IGR indicate the linkage of political and economic problems and the growth and development that have occurred since the initial legal formulation of the Republic in 1789. This linkage is most readily identifiable as a result of the federal assistance or grant-in-aid system. Grants-in-aid, used somewhat synonomously with federal assitance, are defined as "...the payment of funds by one level of government to be expended by another level for a specified purpose, usually on a matching basis and in accordance with prescribed standards or requirements."[7]

Table 2

Federalism in Transition

THEORY OF FEDERALISM (Approximate Dates)	PHASE DESCRIPTION	POPULAR METAPHOR
Nation-Centered 1787-1840	Autonomy and Conflict	Legal Federalism
State-Centered 1840-1861		
Dual 1861-1930		Layer Cake
Cooperative 1930-1962	Cooperation	Cooperative
Creative 1962-1968		
New Federalism 1968-1972	Partnership (with the National Government, the Senior Partner) or Intergovernmental Relations	Marble Cake
Pragmatic Federalism 1972-1974		
Administration and Management 1974-Present		Picket Fence

The eras of federalism are not distinct nor clearly separable. The above table represents an amalgamation of the more popular current theories and phrase descriptors. See: Deil S. Wright, "Intergovernmental Relations: An Analytical Overview," *The Annals,* (November, 1974), p. 5; Richard H. Leach, *American Federalism* (New York: W.W. Norton & Co., 1970), pp. 1-10; and Advisory Commission on Intergovernmental Relations, *Pragmatic Federalism: The Reassignment of Functional Responsibility,* M-105 (Washington, D.C. GPO, July, 1976).

The complexity of this unique federal system can be seen further in the grant-in-aid process. Federal aid to state and local governments has increased from $2.3 billion in 1950 (or 10.4% of state and local expenditures) to $83 billion today (or approximately 27.0% of state and local expenditures).[8] It is through this cash transfer process and the funding assistance or grant-in-aid programs that this process represents that "...the federal government seeks to influence the conduct of state and local governments in such a way as to promote the realization of its own goals."[9] Within a complex legal framework of separate and shared powers, unbalanced financial powers become a part of the forces defining government.

Federal Influences

Federal influence in the grant-in-aid system is exerted directly by at least two means. The first is related to the purpose of the specific program. The program has a basis in a law passed by Congress and funded through an appropriation. The act is usually designed to accomplish some broad national purpose such as improvement of state and local personnel systems or provision of aid to families (meeting certain financial assistance needs). To implement the program, draft regulations or guidelines (rules) which administratively interpret the act, hopefully in accordance with the intent of Congress, are issued by the federal agency responsible for such implementation and are published in the *Federal Register* to allow for public comment. In implementing the program, the agency provides assistance to eligible recipients in accordance with these finalized guidelines. The award is given for the *specific* purpose(s) as described in the act. In short, the federal government offers money to induce the recipient to perform a specific activity that has been defined by statute. Certain recipient actions or characteristics are required as a condition of obtaining this federal assistance.

A second direct means by which federal influence is exerted on a recipient is through conditions which may be attached as a requirement to the receipt of funds. These conditions may not be related to the purpose of the award but are legally binding on the recipient. Implementation of national policy related to such areas as equal employment opportunity, environmental protection, and occupational health and safety is required under provisions accompanying each award. Administrative conditions attached to awards include auditing and bookkeeping procedures, area-wide (local or sometimes state) coordination or clearance, and reporting requirements that often may lead to record-keeping procedures of such magnitude that some jurisdictions and universities have refused to accept federal grants.[10] Federal goals are realized to the extent that state and local governments accept and fulfill these conditions. Federal influence is exercised when recipient governments alter their priorities, spending policies, and ways of doing things in order to conform to federal mandates.

Grant-in-aid programs designed to assist state and local governments in enhancing their service-delivery capabilities exist in many federal "mission" agencies, e.g., the U.S. Department of Health, Education, and Welfare(HEW), now the Departments of Education and Human Resources; the Department of Labor (DOL); the Department of Transportation (DOT); etc.). Mission agencies are those that are assigned specific functions designed to assist recipients while furthering national goals. While no clear delineation is apparent, a non-mission agency in the sense used here might be the Office of Personnel Management (OPM), formerly the U.S. Civil Service Commission, which serves the personnel, training, and staffing needs of the federal bureaucracy. A grant program is assigned within a specific operating division, bureau, or office in each agency charged by Congress with administration and management responsibilities for that program. In most cases the responsible federal agency will deal directly with a recipient government. This situation creates a one-to-one, vertical relationship, which sometimes bypasses an intermediate level, such as the state. Hence, the concept of "picket fence" federalism is used as a descriptor.

While most transfers of functions have been vertical in nature, there also have been many horizontal (between governmental units at the same level) transfers. These transfers usually take the form of contractual arrangements where jurisdictions share the costs of providing a specific service or where one agrees to provide a service to another for a fee and both can benefit from economies of scale. The Advisory Commission on Intergovernmental Relations has labeled these horizontal transfers as "pragmatic" federalism, which also can be viewed as a subset of "picket fence" federalism.

In "pragmatic" federalism, functional reassignment of responsibilities is based on consideration of such criteria as economic efficiency, fiscal equity, political accountability, and administrative effectiveness.[11] While some functions have been transferred between governments voluntarily because of cost-saving considerations or other mutually advantageous factors, some have been mandated by state legislatures or caused by federal grant requirements. The reasons municipalities have engaged in transfers of responsibilities are varied but usually are based upon their perceived savings, needs, or political factors. While only about 15% of these transfers have been brought about as a direct result of federal aid requirements, indirect federal influences promote tangential concerns leading to a much greater percentage of functional transfers, i.e., federal auditing or personnel standards may lead a small jurisdiction to adopt a shared computer system with another small jurisdiction because it will need the system at a later time to meet requirements for federal aid.

The concepts of federalism and intergovernmental relations have become intertwined with the external influences brought about by independent realities such as the rising costs of energy and environmental awareness, as well as by many other factors which are beyond the control of government. For state and local governments, IGR relationships are further compounded by the complexity and rigidity that have been created by the federal grant-in-aid system.

This complexity is further compounded by the independence and autonomy of individual federal agencies. Each agency has been chartered as a separate entity by the Congress with a unique mission. For various reasons, however, there are times when agencies are given programs that overlap the functions or mission of another agency. For example, sewage treatment plant construction grants awarded by the Environmental Protection Agency (EPA) may impact directly on urban development patterns which are promoted by the U.S. Department of Housing and Urban Development (HUD). The two agencies must then resolve their programs in the best interests of the community. Unfortunately, the resolution is not an easy task because the two agencies may have conflicting perspectives of the situation; then the community is given the task of resolving the federal agency differences. Program competition between federal agencies has been said to result in "vertical functional autocracies, Balkanized bureaucracies, feudal federalism, and autonomous autocracies," among other things.[12] Some agencies have become separate domains of power, disbursing funds and enforcing rules and regulations which bare down through all levels of government and the private sector. The framers of the Constitution could hardly have envisioned this dimension and evolution of federalism.

THE BUREAUCRATS

Copley News Service

'WE GOT A FEDERAL GRANT TO HIRE FOUR PEOPLE AND IT TAKES FIVE PEOPLE TO DO THE REPORTS TO KEEP THE GRANT'

Reprinted with permission of Copley News Service and Mr. Knudsen.

This problem has been caused in large part by the federal government itself. One reason for the confusion that exists in program coordination is the lack of clear guidelines under which the executive branch of government operates. Our founding fathers failed to prescribe or even to discuss the organization of the executive branch of government. There has been no guidance or precedent upon which a management infrastructure could be established. In short, there is little agreement "as to what ground rules should be applied to the principal officials of the executive branch and to the Congress in the prescription of the administrative arrangements for the execution of programs."[13]

The Constitution of the United States provides little guidance on the establishment of administrative structures and procedures in the executive branch. Under Article I, Section 8, Congress is given authority to make all laws "necessary and proper" for carrying out the other responsibilities designated in the Constitution. There is nothing specified in the Constitution about the administrative responsibilities of federal agencies and little about the role of the President, other than his charge to faithfully execute the law of the land. There is also no policy guidance provided to assist the Congress in determining its rule-making relationship with the executive agencies administering the programs established by Congressional acts. Further, the undefined relationship between the executive and legislative branches is subject to personalities and political motivations guiding the individuals involved. The President is relatively free to determine, within existing law, how executive departments will operate. However, Congress can make or change laws, forcing the reorganization or creation of executive agencies. Furthermore, Congress has powerful control over appropriations. The mixed nature of this relationship in the grant-in-aid system can be seen in Figure I.

The character of presidential leadership, political reality, and national priorities and problems have changed the *modus operandi* of the executive branch from term to term and affected operating policy with the mission agencies. Each change in presidential leadership and concomitant philosophy has been accompanied by a different perspective of the role of the executive branch in the intergovernmental system. Most scholarly analysis advocating an increase in the effectiveness of the executive branch as it relates to intergovernmental concerns has centered upon strengthening the presidential role. A number of studies, study groups, and commissions have examined the intergovernmental administrative machinery and have agreed upon a need for strengthening the President's capacity to control the farflung domestic empire for which he is responsible.[14]

Evolution of IGR Management in The Executive Branch

The first group to study the problems of administrative management in the executive branch was the Commission on Economy and Efficiency, appointed by President Taft in 1912. The Taft Commission concluded that effective executive control and coordination was possible only through a unified executive budget. Control of the budget would permit the President to allocate resources in a more efficient manner. The Commission's recommendations eventually led to passage of the Budget and Accounting Act of 1921, the central source of Presidential control today over executive branch agencies.[15] Increased operating efficiency (defined roughly as how to do things better) remained the focus of attention in governmental administrative reform efforts until new pressures were brought about by the

Figure I

Primary Actors in Administration of the Grant-In-Aid System, 1980

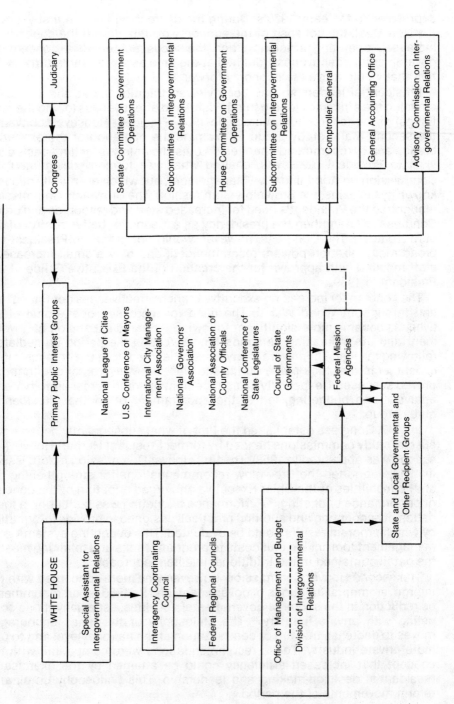

depression in the early 1930's. During the depression and the first years of the New Deal, the collapse of the economy overshadowed the concern for increased operating efficiency; and the focus shifted to a concern for governmental effectiveness (defined at the time as any administrative solution that would move the economy forward).[16]

Presidential leadership has been viewed traditionally as the key to increasing the efficiency (doing things right) and effectiveness (doing the right things) of the federal bureaucracy. In 1936, President Roosevelt convened the second major study group to examine the operation of the executive branch and to recommend changes.[17] Louis Brownlow, a well-respected advisor to President Roosevelt, chaired what was formally designated the Commission on Administrative Management, but which eventually became known by his name, the Brownlow Commission. The Brownlow Commission recognized the President's need for increased staff and resources and urged Congress to strengthen the presidency as a means for better control of the bureaucracy.[18] The Congress, however, would not grant the President the broad reorganization powers recommended, and only a small increase in staff resulted with approval for the creation of the Executive Office of the President in 1939.

The concern for increasing executive branch effectiveness continued into and throughout World War II. The need for increased operational effectiveness became more significant following the rapid expansion of government and the increasing demands for services in the period immediately following the war. There were many lessons learned from the administrative experiments that took place during the war. Innovative practices that had proved successful, especially in management operations research, systems analysis, and budgeting, led to the appointment of another presidential study group.

In 1947, Congress established the first of what subsequently became two special study commissions headed by former President Herbert Hoover (the second was appointed in 1953). The first Hoover Commission report, issued in 1949, supported the Brownlow recommendations for strengthening the staff capabilities of the Chief Executive and urged adoption of the concept of performance budgeting.[19] Performance budgeting was built upon a foundation of accounting and auditing practices designed to provide information by which program results could be evaluated. This budgeting system was a management tool linking unit costs to program results and retaining most of the detail contained in the traditional line-item approach.

The second Hoover Commission, however, was more concerned with the intergovernmental functions of government, and its 1955 report recommended reduction in the scope of governmental activities, especially those competing with private industry.[20] The philosophy of the times encouraged moves to decrease the rate of centralization at the national level and to promote private industry. These recommendations were compatible with the concept that increased efficiency could be attained by the exercise of presidential decision-making and leadership. This philosophy dominated reform movements of the period.

The second Hoover report had little impact. Subsequent governmental reorganization efforts did follow many of the Brownlow suggestions, those in the first Hoover Commission report, and, to a lesser extent, those of the second Hoover report, but significant changes in the management of the federal bureaucracy did not occur. In 1949, however, Congress passed the Reorganization Act which gave the President significant power to reorganize by executive order and allowed him, within prescribed limits, to bypass the cumbersome procedure of seeking this authority from Congress on a piecemeal basis. A second change also may be attributed to the Brownlow and Hoover studies: general governmental activities were reorganized on a more logical basis. For example, the Bureau of Public Roads (which ultimately became a major unit of the Department of Transportation) was transferred to the Department of Commerce, and the U.S. Employment Service was moved to the Department of Labor, thus bringing these relatively autonomous agencies under the administrative control of a central authority. A final residual of the Brownlow/Hoover Commissions was the formal introduction of performance budgeting into the federal government by the Budget and Accounting Act of 1950. This approach to financial management grew into the concept of Planning, Programming and Budgeting (PPB), a systems approach to budgetary decision making that was taken from the private sector, and applied to the Department of Defense in 1961 by Secretary Robert S. McNamara.[21]

Perhaps the greatest impacts of the Brownlow and Hoover Commissions were the attention they focused on the role of the federal government and its impact on subnational units, as well as reorganization to accommodate the nature of federal-state-local relationships that were emerging. Brownlow may be credited with recognizing the interface between politics and administration and working toward upgrading governmental effectiveness through instilling greater professionalism in its employees.[22] The First and Second Hoover Commissions, and later the Kestnbaum Commission and President Eisenhower's Joint Federal-State Action Committee, may be credited with initiating widespread interest in intergovernmental cooperation through better management.[23] The latter studies focused more exclusively on the nature and impacts of the grant-in-aid system, but remedial recommendations took the form of management reform.

The management tools of reorganization and the technological advances available to the Chief Executive following World War II took new directions in the early1950's under President Eisenhower. While most suggestions for increased operating effectiveness and efficiency ultimately resulted in more centralized control at the national level, complaints by the business community and by state governors indicated some reassessment was in order. The federal government was assuming functions more traditionally in the domain of the states or private industry, and a movement toward program decentralization began. President Eisenhower, a sincere believer in a philosophy of governmental decentralization and an adherent to the traditional Republican Party predeliction for laissez-faire, affirmed this commitment when he told the National Governors' Conference (now the National Governors' Association) that:

> ...unless we preserve, in this country, the place of the State
> Government, its traditional place - with the power, the authority,

the responsibilities and the revenue necessary to discharge those responsibilities, then we are not going to have an America as we have known it; we will have some other form of government.[24]

Eisenhower implied a "zero-sum" relationship between the federal and state governments, which was characteristic of the system under the philosophy of dual federalism by which one could only gain or lose at the expense of the other. In fact, however, there could be no return at that late date to a system of separate responsibilities for each level of government (that had characterized the antebellum period following the Civil War). The new interrelationships and interdependencies between levels of government brought about by the grant-in-aid system alone prohibited clear separation. Each governmental level was linked to and dependent upon the others economically, as well as administratively. Cooperation between levels of government was imperative if the system were to continue to function. Eisenhower's efforts were at odds with the reality of the system that had evolved following World War II when the United States entered an era where more complex and necessary intergovernmental cooperation had become essential.

Eisenhower was attempting to turn back the clock by calling for a reappraisal of the role of the national government in relation to the states and their political subdivisions. Although this reevaluation had been attempted previously, in part, by the National Governors' Conference, the lobbying efforts of civic groups, and the assessment by the first Hoover Commission, Eisenhower requested a complete reexamination of the programmatic relationships between levels of government. What Eisenhower sought was not merely a report but, rather, a massive shift in operational procedures that had already been solidified through precedent. This reappraisal represented the first undertaking of this magnitude since the Constitutional Convention of 1787. In an address to Congress on March 30, 1953, President Eisenhower recommended "...the creation of a commission to study the means of achieving a sounder relationship between federal, state, and local governments." An act subsequently passed by Congress created the U.S. Commission on Intergovernmental Relations.[25]

The Kestnbaum Commission

The Kestnbaum Commission, or the U.S. Commission on Intergovernmental Relations, was named after its chairman, Meyer Kestnbaum. It was comprised of 25 prestigious members and a professional staff of 40. It was asked to study federal-state and federal-local relationships and interactions "...to the end that these relations may be clearly defined and the functions concerned may be allocated to their proper jurisdictions...."[26] The Commission issued 16 reports prior to submission of its final report in 1955. In more realistically redefining Eisenhower's desire for program decentralization, the Commission's final report noted that "The National Government and the states should be regarded not as competitors for authority, but as two levels of government cooperating with or complementing each other in meeting the growing demands on both." The Report further noted that "...in our present highly interdependent society, there are few activities of government indeed in which there is not some degree of national interest, and in which the national government is without constitutional authority to participate in some manner."[27] This wording was not to imply a lack of recognition of the responsibilities residing at each level of government. In a later section, the report warned:

> The states must be alert to meet the legitimate needs of their citizens, less [sic] more and more of the business of government fall upon the national government. At the same time, the national government must refrain from taking over activities that the states and their subdivisions are performing with reasonable competence, less [sic] the vitality of state and local governments be undermined.
>
> The division of responsibilities between the nation and the states is not and cannot be set by any authority over and above both, apart from the constitution itself and the people.[28]

The Kestnbaum Commission's reports proved highly creditable and brought public attention, as well as meaning, to the new phrase "intergovernmental relations," used to describe the management infrastructure that had evolved since 1789. The Kestnbaum Commission is noted perhaps as much for its failures as its successes. The Commission's assignment was to alter the *direction* of the federal system by designating programs that could be remanded to the states or to the private sector. Its failure was not so much that the federal agencies blocked this devolution of functions, but that the governors would not accept them.[29]

Turning Back The Tide

The difficulties inherent in the uncontrolled, proliferating system of grants-in-aid made Eisenhower's attempts to promote governmental decentralization and separation of functions incongruent with the realities of increasing governmental interdependence. This analysis is not to say that the concept was without merit, but a Democratic Congress was not responsive to a Republican President. A much more sophisticated attempt to decentralize responsibilities from the national level was to appear again some twenty years later under the guidance of President Richard M. Nixon and the philosophy of "New Federalism," which will be discussed in the next two chapters.

President Eisenhower's efforts to reverse the tide of increasing governmental centralization were not restricted to the Kestnbaum Commission. The Commission's report brought new attention to and concern about federal-state relationships and highlighted the need for increased presidential attention to domestic affairs. Eisenhower created a special post to deal with these concerns. Howard Pyle, former Governor of Arizona, was brought to Washington, D.C. to serve as Eisenhower's deputy assistant for intergovernmental relations. Eisenhower also utilized Meyer Kestnbaum as a special assistant to continue the work initiated by his Commission.

The Joint Federal-State Action Committee

President Eisenhower was not deterred from continuing his pursuit of decentralization. In a 1957 address before the National Governors' Conference in Williamsburg, Virginia, he expressed his confidence that the governors of the states could identify federal programs that would be accomplished better at the state level and would support a move to decentralize them. In his address, Eisenhower proposed creation of a joint federal-state committee for the study of federal programs. This committee soon was formed under the auspices of the National Governors' Conference. The Joint Federal-State Action Committee, as it was named, consisted of nine governors and seven top federal administrators. However, in spite of its status and charge, the Committee produced only modest results. It recommended a greater state role in regulating non-military applications of atomic energy and the creation of an agency in each state to handle urban housing problems. It also proposed that the federal government eliminate grants-in-aid for sewage treatment plants and for vocational education.[30] Although the first two recommendations received some support, the latter two did not, especially when the groups that would have been affected mobilized their forces to lobby against these changes.

For all of the efforts of the Federal-State Action Committee, its recommendations do not appear significant today. Terry Sanford, Governor of North Carolina during this period and a perceptive analyst of the federal system, attributes the Committee's lack of impact to its failure to focus on the reality of the increasingly interdependent federal-state relationship that was emerging. Sanford notes that the Committee's recommendations "...were not soundly based on the concept of shared responsibilities, a procedure even then firmly embedded, even if not fully comprehended."[31] The practice of federalism, always fluid and dynamic, could not be defined in terms of distinct and autonomous responsibilities. The growing tide of intergovernmental complexity could not be reversed. While some federal activities could be decentralized, the vast majority could not. The nation had evolved into an era of federalism marked by the need for a high order of cooperative effort. We had entered the era of cooperative federalism. Dual federalism was dead, and Eisenhower's efforts to arrest the growth of increasing program centralization failed.

In the next few years, presidential reform efforts in the intergovernmental arena shifted to mechanisms designed to gain control of this elusive administrative system, especially through financial management. At the same time, there was increasing Congressional action to reassess and understand the changing federal system and to cope with the increasing number of legislative proposals having intergovernmental significance and impact.

Congressional Intergovernmental Concerns

Under the Legislative Reorganization Act of 1945, the House Committee on Government Operations was charged with the study of intergovernmental relationships between the federal government and the states and their municipalities. To execute this responsibility, the House established a standing Subcommittee on Intergovernmental Relations. The House Subcommittee, chaired by Representative L.H. Fountain (D., N.C.), began its assessment earlier than its Senate counterpart, chaired by Senator Edmund S. Muskie, (D., Maine). In 1956 Representative Fountain's subcommittee surveyed the views of federal administrators on existing grant programs and solicited comments on the recommendations of the Kestnbaum Commission.[32] The survey was followed one year later by a report based on replies received to a questionnaire sent to the executive agencies of state and local governments.[33] Like the Kestnbaum Commission report, the Fountain subcommittee report called for the establishment of better liaison between the two branches of government. This liaison was formally sanctioned several years later with the creation of the Advisory Commission on Intergovernmental Relations (ACIR). The Subcommittee's final report was submitted in 1968 to its parent committee, Government Operations, as a summary of a series of studies on intergovernmental relations. This report, entitled *Federal-State-Local Relations, Federal Grants-In-Aid,* emphasized for the first time the vertical character of grant-in-aid programs and contained a series of recommendations for improving the system.[34]

The Fountain Subcommittee's 1968 studies addressed two problems which previously had been considered by the Kestnbaum Commission in 1955: first, the studies explored the division of responsibility between the national and state governments; and, second, they discussed methods for improving intergovernmental cooperation and efficiency in the grant-in-aid system. Exploration of the federal-state separation or decentralization-of-functions question led to the same conclusions reached by the Kestnbaum Commission, and the topic was finally laid to rest.

Analysis of the second problem, improvements to the grant-in-aid system, led to proposed legislation calling for periodic Congressional review of all grant-in-aid programs. The legislation was not acted upon by the Government Operations Committee because of strong opposition by organized labor interests which were apprehensive about a proposed "sunset provision." Under the sunset concept, a five-year expiration limit was recommended for all grant programs. At the end of this period, each program was to be rejustified and reconsidered by Congress, as if it were a new program but with the disadvantage of having to prove relevancy, accomplishments, and need. The labor interests were unhappy because this review process threatened possible elimination of or reduction in some programs and might have necessitated lobbying efforts every five years in other programs. Many other public interest groups joined the labor organizations in opposng this recommendation.[35] For all practical purposes, the Fountain subcommittee became inactive from this point on. Legislative leadership in exploring intergovernmental relationships would, at a later date, shift to the Senate Intergovernmental Relations Subcommittee.

Linkages and coordination between the executive and legislative branches as related to intergovernmental concerns have been conducted historically through personalized informal contacts. The traditional method of coordinaton was for bureau heads to individually discuss changes in administrative regulations with members of Congress or their staff. The same informal arrangement also has existed with state and local administrators and the Congress. In many instances the efforts of federal agency officials in seeking Congressional attention or information became competitive with or duplicative of state and local ones. In recognition of the growing time and resource demands placed on Congressional staff personnel, the Congress formally sanctioned already extensive federal-state-local interaction through the establishment of the Advisory Commission on Intergovernmental Relations (ACIR).

Advisory Commission on Intergovernmental Relations (ACIR)

The impetus for creation of a research and linking mechanism between federal agencies and the Congress came from Congress and not from the President. The Intergovernmental Relations Subcommittee of the House Committee on Government Operations drafted H.R. 6904 (86th Congress, 1st Session), which was enacted in relatively unchanged form as P.L. 86-380 (86th Congress), to establish the Advisory Commission on Intergovernmental Relations (ACIR). For two reasons, there was little Executive effort to coordinate the House bill. First, the Eisenhower Administration was relatively satisfied with the Joint Federal-State Action Committee, and, second, the broad representative base of the Commission and its system of member selection made Executive control ineffective.[36] In spite of Presidential indifference, the ACIR became the intergovernmental study arm *of Congress* on September 25, 1959.

ACIR has several roles. It serves as a permanent advisory body to Congress, functions as a research agency, and provides an information base for state and local governments and the various organizations representing these constitutencies. It is a 26-member, bipartisan body of representatives from federal, state, and local governments and the general public; the members serve two years and may be reappointed. The President may appoint three private citizens and three members of the executive branch to ACIR, as well as 14 state-local members from a list submitted by the national organizations representing state and local goverment (those appointed include four governors, four mayors, three county representatives, and three state legislators).[37] The process of selecting persons for ACIR membership has enhanced greatly the status of these state and local public interest groups with their membership. The creation of ACIR also increased the role of the state and local public interest groups in providing information on clientele group concerns and representing them when testifying before Congress. The remaining six members of the Commission's board are appointed directly by Congress, three by each House. The ACIR's diversified composition and the selection process for the Commission strengthen the possiblity that ACIR's mission will be realized.

The purpose and responsibilities of the ACIR, as set forth in Section 2 of Public Law 86-380 which formally established the Commission, centered on the need and importance of better "coordination and cooperation" between all levels of government. The full scope of responsibilities is mandated in its broad charter:

(1) to bring together representatives of the federal, state, and local governments for the consideration of common problems;

(2) to provide a forum for discussing the administration and coordination of federal grant and other programs requiring intergovernmental cooperation;

(3) to give crucial attention to the conditions and controls involved in the administration of federal grant programs;

20

(4)to make available technical assistance to the executive and legislative branches of the federal government in the review of proposed legislation to determine its overall effect on the federal system;

(5)to encourage discussion and study at an early stage of emerging public problems that are likely to require intergovernmental cooperation;

(6)to recommend, within the framework of the Constitution, the most desirable allocation of governmental functions, responsibilities, and revenues among the several levels of government; and

(7)to recommend methods of coordinating and simplifying tax laws and administrative practices to achieve a more orderly and less competitive fiscal relationship between the levels of government and to reduce the burden of compliance of taxpayers.

The Commission fulfills its responsibilities by selecting specific intergovernmental problems for staff analysis and research.[38] Suggestions for ACIR study may be proposed by members of the Commission, Congress, public officials, professional organizations, academic scholars, or members of the Commission's staff. Topics are selected for Commission action on the basis of a majority vote by the 26 members. The topics selected over the Commission's 20-year history have proved usually prophetic, relevant, and farsighted.[39]

Executive Agency Developments and Intergovernmental Problems In The Great Society

The advent of the "Great Society," proclaimed by President Lyndon B. Johnson in a May 22, 1964 address at the University of Michigan, introduced an era of new grant programs and the federal government's assumption of new social responsibilities which dramatically enlarged the number, cost, scope, and aim of federal programs. This shift from an intergovernmental focus on cooperative efforts between levels of government to a new concern about solving the ills of society with new and innovative programs ushered in an era of federalism that has been labeled by some scholars as "Creative Federalism." The era was creative in the sense that President Johnson attempted new ways to achieve national goals and objectives through the actions of state and local governments that are legally independent and which may be politically hostile. State and local governments are subject to no federal coercion except through the granting or denial of federal aid. To achieve national goals, the federal government must rely, for the most part, on the cooperation and motivation of state and local elected officials who can be induced or persuaded, but not controlled.

The "war on poverty," which was President Kennedy's program, evolved into Johnson's "Great Society." The promises of a better life for the nation's poor raised expectations and opened doors for groups that previously had little conception of governmental processes.[40] The requirement that many programs be staffed and operated by local persons involved in the receipt of these services also created a number of new management problems. The federal bureaucracy, as well as Congress, was quick to feel the impact of these initiatives on the balance of power between federal, state, and local authorities, especially through the demands presented by citizen and public interest groups that formed to represent this constituency, but failed to anticipate the impact on the community power structure and the increasing local demands for these expanded services. Also unanticipated was the significance of these program additions to the rule-making mechanisms necessary to ensure compliance with the basic legislative intent of each new program.

This problem was caused in large part by the federal government. By the mid 1960's, following the explosion of programs that characterized the "Great Society," each federal agency developed its own strategy for coping with the problem of coordinating with state and local level program counterparts (or recipients of grant funds). In the absence of a central, federally initiated, and general organizational philosophy or a presidential directive applicable to all federal agencies, management and coordination of community level programs were attempted piecemeal, program-by-program.

Federal mission agency management strategies often conflicted with each other. Each agency developed a separate counterpart organization for coordination at the local level, and a hodge-podge of new entities sprang into being. In the late 1960's in Washington, this piecemeal effort was referred to as the "coordinating structure of the month."[41] The Office of Economic Opportunity (OEO) developed Community Action Agencies (CAA's); the Department of Agriculture originated Resource Conservation and Development Projects (RC&D's), Rural Renewal Projects (RRP's), Rural Area Development Committees (RAD's), and Technical Action Panels (TAP's); the Commerce Department had Economic Development Districts (EDD's) and Economic Development Program Committees (EDPC's); HEW established Comprehensive Health Planning Agencies (CHPA's); HUD established Community Demonstration Agencies (CDA's); the Department of Labor formed the Cooperative Area Manpower Planning System (CAMPS) and Concentrated Employment Program (CEP); and the Appalachian Regional Commission formed Local Development Districts (LDD's). Several agencies (HUD, DOL, HEW, and OEO) attempted jointly-sponsored neighborhood centers, and in 1968, HUD, with the Departments of Agriculture and Commerce, organized Nonmetropolitan Districts (NMD's).[42] Lacking a centrally initiated coordination policy, the agencies created and funded new organizations designed to best fulfill their mission objectives.

Further confusing attempts at program coordination resulted when several states independently developed coordinating organizations of their own. At the same time, moreover, regional coordination mechanisms called Councils of Government (COG's) were encouraged and developed with funds awarded under Section 701 of the Housing and Community Development Act of 1965.[43] The COG's eventually became the regional coordinators of many federal programs and exist today in most states as independent public or non-profit agencies.

These newly formed Councils of Governments sought to reconcile federal agency goals with the realities of urban and rural politics. Theoretically, grant applications for projects having regional impacts now could be coordinated by all affected parties. Within the COG's, local elected officials who had never before met, although they might be from adjacent jurisdictions, were asked to work together (often, for the first time) to coordinate programs.

The complexity of federal rules and regulations applicable to each program was compounded, not reduced, by the coordinating systems designed to simplify the program delivery process. The more dedicated local program managers, or at least those attempting to mesh programs and federal administrative requirements, were having difficulty fulfilling federal agency expectations in a real and legal sense. At this same time, the community action agencies, which were created by the major executive departments to deliver services and were largely independent of local government control, began to exert pressures against local goverments as representatives of the community groups they were serving. A two-way push on the administrative infrastructure began as federal agencies initiated more rules and regulations in an attempt to gain administrative control. More local agencies were created to administer these rules and to perform specific service delivery functions, while the newly created agencies sought an independence of their own. Communities became torn by conflicting interests as well as specific agency (program) loyalties as these community-level agencies struggled year by year for survival. The roles of state and local government in this hodgepodge of community agencies became increasingly blurred.

Coordinating the Coordinators
It soon became apparent to federal program planners that the local level problems in coordination were national in origin and demanded a national solution. No state or local agency could be expected to correct what were essentially external pressures on the system. At the national level, part of the problem was a lack of coordination between and within federal agencies. There was no coherent central guidance; each agency owed its existence to its own grant-in-aid programs, which were created and funded by Congress; and each had little incentive to cooperate with other mission agencies.

Federal agency grant allocation strategies included actions to ensure administrative control and direction of the funds they distributed to lower levels of government with no regard for grant-application or reporting requirements imposed by other agencies. It was apparent to even the most casual observer that each department intended to pursue its own interests. Inquiries concerning an agency's administrative requirements were answered only in terms of the logic of program perpetuation and the individualized concerns of that agency. Part of the agency strategy was to retain control of programs with little or no thought of interagency coordination with similar programs, regardless of the problems inherent in this approach.

This attitude, combined with a lack of incentives for interagency cooperation at the national level, highlights the basic weakness of the entire grant-in-aid system - the lack of both a unified intergovernmental system with presidential leadership and an organizational infrastructure to carry out national policy.[44] Government bureaucracy, to the grant applicant or recipient, had become an amorphous mass lacking direction or control.

The Federal Perspective

In the period 1965-67, all agencies experienced considerable difficulty in implementing the rush of programs that accompanied "Great Society" initiatives. Several studies were conducted in an attempt to define these changing relationships and new responsibilities thrust on federal agencies. In 1965, Bureau of the Budget (BOB) Director Charles Schultze appointed a Task Force on Intergovernmental Program Coordination to deal with the intergovernmental and interagency issues that emerged. The Task Force, comprised of public administration experts, stressed the need for attention to this area, but little actually occurred as a result of the Task Force's recommendations, and the situation remained unchanged throughout the Johnson administration.

Another intergovernmental program study was conducted by the Senate Subcommittee on Intergovernmental Relations of the Committee on Government Operation. The Senate report coincided with the more detailed survey and findings of the House Intergovernmental Relations Subcommittee report initiated by Representative Fountain. Both studies urged improvement of federal program coordination. The Senate report also focused on the vertical structure of federal programs. While federal, state, and local officials had some idea about the theoretical foundations of the concept of federalism (or the relationships between levels of government), these views differed radically at each level.[45] Federal officials were concerned with administering their own programs, generally held an anti-state or anti-local bias, and had little subjective knowledge or interest in the problems of officials at other levels.[46] This view made it exceedingly difficult for these administrators to focus on "...such niceties as cooperative planning, appraisal, and administration," of the programs they were charged to administer.[47]

Another reason for the truncated federal view was that program administrators often were not attuned to the intergovernmental repercussions or impacts of their actions. There had been little reason for their concern because the legislation upon which programs had been based did not (does not yet) take intergovernmental factors into consideration. The cause of this oversight resides partly in the Congressional lawmaking process, itself. Congress is geared to formulate legislation through an assessment process which begins with hearings by special committees. These committees are concerned with narrow topics and not with the cross-cutting aspects of programs that affect each level of government differently. Further, there are jurisdictional disputes between committees and subcommittees. The decision as to where a program should be assigned, whether there should be hearings, and even how the matter should be studied has been and remains a political one. Through the mid 1960's, there was no general system of prior consultation with representatives of different levels of government to assess the potential impact of program-policy decisions, nor did Congressional or federal officials formally solicit state and local opinions in the development of programs.[48]

In recognition of this systemic deficiency, President Johnson issued a memorandum on November 11, 1966 to the heads of all federal agencies concerning relations with state and local governments.[49] The President indicated that joint planning between executive departments and their program counterparts at the state and local level was essential to the organization and administration of the intergovernmental system. Federal level administrators were to consult with these officials in the "...development and execution of programs which directly affect the conduct of state and local affairs."[50] Federal agency heads claimed that prior consultation and coordination were taking place already. From a Washington perspective, there was no problem.

BOB Director Schultze was assigned responsibility for developing procedures to implement the President's directive.[51] Schultze warned that the new directive must promote program coordination beyond the long-established channels of consultation between counterpart agencies in federal, state, and local governments. Agency and bureau heads immediately realized the implication of complying with formalized clearance procedures in terms of increased costs, time delays, and added paper work. They felt that only "professionals" should be involved in the formulation of rules and regulations. The added threat of giving state and local elected officials more knowledge and control of the grant-in-aid process also caused despair among federal program heads. The public interest groups, too, were not satisfied. They requested that prior consultation must be extended to the drafting of legislation and even to federal budget considerations. The states' governors requested that they, and not senators and congressmen as was the long-standing custom, be given the prerogative to announce the award of federal grants in their states.[52] A compromise BOB Circular addressing most of these problems finally was drafted and a federal policy developed that, in part, solved many of these concerns.

Circular A-85, "Consultation with Heads of States and Local Governments in Development of Federal Rules, Regulations, Standards, Procedures, and Guidelines," was an initial attempt to solve the problem of intergovernmental coordination. By giving public interest groups, as organized spokesmen of the various clientele they represented, an opportunity to comment on federal regulation changes directly affecting the administration of programs before they took effect, the BOB hoped to develop more meaningful regulations and to decrease criticism that arose after regulation changes had been made. For a number of reasons, the Circular proved ineffective, and the President was left to find other means to effectuate meaningful intergovernmental coordination.[53]

Development of the Intergovernmental Cooperation Act (ICA)

President Johnson's efforts to promote intergovernmental coordination continued beyond the establishment of Circular A-85. On March 17, 1967, he sent Congress a message entitled "Quality of American Government" which was an attempt by the President to gain Congressional support in the development of legislation aimed at improving the administrative machinery of government. In this message, he addressed the problems of increasing red tape, bureaucratic delay, and the confusion that had accompanied program expansion with the war on poverty.[54]

President Johnson's "Quality of American Government" address was the stimulus needed by Congress to promote a new effort in drafting intergovernmental reform. Senator Muskie, working with Budget Director Schultze, Congressman Blatnik (Chairman of the Government Operations Subcommittee on Executive and Legislative Reorganization, which had been assigned review power over the original bill), the ACIR, and several public interest groups drafted a new, more comprehensive piece of legislation which he reintroduced in 1967.[55] After considerable compromise, the Intergovernmental Cooperation Act of 1968 became law.

The passage of the Intergovernmental Cooperation Act (ICA) came at a time that may be considered the end of the "Great Society" era which has been labeled "Creative Federalism." While periods in the evolution of federalism are not easily delineated, the frustration that was expressed when "Great Society" programs failed to solve social ills, when the war in Vietnam had inflamed the nation's youth to the point of civil insurrection, and when the nation's largest cities were experiencing open rioting, indicated that a time of transition had come. Change was badly needed. The nation responded, and a new President took office in 1969 with new hopes, aspirations, and promises. President Nixon arrived in the White House with much of the legal machinery in place and a climate conducive to broad and sweeping change in the intergovernmental arena. The most prominent tool available to him was the Intergovernmental Cooperation Act. The legal authority was now in place, and it was the responsibility of the new President to focus his attention on intergovernmental domestic problems.

Notes

1. Michael D. Reagan, The New Federalism (New York: Oxford Univiersity Press, 1972), p. 3.
2. For a discussion of the historical nature of the federal relationship, see Richard H. Leach, American Federalism (New York: W.W. Norton & Co., Inc., 1970), pp. 1-10. Perhaps the best discussion of the workings of a federal system is contained in Morton Grodzins, The American System: A New View of Government in the United States, Ed. Daniel J. Elazar (Chicago: Rand McNally, 1966).
3. See Senate Committee on Government Operations, Subcommittee on Intergovernmental Relations, "The Federal System as Seen by Federal Aid Officials," (December 15, 1965), p. 95.
4. Richard H. Leach outlines five historical stages in the evolution of federalism - nation-centered, state-centered, dual, cooperative and creative federalism and new federalism, pp. 1-10. At this point, Leach's model of new federalism follows Deil Wright's analogy of picket fence federalism which will be discussed later.
5. Reagan, p.3.
6. Deil S. Wright, "Intergovernmental Relations: An Analytical Overview," Annals of the American Academy of Political and Social Science. (November, 1974), pp. 2-5.
7. Federal-State-Local Relations: Federal Grants-In-Aid, Thirtieth Report by the Committee on Government Operations, Subcommittee on Intergovernmental Relations, House Report 2533, 85th Cong. 2d Sess., (August 8, 1958), p. 7.
8. Advisory Commission on Intergovernmental Relations, Significant Features of Fiscal Federalism 1976-77, Vol. II, M-110 (Washington, D.C.: GPO, March, 1977), p. 7.
9. Martha Derthick, The Influence of Federal Grants (Cambridge, Mass.: Harvard University Press, 1970), p. 7.
10. James M. Kramon, "Where are Federal Grant-In-Aid Programs Headed?" American Bar Association Journal, 57 (May 1971), p. 438.
11. See Advisory Commission on Intergovernmental Relations, Pragmatic Federalism: The Reassignment of Functional Responsibility, M-105, (Washington, D.C.: GPO, July 1976).
12. Wright, pp. 15-16. Also, Advisory Commission on Intergovernmental Relations, Tenth Annual Report, (January 31, 1969), p. 8.
13. Alan Dean, "Administrative Flexibility and Statutory Restraints," in New Directions in Public Administration: The Federal View. Proceedings of "Opposing Forces in Public Administration" Fifth annual Conference of the National Capital Chapter of the American Society of Public Adminstration, November 14-15, 1974 (Reston, Virginia: The Bureaucrat, Inc.), p. 105.
14. A few of the more recent study groups convened to assess the management of the intergovernmental system including the Ash Commission (1970); the President's Advisory Commission on Management Assistance (1974). See also Advisory Commission on Intergovernmental Relations,

Improving Federal Grants Management, (A-53) (Washington, D.C.: GPO, February 1977). The question of the administrative impact of the federal government brought about by the grant-in-aid system has also been relatively ignored. One of the first studies was by the National Municipal League in 1928 (Reports of the Committee on Federal Aid to the States of the National Municipal Review, Vol. XVII, No. 10, October). The next significant work appeared in 1937 by the honored scholar of the American governmental system, V.O. Key, Jr., The Administration of Federal Grants-in-Aid (Chicago: Public Adminstration Service). The Council of State Governments' Committee on Federal Grants-in-Aid published their report, Federal Grants-in-Aid: Report of the Committee on Federal Grants-in-Aid (Chicago: 1949) on the budgetary problems within the administrative apparatus. These reports received little attention and the question of the effects of federal intervention is coming only recently once again into vogue.

15. The Budgeting and Accounting Act of 1921 also created the General Accounting Office (GAO) which is known today as the "Watchdog of Congress." It serves as an outside auditor of the executive branch and reports to Congress.

16. Harvey C. Mansfield, "Reorganizing the Federal Executive Branch: The Limits of Institutionalism," Law and Contemporary Problems, 35 (Summer, 1970), p. 494.

17. For the full text of the report, see the President's Commission on Administrative Management, Report of the Committee With Studies of Administrative Management in the Federal Government (Washington, D.C.: GPO, 1937).

18. Robert C. Fried, Performance in American Bureaucracy (Boston: Little, Brown and Co., 1976), p. 59.

19. Commission on Organization of the Executive Branch of the Government, General Management of the Executive Branch (Washington, D.C.: GPO, 1949).

20. Commission on Organization of the Executive Branch of the Government, Personnel and Civil Service (Washington, D.C.: GPO, 1955).

21. The differences between the two concepts are explained in a number of sources but perhaps most clearly in Alan Schick's, "The Road to PPB: The States of Budget Reform," Public Administration Review, 26 (December, 1966), pp. 243-258.

22. See Louis Brownlow, A Passion for Anonymity (Chicago: University of Chicago Press, 1958), p. 237

23. See Report to Congress by the Committee on the Organization of the Executive Branch of Government (Washington, D.C.: GPO, 1949); and a Report to the President of the U.S. and to the Chairman of the Governors' Conference by the Joint Federal-State Action Committee (Washington, D.C.: GPO, 1958).

24. Address at the National Governors' Conference, Seattle, Washington, August 4, 1953, Public Papers of the President, 1953, p. 536, quoted in Sundquist, p. 7. Also, see President Eisenhower's Message to Congress, March 30, 1973.

25. July 10, 1953 (Public Law 109 (83rd Cong., 1st Sess.)). Section 3(b). The Commission shall study and investigate all of the present activities in which federal aid is extended to state and local governments, the inter-relationships of the financing of this and the sources of the financing of governmental programs. The Commission shall determine and report whether there is justification for federal aid in the various fields in which federal aid is extended; whether there are other fields in which federal aid should be extended; whether federal control with respect to these activities should be limited, and, if so, to what extent; whether federal aid should be limited to cases of need; and all other matters incident to such federal aid, including the ability of the federal government and the states to finance activities of this nature.

26. Ibid., Section1. See also, U.S. Commission on Intergovernmental Relations, A Report to the President for Transmittal to the Congress (Washington, D.C.: GPO, June 1955).

27. Ibid., pp. 2, 5.

28. Ibid., p. 59

29. Morton Grodzins in The American System, ed. Daniel Elazar (Chicago: Rand McNally, 1966), p. 381.

30. "Atomic Energy Proposals," State Government News, Volume X, (March, 1967); and U.S. Advisory Commission on Intergovernmental Relations, State Agencies and Activities for Local Affairs: A Report (Washington, D.C.: GPO, February 8, 1966). For a full report of the Committee, see A Report to the President of the U.S. and the Chairman of the Governors' Conference by the Joint Federal-State Action Committee (Washington, D.C.: GPO, 1958).

31. Terry Sanford, Storm Over the States (New York: McGraw-Hill Book Company, 1967), p. 162. The Committee disbanded with the creation of the Advisory Commission on Intergovernmental Relations in 1959.

32. See Staff Report on Replies from Federal Agencies to Questionnaire Intergovernmental Relations, Intergovernmental Relations Subcommittee, Committee on Government Operations, U.S. Congress, House, 84th Cong., 2d Sess., August 1956.

33. See Replies from State and Local Governments to Questionnaire on Intergovernmental Relations, Sixth Report of the Committee on Government Operations, June 17, 1957.

34. Thirteenth Report by the Committee on Government Operations, August 8, 1958.

35. Donald H. Haider, When Governments Come to Washington (New York: The Free Press, 1974), pp. 124-5. The recommendation for a 5-year review of grant-in-aid programs was also contained in one of the first commission reports to Congress. See Periodic Congressional Reassessment of Federal Grants-in-Aid to State and Local Governments (Washington, D.C.: GPO, July 10, 1967).

36. Deil S. Wright, "The Advisory Commission on Intergovernmental Relations: Unique Features and Policy Orientation," Public Administration Review, 25 (September 1965), pp. 196-98. See also 10-year Record of the

Advisory Commission on Intergovernmental Relations Hearings, Joint Hearings by the Intergovernmental Relations Subcommittees of the House and Senate Government Operations Committee, 92nd Cong., 1st Sess., 1971.

37. Candidates are nominated by the National Governors' Association, Council of State Governments, the National League of Cities/U.S. Conference of Mayors, and the National Association of Counties.

38. For example, recent investigations by ACIR have centered around the concept of sub-state regionalism and the federal system. The Commission produced a conclusive four volume series of the subject area entitled: Regional Decision-Making: New Strategies for Substate Districts, Vol. 1, A-43 (October 1973); Regional Governance: Promise and Performance, Volume II - Case Studies, A-41 (May, 1973); The Challenge of Local Governmental Reorganization, Volume II, A-44 (February, 1974); Governmental Functions and Processes: Local and Areawide, Volume A-45 (February, 1974).

39. Executive Office of the President, Strengthening Public Management in the Intergovernmental System (Washington, D.C.: GPO, 1975) p. 35.

40. Perceptions of program impacts and the development of the war on poverty are contained in Daniel P. Moynihan, Maximum Feasibility Misunderstanding, (New York: The Free Press, 1970).

41. James L. Sundquist and David W. Davis, Making Federalism Work (Washington, D.C.: The Brookings Institute, 1969), p. 25.

42. Ibid. Also, see the Economic Opportunity Act of 1964, Section 2, 611, 604(a)(b); E.O. 11297, August 11, 1966, Section 1, Coordination of Federal Programs; E.O. 11307, September 30, 1966, Section 1, Coordination of Federal Programs Affecting Agricultural and Rural Area Development; and E.O. 11422, August 15, 1968, Section 1(a) 2(c), Cooperative Area Manpower Planning System.

43. Ibid., p. 26.

44. The internal agency problems, lack of a national strategy and leadership as well as suggestions for correcting the problems are contained in Executive Office of the President, Strengthening Public Management in the Intergovernmental System.

45. The Federal System as Seen by Federal Aid Officials, Senate, 89th Cong., 1st Sess., (December 15, 1965), p. 95. State and local views had been determined two years earlier in a previous subcommittee report entitled The Federal System as Seen by State and Local Officials.

46. Ibid., p. 22.

47. Ibid. For other views of this relationship, see J. Leiper Freeman, The Political Process: Executive Bureau-Legislative Committee Relations (2nd ed.) (New York: Random House, 1975).

48. See, for example, Stephen K. Bailey, "Coordinating the Great Society," The Reporter, March 24, 1966.

49. Under President Johnson, the responsibility for Intergovernmental Relations was divided between the Vice President and the Office of Emergency Planning (later called the Office of Emergency Preparedness). Under

this arrangement, the mayors achieved liaison through the Vice President's Office, while the governors were heard through the Office of Emergency Planning.

50. Subcommittee on Intergovernmental Relations, Government Operations Committee, Creative Federalism, Hearings, Senate, 89th Cong., 2d Sess. (1966), pt. 1, p. 397. A summary of intergovernmental problems encountered in administering federal programs in this era is contained in Executive Office of the President, Bureau of the Budget, "Creative Federalism, Report on Field Surveys of Problems in Administering Intergovernmental Programs," The Bureau of the Budget During the Administration of President Lyndon B. Johnson, Vol. II (November 14, 1968).
51. The Bureau of the Budget, now the Office of Management and Budget, was placed within the newly created Executive Office of the President in 1939, as the budgeting and management arm of the President. Following the growth and expansion of other executive agencies during World War II, the management function became subordinated to budget preparation and legislative clearance. As subsequent presidential staffs assumed a greater role in policy issues and affairs, legislative clearance was further subordinated to budget preparation.
52. Haider, pp. 120-2
53. See Chapter 2 for a discussion of the shortcomings of Circular A-85.
54. "Quality of American Government," House Document, March 20, 1967. See also, Harold Seidman, Politics Position and Power—The Dynamics of Federal Organization, 2nd ed. (New York: Oxford University Press, 1976), p. 179.
55. See Federal-State-Local Relations, Hearings Before a Subcommittee, House Committee on Government Operations, 85th Cong. 2d. Sess., 1958; and Subcommittee on Intergovernmental Relations, Government Operations Committee, The Effectiveness of Metropolitan Planning, Senate, 87th Cong., 2d Sess., 1962.

CHAPTER I SELECTED BIBLIOGRAPHY
Articles/Documents

Advisory Commission on Intergovernmental Relations. Annual Report on Operations Under OMB Circular A-85. Washington, D.C.: GPO, January 31, 1975.

____. The Challenge of Local Governmental Reorganization, Vol. II, A-44.Washington, D.C.: GPO, February 1974.

____. Governmental Functions and Processes: Local and Areawide, Vol IV, A-45. Washington, D.C.: GPO, February 1974.

____. Improving Federal Grants Management. A-53. Washington, D.C.: GPO, February 1977.

____. Periodic Congressional Reassessment of Federal Grants-In-Aid to State and Local Governments. Washington, D.C.: GPO, July 10, 1967.

____. Regional Decision-Making: New Strategies for Substate Districts, Vol. I, A-43. Washington, D.C.: GPO, October 1973.

____. Regional Governance: Promise and Performance, Vol. II, A-41. Washington, D.C. GPO, May 1973.

____. Significant Features of Fiscal Federalism 1976-77, Vol. II, M-110. Washington, D.C.: GPO, March 1977.

Bailey, Stephen K. "Coordinating the Great Society," The Reporter. March 24, 1966.

Commission on Organization of the Executive Branch of the Government. General Management of the Executive Branch. Washington, D.C.: GPO, 1949.

____. Personnel and Civil Service. Washington, D.C.: GPO, 1955.

Council of State Governments. "Atomic Energy Proposals," State Government News, Vol. X (March 1967).

Council of State Governments, Committee on Federal Grants-In-Aid. Federal Grants-In-Aid. Chicago: Council of State Governments, 1949.

Executive Office of the President. Strengthening Public Management in the Intergovernmental System. Washington, D.C.: GPO, 1975.

Intergovernmental Relations Subcommittee, Committee on Government Operations. Staff Report on Replies from Federal Agencies to Questionnaire on Intergovernmental Relations. Washington, D.C.: U.S. Congress, House, August 1956.

Intergovernmental Relations Subcommittee of the House and Senate Government Operations Committees, 92nd Cong. 10-Year Record of the Advisory Commission on Intergovernmental Relations Hearings. Joint Hearings. Washington, D.C.: GPO, 1971.

Mansfield, Harvey C. "Reorganizing the Federal Executive Branch: The Limits of Institutionalism," Law and Contemporary Problems, 35 (Summer 1970).

National Municipal League. Reports of the Committee on Federal Aid to the States of the National Municipal Review, Vol. XVII, No. 10. Chicago: National Municipal League, October 1928.

President's Commission on Administrative Management. Report of the Committee with Studies of Administrative Management in the Federal Government. Washington, D.C.: GPO, 1937.

Schick, Alan. "The Road to PPB: The States of Budget Reform," Public Administration Review, 26 (December 1966).

U.S. Advisory Commission on Intergovernmental Relations. State Agencies and Activities for Local Affairs, A Report. Washington, D.C.: GPO, February 8, 1977.

U.S. Bureau of the Budget. "Creative Federalism, Report on Field Surverys of Problems in Administering Intergovernmental Programs," Bureau of the Budget During the Administration of President Lyndon B. Johnson, Vol.II. Washington, D.C.: GPO, November 13, 1968.

Wright, Deil S. "Intergovernmental Relations: An Analytical Overview," Annuals of the American Academy of Political and Social Science. November 1974.

Books

Dean, Alan. "Administrative Flexibility and Statutory Restraints," New Directions in Public Administration: The Federal View. Proceedings of "Opposing Forces in Public Administration," Fifth Annual Conference of the National Capital Chapter of the American Society of Public Administration, November 14-15, 1974. Reston, Virginia: The Bureaucrat, Inc., 1974.

Derthick, Martha. The Influence of Federal Grants. Cambridge, Mass: Harvard University Press, 1970.

Freeman, J. Leiper. The Political Process: Executive Bureau-Legislative Committee Relations. 2nd ed. New York: Random House, 1975.

Fried, Robert C. Performance in American Bureaucracy. Boston: Little, Brown, and Co., 1976.

Grodzins, Morton. The American System: A New View of Government in the United States. Edited by Daniel J. Elazar. Chicago: Rand McNally, 1966.

Haider, Donald H. When Governments Come to Washington. New York: The Free Press, 1974.

Leach, Richard H. American Federalism. New York: WW Norton and Co., Inc., 1970.

Moynihan, Daniel P. Maximum Feasible Misunderstanding. New York: The Free Press, 1970.

Reagan, Michael D. The New Federalism. New York: Oxford University Press, 1972.

Sanford, Terry. Storm Over the States. New York: McGraw-Hill Book Co., 1967.

Seidman, Harold. Politics, Position and Power—The Dynamics of Federal Organization. 2nd ed. New York: Oxford University Press, 1976.

Sundquist, James L. and Davis, David W. Making Federalism Work. Washington, D.C.: The Brookings Institute, 1969.

Hearings

U.S. Congress, House, Subcommittee on Government Operations, 85th Cong. Federal-State-Local Relations, Hearings Before a Subcommittee on Government Operations. Washington, D.C.: GPO. 1958.

Chapter Two
Integovernmental Cooperation and Coordination

I believe that the federal government cannot go on much longer with its present organization of agencies on the domestic side of government....For the past twenty years, the problems of overlap and conflict of mission have grown steadily worse.

John Gardner
Secretary HEW, 1968

Introduction

This chapter focuses on intergovernmental impacts during the years of the Nixon Administration and the changes that were brought about through the expanded administrative authority granted the chief executive through the Intergovernmental Cooperation Act of 1968. The federal responses to the intergovernmental and grant-in-aid program problems of the "Great Society," an era also known as the descriptor "Creative Federalism," are discussed as a prelude to the inauguration of President Nixon's strategy to decentralize the administration of the grant-in-aid system. This strategy eventually became known as the "New Federalism," the subject of Chapter III.

The purpose of Chapter II is to provide information about the continued efforts of the federal government to gain control of the grant-in-aid system and to lay the foundation for the transition between the Johnson and Nixon administrations, which is also the change in philosophical eras between "Creative" and "New" Federalism. In this chapter the more active and pronounced role of the Office of Management and Budget (OMB), as an agency of intergovernmental coordination and management, is discussed. Several key tools of this effort included OMB circulars, the Federal Assistance Review program, development of standard federal regions and the Federal Regional Councils, the Integrated Grants Agreement pilot projects, the Regional Management Information System, and, perhaps most significant, the regional clearinghouse system and OMB Circular A-95. Each of these administration mechanisms is described, and its successes and failures noted where appropriate.

Intergovernmental Cooperation Under the ICA

The problems created by the "Great Society" programs of the Johnson Administration were an extension of the administrative problems already in the grant-in-aid system. The increasing number of programs, the efforts of Congress inspired by a new sense of national conscience, and the patchwork system of administrative rules and regulations that characterized two previous administrations' efforts to cope with the system compounded to blur any clear picture of the state of federalism in the late 1960's and early

1970's. Previous studies provided ample evidence to substantiate the need for wholesale reform and change in the grant-in-aid system. However, because of the nature of the system - how it evolved and the stake in the current system held by the numerous beneficiaries of the aid programs - the movement for meaningful reform was diffused, uncoordinated, and subject to defeat at every turn and before every committee of Congress. It was through this maze, after considerable compromise, that substantial meaningful reform finally was inaugurated. The first significant reform to the grant-in-aid system occurred with the passage of the Intergovernmental Cooperation Act of 1968 (ICA).

The ICA (P.L. 90-577) represented the first serious attempt by Congress to improve the administration of the federal grant-in-aid system. The Act was designed to address a number of problems that were well known to the Congress. In its final form, the Act represented a great deal of compromise between the state and local public interest groups and Congressional reformers. In total, many of the previous systemic deficiencies, as well as the complaints of state and local decision-makers, were addressed.[1]

The ICA contained five key provisions representing a Senate-House compromise and was based primarily upon the efforts of Senator Muskie and the ACIR. The main provisions included the following:

- *mandatory notification of the purpose and amounts of grants-in-aid and support provided to a specific state, upon the request of a governor or state legislature*
- *removal of the requirement that states keep federal funds in separate bank accounts*
- *a requirement that federal agencies schedule the disbursement of funds to recipient governments so as to minimize the time between disbursement and use*
- *a requirement that agencies coordinate the planning provisions of separate federal programs and incorporate them into local and regional comprehensive planning efforts*
- *authority for the President to establish rules and regulations to govern the formulation, assessment, and review of federal grant programs having area-wide significance*[2]

As enacted, the ICA pleased no one entirely. Governors attained most of what they sought, except for additional grant program consolidation and authorization for joint funding of programs. Mayors were relatively satisfied with the Act's attention to community development problems, but they felt that the enforcement provisions assigned to the Bureau of the Budget (BOB) were not clear. Both groups, however, greeted the ICA as an improvement.[3] Although the Act was a piecemeal solving of comprehensive administrative problems characteristic of the legislative process and reflective of BOB (now Office of Management and Budget) management decisions today, it laid the foundations for more effective intergovernmental cooperation.[4] More important, it established the legal basis for subsequent administrative regulation of the grant-in-aid system. The ICA also provided the legal authority for development of subsequent coordination and management within the intergovernmental system.

Following passage of the ICA, intergovernmental coordination and management activities moved forward on several fronts. The first advance was creation of a top level focal point for intergovernmental concerns; the second involved reorganization of the BOB.

Office of Intergovernmental Relations

On February 14, 1969, the Office of Intergovernmental Relations was established by Executive Order 11455 and was placed under the immediate supervision of the Vice President. The purpose of this office was to improve federal, state, and local relationships through top level attention to problems presented by state and local government representatives. It also was assigned to review the procedures of federal executive agencies, which afforded state and local officials opportunities to confer and comment on feeral assistance programs and other integovernmental issues. The selection of a former governor of South Dakota to hed the office, under the supervision of Vice President Agnew, placed the office nder two ex-governors. The appointment did not please the nation's mayors, who had urged that a person with impartial credentials and identification be named, "...one who has not been identified as a 'state' man or as a 'city' man or a 'county' man."[5] Unfortunately, the office lacked significant authority and accomplished little during its existence.[6] In late 1972, under Executive Order 11690, the Office of Intergovernmental Relations was abolished, and its functions were transferred to the Domestic Council.

Reorganization Plan #2 (OMB and the Domestic Council)

On a second front, administration of the intergovernmental system was given added attention in 1970 when President Nixon implemented the recommendations of the Ash Council. Roy Ash, a management specialist who headed Litton Industries, chaired the President's Advisory Council on Executive Reorganization which had been appointed by President Nixon on April 5, 1969.[7] The Council's recommendations were designed to strengthen federal management and control of the domestic intergovernmental system.

The Council called for a Domestic Council patterned after the internationally-oriented National Security Council which had proved so successful under President Eisenhower. It also recommended a reorganization of the Bureau of the Budget into the Office of Management and Budget (OMB) to emphasize the growing management responsibilities of that agency. The division of responsibilities between the two organizations, explained by President Nixon in a message that accompanied the reorganization proposal before Congress, was that the Council "...will primarily be concerned with what we do," while the OMB "...will primarily be concerned with how we do it and how well we do it."[8]

The Domestic Council was formed to assess national domestic needs, define national goals, analyze specific problems, monitor compliance with existing policies, and provide the President with policy recommendations in response to domestic problems.[9] It would operate through task forces designated by the President and charged to present a complete picture of the problem in such areas as the environment, welfare, energy, crime, housing, etc. The task forces would report directly to John Erlichman, the Council's Executive Director and the President's advisor for domestic affairs. The Domestic Council was intended not only to establish an integrated domestic policy, but also to attempt for the first time to manage the intergovernmental system.

Unfortunately, as circumstances proved, domestic policy became secondary to a President more concerned with international affairs and the war in Vietnam. Therefore, while the idea of the Domestic Council was sound, it was not supported strongly by President Nixon, who felt that the domestic affairs were something better left to the Cabinet. Nixon noted, "All you need is a competent Cabinet to run the country at home. You need a President for foreign policy; no Secretary of State is really important; the President makes foreign policy."[10] The final formulation of the Council was left to John Erlichman, who structured the organization as a personnel staff element and staffed it with political appointees, thus formalizing a trend toward centralizing power in the President's personnel staff.[11]

Perhaps because of its political underpinnings, the Domestic Council failed to live up to its charge. Its responsibilities were relegated to other groups, and it became involved in political concerns at the beginning of President Nixon's second term.[12] However, the Domestic Council was not a total failure. During its first two years of existence, there were some noteworthy successes. For the first time in history, the President, along with the OMB, had a significant mechanism for developing innovative domestic policy initiatives. At its height, the Domestic Council employed 47 staff members and sent the President 13 reports between August 1969 and November 1970. The Council produced a number of legislative proposals and gave form to what later became President Nixon's "New Federalism" approach to domestic affairs. It also made it easier for domestic policy issues to be brought up for consideration in the White House.[13].

Adding the "M" to OMB

During his first term in office, President Nixon promoted a domestic policy that included plans to "devolve" and decentralize funds and authority away from Washington and toward state and local governments. This goal was to be accomplished through a "New American Revolution," whereby power would be returned to the people.[14] The "revolution" was to begin with executive level reorganization, starting with the BOB.

Following the recommendations of the Ash Council, the Bureau's management functions were strengthened under Reorganization Plan No. 2. The plan took effect on July 1, 1970, and the term "management" was added to the title of the Bureau, emphasizing its expanded role. The statutory functions of the BOB were transferred to the President and returned to the Director of OMB under Executive Order 11451.[15]

As previously noted, OMB was to be concerned with *how* and *how well* the objectives and policies that would be established by the Domestic Council were carried out by executive agencies. A March 12 Presidential message to Congress also stressed new roles for OMB related to fiscal analysis, program performance, evaluation, field-level interagency cooperation, executive manpower development, and improvements in governmental organization and management.[16] These changes were intended to broaden OMB's management role considerably beyond its traditional budgetary functions.

On the surface, this new direction appeared logically related to the President's desires for greater management control over domestic affairs. However, some reviewers of the reorganization noted that powers previously conferred by statute to OMB were transferred to the President. This transfer made OMB officials less accountable and responsive to Congress. Also, some administrators within OMB were unhappy to see their policy-making roles shifted to the Domestic Council. The Domestic Council appeared to be structured to formalize a process requiring legislative clearance by the White House, rather than through the staff of OMB, as had been done previously.[17] In response to these changes, Roy Ash in testimony before Congress noted "... we do not believe this is centralizing the governmental process....Quite the contrary. The President intended to delegate more power, but to do so he must first centralize managerial control."[18] Recognizing the need for executive reorganization, Congressional criticism was quieted, but not eliminated.

In 1973, following the appointment of Roy Ash as OMB Director, the two-sided arrangement of a deputy director over the budgetary functions and an associate director over management functions was eliminated to permit a single, straight line of control over both. Management associates were added to each budgetary division of OMB to incorporate a management thrust into those areas. An assistant director for operations was made responsible for the four management divisions, including a small Division of Intergovernmental Relations. At this same time, some grant-in-aid related administrative responsibilities and the corresponding management circulars in these areas were transferred to the General Services Administration (GSA) and the Department of Treasury. Several OMB circulars were redesignated as GSA circulars or Treasury circulars.[19] These changes coincided with President Nixon's attempt to tighten control of the Executive Office by shifting "line" activities to other agencies.

The OMB has been used not only to implement presidential policy, but also to bring order to the entire executive establishment. One of the most prominent tools in this process is OMB's use of the management circular. Circulars are administrative rules and regulations specifying actions or constraints on federal executive agencies and promoting uniform national policies. Agencies, in turn, develop internal rules and regulations based on these circulars, which are enforced through periodic audits by OMB (previously BOB) examiners. State and local agencies, as recipients of federal assistance, are held accountable for compliance with these circulars, as well as agency regulations.

Significant OMB Circulars Through 1970

At approximately the same time that the debates over the Intergovernmental Cooperation Act were nearing conclusion, in the spring of 1967, BOB formally released an administrative circular designed to address some of the issues raised during these debates. The new BOB circular was designed to address the complaints by state and local officials that they had no opportunity to participate in the rule-making process prior to the formalization and publication of agency rules. After more than six months of negotiations, the BOB formally released Circular A-85 (*Consultation with Heads of States and Local Governments in Development of Federal Rules, Regulations, Standards, Procedures, and Guidelines*) with instructions concerning its intent and implementation procedures for federal agencies to follow in obtaining state and local review and comment on proposed program changes, administrative rules, regulations, standards, procedures, or guideline changes.

Section of Intergovernmental Administration and Management, American Society for Public Administration. *Intergovernmental News,* Vol. 3, No. 2 (September, 1979), p. 5. Reprinted with permission.

Circular A-85, which went into effect on July 28, 1967, covered both old regulations and new ones that would be issued by federal agencies. Federal agencies were directed to consider requests from state and local governments "...to review and revise regulations already in effect, and to consult with such officials upon request."[20] The ACIR was persuaded to act as an intermediary or secretariat in coordinating draft regulations between the state and local government public interest groups and executive agencies and to serve as the administrator of the Circular.

Under the Circular, the federal agencies, themselves, decided which regulations were to be channeled through the A-85 consultation process. The ACIR transmitted draft regulations to appropriate public interest groups whose members served as spokespersons for state and local government interests and forwarded the comments returned to the federal agency initiating the regulation. ACIR also was required to submit an annual report on A-85 activity to the Director of BOB.

The first evaluation of the effectiveness of A-85 was made in 1975. In this report which covered calendar year 1974, ACIR noted that the primary user of the system was the U.S. Department of Health, Education, and Welfare (37 issuances) followed by the Environmental Protection Agency (16 issuances), and the Law Enforcement Assistance Administration (14 issuances).[21] The total number of possible issuances was not estimated. The total number of consultation issuances under the Circular totalled 114 for all agencies. The response record to these issuances by the public interest group representatives of state and local governments was not good.

In the final report on A-85, which was replaced with the issuance of Executive Order No. 12044 in March 1978, the ACIR noted some possbile reasons for this poor response record. Some public interest groups (PIGS) did not wish to reply to draft regulations; some replied, but rarely commented on agency issuances; others felt that most agency issuances were irrelevant to their interests.[22] However, much of the failure of A-85 can be blamed on a lack of federal level enthusiasm:

- *Agencies do not seriously consider major changes to circulated drafts suggested by the public interest groups.*
- *There is inadequate pre-consultation with the public interest groups by the agencies.*
- *OMB almost always exempts agencies from the provisions of the Circular whenever requested.*
- *Final regulations are circulated infrequently, and when they are, it is usually all at once at the end of each calendar year.*
- *OMB has refused to clarify ambiguous language in the Circular around which most compliance questions revolve.*
- *Agencies use the A-85 process simultaneously with, or even after, a draft regulation appears in the **Federal Register** where it becomes law in 30 to 60 days.*[23]

Circular A-85 continued in effect until agency procedures for implementing Executive Order No. 12044 had been developed. However, without OMB leadership or more substantial presidential interest, the chances of enforcing the intent of A-85 (substantive state and local input to the rulemaking process) were slight. Given the effort required in the pre-consultation clearance of rules and regulations, there are serious questions as to whether A-85 was worth the effort.[24] Today, A-85 and E.O. 12044 require publication of proposed rules in the *Federal Register* (which will be discussed later) as a better, broader method of comment than ACIR's previous distribution role.

Another significant circular was directed at encouraging intergovernmental cooperation in the provision of services to state and local governments (OMB Circular A-97, 1969). A third circular was prepared in response to the dictates of the Intergovernmental Cooperation Act. In Circular A-98 (1970), OMB developed a standardized reporting form that required federal agencies to provide information on their grant-in-aid actions. Finally, a fourth circular established uniform principles for determining costs applicable to grants and contracts (OMB Circular A-87, 1970).

These OMB management efforts came at a favorable time. By 1970, the number of categorical grant programs had escalated to almost 1,000, and there was little that had been done to consolidate existing programs or to assist state and local officials in understanding or coping with them. OMB's goal was to strike a balance between centralized management control and direction and those decentralized operations that would be left to the executive line agencies. These four circulars, while inadequate in addressing the full range of intergovernmental administrative problems, moved the system in the right direction. By 1970, individual agency decisions based on programmatic concerns resulted in over 200 different federal field structures. State and local officials were forced to travel to different parts of the country to discuss programs and needs with the appropriate federal agency program representatives. There was no focal point for information located as a convenience to the users of federal program funding. The lack of a uniform federal field structure was readily apparent.

Management Centralization, Administrative Decentralization Under Nixon

President Nixon reviewed the results of these problems in a special address on March 27, 1970:

> *The organization of federal services has grown up piecemeal creating gaps in some areas, deficiencies across the country....Coordination cannot flourish under conditions such as that. Yet without real coordination, intelligent and efficient government is impossible; money and time are wasted and goals are compromised.*[25]

In a vigorous movement toward reform, the President inaugurated a series of steps designed to provide administrative control of the grant-in-aid system while decentralizing program responsibilities, the key to what later became the philosophy of "New Federalism."

Federal Assistance Review (FAR)

A first step toward resolving these deficiencies was a move in the direction indicated by the Intergovernmental Cooperation Act. President Nixon initiated the Federal Assistance Review (FAR), a three-year experimental program to decentralize administrative procedures in the grant-in-aid program, to place greater reliance on state and local governments, and to standardize and simplify the grant administration process. FAR was conducted by OMB and the Domestic Council between 1969 and 1973. Based on earlier recommendations by BOB and its own findings, the FAR teams proposed the establishment of ten federal regions to bring together 75 regional federal agencies and bureaus (Figure 1).[26]

The purpose of FAR was to allow state and local governments to assume more responsibility in coordinating grant proposals while standardizing and simplifying application procedures. The participating federal agencies were told to cut "red tape" in the application process as much as possible and to encourage joint funding proposals from one governmental unit when it involved two or more federal agencies. Following the provisions of the ICA, the FAR effort also served as an action catalyst within each of the 14 par-

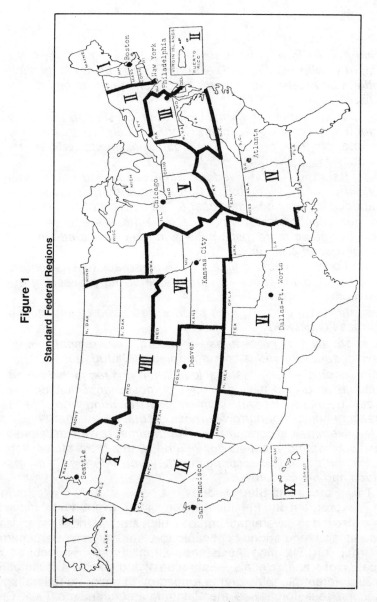

Figure 1

Standard Federal Regions

ticipating federal agencies by bringing about internal coordination while facilitating the implementation of standard federal regional boundaries. Internal management improvement programs within each agency concentrated on the reduction of paperwork imposed on state and local governments, implementation of the regional boundaries concept, and support of the Federal Regional Councils.

The results of the FAR program were impressive. FAR can be credited with the following:

- *Common regional boundaries—Those agencies concerned primarily with social and economic programs established uniform boundaries and common locations for their regional offices.*
- *Regional Councils—Regional Councils representing the major federal grant-making agencies were established in the new regional centers to improve coordination among federal programs.*
- *Decentralization—Some federal agencies moved operational authority from Washington, D.C. to their field offices to ensure that decision making was closer to the delivery of services.*
- *Greater reliance on state and local governments—These levels were delegated more responsibility in the detailed administration of federal programs.*
- *Reduction in processing time—The federal assistance agencies were directed to reduce the time required for processing applications.*
- *Reduction in red tape—High priority was given to eliminating needless paperwork.*
- *Consistency in procedures—Standard requirements were developed for functions common to several programs.*
- *Joint funding—Congressional legislation was requested to consolidate programs having similar purposes and recipients in order to offset program fragmentation resulting from the increasing number of narrow-purpose grants.*
- *Intergovernmental cooperation—Arrangements were developed for coordinating requests for federal grants with states and communities, and for ensuring that they were informed of grants which had been approved.*[27]

Other Task Forces and Study Groups

The FAR program and President Nixon's intergovernmental management strategy also led to several task forces which studied the standardization of procedures and regulations applicable to planning. The Interdepartmental Task Group on Planning Assistance Grant Programs focused on the clarification of planning goals, elimination of duplication, and simplification of the 36 different planning grants funded by 11 separate federal agencies. The second task force was the Planning Requirements Task Group. It studied the planning requirements that were imposed on state and local recipients by each planning grant program. Both groups developed recommendations for simplfying the paperwork associated with planning grants, and they completed their work in 1970. Their reports were released through the Planning Assistance Requirements Coordinating Committee (PARC), which had been established by HUD in 1967 to coordinate and oversee planning requirements and assistance programs. Some paperwork savings and standardization resulted from the recommendations of these groups, but no significant changes were indicated.

Another effort at studying aspects of the grant-in-aid system was the Joint Financial Management Improvement Program (JFMIP). The JFMIP began in 1948 as an attempt to improve the financial management, planning, and control of federal funds. Direction of this program was shared by the Comptroller General, the Secretary of the Treasury, the Director of OMB, and the Chairman of the U.S. Civil Service Commission. The study involved the review of procedures and requirements related to auditing, accounting, and financial reporting under grant-in-aid programs. It resulted in several recommendations to simplify and improve these aspects of grant programs.

The Interagency Audit Standards Working Group (IASWG), also was formed during this same period as a result not only of the increasing complexity and proliferation of grant programs, but also of growing concern about the use of federal funds. It included representatives from the General Accounting Office (GAO); Health, Education, and Welfare (HEW); the Office of Management and Budget (OMB); the Departments of Commerce (DOC), Agriculture (DA), Labor (DOL), Transportation (DOT), and Housing and Urban Development (HUD); the Office of Economic Opportunity (OEO); state and local governments, and universities. This group addressed intergovernmental audit standards and issued a report through the GAO in 1972 entitled "Standards for Audit of Governmental Organizations, Programs, Activities, and Functions." This report served to standardize audit requirements and promote some uniformity.

Additionally, the Commission on Government Procurement, (CGP) was created under P.L. 91-129. It was comprised of representatives of the legislative branch, the executive branch, and the public, and it employed a professional staff. The Commissions studied federal grant programs and use of grants and contracts, as well as the applicablilty of procurement rules and regulations related to grant programs. It documented what everyone already knew: the existence of considerable confusion in the relationship between the federal agencies, their contractors, and the recipients of assistance. The Commission suggested legislation to clarify, first, the distinction between contracts and grants for assistance programs and, second, the different types of assistance available. For various reasons, most federal line agencies did not support clarification of the distinction between grants and contracts. Lacking a clear definition, each agency had the prerogative to interject and utilize the relationships established by these instruments to its own advantage. It was almost 10 years before an acceptable distinction emerged in the Federal Grant and Cooperation Act of 1977 (see Chapter VII).

In summary, during the late 1960's, the federal response to the proliferation of grant programs which characterized the "Great Society" was a series of study groups which developed recommendations for standardizing and simplifying the grant system. OMB took the leadership in this effort by organizing and coordinating the various interagency bodies and their work. With the new management responsibilities it had been given under President Nixon, OMB began to implement changes authorized by the Intergovernmental Cooperation Act of 1968.[28] Its principal efforts, however, to actually carry out its administrative and management responsibilities were through the Federal Regional Councils and the development, issuance, and control of management circulars.

Federal Regional Councils (FRC's)

Complaints emanated from state and local officials following the rapid rise in the number of categorical grant-in-aid programs and the accompanying rules and regulations that grew out of the "Great Society." The more prevalent complaints noted that federal agencies pursued program goals without regard to local needs; that certain needs could be met only by application to several federal agencies; that the application process was too complex; that the general deluge of federal information and reporting requirements was becoming too complicated to understand; and that federal programs frequently overlapped or even failed to meet the key needs of the recipient governments.[29] In addition, the number of interagency study groups, organized to formulate recommendations to resolve these problems, began to present a coordination problem.

To address these concerns, in September 1968, BOB requested that regional representatives of HUD, DOL, OEO, and HEW in Atlanta, Chicago, New York, and San Francisco meet on a regular basis to deal with interdepartmental grant-in-aid program conflicts and to assist in developing joint funding strategies with governors and other elected officials. The representatives also were requested to study and learn about the programs and problems of each other's agencies. These meetings became the foundation for the establishment of the Federal Regional Councils (FRC's).[30]

The FRC's appeared to be the answer to a need for program coordination at the regional level that would assist the new Nixon Administration in responding to state and local complaints, solve some interagency problems, and promote administrative decentralization. The mission of the FRC's, articulated formally when chartered after a 3-year "pilot" or test period was, "...to foster and promote the utilization of multi-agency programs and funds so that the needs of the citizens and the directives of Congress [could] be more efficiently addressed and carried out."[31] In short, the FRC's central mission was to promote interagency program coordination at the regional level.[32] The Councils were directed to develop short-term, regional strategies and mechanisms for program delivery; to develop integrated program and funding plans with the assistance and participation of governors and local chief executives; to encourage joint and complementary grant applications in related programs; to evaluate interagency programs; to develop long-range allocation strategies responding to state and local needs; to supervise other regional interagency coordinating mechanisms; and, finally, to develop administrative procedures to facilitate day-to-day intergovernmental interagency cooperation.[33]

The translation of this mission into operational activities was left to each FRC. For example, the Region V (refer to Figure 1) FRC operating plan reflects specific needs in the Great Lakes Region, a high-density, industrial complex. For FY 1976, the Region V FRC plan included the following specific activities designed systematically to manage and coordinate federal program activities within the region. The 17 activities indicated were:

1. Joint Funding Programs – to simplify delivery and administration of joint funded federal assistance to state and local governments and private, non-profit organizations.

2. Intergovernmental Relations – to assist state and local units of government in improving their overall capability to manage resources received by federal agencies and to increase agency sensitivity to state and local needs.

3. A-95 – to assist the FRC in improving the implementation of OMB Circular A-95 within Region V.

4. Comprehensive Planning – to develop recommendations for resolving conflicting federal agency requirements in the area of comprehensive planning.

5. Rural Development – to implement the Rural Development Act by providing technical assistance to improve the quality of life and economic opportunity in rural areas.

6. Migrants – to improve opportunities for migrant agricultural workers in Region V and to cooperate with the Dallas FRC in developing continuity of services for migrant people who follow the crops between Texas and Region V states.

7. Indians (Reservation) – to strengthen tribal government planning and management capacity in selected Indian tribes and provide tribal representatives with periodic briefings on federal programs for which they are eligible.

8. External Affirmative Action – to develop guidelines to further and ensure affirmative action by FRC grantees and contractors.

9. Construction Grants – to provide information concerning the projected outlays of federal grants for capital improvement projects to states and municipalities for use in projecting the number and type of jobs to be created and in planning training programs needed to ensure the existence of a pool of skilled workers.

10. Great Lakes Shoreland Damage Reduction – to coordinate the efforts of various federal, state, and regional entities acting to reduce shoreland damage due to erosion and to develop alternative strategies for abating damage.

11. Environmental Impact Study – to serve as the FRC's focal point for environmental issues of multi-agency concern relating to federal loan, grant, permit, and contract programs.

12. FEB/FRC Preventive Health Measures - Health Projects — to continue cancer education and screening and the development of campaigns to combat heart disease, drug abuse, and alcoholism.

13. Title XX – to develop interagency cooperation in the implementation of the Title XX state plans that will supplement and/or complement the actions of the HEW Title XX efforts.

14. Spanish Speaking (Urban) – to examine existing programs for the Spanish-speaking and to develop a method to integrate them with FRC

efforts.

15. Indo-Chinese Refugee Resettlement Program — to improve the present services provided by all agencies assisting in the Indochinese resettlement effort.
16. Uniform Relocation Assistance—to facilitate uniform implementation of the Uniform Relocation Assistance and Real Property Acquisition Policies Act of 1970.
17. Special Issues and Programs—to coordinate all available agency resources to alleviate crisis situations and/or matters of an emergency nature.

Generally, the FRC's have not been viewed as succesful. Their performance is limited, in part, by organizational constraints. The FRC chairperson is presidentially appointed for only a one-year term in accordance with the original recommendation of the Undersecretaries Group. (The Undersecretaries Group is comprised of the persons who are second only to the secretary of each federal domestic agency and are, thus, a highly potent, but political group.[34]) While the chairperson of an FRC may be reappointed, the position is political and is usually filled by a politically appointed agency regional director rather than a career professional administrator. Turnover of agency regional directors usually occurs with each change of presidency. Furthermore, FRC staff are provided and funded by several of the participating federal agencies, diffusing the chairperson's control. Promotions and job tenure for FRC staff are determined by the parent agency. Finally, the scope of decisional authority delegated by parent agencies to regional representatives varies from agency to agency. Thus, for example, HUD's regional representative is not only autonomous from the FRC chairman but also has considerably different authority than the Environmental Protection Agency's representative. Superimposed upon this staff autonomy is the policy guidance of the Undersecretaries Group, which is located in Washington, D.C. and not in the field, where the perspective may be very different.

The performance of FRC's also is limited by regional factors, the character or personality of the executive director and staff personnel of each region, and the willingness of governmental representatives within the region to cooperate with the FRC. There have been complaints that local governmental managers have not heard of the FRC, that federal representatives at the FRC's do not recognize the problems of local governments, and that grant-coordination efforts are infrequent and not vigorous enough or are of an ad hoc nature.[35] As might be expected, some FRC's are considered highly successful by state and local governments, while others are not.

Inspite of managerial difficulties, the FRC's have made some gains. Several have been able to meet some needs of their regions and have received regional acceptance. As time passes, the existence of the FRC's has gained increased attention, and they appear to be better fulfilling the role for which they were created. The FRC's serve an important information dissemination role concerning specific federal program objectives and are receiving increasing recognition by OMB. Their future, however, is uncertain and dependent upon presidential interest and attention (see Chapter VII).

The Integrated Grant Administration Program (IGA)

One area in which the FRC's have been useful in simplifying the grant-in-aid application process has been the Integrated Grant Administration Program (IGA), which also was created under the legislative authority of the Intergovernmental Cooperation Act of 1968. The Integrated Grant Administration pilot or test program was initiated in January 1972 by OMB with the support of the Undersecretaries Group. Under the IGA, the FRC's were assigned the administration of 26 pilot projects which permitted state and local agencies to submit single applications for multiple, related grants. The review process of those applications was greatly simplified by using a single set of financial controls, as well as auditing and record-keeping requirements, which were usually those of the lead agency.

The IGA experiment evolved from a test project in which four state and local applicants were permitted to submit single assistance applictions to obtain funding from several federal funding sources.[36] After two years of experience, the original four test projects were expanded to 24, or two in each FRC and four from the Seattle and Chicago FRC's. During the trial period an interagency group, supervised by OMB, evaluated the projects and furnished the results of these tests to all participating federal and state agencies. The results were generally favorable.

Administrative responsibility for the IGA experiment was transferred to the General Services Administration (GSA) in November 1973.[37] OMB's first-year assessment of the IGA pilot program was issued simultaneously with the November transfer. The assessment included recommendations for several administrative adjustments to be carried out by GSA in addition to its responsibility for training participants and monitoring the program.

The IGA, while not a grant program per se, attempted to bring about administrative simplification of the application process. IGA was simply a process designed to overcome restrictive administrative constraints associated with applications for assistance involving more than one agency. It involved three phases: 1) multi-agency project funding requests by state or local applicants were made by means of a single application to the appropriate FRC; 2) projects selected by the FRC for processing were reviewed by an interagency task force of representatives from the potential granting agencies; and 3) approved projects were administered by a lead federal agency.[38] A detailed work plan of this complex process, from application to project execution, is contained in Exhibit I.

While this process may appear formidable, it is not as complicated as processing an application involving multiple funding sources when the burden rests entirely on the applicant. For example, when attempting to obtain funding from several agencies to support a single project, the applicant must submit a separate application to each agency using that agency's forms and meeting its auditing and control requirements. Each agency that is part of the package exercises a veto at any stage of the process on the application. Applications to multiple funding sources are thus extremely complex and time-consuming to prepare. Under the IGA pilot, however, the FRC selected

Exhibit I

Integrated Grant Administration Program System Flow Chart

			A. NOTIFICATION
1.	Applicant	(a)	prepares notification of proposed project and submits to Federal Regional Council (FRC)
		(b)	prepares notification information required under OMB Circular A-95 and submits to clearinghouses
2.	FRC	(a)	accepts or denies proposal
		(b)	appoints coordinating officer for accepted proposals
3.	Coordinating officer		
		(a)	contacts Federal agencies to confirm availability of grant funds requested or locate alternate funding possibilities for proposal
		(b)	coordinates the relationship between Federal and State grantor agencies
		(c)	assists applicant in preparation of application
4.	Applicant submits application to FRC (Through A-95 clearinghouse if issue remains)		

			B. APPLICATION PROCESSING
1.	FRC assembles task force of representatives from Federal agencies from whom funds are requested and from State agencies participating as State grantor agencies.		
2.	Task force	(a)	recommends a lead agency to FRC
		(b)	reviews entire application and assures it has received clearinghouse coordination
		(c)	obtains decisions on program funding from grantor agencies
		(d)	recommends approval or disapproval to FRC
3.	FRC	(a)	selects lead agency
		(b)	approves or disapproves application
		(c)	transmits approval or disapproval decision to applicant. Approval letter includes amount of award and identification of the lead agency
4.	State agencies participating as grantor agencies notify grantee of decisions on State support. Approved project will receive State funds under established State procedures.		
5.	Federal grantor agencies submit the notifications of grant-in-aid action (OMB Standard Form 240) to the appropriate State central information reception agency.		
6.	Lead agency	(a)	establishes working fund and arranges for advances of funds from amounts obligated by Federal participating agencies to support project
		(b)	issues integrated grant award to grantee

Submits continuation application

			C. PROJECT EXECUTION
1.	Lead agency		
		(a)	issues letter of credit as funding mechanisms for project
		(b)	arranges for and coordinates program monitoring
		(c)	receives and processes fiscal reports
		(d)	reports to participating Federal agencies on project programs
		(e)	handles requests for project revisions
		(f)	monitors compliance with special conditions imposed with grant award
		(g)	arranges for single Federal audit
		(h)	monitors timely submission of continuation application
2.	Grantee agency		
		(a)	performs projects in substantial conformance with approved work plans and in compliance with any special conditions imposed with award
		(b)	prepares and submits required reports promptly
		(c)	consults with lead agency concerning deviations from work plans, possible revisions in project, any problems related to use of proposed funds
		(d)	revises annual work program

Source: The Integrated Grant Administration (IGA) Program, Washington, D.C., Office of Management and Budget, January 14, 1972, Exhibit B.

projects which seemed suitable for the special IGA assistance. It then appointed and steered the task force responsible for the application and generally coordinated the progress of the application to conclusion (i.e., to project execution). Projects were selected on the basis of dollar value (they had to total over $200,000 and be interagency in nature).

An additional assessment of the first 26 IGA projects covering the period January 1972 to September 1973 was reported by OMB in November 1973. The report indicated generally positive results but also several needed areas of administrative adjustment. GSA responded to the recommendations by establishing a full-time staff responsible for IGA, which was located in its Office of Federal Management Policy. GSA also issued a management policy directive (May 7, 1974) that rescinded exclusions contained in the original pilot project selection guidelines against land acquisition and construction grant projects and that required the use of uniform application and reporting forms. GSA also expanded the number of IGA pilot projects from 26 to 34, created an IGA information center and clearinghouse (at GSA), and began publication of an IGA newsletter. (The IGA newsletter was subsequently discontinued following passage of the Joint Funding Simplification Act in 1974).

The OMB assessment report also recommended that GSA conduct a second-year evaluation. The GSA evaluation was initiated in August 1974 and completed in December. The purpose of this assessment was to evaluate the IGA program's effectiveness and to recommend improvements or, in case of negative findings, the termination of the pilot effort. This second assessment encompassed a view at four governmental levels: 1) a field assessment of participants, including grantees, state grantor agencies, and federal regional officials; 2) FRC staffing and management practices, including staffing, project management patterns, and work priorities; 3) central office assessment of participating federal agencies; and 4) analysis of the participation of public interest groups and related professional organizations.[39] Shortly before the draft assessment report was issued in December 1974, President Ford signed the Joint Funding Simplification Act (JFSA).[40] The question of extending or amending the IGA became moot because the pilot was superseded by legislative authority for a program of government-wide joint funding built upon the experience of the IGA pilot program.

Was the IGA a success? Perhaps the better question is: Was it worth the effort? The survey results of the second IGA assessment indicated that state and local officials favored the process, while federal level officials generally felt it was too much trouble. The comments of one federal official at the operating level seemed to capture the ambivalence, "IGA is worth the effort in the minds of local public administrators.... Thus, it is worthwhile for federal officials to accept the grief of testing new support systems with state and local administrators."[41]

At the federal level, agencies adhered to separate application, reporting, auditing, and evaluation requirements unique to their operations and established by their administrative rules, thereby facilitating the vertical, functional, or "picket fence" approach to grants administration. The IGA assessment found a "lack of clear policies and procedures [which] inhibited consistent application of the IGA process by federal agencies and Federal Regional Councils."[42] The assessment report also indicated that federal agencies failed to identify clearly programs suitable for joint funding, that internal procedures for processing IGA applications were inadequate, that IGA projects were not audited uniformly, and that the development of expertise was hampered by federal staffing limitations and turnover both within the federal agencies and the FRC's. Because of a lack of adequate staff, several FRC's even refused to accept applications for new projects under the pilot program.[43]

The reaction to the IGA pilot program by state and local representatives was extremely positive. One of the more successful projects—a program originated by the Metropolitan Council of Municipalities and the City of St. Paul—resulted in a savings of 14 man-years of administrative time at a cost of $140,000. It was noted that "... the integration of all the funding sources enabled the Council to more closely coordinate its multifaceted planning effort by requiring the separately funded program elements to relate to the overall program." [44]

Following passage of the Joint Funding Simplification Act on December 31, 1975, the IGA program ceased to exist in name. Responsibility for the IGA program, at that time, was transferred to OMB and a management circular was issued to standardize the use of this process (A-III, Jointly funded Assistance to State and Local Governments and Non-Profit Organizations.).

The Joint Funding Simplification Act (JFSA)

The Joint Funding Simplification Act (JFSA) or P.L. 93-510, which incorporated many of the recommendations of the IGA assessment report, represented a signficant administrative step forward in intergovernmental cooperation. Unfortunately, the JFSA is broad in language, and this fact has allowed individual federal agencies to interpret how *they* believe programs should be best coordinated to serve grantees.[45] The JFSA builds upon the experience of the IGA program in promoting simplification in the coordination of jointly-funded grant-in-aid programs. It permits a single application, audit, and federal agency point of contact for grant applications involving multiple programs or agencies. Like the IGA pilot, the Act seeks to "streamline" the grant application process by cutting red tape. Its purposes, as stated in the Act, are:

...to enable state and local governments and private non-profit organizations to use federal assistance more effectively and efficiently, and to adapt that assistance to their particular needs through the wider use of projects drawing upon resources available from more than one federal agency, or appropriation. It is the further purpose of this Act to encourage federal-state arrangements under which local governments and private, non-profit organizations may more effectively and efficiently combine state and federal resources in support of projects of common interest to the governments and organizations concerned.

The JFSA is designed to accomplish these purposes by:

- *meeting interrelated needs for receiving grants from several federal agencies through one funding source,*
- *establishing work plans and priorities geared to the needs of the grantees,*
- *coordinating federal funds to meet the grantees' own planning and funding cycles,*
- *simplifying and standardizing grant administrative requirements,*
- *requiring reports to one federal agency versus several,*
- *replacing several federal audits with one by the lead agency.*[46]

The Act is similar to, but not the same as, the IGA pilot program. Under the JFSA, private, non-profit organizations are eligible applicants and projects supported by only one federal agency are not eligible if state assistance is also part of the project plan.

The joint-funding process has advantages and disadvantages. It is geared toward large, multi-year projects (most projects will have a life of three to five years) and generally is not feasible for one-year projects costing less than $200,000. Also, the Act does not clarify the relationships between the OMB, GSA, the Undersecretaries Group, and the FRC's. The effect of these new procedures on federal department operations also is not clear. The administrative burden of participating agencies is sure to increase, and the IGA was not popular at the very level assigned major responsibility for implementing the program.[47]

JFSA had an expiration date of February 1980. In February 1979, the President reported his recommendations to the Congress regarding continuing, modifying, or terminating the Act. While not completely satisfied with the results of the JFSA, President Carter recommended its continuation at least for the present, and Congress concurred by renewing the charter.

The need for joint funding has been reduced by the passage of several block grant programs and some uniformity in administrative procedures brought about by OMB Circular A-102, but over 1,000 categorical programs remain. Joint application permits the packaging of different grant programs which may become unique single state or local projects transcending functional program lines. Although some difficulties with the process remain, joint applications are clearly advantageous to the participating state and local governments and simplify their grant application tasks. Final success of the JFSA, however, will rest on how willing the federal agencies, OMB, and the FRC's are to promote joint funding and make the system work. The prognosis is not favorable.

Regional Management Information System (RMIS)

The Federal Regional Councils also have been used to test other devices for evaluating the flow of grant-in-aid applications under the legal structure created by the Intergovernmental Cooperation Act. Executive Order 11731, which formally established the FRC's, also broadened their mandate to include direct responsibility for providing federal program coordination assistance to state and local governments.

To fulfill this mandate, a regional information network was established in March 1972 by OMB to aid state and local governments in planning, program analysis, and program evaluation, as well as to improve the coordination of federal grants among federal agencies. The system was to provide up-to-date federal budgeting information and appropriations data to assist state and local planners in establishing funding priorities based upon a knowledge of the progress and status of grant-in-aid programs and funding within federal agencies. It was called the Regional Management Information Sytem (RMIS) project and consisted of three subsystems: REGIS, SEDS, and BIS.

REGIS (Regional Grant Information System) was an automated computerized grant information system (a subsystem of RMIS) covering 48 programs. The REGIS was tested by the Boston and Dallas FRC's in 1972. The pilot test was eventually extended to 139 programs. Using REGIS, selected grant applications could be tracked accurately by the FRC's from the time of pre-application through final notification of the grant award or disapproval. This information was useful in monitoring A-95 compliance and the flow of applications through the system. While OMB saw the system as useful, a GAO report categorized it as being superfluous to existing internal agency information systems and it was eventually terminated.[48]

Another of the RMIS subsystems, Social, Economic, and Demographic Subsystem (SEDS), was tested but never operationalized. In its developmental stages, SEDS was to identify social, economic, and demographic statistical data and analytical tools of use to the FRC's related to the needs of federal programs. it was tested in four regions but rejected as being too complex to institute on a nationwide basis.

The remaining RMIS subsystem, BIS (Budget Information Subsystem), although not heavily endorsed, has been continued. The BIS subsystem was to provide federal budgetary information on formula grants (see Chapter VI) by state and region. Under BIS, federal agencies must submit program budget figures (once approved by the President) to the FRC's. The FRC's forward this information to the states within their regions, which helps reduce the uncertainty of anticipated federal revenues in the preparation of state budgets. State governments can then make more realistic budget projections based on this information and can change projections as federal appropriations are changed.

Total direct expenditures for RMIS between March 1972 and June 1974 were approximately $992,000. Indirect expenditures (those costs generated by, but not charged to the project) were not calculated. While state and local governments generally supported the project, its success was questionable.[49] In effect, the RMIS subsystems were never operationalized (with the exception of BIS), and the project eventually was dropped in late 1974, largely because of its projected costs.

Today, the informational purpose of the RMIS system is accomplished through the Federal Assistance Programs Retrieval System (FAPRS) of OMB. FAPRS was developed by the Department of Agriculture in March

1976, as a computerized means of identifying federal programs that can be used to meet the developmental needs of state and local governments, public and private profit and non-profit organizations, and individuals. Upon request, the FAPRS matches the characteristics of the applicant with the requirements of federal programs that are most likely to be of assistance. The FAPRS program was moved from Agriculture to OMB in 1979 as part of the implementation of the Federal Program Information Act (P.L. 95-220).

Standardization and Control of the Grant-in-Aid System, CIRCA 1970

The administrative tools represented by FAR, the development of standardized federal regions, Federal Regional Councils, several key management circulars, the IGA program, and the REGIS information system were indications of President Nixon's efforts to gain management control of the grant-in-aid system. However, the most significant advance was the new administration and management authority over this system granted to OMB as a result of the Intergovernmental Cooperation Act. OMB was quick to utilize this authority by adapting existing management circulars or developing new ones designed to promote standardization, uniformity, and control. OMB circulars provide an example of a system within a system.

The federal rule and regulation system represents an intermix of statute and administrative law (see Figure 2). While there is considerable legal distinction between statute and administrative law, for all practical purposes the circular system has the same effect on the grant recipient. All law, whether statute or administrative, must be consonant with the U.S. Constitution. Complementary federal, state, or local administrative regulations merely expand or define procedures in any given area. (Lower level [government] laws and regulations may be *more* restrictive, but *not less* definitive or restrictive then higher level ones.) The grant recipient is held responsible for all laws and regulations issued by higher level agencies; and each award instrument either will contain copies of applicable OMB circulars as well as agency rules and regulations or reference to them and their publication in the *Federal Register.* (The *Register* is the official publication of the federal government, published daily, in which all agency rules and regulations must be announced and drafts presented for review and comment. Citizens and public interest groups are invited to comment on each proposed change.)

An annual cumulation of executive agency regulations, published in the *Federal Register* is found in the *Code of Federal Regulations* (CFR). The CFR is divided into 50 titles, each representing a broad subject area. Individual volumes of the CFR are revised at least once each calendar year and are issued on a staggered, quarterly basis. Thus, the *Code* serves as an additional source of reference for general and permanent federal regulations.

OMB circulars are developed pursuant to the authority of the Intergovernmental Cooperation Act and to support the Act's goals and objectives. In essence, although they are technical, administrative instructions, the circulars bear the force of law. State and federal agencies, as well as grant recipients, are held legally responsible for complying with the provisions and requirements of these regulations. The OMB circulars form the basis for federal agency rules and regulations. Circulars are the key links in providing

Figure 2

The Dual Nature of Statute and Administrative Law

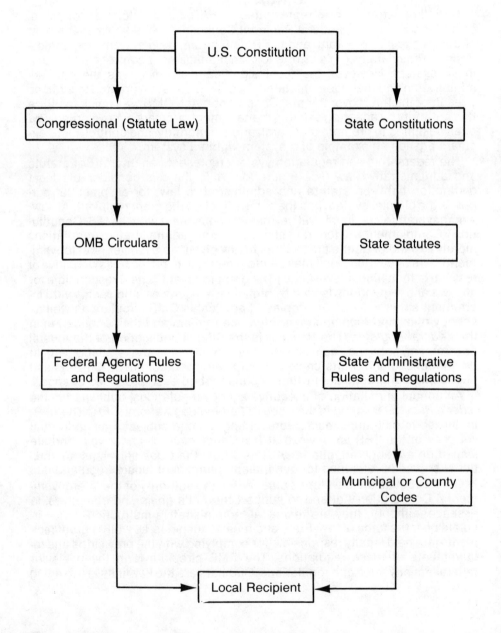

guidance between statute law and implementation and compliance procedures and regulations which are developed by federal agencies. Thus, circulars form the administrative infrastructure, the "marrow" of the grant-in-aid administrative system.

During the first years of the Nixon Administration, OMB developed four key management circulars which were designed, in part, to promote uniformity as well as to further the intent of the Intergovernmental Cooperation Act. The purpose of these circulars was to promote consistency in federal agency administrative requirements, as well as to simplify the growing paperwork burden that had become part of the grant application process.[50]

- *FMC 73-2 (A-73), Audit of Federal Operations and Programs by Executive Branch Agencies*
- *FMC 74-7 (A-102), Uniform Administrative Requirements for Grants-in-Aid to State and Local Governments*
- *FMC 74-4 (A-87), Cost Principles Applicable to Grants and Contracts With State and Local Governments*
- *TC-1082, Notification to States of Grant-in-Aid Information*

Circular 73-2 (A-73), Audit of Federal Operations and Programs by Executive Branch Agencies

In 1965, OMB (then BOB) issued Circular A-73 (later changed to FMC 73-2 and then back to A-73) in an effort to develop intergovernmental audit coordination. By 1970, OMB, GAO, and several other federal agencies had developed audit procedures applicable to all agencies involved in the auditing of governmental activities at all levels. By 1972, after considerable negotiation between OMB and the agencies, one set of standards finally was formulated to apply to all internal federal agency audit programs. These standards were published by GAO in a landmark booklet entitled "Standards for Audit of Governmental Organizations, Programs, Activities and Functions." GSA re-issued OMB Circular A-73 as FMC 73-2 in 1973, and following earlier recommendations of the Advisory Commission on Intergovernmental Relations, the General Services Administration expanded audit authority to permit reliance on non-federal audits and performance auditing.[51]

The parallel audit standard which is applied to recipients of federal funds is contained in Attachment P to Circular A-102. Audits of federally funded programs may be performed by state or local agencies, independent public accountants, or the *cognizant* federal agency (that agency designated as the responsible auditing agency within the region). Federal agencies must coordinate their audit requirements with state and local goverments and must accept reports performed by non-federal auditors as long as these audits fulfill agency requirements. The Circular requires a broad and complete audit of a grant program to include not only the correctness of financial operations and compliance with applicable laws and regulations, but also an evaluation of the efficiency and effectiveness of the program funded by the grant (essentially a cost-benefit evaluation of the grantee's performance under the grant). The Circular allows auditing organizations to balance audit requirements between the need to collect information for management purposes and the need to review the capabilities and compliance procedures of the audited agency. The intent of this balancing is to reduce the data collection requirements imposed on agencies being audited.

Circular 74-7 (A-102), Uniform Administrative Requirements for Grants-in-Aid to State and Local Governments

A second significant circular which helped to bring order to the grant-in-aid system was FMC 74-7. Issued first as OMB Circular A-102 in October 1971, it was re-issued by GSA as FMC 74-7 on September 13, 1974, and is now again A-102. The Circular was developed under the Federal Assistance Review Program to alleviate 16 problem areas that had been identified as obstacles in the administration of grants and to check the imposition of excessive additional administrative requirements by federal mission agencies. It was intended to promote uniformity and consistency among federal agencies in the administration of grants. The subject areas addressed include records retention, matching, standards for grantees financial management systems, financial reporting requirements, standard assistance application forms, and audit standards.

The Circular attempted to accomplish four objectives:
- *to ease the burden of requirements on grantees;*
- *to emphasize performance rather than administrative procedures;*
- *to require only essential information in reports and applications, etc; and*
- *to decentralize managerial responsibility but still permit effective federal oversight.*[52]

Circular A-102 has done much to streamline the grant-in-aid system. However, a 1975 GAO report noted that while the Circular had reduced state and local complaints, some administrative problems still remained.[53] The GAO report indicated that not all federal agencies had implemented the preapplication process outlined in the Circular, that some federal agencies imposed requirements which duplicated those contained in standard application forms, and that agencies required additional reports or forms and at intervals not in compliance with the Circular. The agency response to this criticism was that the complexity of the standardization process imposed by the Circular caused problems and that only "minor instances" of noncompliance existed.[54] In short, agencies felt that GAO was being too critical. While a number of other criticisms have been directed at federal agency compliance with the Circular, it represents a significant step in the reduction of paperwork and simplification in an extremely complex system and promotes a level of standardization that, unfortunately, had not existed previously.

Circular 74-4 (A-87), Cost Principles Applicable to Grants and Contracts with State and Local Governments

The third significant OMB Circular affecting grants administration was FMC 74-4, which originally was issued as OMB Circular A-87 and again as A-87. This Circular attempted to standardize allowable and non-allowable costs of programs administered by state and local governments and funded by federal grants and contracts. It permits a single federal department (the cognizant agency) to represent all federal departments in auditing programs associated with federal funding support. Perhaps more important, the Circular establishes policies for the reimbursement of eligible indirect costs of the grantee. (Indirect costs are those not clearly identifiable, but nevertheless real, such as administrative overhead, heating, and lighting costs of a building used, in part, for a grant project.)

Prior to the issuance of OMB A-87 (FMC 74-4), each federal agency determined which costs would be allowable for its grant recipients according to its own policies. For grantees dealing with more than one federal agency, what may have been allowable in one instance may not have been in another. Thus, considerable extra work, record-keeping, and documentation were required of recipients. Today, as a result of the Circular, a single federal agency is designated as responsible for approving cost allocation plans which are submitted by individual state and local governments. The agreements that are negotiated by the cognizant agency covering these plans constitute authority to other federal grantor agencies to accept grantee claims for services and indirect costs. The cost allocation plan also represents protection to the grantee should individual federal agency challenges to indirect cost rates arise.'

Circular 1082, Notification to States of Grant-in-Aid Information

Another circular having significance to the administration and management of the grant-in-aid system is related to the informational needs of state and local governments. Treasury Circular (TC) 1082 was issued pursuant to Section 201 of the Intergovernmental Cooperation Act of 1968 which provides that:

Any department of the United States government which administers a program of grants-in-aid...shall, upon request, notify in writing the governor, the state legislature, or other official...of the purpose and amounts of actual grants-in-aid to the state or to its political subdivisions.

TC 1082 establishes procedures for federal agency notification to the State Central Information Reception Agency (SCIRA) within each state. The state agency must be informed of the purpose and amount of grants awarded to the state or its local governments. Also reported are all other types of federal financial assistance (loans, loan guarantees, and insurance) awarded to state-affiliated institutions of higher education, quasi-public agencies, and non-profit institutions. This information is provided to facilitate state and local government planning, budgeting, and program administration.

Although considerable information is supplied to the state through this process, a 1975 GAO study indicated that the states received an incomplete picture.[55] Due to the restrictive definition of financial assistance, the GAO report noted that federal agencies failed to supply full and complete funding information. In most cases, federal agencies failed to complete the required notification (Form 240). The report recommended legislation to *require* federal agencies to report *all* financial assistance to state and local governments. It was suggested that OMB assume leadership in monitoring compliance with the Circular.

In late 1974, OMB initiated an interagency study to consider the GAO recommendations, as well as to review program coverage under Circular A-95 (a circular requiring state and local coordination of grant applications for certain grant programs) and to study the informational aspects of Circular A-87 and TC 1082. A team of representatives from OMB, the Treasury Department, and GSA participated in a study known as the Intergovernmental Information Systems Project. The interagency group's final report recommended revisions to A-87 and TC 1082 and added several programs to be covered under Circular A-95.[56]

Comprehensive Planning (A-95)

Perhaps one of the most significant coordination devices instituted by OMB during this period, and one that has created considerable apprehension among state and local governments, is OMB Circular A-95. OMB Circular A-95, *Evaluation Review, and Coordination of Federal and Federally Assisted Programs and Projects,* was issued on July 24, 1969, in partial implementation of the Intergovernmental Cooperation Act.[57] Its purpose was to provide guidance to federal agencies to promote "...cooperation with state and local governments in the evaluation review and coordination of federal and federally-assisted programs and projects."[58] The Circular sets forth implementation regulations in four parts which provide for the following:

Part I — Project Notification and Review System—*To encourage the establishment of a project notification and review system to facilitate coordinated planning on a state and local basis for certain federal programs.*

Part II — Federal Development Programs—*To provide for the direct coordination of federal development programs and projects with state, regional, and local planning and programs.*

Part III — State Plans and Multisource Programs—To provide federal agencies with information about the relationship to state or area-wide comprehensive planning of state plans which are required or form the basis for funding under various federal programs.

Part IV — Coordination of Planning in Multi-jurisdictional Areas—*To encourage and facilitate state and local initiative and responsibility in developing organizational and procedural arrangements for coordinating comprehensive and functional planning activities.*

A-95 was developed partially as a response to the complaints of state and local officials that they had no control, and sometime no knowledge, of federally-funded projects in their areas. Without knowledge about development activities in adjacent areas, coordinated area-wide development was impossible. For example, construction projects funded by one federal agency might cause problems to an adjacent jurisdiction or level of government. A county with federal funding assistance might resurface a road, while a municipal public works crew shortly thereafter would tear up the road to lay sewer lines. This lack of coordination was both costly and inefficient. A-95 was developed to *require* local and state coordination of grant applications to forestall situations of this nature. Part I of the Circular, the Project Notification and Review System (PNRS), was the vehicle for this coordination.

PNRC is based on an earlier Act, Section 204 of the Demonstration Cities and Metropolitan Development Act (Model Cities) of 1966, which requires that all state and local applications for federal grants to assist in the planning or building of public projects under 36 specified programs be referred to a policy or review board comprised of locally elected officials in the affected area. Applications from metropolitan areas must be accompanied by review comments (concerning the project's impact on the planned development of that region) by an area-wide comprehensive planning agency. The intent of this Act was to bring local policy-makers together to weigh project impacts and to promote the growth of area-wide planning.

Under programs covered by A-95, when an applicant decides to seek federal funding assistance, a "Notification of Intent" (NOI) to apply is submitted to the state and area-wide clearinghouse established for this purpose (see Figure 3). The NOI is a brief description (but not a formal application) of the proposed project. The clearinghouse circulates the NOI to state and local organizations which might have an interest in the project and receives comments within 30 days. If there are no comments, the applicant completes and submits a formal application to the granting agency. If there are comments concerning problems, the clearinghouse attempts to resolve the issues. If the problems are resolved, the review and comments are returned to the applicant and the application may be completed and forwarded to the funding agency. If the problems cannot be resolved, the applicant still may complete a formal application which may be commented on by the clearinghouse and other concerned agencies in a second 30-day period. The application and comments are then forwarded to the appropriate funding agency.

The project notification and review process provides an opportunity for governors, mayors, and other officials to assess the potential or real impact of proposed projects on state and local plans and programs. In this manner, these officials are able to influence federal funding decisions. The comments made by the clearinghouse are only advisory in nature and do not assure federal approval or disapproval of applications. The PNRC process is merely an "early warning system" to identify possible conflicts, problems, and issues and to force agencies and jurisdictions to work together in the comprehensive planning and development of regional activities.

Implementation of the PNRS portion of OMB Circular A-95 has not been without problems. A recent GAO report indicated that the complexity of the review process has been increased especially from the perspective of the applicant.[59] Applicants must determine which clearinghouses are to be contacted; minimally two clearinghouses, state and area-wide, must receive copies of the NOI. The applicant also must keep track of two, separate

Figure 3

Project Notification and Review System

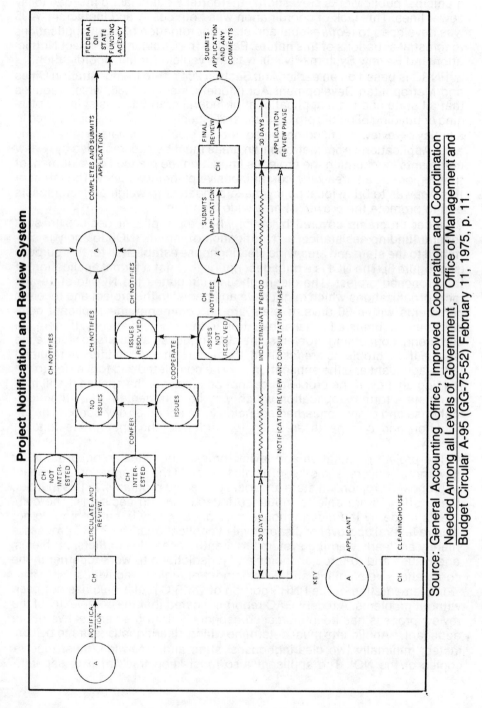

Source: General Accounting Office, Improved Cooperation and Coordination Needed Among all Levels of Government, Office of Management and Budget Circular A-95 (GG-75-52) February 11, 1975, p. 11.

30-day periods (one for each clearinghouse), and if other clearinghouses are interested, the applicant must keep track of additional 30-day periods. Finally, the applicant must attach a statement to the final proposal that all review comments have been considered. Needless to say, the added time for the clearance process imposes considerable stress on the applicant; however, in unusual circumstances applications may be submitted to the federal agency concurrently with A-95 review.

The GAO report also indicated that the PNRS process causes confusion among applicants in deciding which programs are covered. It is not always clear from the agency solicitation or application guidelines which program will require A-95 review. While the *Catalog of Federal Domestic Assistance* indicated programs requiring review, it often is outdated. The Catalog is completed and published annually by OMB pursuant to the Federal Program Information Act (P.L. 95-220). It is updated semiannually and includes the most current data available on the staus of 1074 assistance programs administered by 56 federal agencies. It is a voluminous source of information about these programs and includes eight separate indices to assist in the location of specific information.

The A-95 process also limits the effectiveness of the clearinghouse in determining the impact of federal assistance on an area. It also hampers planning by state clearinghouses by limiting their ability to compile complete data on federal assistance being sought within the state because all programs are not required to undergo the A-95 process. Even for programs requiring the A-95 process, the information not only is incomplete, but what information is provided is too extensive to be meaningfully assimilated by the clearinghouses.

Clearinghouses Resulting From the PNRS

Circular A-95 specifies that clearinghouses should be multijurisdictional, with comprehensive planning capabilities and an administrative and planning staff. The functions of clearinghouses include:

a) *evaluating the significance of proposed projects to state, area-wide, or local plans and programs;*

b) *assessing and disseminating project notifications to appropriate state and multi-state agencies, local governments and agencies, and regional organizations;*

c) *providing for the appropriate state agency review of projects covered by the Coastal Zone Management Act of 1972;*

d) *assuring that responsible agencies under Section 102(c) of the National Environmental Policy Act of 1969 are given the opportunity to review and comment on the environmental significance of proposed projects;*

e) *providing for review by agencies responsible for enforcing state and local civil rights laws;*

f) *providing liaison between federal agencies contemplating direct federal development projects and the state or local agencies or governments that may be affected by the project; and,*

g) in the case of projects initiated by special purpose governments, assuring that units of general or local governments having jurisdiction over the area in which projects will be located have an opportunity to confer, consult, and comment on the project application.[60]

Circular A-95 is not specific in defining what a clearinghouse should be; thus, states are given broad discretion in establishing organizations best suited to their needs. Clearinghouses are usually of two types: state and area-wide. State clearinghouses are designated by the governor. Area-wide clearinghouses may cover individual cities, counties, groups of counties, or regions within a state; and usually they also function as regional comprehensive planning agencies. There are also several multi-state clearinghouses covering a bi- or tri-state metropolitan region.[61]

Most clearinghouses are voluntary associations of area governments and are organized as Regional Planning and Development Organizations (RPDO's) or Councils of Governments (COG's).[62] Technically, a COG can be a council of governments, a governmental conference, an association of governments, or any variety of organization representing several governments. COG's usually are governed by the elected officials of the participating governments and employ a full-time professional planning and administrative staff. Their activities are funded, in part, by fees paid by participating agencies. These fees are determined by a formula based on a number of factors, such as anticipated use of the COG staff, number of voting units the agency will have on the COG (which is determined by the population represented), and other factors. Direct federal support for RPDO's and COG's has been diminishing, thus placing a greater financial burden on the participating governments.

While COG's owe much of their current status and existence to the regional clearinghouse incentives of Circular A-95, their origins go back over 20 years and address local attempts to promote area-wide coordination and planning. The fastest-growing areas in America today are the "urban counties," those 500 counties that lie within metropolitan regions. These counties function much the same as cities, but most coordination mechanisms that are developed tend to ignore them. While the National Association of Counties (NACo), a public interest group, aids in technical assistance and informational needs of these governments, the challenges and problems of these fractionalized metropolitan areas go beyond the informational capabilities of one external group. Intergovernmental coordination is needed among the central cities and their suburbs, adjacent towns, counties, and special districts. However, fear of an infringement on local autonomy has hampered intergovernmental coordination efforts. The result has been the proliferation of special district governments (governments created to perform a single or specialized service), and additional fragmentation has ensued. This intergovernmental fractionalization is called "Balkanization" by some scholars.

The early 1960's saw the development of organizations and associations to promote intergovernmental coordination. While differing in form, these voluntary, fledgling, area-wide planning organizations were sufficiently alike to become known eventually as Councils of Governments or COG's. Some COG's were informal forums organized to protest the movement toward a "metro" government, while others were associations of elected officials meeting to discuss common area-wide problems. The COG's potential for metropolitan cooperation and planning was recognized and given impetus through federal programs requiring area-wide planning (such as projects involving highways, sewer and water projects, health care, crime prevention, and more recently, environmental protection). Section 701 of the Housing and Community Development Act of 1965 made COG's eligible for planning funds for area-wide projects involving open space and others having area impacts. The Demonstration Cities and Metropolitan Development Act of 1966 gave COG's review powers over certain locally-initiated federal loan and grant applications. Section 204 of the Act specifies that these applications "...shall be submitted for review to any area-wide agency which is designated to perform metropolitan or regional planning for the area within which the assistance is to be used...." This requirement and the PNRS provisions of A-95 have made the COG's the hub of local planning activities. By 1976 over 585 regional clearinghouses had been identified. The fledgling National Association of Regional Councils (NARC), established in 1968, soon became known for speaking out on regional concerns. NARC provides services similar to other national organizations of local elected officials which serve as public interest groups, such as NACo and the National League of Cities (NLC).

Part II of Circular A-95 requires that federal agencies engaged in *direct* development of projects or in projects undertaken for the use of the federal government (such as military or scientific installations, public buildings, or other civil works) must consult with state and local governments that might be affected by these projects. Further, projects must conform with state, regional, or local plans, or the federal agencies are required to justify departures from those plans. Federal development agencies also are required to prepare environmental impact statements and to solicit the views and comments of state and local environmental agencies.

The third part of Circular A-95 requires the submission of state plans with information about state or area-wide planning, as required by some federal programs. Federal programs requiring state plans are listed in Appendix II of the *Catalog of Federal Domestic Assistance.* The existence of a state plan permits the governors, or their designated representatives, to comment on the relationship of the proposed activity to other state or area-wide plans or activities which have a state-wide impact. A-95 also encourages intrastate coordination by urging governors to involve area-wide clearinghouses in the review of state plans as they may affect or relate to area or local plans or programs.

Part IV of the revised OMB Circular A-95 encourages and facilitates coordinated, comprehensive, functional area-wide planning by state and local institutions. It urges the most effective use of state and local planning resources and the elimination of overlaps, duplication, and competition in area-wide planning activities. It also is designed to manage inconsistency among federal administrative and approval requirements placed on area-wide planning activities.

The states are encouraged to develop systems of substate planning and planning regions to facilitate the Project Notification and Review System (PNRS) provisions described in Part I above. Part IV places increased emphasis on these coordinating arrangements in order to encourage the establishment of conforming boundaries and internal (area-wide) communications. It encourages, but does not require, federal agencies to utilize the substate district organization (which are usually A-95 clearinghouses) to carry out such planning. It also requires that regulations of programs supporting area-wide planning provide for a memorandum of agreement between that organization and the district organization when the organization being funded for area-wide planning is not the district organization.[63]

Part IV does not prescribe the form or substance of state agreements. In case of conflicts in negotiation, problems are to be resolved by the funding agency in cooperation with the appropriate Federal Regional Council and the state clearinghouse.

Part IV does provide maximum opportunity for governors "to develop a system of useful, coordinated, and workable substate districts that can coordinate federal and state-local activities below the state level."[64] Perhaps more important, it permits each governor maximum flexibility in creating and structuring those organizations to fit the needs of his/her state. [65] Thus, each state is able to tailor its regions to meet its own unique political, geographic, and physical differences with minimum direction or influence by federal agencies.

Many states appear to have made a commitment to the concept of regionally coordinated planning under the federal arrangement. However, some seem to prefer their own regional presence or regional, single-purpose agencies established by their state legislatures for this purpose. While there are a number of issues relating to the COG concept and the view of state governments, the most common problem is the lack of a commonly accepted definition of a region as well as knowledge of what constitutes a regional rather than a local issue.

Federally Assisted Coordination of Projects

The process developed under OMB Circular A-95 to promote effective coordination of federally funded planning and development activities, especially the project notification and review system, has been subject to a wide range of criticism. Private, non-profit organizations claim that the A-95 process promotes a *de facto* veto by local governments over their proposals. Local comments often are based on a lack of knowledge or on political reasons. (A-95 clearinghouses do not have a veto power over proposals, but negative comments *can influence* a federal agency's funding decision.) Others feel that A-95 complicates, rather than assists, the application process; that it is another level of government superimposed over a local jurisdiction; that it is an insidious federal (or Communist) plot to steal the autonomy of local government; and that it is an unwarranted federal intervention into local affairs.[66] Racial and ethnic minorities have pointed out that there is usually sparse minority representation on clearinghouse boards and staff and that their (minority) interests and opinions are not fairly represented. Other criticisms can be viewed from the perspective of at least four other parties: the federal agencies engaged in the process, the clearinghouses that circulate the notification of intent to apply for federal assistance, the respondents to circulated proposals, and the applicants themselves.[67]

Many federal agencies do not understand sufficiently the A-95 process nor its significance in promoting regional planning at the substate level. In some instances, there are indications that they do not care.[68] This lack of seriousness is evidenced by awards that are made while (or even before) the review process is in progress. Also, review comments of a substantive nature and clearinghouse recommendations frequently are ignored. These problems may be internal. A GAO investigation of these processes indicated significant inaccuracies in internal agency instructions regarding A-95. The inaccuracies have led to interagency confusion and to confusion and misconceptions by applicants and clearinghouses. This internal confusion, to some degree, explains a lack of uniformity in agency interpretation of A-95. In fairness to the agencies, however, many programs do not lend themselves readily to the A-95 process; and the required "forced fit" causes difficulties in itself.

Regional clearinghouses also have had problems with the A-95 process. They have complained that there is a lack of federal funding support activity and that local agencies are pressured to finance the process. A more serious complaint is that the A-95 process is essentially voluntary and not strong enough to foster regional planning because it relies on applicants responding to comments, not to directives. One clearinghouse director recited the following litany of complaints from a regional perspective that is quite revealing. He noted that elected officials do not understand the need for regional planning nor do they understand A-95; townships and small cities are least active in the review process and fail to assess project impacts in their areas; local politics and backscratching are a part of the review process; strong comments are unwelcome and viewed with hostility by the submitting agency; commentors tend to focus on small details and even rewrite someone else's application instead of addressing the broader concerns of integrating area-wide projects; submitting agencies spend too much time in justifying actions or responding to the complaints of reviewers even when the items are insignificant to the project; and finally, some citizen groups use the A-95 process as a form for furthering their own causes rather than for constructive purposes.[69]

As a former member of a regional review board, the author's own complaint is that the members of review panels are not knowledgeable about the intent of region-wide coordination of projects and sometimes do not bother to read the proposals they must act upon. Worse yet, members may approve project applications wholesale, using the rationalization that it is "only federal money," and, thus, they negate the intent of the review process and lend support to its detractors. Finally, review boards often spend an interminable amount of time discussing proposals about which they have some knowledge and totally ignore those about which they do not, regardless of the magnitude or significance of the projects involved.

The third area of complaint about the A-95 process emanates from the respondents to circulated proposals. While some of the same problems previously noted apply equally to this group (and to applicants as well), there are also genuine and unique concerns. Perhaps the most critical concern voiced by respondents is a fear that criticism of a circulated proposal will lead to retaliation in some manner by counterpart organizations or the regional clearinghouse (if it is a "pet" project). Also, criticism is not viewed as constructive, and they believe that comments are ignored. Thus, most respondents do not take time to write substantive comments, if they write any comments at all. Finally, respondents feel overwhelmed by the number of notifications of intent to which they are asked to respond, many of which have no meaning or significance to their interests. In summary, the time demands for adequate review are often too great for non-paid, nonprofessional officials with no commitment to the process.

The final group of complaints about the A-95 process came from the applicants. Simply stated, A-95 is seen as a bother and irritant, and most applicants do not understand the overall significance of the process. Basically, this group views A-95 as an infringement on, or even a threat to, their autonomy. Many applicants refuse to supply clearinghouse staff personnel with information about their proposed projects and they may not even appear at the area-wide agency hearings on their proposals. At times, if project representatives are sent, they may be openly hostile, defensive, or uninformed about the proposal. Criticism or requests for further study or coordination are viewed as personal attacks. This attitude seems to predominate in smaller jurisdictions or jurisdictions with little or no professional staff—the very group that could benefit most from the process.

Unfortunately, too, there have been some indications that clearinghouse personnel have slanted the review process by sometimes deliberately selecting either hostile or friendly reviewers. There is some indication that project ideas can be discouraged by the process and even "stolen" by reviewers who may have a more favorable chance of obtaining funding because of the nature of their organization. For example, a small, unknown community service, non-profit agency may submit an idea and receive very negative responses, only to discover that the same idea, submitted several months later by a counterpart, but larger and more established organization, has received positive comments and is subsequently funded. The academic community is especially concerned about this aspect of the process when discussions are held about bringing university research proposals under the A-95 process.

Fortunately, the A-95 process is overcoming many of these hardships. It is not only gaining acceptance, but also winning over many formerly antagonistic participants. A-95 has listed many successes. The project notification process permits clearinghouses to provide technical assistance and support to applications. Thus, a clearinghouse staff is better able to communicate with area governmental representatives and to facilitate improved applications which incorporate reviewer comments into the final proposal.[70] Review Board members are becoming more sophisticated and aware about what is occurring in the area; and finally, all participants have more information on the availability of federal funding.

The A-95 process has considerable potential to accomplish its objectives of promoting knowledge and area-wide coordination for federally funded projects. It also serves a subsidiary effort in promoting other federally mandated policies related to such concerns as environmental standards and civil rights. While some evaluators claim that A-95 is not working, others who are equally qualified claim that it is. In either case, there is ample evidence to prove that jurisdictional managers are beginning to communicate together, in some instances for the first time in the history of those jurisdictions.

It is evident that A-95 and the OMB management circular system opened many doors to intergovernmental cooperation and coordination in the early 1970's. The key to this new effort was the expanded administrative authority granted to the executive branch under the Intergovernmental Cooperation Act of 1968. For the first time in history, the President was given the legislative authorization to manage the intergovernmental system. By the early 1970's, the label "Creative Federalism" was no longer an accurate descriptor because the circumstances—the relationships among levels of governments—had changed from what they were in the 1960's. The era of "New Federalism" had arrived.

NOTES

1. Advisory Commission on Intergovernmental Relations, Improving Federal Grants Management, A-53 (Washington, D.C.: GPO, February 1977), p. 98.
2. Ibid.
3. Conley H. Dillion, "Needs and Prospects for Research in Intergovernmental Relations" Symposium, Public Administration Review, Vol. XXX, No. 3 (May/June 1970), p. 265.
4. Ralph C. Bedsoe, "MBO and Federal Management: A Retrospective," The Bureaucrat, Vol. 2, No. 4 (Winter, 1974), p. 404.
5. Nations Cities, March, 1969, p. 5.
6. Harold Seidman, Politics, Position and Power—The Dynamics of Federal Organization, second edition (New York: Oxford University Press, 1976), p. 181.
7. Roy Ash later became Director of the Office of Management and Budget. Ash chaired the Advisory Committee on Executive Reorganization which became known as the Ash Council.
8. "Message to Congress Transmitting Reorganization Plan #2 of 1970," March 12, 1970, Public Papers of the President, Richard M. Nixon, 1970 (Washington, D.C.: GPO, 1971), pp. 260-261.
9. Advisory Committee on National Growth Policy Processes, Forging America's Future: Strategies for National Growth and Development (Washington, D.C.: GPO, December 1976), p. 19.
10. Rowland, Evans, Jr. and Robert D. Novak, Nixon in the White House (New York: Random House, 1971), p. 238.
11. Harold Sidman, p. 181.
12. Raymond J. Waldmann, "The Domestic Council's Innovation in Presidential Government," Public Administration Review, Vol. 36, No. 3 (May/June 1976), p. 261. Waldmann provides an intimate insider's view of the formulation and functioning of the Domestic Council.
13. Ibid., p. 266.
14. Budget Message of President Richard M. Nixon to Congress, January 29, 1971, p. 162.
15. The Bureau of the Budget, now the Office of Management and Budget was established under the Budget and Accounting Act of 1921. Originally housed in the Treasury Department, it was placed within the newly created Executive Office of the President in 1939, following the recommendations of the Brownlow Committee. From its inception, the BOB enjoyed a position of high regard as the budgeting and management arm of the President, but its stature eroded following the growth and expansion of other executive agencies during World War II. The management function of BOB became subordinated to its two other missions: budget preparation and legislative clearance; furthermore, even the latter of these missions was subordinated to the budgetary function as subsequent presidential staffs assumed a

greater role in policy issues and affairs.

16. "Message to Congress Transmitting Reorganization Plan #2 of 1970," March 12, 1970, pp. 260-261.

17. Robert S. Gilmour, "Central Legislative Clearance: A Revised Perspective," Public Administration Review, Vol. XXI, No. 2 (March/April 1971), p. 159.

18. House Committee on Government Operations, Hearings on Reorganization Plan #2 of 1970, 91st Cong., 2d Sess., April/May 1970 (Washington, D.C.: GPO, 1970), p. 61.

19. Congressional action in 1975 brought these circulars back to OMB.

20. U.S. Bureau of the Budget, "Bureau of the Budget Circulars of Interest to State and Local Governments," Washington, D.C.. 1968, Memo from the Director of the Bureau of the Budget Charles L. Schultze to the Heads of Executive Departments and Establishments, dated June 28, 1967, as quoted in Haider, p. 122.

21. Advisory Commission on Intergovernmental Relations, Annual Report on Operations Under OMB Circular A-85 (Washington, D.C.: GPO, January 31, 1975), p. 2.

22. See Advisory Commission on Intergovernmental Relations, Annual Report on Operations Under Office of Management and Budget Circular A-85 (Washington, D.C.: ACIR, January 31, 1979).

23. Advisory Commission on Intergovernmental Relations, Annual Report..., p. 5

24. Advisory Commission on Intergovernmental Relations, Improving Federal Grants Management A-53 (Washington, D.C.: GPO, February 1977), p. 137

25. House Subcommittee on Intergovernmental Relations, Hearings on "New Federalism," 93rd Cong. 2d Sess., January/February, 1974 (Washington, D.C.: GPO, 1974), p. 12.

26. See OMB Circular A-105 Standard Federal Regions, April 4, 1974. Agencies participating in the FAR project included the Departments of Agriculture, Commerce, Justice, Interior, Labor, Transportation, HEW, HUD, the EPA, Small Business Administration, Civil Service Commission, Office of Economic Opportunity, and the Office of Intergovernmental Affairs. An interesting commentary on the origins of FAR is made by the originator of the project, Dwight Ink. See "Federal Assistance Review: Did it Make a Difference?" in Intergovernmental Administration: 1976, Eleven Academic and Practitioner Perspectives, eds. James D. Carroll and Richard W. Campbell (Syracuse, New York: Maxwell School of Citizenship and Public Affairs, 1976), pp. 193-208.

27. Advisory Commission on Intergovernmental Relations, Improving Federal Grants Management, p. 98.

28. Ibid., pp. 98-104.

29. The section on Federal Regional Councils is taken in part from the testimony of Frederick V. Malek, Deputy Director, OMB, in testimony before the Subcommittee on Government Operations. See Hearings

on "New Federalism," p. 12.

30. The concept of federal coordinating mechanisms at the regional level was not new. Special-purpose coordinating bodies had existed during the 1960's in large metropolitan areas. President Kennedy established Federal Executive Boards (FEB's) in ten of the nation's largest cities in 1961. By 1969, the number had been increased to 25. These Boards were comprised of the highest ranking civilian and military officials located in the geographic area. Thus, some agencies, such as HUD, HEW, or DOL might not have a Board representative unless they had staff already located in that region. These Federal Executive Boards were (and still are) largely concerned with encouraging cooperative efforts between federal agencies and expressing some local civic concerns. Other groups assigned coordination responsibilities included the Federal Executive and Federal Business Associations, some of which began as early as the 1920's. For a discussion of why the FEB's have been ineffective, see Harold Seidman, pp. 205-206.

31. Pamphlet, Federal Regional Council, Region V (October 1, 1975).

32. Original membership in the pilot FRC's included regional representatives of OEO, DOL, HEW, DOT, and HUD. Under Executive Order No. 11647, the Law Enforcement Assistance Administration (LEAA) and Environmental Protection Agency (EPA) were added to the Councils; FRC Chairmen were to be designated by the President; and the Under secretaries Group for Regional Operations was formalized. Under Executive Order No. 11731, July 25, 1973, the Departments of Agriculture and Interior were added to Council membership. Also, the Councils were tasked with the added responsibility of coordinating intergovernmental programs originated by state and local governments, as well as coordinating grants. Membership on the FRC's was increased by President Carter in September, 1979.

33. Pamphlet, Federal Regional Council.

34. Under President Carter, the USG role has been reappraised. President Carter's Cabinet Secretary and Intergovernmental Relations Coordinator, Jack H. Watson, Jr., will co-chair the USG along with Harrison Wellford, the Executive Associate Director of OMB, thus lending even stronger support for this group, if it is utilized in establishing domestic policy. For hints on the reactivation and role of USG, see Neal R. Pierce, "Watson Sees Closer Ties in The Intergovernmental Arena," National Journal, April 9, 1977, pp. 557-559.

35. See Hearings on "New Federalism," p. 8.

36. Indianapolis—Marion County Unified Government, Lane Council of Governments, Ohio Department of National Resources and the Puget Sound Governmental Conference.

37. Executive Order No. 11717, May 9, 1973, "Transferring Certain Functions from the Office of Management and Budget to the General Services Administration and the Department of Commerce." A number of former OMB circulars dealing with grants management were also

transferred by this Executive Order and re-issued as Federal Management Circulars (FMC's) under GSA as follows (They were returned to OMB in January 1976):

OMB #	Title	FMC#	CRF Reference
A-73	Audit of Federal Operations and Programs by Executive Branch Agencies (Superceded and re-issued as OMB Circular on March 15, 1978. See, the Federal Register, Vol. 43, No. 58, March 24, 1975).	73-2	34 CFR 251
A-100	Cost Sharing on Federal Research	73-3	34 CRF 211
A-88	Coordinating Indirect Cost Rates and at Educational Institutions	73-6	34 CFR 252
A-101	Cost Principles for Educational Institutions	73-8	34 CFR 254
A-87	Cost Principles Applicable to Grants and Contracts with State and Local Governments	74-4	34 CFR 255
A-102	Uniform Administrative Requirements for Grants-in-Aid to State and Local Governments	74-7	34 CFR 256

Administrative responsibility for the IGA program was also transferred to GSA pursuant to Executive Order No. 11717 in November, 1973.

38. Detailed program objectives, definitions, guidelines and procedures, and applications are contained in Integrated Grant Administration (IGA) Program, Office of Management and Budget (Washington, D.C.: GPO, January 14, 1972).

39. Statistical assessment results and recommendations were distributed in a draft report entitled Integrated Grant Administration: Second Year Assessment Report, Office of Program Management Systems and Special Projects, General Services Administration, December 27, 1974. The final assessment report was a condensed version of the draft. See Integrated Grant Administration, Office of Federal Management Policy, GSA, April, 1975.

40. P.L. 93-510, December 5, 1974.

41. Quoted in Integrated Grant Administration...,p. 1.

42. Ibid., p. 17.

43. Leigh E. Grosenick, "News from the States and Local Governments," News and Views, American Society for Public Administration (June 1975), p. 9.

44. Ibid.

45. Both the Intergovernmental Cooperation Act amendments of 1969 and 1972 contained joint funding simplification titles which were not enacted. The House (of the 91st Cong.) also passed a joint funding bill similar to the JFSA which was not passed by the Senate.

46. For interpretations of the meaning of the JFSA and additional background information, see Advisory Commission on Intergovernmental Relations, "Joint Funding Act Simplified Federal Assistance Process" Information Bulletin No. 74-10 (December 1974); Dwight A. Ink, Deputy Administrator, GSA, letter to Bernard Rosen, Executive Director, US. Civil Service Commission, January 7, 1975; and Office of Federal Management Policy, "Special Joint Funding Issue," IGA Newsletter, General Services Administration, April 1975.

47. GSA and IGA Interagency Systems Group worked together to develop the implementing regulations. See "Jointly Funded Assistance to State and Local Governments and Private Non-Profit Organizations," Proposed Rulemaking, Federal Register, December 24, 1975.

48. See U.S. General Accounting Office, States Need, But Are Not Getting, Full Information on Federal Financial Assistance, B-146285 (Washington, D.C.: March 4, 1975).

49. Hearings on "New Federalism," pp. 110-105.

50. These Circulars were administered by OMB until May, 1973, at which time they were transferred to GSA as part of Executive Order No. 11731. The Circulars were returned to OMB pursuant to Executive Order No. 11893, on January 2, 1976.

51. See Fiscal Balance in the American Federal System, A-31 (Washington, D.C.: GPO, 1967), Vol. 1.

52. Advisory Commission on Intergovernmental Relations, Improving Federal Grants..., p. 106.

53. See General Accounting Office, Fundamental Changes are Needed in Federal Assistance to State and Local Governments, GG 75-75 (Washington, D.C.: August 19, 1975).

54. Ibid., pp. 111-112.

55. General Accounting Office, States Need,..., p. 12.

56. OMB Memorandum, "Final Report—Intergovernmental Information Systems Improvement Project" (December 15, 1975).

57. Major revisions occurred on February 9, 1971, March 8, 1972, November 13, 1973, and January 2, 1976.

58. Federal Register (January 13, 1976), pp. 2052. This revised circular incorporates many of the changes suggested in a February 11, 1975 General Accounting Office review of A-95; see Improved Cooperation and Coordination Needed Among All Levels of Government, Office of Management and Budget Circular A-95 (GGS-75-52); Executive Office of the President, Office of Management and Budget, Circular

A-95. What It Is—How It Works (undated), p. 2.

59. General Accounting Office, Improved Cooperation..." 12-13 and 21.

60. Federal Register, p. 2052. The purpose and function of clearinghouses is also discussed in the Advisory Commission on Intergovernmental Relations, Improving Federal Grants Management (A-53) February 1977, p. 219. Substate regionalism is exceptionally well covered in the ACIR four reports on that topic; Regional Decision-Making: New Strategies for Substate District, Vol. 1 (A-43), October, 1973; Regional Governance: Promise and Performance, Vol. II (A-41), May, 1973; The Challenge of Local Governmental Reorganization, Vol. III (A-44), February, 1974; and Governmental Functions and Processes: Local and Area-wide, Vol. IV (A-45), February, 1974.

61. Office of Management and Budget, Circular A-95, What It Is..., p. 7.

62. In most cases, clearinghouses are financed by using federal funding assistance under Section 701 of the Housing and County Development Act of 1965. They are also organized to respond to requests of Section 204 of the Demonstration Cities and Metropolitan Development Act and Title IV of the Intergovernmental Cooperation Act.

63. Office of Management and Budget, Circular A-95, What It Is..., p. 25.

64. House Subcommittee on Intergovernmental Relations, Hearings on "New Federalism," p. 49.

65. Ibid., p. 50.

66. See for example, "Regionalism a Nixonian 'Monster'," Akron Beacon Journal, January 1977, p. A6.

67. Most of the following comments were taken from interviews with federal aid applicants, review groups, and clearinghouse staff personnel in Northeast Ohio.

68. General Accounting Office, Improved Cooperation and Coordination Needed..., pp. 25ff.

69. Richard Stall, Director, Stark County Planning Commission. [a subregional clearinghouse in the Northeast Four County Regional Planning and Development Organization (NEFCO)]. In Ohio, the review process has been "sub-regionalized." Review and final recommendations for all local (one county) projects are made by an area-wide county regional planning commission. Projects having area-wide scope or impact are reviewed by the regional state designated area-wide clearinghouses, NEFCO.

70. Considerable information has been developed to explain A-95 to potential applicants by state, as well as area-wide clearinghouses. See for example Division of Planning and Evaluation, Office of Management and Budget, State Clearinghouse Applicants' Guide (Columbus, Ohio: November 1, 1974) and Northeast Ohio Four County Regional Planning and Development Organization, NEFCO Report: NEFCO A-95 Review Process—A Guide for Participants, Vol II, No. 1 (January 1975).

CHAPTER II SELECTED BIBLIOGRAPHY
Articles/Documents

Advisory Commission on Intergovernmental Relations. Fiscal Balance in the American Fiscal System, Vol. II, A-31. Washington, D.C.: GPO, 1967.

_____ . Government Functions and Processes: Local and Area-Wide, Vol. II, A-45. Washington, D.C.: GPO, February 1974.

_____ . Improving Federal Grants Management, A-53. Washington, D.C.: GPO, February 1977.

_____ . "Simplified Federal Assistance Process," Information Bulletin, MO-74-10. Washington, D.C.: GPO, December 1974.

_____ . Regional Decision-Making: New Strategies for Substate Districts, Vol. I, A-43. Washington, D.C.: GPO, October 1973.

_____ . Regional Governance: Promise and Performance, Vol. II, A-41. Washington, D.C.: GPO, May 1973.

_____ . The Challenge of Local Governmental Reorganization, Vol. III, A-44. Washington, D.C.: GPO, February 1974.

Advisory Commission on National Growth Policy Processes. Forging America's Future: Strategies for National Growth and Development. Washington, D.C.: GPO, December 1976.

Bledsoe, Ralph C. "OMB and Federal Management: A Retrospective", The Bureaucrat, Vol. II, No. 4 (Winter 1974).

Budget Message of President Richard M. Nixon To Congress. January 29, 1971. Washington, D.C.: GPO, 1971.

Dillion, Conley H. "Needs and Prospect for Research in Intergovernmental Relations," Symposium, Public Administration Review, Vol. XXX, No. 3. (May/June 1977).

Division of Planning and Evaluation, Office of Management and Budget. State Clearinghouse Applicants Guide. Columbus, Ohio: November 1, 1974.

General Accounting Office. Fundamental Changes Are Needed in Federal Assistance to State and Local Governments, GG-75-75. Washington, D.C.: GPO, August 19, 1975.

Gilmour, Robert S. "Central Legislative Clearance: A Revised Perspective," Public Administration Review, Vol. XXI, No. 2 (March/April 1971).

Grosenick, Leigh E. "News From the States and Local Governments," News and Views. American Society for Public Administration, June 1975.

"Jointly Funded Assistance to State and Local Governments and Nonprofit Organizatons, Proposed Rulemaking," Federal Register. December 24, 1975.

"Message to Congress Transmitting Reorganization Plan #2 of 1970, March 12, 1980," Public Papers of the President: Richard M. Nixon 1970. Washington, D.C.: GPO, 1971.

Northeast Ohio Four County Regional Planning and Development Organization. NEFCO Report: NEFCO A-95 Review Process—A Guide for Participants, Vol. II, No. 1 (January 1975).

Office of Federal Management Policy, General Services Administration. Integrated Grant Administration. Washington, D.C.: GPO, April 1975.

_____. "Special Joint Funding Issue," IGA Newsletter. Washington, D.C.: GPO, April 1975.

Office of Management and Budget. Integrated Grant Administration (IGA) Program. Washington, D.C.: GPO, January 14, 1972.

_____. Circular A-95 What It Is—How It Works. Washington, D.C.: GPO (undated).

Office of Program Management Systems and Special Projects, General Services Administration. Integrated Grant Administration: Second Year Assessment Report. Washington, D.C.: GPO, December 27, 1974.

Pierce, Neal R. "Watson Sees Closer Ties in the Intergovernmental Area," National Journal. April 9, 1977.

"Regionalism a Nixonian 'Monster'," Akron Beacon Journal. January 12, 1977.

Transferring Certain Functions From the Office of Management and Budget to the General Services Administration and the Department of Treasury. Washington, D.C.: GPO, May 9, 1973.

Waldmann, Raymond J. "The Domestic Council: Innovation in Presidential Government," Public Administration Review, Vol. XXXVI, No. 3 (May/June 1976).

Books

Evans, Rowland, Jr. and Novak, Robert D. Nixon in the White House. New York: Random House, 1971.

Ink, Dwight. "Federal Assistance Review: Did It Make a Difference?" in James D. Carroll and Richard W. Campbell (eds.), Intergovernmental Administration: 1976, Eleven Academic and Practitioner Perspectives. Syracuse, NY: Maxwell School of Citizenship and Public Affairs, 1976.

Mogulof, Melvin B. Government Metropolitan Areas: A Critical Review of Council of Governments and the Federal Role. Washington, DC.: The Urban Institute, 1971.

Seidman, Harold. Politics, Position and Power—The Dynamics of Federal Organization. 2nd ed. New York: Oxford University Press, 1976.

Hearings

U.S. Congress, House, Committee on Government Operations. Hearings on Reorganization Plan #2 of 1970. 91st Cong., 2nd Sess., April/May, 1970. Washington, D.C.: GPO, 1970

U.S. Congress, House, Subcommittee on Intergovernmental Relations. Hearings on "New Federalism." 93rd Cong. 2nd Sess., January/February 1974. Washington, D.C.: GPO, 1974.

Chapter Three
The Administrative Impacts of New Federalism

It is time that good, decent people stopped letting themselves be bulldog-ged by anybody who presumes to be the self-righteous moral judge of our society. In the next four years, as in the past four, I will continue to divert the flow of power away from Washington and back to the people.

Richard M. Nixon
October 21, 1972

Introduction

This chapter discusses the origins, strategies, promises, successes, and failures of "New Federalism." The theme of New Federalism was captured in a 1967 article by Richard N. Goodwin, a White House aide to President Kennedy, who wrote that the objectives of government would best be accomplished "by assisting and compelling states, communities, and private groups to assume a greater share of responsibility for collective action. The key to resolving problems that are national in scope," said Goodwin, "was and has been money — how and where to use it."[1] Money is used by the federal government as a lever to entice participation and compliance with national objectives. People are "convinced" to cooperate and work together to solve national problems. Through its taxing powers, the federal government has both the power and funds to attack social problems, although in employing these resources in the era of New Federalism it strove to retain authority in Washington.

The long-term impacts of the "Great Society" programs of the 1960's on state and local governments resulted in an increasing reliance on federal funds. By 1969, federal funds comprised over 25 percent of state and local revenues. The significance of this increasing dependence on federal funds, was not lost on administrative officials who were anxious, in the late 1960's, to promote the national goals of New Federalism. Thus, the proliferation of categorical grant programs that marked the Great Society was paralleled by restrictive administrative rules and regulations, as well as application procedures.

The new Nixon Administration took office with a goal of decentralizing decisional authority for the allocation of federal programs and funds to the levels of government where the problems resided. This goal was altered severely by the Congress, by disillusioned state and local officials and interest groups, and as a result of the problems that followed Watergate.

Origins of the New Federalism

In the last part of the 1960's, as the new Nixon Administration reviewed the role of state and local government officials that resulted from federal program fragmentation, the proliferation of community-level agencies, the spread of special district governments, and other problems engendered by the Great Society programs of the Johnson Administration and now part of the grant-in-aid system, it began a series of administrative adjustments to gain some measure of control. These changes, outlined in Chapter II, focused on a stronger managerial role for the Office of Management and Budget (OMB). The development of the Federal Regional Councils (FRC's) was of particular interest because of the strategic locations of the FRC's, their proximity to state and local officials, and their familiarity with local needs and concerns, combined with the FRC agency representatives' familiarity with present agency grant-in-aid programs. The FRC's offered the opportunity to create a working unit that would be located close to state and local officials and their problems and, yet, would remain responsive to Washington. Thus, they could be used as a linking mechanism between Washington and the user governments. Nixon saw this linking as a first step in reversing the trend of centralization, a goal inherited during his apprenticeship as Vice President under Eisenhower.

Federal Regional Councils became an integral part of the strategy of *devolution* and *decentralization* announced by the President in March 1969. This strategy was the key to his New Federalism philosophy. The Bureau of the Budget (BOB) was asked to lead in this two-pronged effort and launched the Federal Assistance Review Program (FAR) to help plan, test, and coordinate the system which led to the development of the ten Regional Councils.

The results of those efforts were changes in the late 1960's and early 1970's and the beginning of a new era in federalism. A transition could be noted away from an intergovernmental strategy based on creating new organizations for "managing" new programs that were supported by a series of piecemeal regulations to a strategy that was more management oriented. Such concepts as planning, programming and budgeting, organizational development, management by objectives, and public policy anaylsis came into vogue. A great sense of professionalism and a revival of management thought could be seen in the bureaucracy.

President Nixon assumed his first term of office with an ideal of decentralizing federal programs, perhaps instilled by his exposure to a philosophy that had been attempted by President Eisenhower. Noting the more than 40 years of increasing centralization, President Nixon called for a new effort toward reversal. He stated that "...it is time for a new federalism in which power, funds, and responsibility will flow from Washington to the states and to the people...."[2] This new thrust was to be embodied in a bold series of changes which became an agenda of greater significance through Nixon's first term of office and became identified as a "new" brand of federalism. Sounding a traditional Republican anti-centralization theme, Nixon said that his New Federalism would "turn back to the states a greater measure of responsibility - not as a way of avoiding problems, but as a better way to solve problems. [This new philosophy was to be] a cooperative venture among governments at all levels...."[3] With these words, President Nixon not only attempted to inaugurate an era of needed domestic policy reform, but he also created a concept in which practitioners and students of the intergovernmental system found a multitude of different meanings. New Federalism meant different things to different people.

Devolution and Decentralization

Both political parties supported a movement toward reform of the grant-in-aid system, but it was Nixon who seized the initiative in his 1968 campaign for the presidency by calling for a "...dispersal of power - so there is not one center of power, but many centers. I am not saying that the federal government should back off from its responsibilities," Nixon said in a White Plains, New York speech. "I'm saying that it should share those responsibilities and begin breaking up massive problems into manageable pieces." Later, in Oklahoma City, Nixon developed this idea further — the federal government's role should be "...to return to the states and cities the resources to do the job themselves." Following his 1968 election victory, Nixon elaborated on this same theme: "After nearly 40 years of moving power from the states to Washington, we begin in America a decade of decentralization, a shifting of power away from the center whenever it can be better used locally."[4] The shifting of power was to take place in a two-pronged strategy of "devolution" and "decentralization."

The concept of *devolution* was an attempt to shift the responsibility for making operational decisions away from federal agencies to "...those levels best able and willing to serve the needs of the people. Based on an assessment of the appropriate roles for each level, there should be a *devolution* or transfer of federal functions more effectively handled at the state and local level."[5] Implementation of this concept was to be accomplished through such efforts as the block grants (see Chapter VI) and what later became the General Revenue Sharing program (see Chapter V). While national priorities and policy guidelines would still prevail, greater management responsibility and resource allocation discretion could be exercised by state and local officials under block grants (sometimes referred to as Special Revenue Sharing). General Revenue Sharing would permit even greater latitude and discretion in the use of federal funds in line with state and local needs and priorities without the cumbersome accountability procedures that characterized the categorical (or program-by-program) system. In short, although devolution still meant federal control, it represented a shift in distributional or program allocation decision-making responsibility to the state or local level.

In articulating the decentralization part of the strategy, a spokesman for the Administration noted that:

> The federal government should **decentralize** to its field establishments those functions which must continue to rest with the federal government and can be most effectively handled at the field level so the decisions are made as close as possible to the locus of the problem.[6]

The intent of this approach was clear. Washington was developing a strategy to place the focal point of *responsibility* for social policy and program allocation decisions with state and local decision-makers, but within certain limits.

Thus, decentralization meant not only a retention of program and policy responsibilities as a federal function, but also a readjustment or shift of some decision-making responsibilities to a level within the federal field establishment where a better knowledge of local conditions prevailed. This policy resulted, in some cases, in a transfer of management responsibilities away from Washington to federal field offices. The difficulty in implementing decentralization is that the national level offices must be willing to surrender their prerogatives and the field structure must be sufficiently strong and organized to accept this responsibility. Also, national-level policy requirements and management guidelines must be defined clearly. Unfortunately, as the President was to learn, neither of these conditions prevailed. Presidential leadership, the adoption of standard regional boundaries, and the Federal Assistance Review Program (FAR) were used in an attempt to overcome internal federal agency barriers to the decentralization effort.[7] There were, however, other problems that were not anticipated by the Administration which also affected its strategy of devolution.

Reactions to New Federalism

Housing and Urban Development (HUD) Secretary (and former Governor of Michigan) George H. Romney predicted a revolution in federal, state, and local relationships under the New Federalism, but, he cautioned, "There are powerful forces opposed to this shift of direction and power."[8] Among those opposing forces were the U.S. Congress. Romney felt that Congress would resist reduction of its indirect control over local decision-making exercised through the program-by-program review and appropriations process that characterized the categorical grant system. New Federalism, in particular the special revenue sharing measures, was viewed by some "...as a direct assault by the Executive on the role of Congress in determining national priorities."[9] It also was perceived as an Executive intrusion into Congressional "constitutional prerogatives of oversight and legislative interference into program administration."[10] New Federalism also threatened a shift in power away from Congress to the governors and mayors, a shift which did not make the Congress happy.

The potential power shift represented by the New Federalism would alter Congressional roles in three areas. First, it would significantly reduce Congressional oversight. State and local governments would gain increasing control over program execution, and less outside control could be exercised in review and evaluation. Second, and perhaps more important from a Congressional perspective, general purpose funding (either revenue sharing or block grants) would provide less opportunity for individual members of Congress to identify with specific national programs and to take credit for the delivery of grant awards to their constituencies. A third and related threat was the fact that increasing the resources of state and local officials would enable them to improve their political positions and to pose a greater challenge to Congressional incumbents.[11] Special and general revenue sharing, in particular, "raise[d] the prospect of subsidizing political rivals and of loosening the ties that many members have to special interest groups."[12] The governor of a state was viewed as the greatest potential rival to incumbent members of Congress, who were well aware of the possible political uses of unrestricted federal funding at the state level. Mayors also were seen as potential rivals of the future. Through the categorical systems, tight controls in the allocation of funds still could be exercised, but no such checks existed under general or special revenue sharing.

Finally, in Washington it was a recognized fact of life that considerable political activity was indirectly related to and supported by the categorical system. Recipient, clientele, or public interest groups supported directly or indirectly by categorical programs were not anxious to change the nature of the existing system for fear of altering the fundamental balance of power in their particular programs. These groups became Congressional allies when plotting strategies on pending legislation. During the traditional cocktail parties that characterized these strategy sessions, the hosts might have been representatives of medical schools interested in issues related to health funding; local housing authorities involved in public housing; or state highway engineers affected by the Highway Trust Fund. The resulting combination of political forces posed a serious threat to acceptance of New Federalism initiatives. As a result, many of the New Federalism proposals were greeted with little enthusiasm and no serious consideration in the 92nd Congress.[13] Congress also controlled the purse strings through the appropriations process and was more than happy to let many programs die a quiet death by failing to appropriate funds rather than addressing the issues.

Besides indifference or hostility by the Congress, resistance to the New Federalism also came from the bureaucracy. Nixon felt that the bureaucracy was too powerful and that the Executive Office was unable to assume a leadership role under the existing structure. His solution was to break up or disburse the current relationships between individual bureaucrats and members of Congress by attempting to move decision-making authority away from Washington (both devolution and decentralization).

To implement the decentralization part of New Federalism, the President exercised his administrative powers rather than asking for reorganizational authority from the Congress. As a first step, Nixon created the Domestic Council and reorganized the policy-making apparatus of the BOB into OMB (see Chapter II). OMB's response to these new responsibilities was an outpouring of management circulars aimed at cutting "red tape" and strengthening the hand of state and local elected officials. For example, Circular A-102, *Uniform Administrative Requirements for Grants-in-Aid to State and Local Governments,* was designed to reduce some of the prerogatives of federal bureaucrats by instituting uniform administrative requirements for all agencies. The creation of common regional boundaries and the FRC's (see Chapter II) was another step in the decentralization process.

The bureaucracy actively resisted the President's decentralization directives. Some agencies refused to move their regional headquarters into the selected cities or to support the FRC's. A key problem for the FRC's was the inability of the Councils to coordinate programs because of the uneven manner in which agencies decentralized their decision-making prerogatives. At one extreme, several agencies which previously had decentralized some funding decision authority even beyond the regional level (perhaps to a city), were reluctant to move this authority back to the FRC. The U.S. Department of Labor (DOL), for example, granted regional manpower directors authority down to the mayoral level (cities). The Department of Housing and Urban Development (HUD) allowed its regional directors the same prerogatives as DOL and also attempted to delegate its program funding authority to its 42 subregional offices. While regional directors of the Law Enforcement Assistance Administration (LEAA), the Department of Health, Education, and Welfare (HEW), and the Department of Transportation (DOT) were not given the broad range of decision-making authority granted to HUD and DOL representatives, they were allowed certain discretion for some programs.[14] The confusion over responsibilities vexed agency representatives as well as state and local officials.

In an effort to strengthen the FRC's and to bring some uniformity to administrative management of grant-in-aid programs at the regional level, President Nixon created the Undersecretaries Group for Regional Operations (see Chapter II). This group consisted of the second highest-ranking person in each of the seven agencies holding membership on the FRC's and was (originally) chaired by Associate OMB Director Frank C. Carlucci, a key figure in the Administration's decentralization efforts. The group met twice monthly to monitor the decentralization process and to help solve problems encountered between the FRC members and their Washington chiefs. Unfortunately, the group, in effect, diluted the authority of the FRC representatives and was too deeply concerned with interagency funded projects and not familiar enough with regional problems and uniqueness. Its efforts produced little change in the individual operating procedures used by agency representatives in the field.

Decentralization at the State and Local Levels

The decentralization philosophy of New Federalism was ostensibly an effort to delegate new power and authority over the distribution of federal grants-in-aid to state, county, and city government leaders. The first several years of the experiment showed a federal preoccupation with urban social problems to the exclusion of state and county concerns. Funding and program shifts were directed at the cities, while states and counties experienced decreasing allocations. This preoccupation was ironic because the majority of voters who resided in the cities characteristically reflected a Democratic political orientation as opposed to the more Republican orientation of the counties and states. Not only had the Nixon (Republican) Administration concentrated its decentralization efforts on the cities, but it issued no directives, programs, or guidelines involving urban cooperation with the states or counties. Republican supporters of the President did not fail to note this disparity.

State and county representation within the Administration was to take place through the Office of Intergovernmental Relations, located in the White House under the Vice President (Agnew). The Office was to be the chief administration link between the states and counties and the executive branch. However, it carried relatively little clout with federal departments. As one Washington representative of a relatively large industrial state said:

I can get just as quick a response if I go over [to an agency] on my own. Unless a governor gets into Nixon's offices and the man directs action, the departments just don't listen. The New Federalism is no more than rhetoric when it comes to getting agencies to heed governors.[15]

While federal programs generally were designed to provide assistance at the local level (or the level at which a problem resides), the lack of top level support or of a mechanism to assist in coordinated planning between state and county governments proved one of the weaknesses of the New Federalism. Many state leaders, noting the lack of serious implementing actions and follow-up, doubted the President's commitment to the concept and became cool supporters of further decentralization initiatives.

The cities, however, proved to be the primary beneficiaries of the administration's planned decentralization experiments. Deliberately avoiding the need for Congressional legislation and acting under his administrative authority, President Nixon initiated a number of experiments to test and demonstrate what he envisioned as the appropriate pattern for federal grant-in-aid programs. Two primary experiments were managed by HUD and were labeled "Annual Arrangements" and "Planned Variations."

Annual Arrangements involved a negotiation process between HUD field personnel and local, general-purpose government officials in which a written agreement was developed. This agreement was to promote better coordination of HUD's categorical programs to coincide with local priorities, plans, and needs. The process began when the local chief executive was invited by HUD to develop a policy statement or plan as a basis for negotiations. This policy/planning statement generally included the city's community development goals and objectives, the problems in attaining these goals, and the plan to solve the local problems. The subsequent agreement included a request for HUD funding and resource assistance. It then became the basis for a give-and-take, face-to-face negotiation session between the top administrators — federal and city — in which compromises could be reached and decisions made on the spot.

The final "Arrangement" was expressed in a memorandum of understanding which was signed by both parties and formed the basis for a working relationship for the following year. It specified actions by the city and committed resources and funds from HUD. Unlike most federal programs, which seldom can be incorporated into city plans *in advance,* annual Arrangements permitted cities to plan and manage programs as a part of a city-wide, community development strategy. In the short history of the experiment, from its inception in December 1970, over 200 cities negotiated Annual Arrangements with HUD. The Annual Arrangements program was fairly well concluded in FY 1974, when the Nixon administration made severe cuts in community development programs. The experiment expired with passage of the Community Development Block Grant program in 1974 (see Chapter VI).

A comparable devolution experimental program was developed within HEW at both the state and local levels. Individual governors, upon request, were granted waivers and relaxation of federal requirements when they attempted to integrate various intergovernmental programs on grant applications. They also could utilize the A-95 process to strengthen state area-wide planning and coordination and they could use their review and comment powers regarding the impact of federally assisted programs on state planning.

A second HUD experiment in furtherance of the concept of decentralization, "Planned Variations," was perhaps the Administration's most ambitious effort. This effort was an attempt to bypass much of the administrative machinery of the categorical system and to increase the role (and power) of the mayor at the expense of the federal bureaucracy.

Planned Variations was announced in a White House press release on July 29, 1971, as an expansion of the Great Society-initiated Model Cities program.[16] The Model Cities program was an attempt to funnel substantial sums of money into some of the nation's poorest minority neighborhoods in some of the largest cities to stimulate the rebuilding and rejuvenation of these areas. Under the President's Planned Variations experiment, 20 of the 147 cities participating in the Model Cities program were given greater flexibility in the use of federal funds and a greater role in coordinating incoming funds (Table 1). These cities were granted an additional $79 million in Model Cities funds in fiscal 1972 and the same amount in fiscal 1973. The three primary variations included the following:

1. Chief Executive Review and Comment (CERC). In all 20 cities, the chief executive of the city was given greater control over all applications for federal assistance through the right to review and comment on all applications for federal funding assistance affecting the city.
2. City-Wide Model Cities. Supplemental Model Cities grants were given to 16 of the 20 cities, with authority to expand the program to some or all portions of their deteriorated areas.
3. Authority to minimize review. The 20 selected Model Cities were allowed to obtain waivers of federal regulations applicable to categorical programs related to Model Cities projects. Federal agencies took steps to *waive,* or at least minimize, administrative requirements for other related grant-in-aid program applications.

Planned Variations was funded with a total of $158.8 million for a two-year period. These funds were used to support the Chief Executive Review and Comment (CERC) system and the supplemental Model Cities funding to the selected cities with this variation. CERC seems to have been the most effective of these experiments. Its purpose was to increase the ability of the city's chief elected offical to establish local priorities. It was a decrease in the federal bureaucracy's ability to influence the use of funds at the local level; but it permitted a mayor to have more control over developments within a city with less outside interference.

The purpose of CERC was described by HUD Secretary George Romney as:

> By allowing the mayor or other appropriate local chief executive to review and make recommendations with respect to applications from other agencies to federal funding sources,

Table 1

Planned Variations Cities and Funding,
First Year 1972
(In Millions of Dollars)

Full Variations Cities	Regular MC Funding	PV Increase	Total MC Funding
Butte	$ 1.7	$ 1.5	$ 3.2
Dayton	2.9	5.2	8.1
Des Moines	2.1	3.7	5.8
East St. Louis	2.1	3.8	5.9
Erie	1.6	2.9	4.5
Fresno	2.8	4.9	7.7
Indianapolis	6.2	8.5	14.7
Lansing	1.9	3.3	5.2
Newark	5.7	7.0	12.7
Norfolk	4.5	8.0	12.5
Paterson	2.1	4.1	6.2
Seattle	5.2	5.2	10.4
Tampa	4.1	7.1	11.2
Tucson	3.1	5.5	8.6
Waco	2.6	4.6	7.2
Winston-Salem	1.9	3.3	5.2
CERC/Only Cities			
Houston	13.4	.2	13.6
Rochester	3.0	.2	3.2
San Jose	3.1	.2	3.3
Wilmington	1.7	.2	1.9
TOTALS	$71.7	$79.4	$151.1

SOURCE: U.S. Department of Housing and Urban Development, Community Development Evaluation Series No. 7, Planned Variations: First Year Survey (Washington, D.C.: U.S. Government Printing Office, October, 1972), pp. 9-10.

*substantially increased coordination, improved planning, and
more effective utilization of resources at the local level should
result.*[17]

Even Model Cities, which was considered a very flexible categorical program, had been burdened with administrative regulations and controls concerning the activities that could be funded. Areas of need in one part of the
city were aided, while other areas, equally in need, would receive no help.
There was an absence of centralized coordination within the city, and
categorical programs that should have worked together to solve common
problems were frequently at odds. Model Cities had attempted to bring
about strategic planning and centralized coordination through their City
Demonstration Agencies (CDA's), which reported directly to the local chief
executive. However, the CDA's operated in a relatively small section of the
city and possessed insufficient leverage in influencing or controlling other
agencies or special districts, some of which already were completely independent of the local, general-purpose government. CERC was an administrative adjustment designed to correct these problems.

CERC emerged from substantial experience in attempting to strengthen
the hand of the chief executive in each jurisdiction. President Nixon had indicated early in his first term that he wished to strengthen the decision-
making authority of local elected officials. A Task Force on Model Cities,
chaired by the eminent and controversial urbanologist, Edward Banfield,
recommended augmentation of this initiative and laid the foundation for
what later became Planned Variations and other segments of the New
Federalism. Its December 1969 Report of the Task Force on Model Cities
called for changes designed to decentralize federal control and assist local
decision-makers.[18]

The Task Force's recommendations were translated into the Planned
Variations experiment by the fall of 1970. Planned Variations was successful
in allowing a city's chief elected official, for the first time, to exercise a
measure of control over the independent agencies within his jurisdiction.
There were indications, however, that this new discretion and power were
not welcomed by many elected officials.

Discretion meant that the chief executive of the jurisdiction would make a
program or funding allocation decision instead of having that decision
already determined by Washington. This power elevated the status of the
decision-maker, but also brought problems. Established interest groups
began to pressure these officials both to retain existing programs and to expand or increase funding. New interest groups emerged to voice their concerns and demand programs and funds to meet their needs. The mayor, who
previously could blame Washington for controversial allocation decisions,
now was forced to make these choices and to face the consequences of
each decision.

These problems became especially apparent by 1972 with the initial feedback following implementation of General Revenue Sharing (GRS), which
was a New Federalism initiative whereby large blocks of funds, approximately $5 billion each year, were distributed to all the general-purpose units
of government, including states, to spend on an almost "string free" basis.
That is, the funds were given for no special federal purpose, without applica-

tion, and with almost no federal guidance, accounting, or reporting requirements (see Chapter V).

In many jurisdictions, these funds were used to decrease taxes or to avoid needed increases rather than to develop new or needed programs. However, contrary to promises by the Administration, categorical program funds were reduced when GRS was instituted, and the local official was forced to utilize GRS funds to maintain existing programs. The "string free" aspect and the greater discretion promised in the use of GRS were not as real as they appeared. Political leaders suddenly discovered their vulnerability in the face of competing interests when confronted with the loss of the federal shield. Washington, which "...could be successfully used in the categorical grant-in-aid system to divert hostility and dissatisfaction that often arises within local interest groups,"[19] could no longer be blamed, given the nature of GRS.

Finally, it appeared to many local officials that the Administration ultimately did not support its New Federalism initiatives. It appeared to be concerned more with the management systems it was creating than with the actual results and impacts of its initiatives. As one official noted, New Federalism represented "...an efficient management philosophy that appears to weight the efficiency of a service delivery system above characteristics such as responsivenes, flexibility, and quality of that system."[20] Planned Variations, and CERC in particular, was an administrative anomaly in the devolution/decentralization strategy of New Federalism. Whether it ultimately would help develop the capacity of local decision-makers to overcome the politically negative features of their new autonomy remained to be seen.[21]

Executive Branch Reorganization Under New Federalism

The second part of Nixon's devolution and decentralization strategy was to strengthen management control of executive agencies. Control of the bureaucracy was viewed as necessary in order to offset increasing resistance by the bureaucracy to New Federalism initiatives. The White House developed a series of reorganization proposals designed to give the President's trusted lieutenants authority to control the bureaucracy. This tool was utilized to reorganize entire activities out of existence or to change substantially reporting relationships. For example, the Office of Economic Opportunity (OEO) was established as the keystone of the Great Society programs by President Johnson and was placed in the Executive Office of the President. President Nixon had the Office abolished by appointing a director for this purpose without using the Reorganizational Act procedure which would have given Congress 60 days to disapprove such a proposal. The President was adroit at using these tools to promote his own goals and to check the proliferation of agencies of the executive branch which he inherited.

The proliferation of programs during and following the depression of the 1930's led to the creation of a large number of autonomous federal agencies dealing directly or indirectly with state and local governments. By the mid 1960's, approximately 123 separate federal bureaus and divisions were responsible for administering one or more grant-in-aid programs. In 1966, 9 of the 11 cabinet rank departments offered some form of funding assistance to state and local governments.[22] A 1967 ACIR study noted 17 departments or agencies administering grants. Within eight of these could be found 38 different offices directly responsible for grant programs. [23] By 1975, 74 bureaus within 28 federal agencies and departments had these responsibilities.

Executive agency expansion also followed the program and funding initiatives of the Great Society. A number of major executive departments and independent agencies were created to administer grant-in-aid programs that originated during this period. These new organizations included the Departments of Housing and Urban Development (1965) and Transportation (1964); the Appalachian Regional Commission (ARC-1965); and the Environmental Protection Agency (EPA-1970). HUD was created to focus primarily on urban affairs; DOT assumed the functions of seven different departments and agencies in order to provide a mechanism for the development of a needed national transportation policy. The EPA, which was created under Reorganization Plan #3 in 1970, brought together the environment-related functions of eight different agencies in order to mount a concerned attack on the nation's problems in this area. Both OEO and the ARC, like the other new departments, were intended to provide a focal point for functionally-related programs and to serve as coordinators of intergovernmental affairs in their respective mission areas. Although these new departments and agencies were intended to merge related activities, the proliferation of programs and their expanded roles led, instead, to further fragmentation within the intergovernmental system.[24]. Each new agency and department, once created, tended to develop a life of its own.

To consolidate the effects of these spreading organizations, President Nixon attempted to improve the coordination of domestic policy across departmental lines by the appointment of three White House Counselors with special powers. On January 5, 1973, Nixon announced that certain Cabinet officers would be given special roles as "Counselors to the President" in addition to leading their own agencies. The new designations followed the recommendations of the Ash Council. They were to serve in a "supersecretary" capacity. Their responsibilities included those of their own departments—HEW, HUD, and the Department of Agriculture—as well as those of programs run by other agencies. The President's proposal stretched the limits of his reorganizational authority without action by Congress. While the Domestic Council was developed during President Nixon's first term of office for essentially this same purpose, the new arrangement led to a reduction in the Domestic Council's staff, authority, and resources as the new White House Counselors assumed their responsibilities.[25]

In developing this new arrangement, the President followed his propensity for dealing with trusted advisors. Agriculture Secretary Earl L. Butz, a long-time friend of the President, became Counselor for Natural Resources. His responsibilities included natural resource use, lands and minerals, environment, outdoor recreation, water control, and park and wildlife reserves.

Another friend of long standing, HEW Secretary-designate Caspar W. Weinburger, was named Counselor for Human Resources with responsibility for health, education, manpower development, income security, social services, Indian and native peoples, drug abuse, and consumer protection. At his confirmation hearing before Congress on January 11, 1971, Weinburger described his new post as one which attempted to convey the recommendations, reactions, and responses of these Departments to the President. The Counselor's job was "...a liaison task; it is a coordinating task...."[26] James T. Lynn, Secretary of HUD, was named Counselor for Community Development. His responsibility included authority over county institutions, community planning, housing, highways, public transit, regional development, disaster relief, and national capital affairs.

Paralleling these changes within the White House, four men were selected by the President as his principal assistants who were to be responsible for integrating and unifying policies and operations throughout the executive branch. They were H.R. Haldeman, John Erlichman, Roy Ash (the new Director of OMB), and Henry Kissinger. The new Counselors were to speak for the President and represent his interests before the other executive departments and their secretaries. This change also subordinated the other secretaries to the Counselors, a situation that assured tension within the bureaucracy and apprehension by Congress.

In an earlier message to Congress on March 25, 1971, President Nixon proposed consolidation of seven executive departments and a number of agencies into four functionally integrated new departments. His plan called for the creation of four generic superdepartments—Natural Resources, Community Development, Human Resources, and Economic Affairs.[27] The three "Supersecretaries" would head three of these consolidated departments. These men would report to John Erlichman, the President's trusted domestic affairs advisor, but their operations would be monitored by Treasury Secretary George P. Schultz, who was given the added title of Assistant to the President for Economic Affairs. Schultz also would head the fourth department. In his reorganization proposal, Nixon stressed the need to unify and coordinate interdepartmental activities and departmental programs in each of these four areas. He noted that the narrowly-defined missions of the departments as then organized caused them to become advocates of specific interests; that the organizational fragmentation of too many departments made it difficult to concentrate on problems and issues and created a piecemeal approach to addressing public needs; that this inefficient hierarchy caused confusion among state and local governments as well as among the citizenry; and that this fragmentation made accountability an impossibility.[28] His suggestions were logical and followed recognized principles of organization. Nixon's efforts, however, were received with little enthusiasm by Congress and had little support from any constituency or within other executive agencies.[29]

During the Congressional hearings on the reorganization proposals affecting the seven executive departments, the program was attacked by the influential chairman of seven significant House committees.[30] Congress, it seemed, resented the implications of changing relationships between the

91

departments and the relevant oversight committees. Faced with this level of hostility, the proposals, as well as Nixon's use of special counselors, died a quiet death. With the failure of this plan in Congress, the Administration tried unsuccessfully to implement the plan without Congressional approval. This second failure discouraged further reorganizational attempts for the remainder of the President's second term, especially with the increasing demand for White House attention generated by the Watergate scandal.

Special Revenue Sharing and Block Grants

While executive level reorganization was designed to strengthen management control of federal agencies, Annual Arrangements and Planned Variations, especially the Chief Executive Review and Comment variation, were designed to strengthen the position of general purpose local government and its chief executive. These latter two experiments were initiated, in part, to demonstrate how cities could handle enhanced resource allocation roles under one of several special revenue sharing proposals being developed by the President (see Chapter VI). Special revenue sharing was a concept designed to promote local autonomy in broad functional areas, such as education, law enforcement, manpower training, rural and urban community development, and transportation.

Another devolution strategy was that of block grants or grants consolidation. In its simplest form, a block grant is a large allocation of funds to be used in one general program area, such as health. It may be developed by consolidating a number of program or categorical grants under one heading and distributing funds by means of a formula, where each eligible jurisdiction is assured some funding support and minimal federal programmatic control.

The 92nd Congress also viewed Nixon's proposals for special revenue sharing and block grants as a threat. Both measures represented an intrusion into Congressional prerogatives to determine priorities, a diminution of oversight responsibilities, and a threat to Congressional initiatives in grant program administration. The devolution of decision-making responsibility and funds to governors and mayors was, by itself, adequate to bring strong Congressional opposition. Special revenue sharing would have disrupted the delicate balance of interrelationships that connected the interest groups, the bureaucracy, and the members of Congress. In education, special revenue sharing threatened to disturb Congressional sponsors and the hundreds of educational groups benefiting from a myraid of grant programs; transportation revenue sharing would have opened up the Highway Trust Fund for other uses by governors and mayors; urban community development revenue sharing brought opposition from builders, urban renewal interests, minority groups, and others; rural community development revenue sharing posed a threat to the recipients and interest groups for programs administered by the Department of Agriculture and the Appalachian Regional Commission.[31] The Administration's New Federalism proposals failed, one by one.

Other administration efforts to consolidate grant programs failed as well. The proposed Intergovernmental Cooperation Act of 1972, the proposals for grant consolidation in areas such as the comprehensive Headstart Child Development Program, and the programs related to water and sewer facilities, library services, and education became mired down in one or both Houses of Congress. Finally, the Ominibus Housing and Urban Development Act of 1972 and the Allied Services Act did not pass, leaving the President's other attempts to combine federal financial assistance and categorical programs into functionally-related block grants a failure.

The Unfulfilled Promise of New Federalism

There were also a number of criticisms and concerns with other New Federalism initiatives. As indicated earlier, President Nixon's New Federalism meant different things to different people. The fundamental strategy of New Federalism at first seemed clear—in short, *devolving* federal functions to the state and local levels (for example, Planned Variations and Annual Arrangements) and *decentralizing* federal administrative decisions to field locations (for example, establishing the FRC's) along with the responsibility for the operational aspects of programs and grants administration. However, implementing this strategy met with difficulties. Political compromises were necessary as were changes to the Administration's basic proposals because of a hostile and uncooperative Congress and a constituency obsessed with self-interest. The lack of clear national goals and the dilemma of attempting to solve broad-ranged social problems that have no short-term solutions (e.g.,poverty) added to the difficulty. The potential recipients (or beneficiaries) of the changes promised by New Federalism (state and local governments) also began to criticize the Administration for not fulfilling their expectations, and the programs were criticized for not working as expected. These groups seemed most bitter because the Administration failed to fulfill the expectations created by the promises of the President. Together these factors created an atmosphere in which the Administration was forced continually to define, redefine, and clarify its intent; and it was thrust finally into a defensive posture from which it never recovered.

One promise of New Federalism related to the Administration's attempts to provide general and special revenue sharing and block grants was characterized by an article by John Herbers which appeared in the *New York Times* in November 1972:

> The era of the federal government responding to specific needs with resources directed by the federal bureaucracy is giving way to a new era in which the federal government, in the words of one Tennessee official, "leaves the money on the stump" for the local officials to pick up and use for a general or any other public purpose.[32]

Former Governor of Michigan and Secretary of the U.S. Department of Housing and Urban Development under President Nixon, George H. Romney described another (later unfulfilled) promise as "a renaissance of state and local government," in which "we may, in the next decade, see the emergence of a locally-oriented society much different than [sic] that generally expected in the last quarter of this century."[33] Thus, the image that was created for state and local officials was not part of the reality that could be delivered by the Administration.

From the Administration's standpoint, New Federalism was a philosophy of total (but controlled) national decentralization and it proceeded to implement strategies without recognition of what this philosophy implied or of what President Nixon could convince Congress to support. The tools to implement this philosophy were welfare reform, special revenue sharing, decentralization of administrative functions to the regional level, reorganization of the executive departments, and its primary vehicle was general revenue sharing. The long-term fiscal effects of general revenue sharing, the one successful New Federalism program, have led to more significant changes in domestic policy. The effect, however, on the bureaucracy and the structure of government, and subsequently the way programs are administered, has been less profound.

As an unintended effort, New Federalism produced changes in state and local governments that no one anticipated. As envisioned by President Nixon, New Federalism's strategy was to involve general purpose governments and chief elected officials in the decision-making processes of program implementation at the expense of special districts and local functional agencies—particulary those which emerged during the Great Society era. New Federalism adhered to the state's definition of what constituted a general purpose government. It attempted to be neutral in its distribution and allocation of funds under the proposed general and special revenue sharing plans.[34] The intergovernmental linkages, areas of concern, and programmatic responsibilities of each unit of government, as already established, were to remain undisturbed by the Administration's policy under New Federalism.

In reality, some of the New Federalism initiatives did affect the structure of state and local government. The Administration's policies related to regionalism, the creation of regional planning organizations under Section 701 of the Housing and Community Development Act of 1965, and the Comprehensive Community Health Programs were examples in which the fiscal and structural effects of New Federalism exerted an indirect influence. Hundreds of substate clearinghouses were established and planning organizations proliferated. Also, general revenue sharing, the most important legislative enactment of New Federalism, exerted considerable influence on state and local governmental structures and functions by affecting funding allocation decisions, taxing policies, and capital expenditure programs.

Richard Nathan indicated the need to study the long-term effects of this facet of revenue sharing in at least three areas:
1. Distributional—How was money allocated by state and local governments?
2. Fiscal—What have been the real and net effects?
3. Political—What have been the long-term effects of revenue sharing on the structure and processes of state and local governments?[35]

Although the initial assessment of these impacts is still taking place and there is continuing debate on the future of general revenue sharing, the significance of this portion of New Federalism on governmental structures cannot be ignored. The real heritage of New Federalism may not be a decentralization of power away from Washington, but rather a new dependency.

There are indications today that the financial dependency of the nation's largest cities is based upon Great Society programs and New Federalism policies, strategies, and programs. For example, by 1976, 14 of the largest cities in the United States had received almost one-third of their revenues from the federal government.[36]

The End of An Era

Opponents of the philosophy of New Federalism have been outspoken in pointing out possible negative implications and the spectre of hidden intent. Speaking for the AFL-CIO, Arnold Cantor labeled New Federalism as: "A reincarnation of the view that the federal government and the states are competitors; any edge given the federal government is an usurpation of states rights, a threat to freedom and part of a master plot to socialize America.[37]

Another view, that of Edwin Kepler, the executive director of a community action agency, from a slightly different perspective, echoes the same theme:

Although ostensibly a conservative political doctrine well within the bounds of Democratic tradition, New Federalism, as it is now being implemented, contains elements that threaten to destroy the pluralistic counter-balance to government provided by private non-profit organizations in the human service fields.[38]

Both of the above critics were concerned with President Nixon's promise of New Federalism to return power, funds, and authority to those governments which are closest to the people. Mr. Kepler highlighted the flaw in this concept as "rhetoric that distorted, falsified, and ignored realities."[39] These realities included:

- The disorderly structure and limited nature of local government.
- The nonrepresentative character of local politics.
- The history of local governments' neglect of the poor.
- The positive values of pluralism.
- The importance of having a variety of centers of initiatives.
- The positive merits of consumer participation in human service programming.

Kepler argued that New Federalism sidestepped these characteristics of local government in the mistaken assumption that they were not significant or important.

While these arguments had some merit, perhaps the most valid criticism of New Federalism was related to the decisional authority that would be given to local officials. Local officials were to have the power to decide which programs to continue when the categorical program funds were cut and the "string-free" revenue sharing funds were forthcoming. While the original intent of general revenue sharing was to provide new or additional monies to state and local governments and not to reduce current programs or funds, it became painfully obvious by the time of the fiscal year 1974 federal budget that the states and cities would be forced to utilize some of their own funds to take over programs previously funded by Washington.[40] Thus, the freedom to make decisions at the local level was diminished, in large part, by decisions made in Washington. The choices that remained often would be faced with considerable local hostility, and local decision-makers would be forced to make some very difficult and unpopular choices.

While the criticisms raised against New Federalism had some validity, its fatal flaw was a lack of understanding of the reality of state and local capabilities. The problem in transferring funds and decisional authority from the federal to the state and local levels was related to, first, the limited vistas and parochialism of some local officials; second, threatened cuts to programs benefiting minorities and the poor under general revenue sharing; and third, the lack of managerial training or professional preparation of these officials.

Limited Vistas and Parochialism

Many local officials traditionally have held narrow and parochial views concerning decisions related to the services provided to their communities. They have demonstrated a reluctance to experiment with new and innovative programs or to make decisions on programs having impacts outside of their jurisdictional borders. The New Federalism initiatives mandated state and local attention to the "quality of life" factors extending beyond jurisdictional boundaries. Without federal leadership or program specific funding, local officials had few incentives to be concerned with social policies dealing with the needs of the disadvantaged, the poor, and of racial minorities.[41] They had little incentive to worry about the pollution created by industries located within their boundaries so long as the impact of this pollution was felt elsewhere. Finally, they had little incentive to worry about equal employment opportunities, health and safety regulations, and other intangibles that have become part of our national grant-in-aid system. It is largely due to the inattention to these concerns at the local level that federal funding (which today comprises from 25 to 40 percent of most state and local budgets) is used to provide incentives in accomplishing these goals. Attention to these concerns has become a "string" attached as a condition of receiving federal funding support. Thus, simply turning the funds over to state and local officials was destined to failure, as some critics noted, "because it was the failure of local government to act that led to the federal programs in the first place."[42]

The interstate regional planning and interstate coordination movement of New Federalism was designed to attack the lack of interlocal governmental cooperation as well as parochialism. Nixon's decentralization strategy was designed to promote multi-state cooperation through the Federal Regional Councils, again using the grant-in-aid system as a lever. Substate regionalism, as developed through the A-95 clearinghouse procedure, was to bring local officials together to promote uniformity and cooperation in area-wide planning effort. Both thrusts were expected to enlarge the perspectives of local elected officials and, hopefully, to help them to see beyond their own jurisdictions and their own political problems. To some extent these programs were successful. In spite of the high turnover of local elected officials, at least a community awareness was developed which · facilitated the implementation of subsequent federal legislation aimed at these same ends.

Impact on Minorities

New Federalism included a promise that categorical funding would not be reduced with the advent of general and special revenue sharing. With the release of the FY 1974 budget, the nation's minorities were quick to perceive that this was not the case.[43] Critics of New Federalism began a series of attacks on the categorical programs that accompanied general revenue sharing. Minority groups traditionally have believed that their main hope in improving their condition lay with "federal intervention and federal dollars and...their access to federal money would end if it were put under the control of local politicians answering to local white majorities."[44]Wilbur J. Cohen, Secretary of the Department of Health, Education, and Welfare during the last years of the Great Society era argued:

We have to have federal programs with strings attached because it is the only way that the disadvantaged, the poor whites, and poor blacks will get their fair share. If there are not federally regulated programs to disburse money and instead it is handled by local city governments, they won't get their fair share.[45]

Minority groups' fears are related to the unknowns of removing federal controls and the effects of decentralization.[46] For example, general revenue sharing funds are relatively string-free and have few restrictions on the use of the money. State governments, though, could spend their revenue sharing funds as they choose without any restrictions.[47] Thus, from a minority group's perspective, a flaw in the Revenue Sharing Act is the weak provision for enforcement actions in cases of discrimination in the use of funds—a flaw that was not corrected sufficiently with extension of the Act in 1976.[48]

Discriminatory effects of programmatic decentralization, apart from general revenue sharing, are not well documented. E.E. Schattschneider, for one, has argued that minorities fare considerably better at the national level than in a decentralized setting.[49] While there is no proof to validate this contention, the apprehensions remain.

Lack of Managerial Training, Experience

Shifting the burden for programmatic decisions to the state and local level during the first years of the New Federalism accentuated a problem that was suspected but had not been documented—the lack of sophistication and management ability (capability) of officials and decision-makers at the state and local levels. The problem was especially acute at the local level, where an elected official might be asked to administer a budget running into the millions of dollars with a work force of thousands. Few candidates for local office run on a platform of professional expertise to do the job for which they seek office; rather, their main thrust is often to attack the failings of the incumbent. Local politics, thus, becomes issue—or personality-oriented, with little attention to the capability preparation, or training of the challenger to manage effectively. This problem has been addressed, in part, by the movement toward the city manager form of government and the use of chief administrative officers or other professionally trained managers working under the mayor, county commissioners, or other responsible elected officials.

Although the use of the term "management" frequently has been shunned and little research has been directed toward this topic as it is related to state and local elected officials, OMB became concerned with what federal agencies were doing to develop the capacity of state and local decision-makers to handle their new resources and responsibilities as an outgrowth of New Federalism. A study effort was launched by OMB in the spring of 1974 to explore this question, but the appearance of the findings of this study occurred at a point following the resignation of President Nixon, the transitional administration of President Ford, and the start of a new administration under President Carter (see Chapter IV).

The study was a benchmark which came at a time that can be identified as the end of the era of New Federalism. Attention to domestic and world events shifted as President Nixon departed office. Federalism was beginning a period of transition. One of the residuals of New Federalism and a characteristic of this transition period was new attention to the concept of management.

NOTES

1. Quoted in "Nixon, Congress Still at Odds on Decentralizing Power," Congressional Quarterly, C.Q. Guide: Current American Government, Spring 1974, p. 48.
2. The New Federalism: An Address and Statement by the President. Address to the Nation, August 8, 1969.
3. Ibid.
4. U. S. Congress, House, Health and Education Message From the President of the United States, House Document 395, 89th Cong., 2d Sess., (March 1, 1966), pp. 48-49.
5. Ibid.
6. Hearings before a Subcommittee of the Committee on Government Operations, New Federalism, House of Representatives, 93rd Cong., 2d Sess. (January 29-31; February 5-6, 1974), p. 9.
7. Ibid.
8. George H. Romney, "The New Era of Federalism: Challenge for the U.S.," National Civic Review (January 1973), p. 7.
9. See "New Federalism IV: Legislation—Drive to Return Power to Local Governments Faces Hard Struggle Over Control of Programs," National Journal, Special Report (March, 1973) p. 20. Special revenue sharing includes the consolidation of intergovernmental programs into general accounts that may be used more flexibly by state and local recipients with fewer controls by Washington.
10. Donald H. Haider, When Governments Come To Washington (New York: The Free Press, 1974), p 262.
11. See, Jeffrey L. Pressman, "Political Implications of the New Federalism," in Wallace E. Oates, ed., Financing the New Federalism (Baltimore: The Johns Hopkins University Press, 1975), pp. 32-33.
12. "New Federalism IV: Legislative...," p. 20.
13. For a review of Congressional attitudes concerning general revenue sharing, see Intergovernmental Relations Subcommittee of the House Committee on Government Operations, Replies by Members of Congress to a Questionnaire on General Revenue Sharing, Committee Print, April 1974.
14. See "Hearings Before A Subcommittee..." for a discussion of the strengths and weaknesses of the FRC's.
15. Quoted in :"New Federalism VI: Rivalries—Administration's Field Experiments Engender Power Struggles Among Levels of Government," National Journal, Special Report (March 1973), p. 30.
16. Statement by President Nixon, July 29, 1971, Office of the White House Press Secretary.
17. Statement by George Romney, Secretary of HUD, in "Planned Variations Program," July 29, 1971, HUD News.
18. "Banfield Report," New York Times, December 31, 1969.
19. Victor A Capoccia, "Chief Executive Review and Comment: A Preview

of New Federalism in Rochester, New York," Public Administration Review, 34 (September/October 1974), p. 468.

20. Ibid.
21. See HUD, Community Development Evaluation, Series No. 7, "Planned Variations: First Year Survey," 1974.
22. Deil S. Wright, Federal Grants-in-Aid: Perspectives and Alternatives (Washington, D.C.:American Enterprises Institute for Public Policy Research, 1968), p. 54.
23. Advisory Commission on Intergovernmental Relations, Fiscal Balance in the American Federal System, Vol, 1 (Washington, D.C.: GPO, October 1975), pp. 150-151.
24. See Advisory Commission on Intergovernmental Relations, Improving Federal Grants Management, A-53 (Washington, D.C.: GPO, February 1977), pp. 152-153.
25. "New Federalism Report/Nixon Attack on Grant Programs Aims to Simplify Structure, Give Greater Local Control," National Journal, Special Report, (March 1973), pp. 36-37.
26. Ibid., p. 37.
27. See Papers Relating to the President's Departmental Reorganization Program: A Revised Compilation (Washington, D.C.: GPO, 1972).
28. Improving Federal Grants Management...," p. 153.
29. By April 1973, John Erlichman, the primary force behind this reorganization, was gone and the designations of the supersecretaries were removed. White House control over domestic agencies in the last days of the Nixon presidency was essentially nonexistent. See Richard P. Nathan, The Plot That Failed: Nixon and the Administrative Presidency (New York: John Wiley and Sons, Inc., 1975), pp. 68 ff.
30. See Executive Reorganization Hearings, Senate Committee on Governmental Operations, 92nd Cong., 1st Sess., 1971.
31. See "Governmental Reorganization," National Journal, Reprint No. 11 (Spring, 1972). For a detailed discussion of special revenue sharing actions by Congress, see "Nixon, Congress Still at Odds on Decentralizing Power," Congressional Quarterly..., pp. 50-51
32. Quoted in Romney, p. 7.
33. Ibid. Romney's article represents a concise interpretation of President Nixon's New Federalism strategy, but makes no attempt to address some of the key questions which were emerging at that time as to why it did not ultimately succeed.
34. Richard P. Nathan, "Federalism and the Shifting Nature of Fiscal Relations," Annals 419 (May, 1975), pp. 125-126. Nathan's views on "New Structuralism" are elaborated further in the "The New Federalism Versus the Emerging New Structuralism," Publius (Summer 1975).
35. Ibid., pp. 128-129. The "New Structuralist" (Nathan's term) position is shared by the Advisory Commission on Intergovernmental Relations. See Regional Decision Making: New Strategies for Substate Districts, A-43 (Washington, D.C.: GPO, October 1973).

36. See Advisory Commission on Intergovernmental Relations, Significant Features of Fiscal Federalism 1978-79, M-115 (Washington, D.C.: GPO, May 1979).

37. "Revenue Sharing: The New States Rights," AFL-CIO American Federationist (July 1973), p. 16.

38. Edwin Kepler, "New Federalism: A Clear and Present Danger," The Grantsmanship Center News (May- July 1976), p. 35. The citation is from an edited version of an article that originally appeared in the December 1975 issue of the National Center for Community Action Reporter. Mr. Kepler is the executive director of the Massachusettes Opportunity Council in Leominster, MA.

39. Ibid., p. 36.

40. See "Nixon's New Federalism Shapes the '74 Budget," Business Week (Feruary 3, 1973), p. 36.

41. See Richard P. Nathan, "Social Policies in the 1970's," Urban and Social Change Review, Vol. 1 (1974), pp. 3-1.

42. "Nixon's New Federalism...," p. 61.

43. See David A. Caputo and Richard L. Cole, Urban Politics and Decentralization: The Case of General Revenue Sharing (Lexington, Massachusetts: D.C. Health and Company, 1974).

44. "New Federalism III: The Opposition," National Journal, Reprint No. 11 (Spring, 1972) p. 16. See also David A. Caputo, "General Revenue Sharing and American Federalism: Towards the Year 2000," Annals, 419 (May 1975).

45. Ibid., p. 14.

46. Pressman, p. 15.

47. For a detailed listing of these restrictions see the State and Local Fiscal Assistance Act of 1972, Subtitle B: "Administrative Provisions," and Sec. 103: "Use of Funds by Local Governments for Priority Expenditures."

48. See G. Ross Stephens,"Federalism, Federal Aids, and the States," State Government (Winter 1976).

49. E.E. Schattschneider, The Semi-Sovereign People (New York: Holt, Reinhart, and Winston, 1960) pp. 7-9.

CHAPTER III SELECTED BIBLIOGRAPHY
Articles/Documents

Advisory Commission on Intergovernmental Relations. Fiscal Balance in The American Federal System, Vol. I. Washington, D.C.: GPO, October 1975.

_____ . Improving Federal Grants Management, A-53. Washington, D.C.: GPO, February 1977.

_____ . Regional Decision-Making: New Strategies for Substate Districts, A-43. Washington, D.C.: GPO, October 1973.

"Banfield Report," New York Times. December 31, 1969.

Capoccia, Victor A. "Chief Executive Review and Comment: A Preview of New Federalism in Rochester, New York," Public Administration Review, Vol. 34 (September/October 1974).

Caputo, David A. "General Revenue Sharing and American Federalism: Towards the Year 2000," The Annals, 419 (May 1975).

"Governmental Reorganization," National Journal, No. 11 (Spring 1972).

Intergovernmental Relations Subcommittee of the House Committee on Government Operations, House of Representatives, 93rd Cong., 2nd Sess. Replies by Members of Congress to a Questionnaire on General Revenue Sharing. Washington D.C.: GPO, 1974.

Kepler, Edwin. "New Federalism: A Clear and Present Danger," The Grantsmanship Center News. May-July 1976.

Nathan, Richard P. "Federalism and the Shifting Nature of Fiscal Relations," The Annals, 419 (May 1975).

_____ . "Social Policies in the 1970's," Urban and Social Change Review, Vol. 2. (1974).

_____ . "The New Federalism Versus the Emerging New Structuralism," Publius. Summer 1975.

"New Federalism Report/Nixon Attack on Grant Programs Aims to Simplify Structure, Give Greater Local Control," National Journal. Special Report. March 1973.

"New Federalism III: The Opposition," National Journal. Special Report. March 1973.

"New Federalism IV: Legislation—Drive to Return Power to Local Governments Faces Hard Struggle Over Control of Programs," National Journal. Special Report. March 1973.

"New Federalism VI: Rivalries—Administration's Field Experiments Engender Power Struggles Among Levels of Government," National Journal. Special Report. March 1973.

"Nixon, Congress Still at Odds on Decentralizing Power," Congressional Quarterly Guide: Current American Government. Spring 1974.

"Nixon's New Federalism Shapes the '74 Budget," Business Week. February 3, 1973.

Papers Relating to the President's Departmental Reorganization Program: A Revised Compilation. Washington, D.C.: GPO, 1972.

"Revenue Sharing: The New States Rights," AFL-CIO American Federationist. July 1973.

Romney, George H. "A New Era of Federalism: Challenge for the U.S.," National Civil Review. January 1973.

"Statement by George Romney, Secretary of HUD, in Planned Variations Programs," HUD News. July 29, 1971.

Stephens, G. Ross. "Federalism, Federal Aid, and the States," State Government. Winter 1976.

U.S. President, "The New Federalism: An Address and Statement by the President," Address to the Nation, August 8, 1969. Washington, D.C.: GPO, 1969.

U.S. Department of Housing and Urban Development. "Planned Variations: First Year Survey," Community Development Evaluation Series, No. 7. Washington, D.C.: GPO, 1974.

Books

Caputo, David A. and Cole, Richard L. Urban Politics and Decentralization: The Case of General Revenue Sharing. Lexington, Mass: D.C. Health and Company, 1974.

Haider, Donald H. When Governments Come to Washington. New York: The Free Press, 1974.

Pressman, Jeffrey L. "Political Legislations of the New Federalism," in Wallace E. Oates (ed.), Financing the New Federalism. Baltimore: The Johns Hopkins University Press, 1975.

Wright, Deil S. Federal Grants-In-Aid: Perspectives and Alternatives. Washington, D.C.: American Enterprises Institute for Public Policy Research, 1968.

Hearings

U.S. Congress, Senate, Committee on Governmental Operations, 92nd Cong., 1st Sess. Executive Reorganization Hearings. Washington D.C.: GPO, 1971.

U.S. Congress, House, Committee on Government Operations, Subcommittee of the Committee on Government Operations, 93rd Cong., 2nd Sess. Hearings on New Federalism. January 29,30,31; February 4,5, 1974. Washington, D.C.: GPO, 1974.

Chapter Four
Management Capacity Development: Administrative Adjustment Following the Era of New Federalism

Yet the principle of decentralization is sound. Decisions on community problems made at the community level are <u>potentially</u> better than those made at the national level, because only at the community level can the community be seen whole, only there can all the community programs be interrelated, only there can the systems of comprehensive planning and program coordination be established and operated, and only there can widespread citizen participation be organized and the contributions of the citizens blended with those of the professionals in the decision-making process.

James L. Sundquist
1969

Introduction

Federal agencies made little effort to assess the administrative effects of the Great Society programs of the early 1960's.[1] There was also little attention to the impacts of the New Federalism initiatives of the late 1960's and early 1970's on state and local decision-makers' (primarily elected officials) capabilities to manage the new and considerable responsibilities resulting from both of these significant efforts.[2] Nor was there any concerted effort to assess the grants-in-aid going to these governments in terms of the amounts available for management training or funds to develop the capacity of these officials to manage resources. Federal agencies remained concerned with their own missions or responsibilities. Programmatic evaluations involving grant recipients were conducted primarily in terms of financial audits or the assessment of compliance with federal rules and regulations. Additionally, because of political reasons, state and local elected officials were reluctant to request assistance or to identify management needs. They also realized that management training was considered of lower importance than many of the other frustrations, time consuming activities, or critical problems they faced on a day-to-day basis.[3] Management was by crisis, and management activities centered around the use of resources and the conduct of programs with little attention to long-term integrated policy planning and resource utilization for the future.

By 1974, it became apparent to officials at OMB that state and local managers were being subjected to considerable pressure and increasing demands as a result of the new decision-making responsibilities thrust upon them by the New Federalism strategy of devolution and decentralization, inflation, the high costs of energy, and the ever-increasing number of federal categorical grant programs with their individualized rules and regulations. The grants themselves posed a significant problem. A high order of technical and legal knowledge was required in order to navigate the maze of federal application and compliance procedures, but more important, management expertise also was needed.

The purpose of this chapter is to discuss the state of the grant-in-aid system as it appeared to federal program decision-makers in the period following the resignation of Richard M. Nixon as President of the United States. This transitional period, as President Ford assumed the reins of government, signaled the end of the era of New Federalism and the awakening of a new management consciousness in government. This chapter discusses the impacts of New Federalism initiatives, and OMB's attempt to measure these impacts and to assess what federal agencies were doing to provide management assistance to state and local jurisdictional managers.

The Setting: Post New Federalism

Following the federal program "boom" of the early 1960's, most metropolitan areas experienced a mushrooming of single and multi-purpose area-wide districts encouraged by the grant-in-aid system. For example, according to the Advisory Commission on Intergovernmental Relations (ACIR), over 4,000 geographic program areas across the country were recognized under 24 federal programs. The more common single-purpose district organizations included 481 Law Enforcement Planning Regions, 957 Community Action Agencies, 419 Cooperative Area Manpower Planning System Councils, 195 Comprehensive Area-Wide Health Planning Agencies, 115 Economic Development Districts, 56 Local Development Districts, 165 Resource Conservation and Development Districts, and 247 Air Quality Regions. ACIR has stressed the need for more regional level coordination to bring together this hodge-podge of independent agencies in order to promote at least minimal systematic planning for development within a region.[5]

The growing complexity of governmental functions and structures was matched by increases in the costs of operation. Between 1946 and 1972, when they reached $368.3 billion, governmental *outlays* multiplied more than seven times. At the same time governmental *receipts* totaled $361.4 billion (a six-fold increase), and taxes increased by a magnitude of four to $274.7 billion. Federal grants to state and local governments in the 1970's were 16 times as great as total federal expenditures in the 1930's (see Figure 1 and Table 1). More generally, local government expenditures increased 135 percent between 1960-1970.[6] The National Commission on Productivity noted the significance of the expansion of governmental functions on human resource expenditures for this period:

- *Personnel expenditures for state and local government totaled 54 percent of all direct expenditures. Employment rose 140 percent from 1955 to 1972, from 4.5 million to 10.8 million.*
- *80 percent of state and local police budgets was for personnel costs which have increased by approximately 14 percent each year.*
- *66 percent of school budgets and 56 percent of sanitation*

Table 1

Federal Aid in Relation to State-Local Own Source Revenue, 1954, 1964, and 1969 Through 1978

Fiscal Year	Total Federal Aid		Education	Highways	Public Welfare	Housing and Urban Renewal	All Other. (Including Revenue Sharing[1])
	Amount	As a Percent of State-Local General Revenue From Own Sources					
Amount (in millions)							
1954	$ 2,967	11.4	$ 475	$ 530	$ 1,439	$ 90*	$ 433
1964	10,097	17.3	1,371	3,628	2,973	564	1,561
1969	19,421	20.4	4,960	4,314	6,358	921	2,868
1970	23,257	21.4	5,698	4,553	7,574	1,609	3,823
1971	27,121	22.8	5,907	4,738	9,766	1,611	5,099
1972	33,178	24.6	6,250	4,741	13,251	1,981	6,955
1973	41,268	27.3	6,791	4,807	12,097	2,121	15,452[1]
1974	42,854	25.8	7,496	4,555	12,837	2,391	15,575[1]
1975	49,628	27.0	8,959	4,754	14,352	2,734	18,829[1]
1976	69,057	34.4	9.254	6,243	17,225	2,820	33,515[1]
1977	73,045	32.7	10,205	6,173	19,520	2,914	34,233[1]
1978 est.	83,000	33.3	11,230	6,640	21,000	3,030	41,100[1]
Annual Percent Increase or Decrease (−)							
1954	—	—	—	—	—	—	—
1964	13.0[2]	—	11.2[2]	21.2[2]	7.5[2]	20.1[1]	12.9[2]
1969	14.0[3]	—	29.3[3]	3.5[3]	16.4[3]	10.3[3]	14.1[3]
1970	19.8	—	14.9	5.9	19.1	74.7	33.3
1971	16.6	—	3.7	8.2	28.9	0.1	33.4
1972	22.3	—	5.8	0.1	35.7	23.0	36.4
1973	24.4	—	8.7	1.4	−8.7	7.1	122.2
1974	3.8	—	10.4	−5.2	6.1	12.7	0.8
1975	15.8	—	19.5	4.4	11.8	14.3	20.9
1976	39.1	—	3.3	31.3	20.0	3.1	78.0
1977	5.8	—	10.3	−1.1	13.3	3.3	2.1
1978 est.	13.6	—	10.0	7.6	7.6	4.0	20.1
Percentage Distribution							
1954	100.0	—	16.0	17.9	48.5	13.0	14.6
1964	100.0	—	13.6	35.9	29.4	5.6	15.5
1974	100.0	—	17.5	10.6	30.0	5.6	36.3
1978 est.	100.0	—	13.5	8.0	25.3	3.7	49.5

*estimate

[1] Includes Federal general revenue sharing payments of $6,636-million in 1973, $6,106-million in 1974, $6,130-million in 1975, $6,238-million in 1976, $6,758-million in 1977, and $6,827-million in 1978.

[2] Annual average increase 1954 to 1964.

[3] Annual average increase 1964 to 1969.

SOURCE: Advisory Commission on Intergovernmental Relations, *Significant Features of Fiscal Federalism, 1978-79 Edition,* M-115 (Washington, D.C.: GPO, May, 1979) p. 78. ACIR staff a compilation based on U.S. Bureau of the Census, *Governmental Finances,* various years; Budget of the United States Government, various years; and ACIR staff estimates.

Figure 1

**Federal Aid as a Percent of Aggregate
State and Local Government Expenditures,
1930-1974 (Est.)**

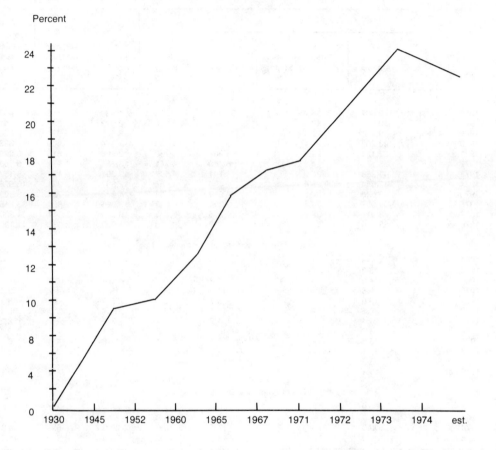

SOURCE: Special Analyses, Budget of the United States, Fiscal
Year 1974, Table N-5, p. 217, and Special Analyses,
Budget of the United States, Fiscal Year 1970, Table 0-3,
p. 209.

department budgets were for personnel.[7]

The task of human resource management was complicated greatly by laws concerning equal employment opportunities, occupational health and safety, collective bargaining, and fair labor standards.[8] The enactment of new laws and regulations also demanded increased managerial skills from local administrators. Each new federal enactment required substantial resource and manpower commitments at the state and local levels.

The pressures of inflation, the energy crisis, and the movement toward municipal employee unionization also accentuated management problems. Demands for higher wages from governmental employees, and a reluctance to increase taxes in the face of soaring demands for services left local administrators seeking ways to improve productivity and to utilize their resources more effectively. These managers turned to the federal government to provide technical assistance, primarily in the solving of day-to-day problems, not for help in managing programs or allocating resources. However, at least in the more sophisticated municipalities, managers began to seek ways to enhance their own capabilities in the more effective management of resources. Planning and productivity improvement became popular workshop activities as many state and local officials sought to acquire new management skills. Unfortunately, the federal effort in providing management assistance to state and local governments was relatively undefined, unplanned, program specific, and at low levels.[9] Consultants, universities, and professional associations began to reap a small bonanza as they attempted to fill this gap.

Management Development Efforts by Federal Agencies

With the growth of the grant-in-aid system by the early 1970's, federal mission agency officials increasingly became aware of the differing management skills and abilities of decision-makers at the state and local levels who were to implement the programs so carefully designed by Congress and articulated by the federal agencies. Where management skills were good, programs were conducted with few or no problems. Where they were poor, programs did not achieve their primary purpose; they did so only with additional federal intervention, or they presented problem after problem to the responsible officials. While there were no studies to support these generalities, federal agencies began to channel some of their programmatic resources into training and technical assistance efforts for these officials. Training was the smaller part of this effort. Technical assistance, while a more substantial effort, still was designed to provide information, consultation, or other direct assistance to these same officials. Few agencies were authorized specifically to provide the types of training or programs that were designed to impact management skills.

The root of many of the problems faced by these officials was thought to reside in a lack of management skills, and yet, management development efforts by a number of federal agencies aimed at assisting state and local officials were relatively uncoordinated. HUD took the lead in exploring the management development needs of these managers.[10] HUD was the logical agency for management development initiatives because of its mission, the efforts of its key personnel, and its historical experience with the Housing

Needs Analysis and Planning Effort, the Community Renewal Program, Model Cities, "701" grants, Planned Variations, and Annual Arrangements. Other agency efforts included those of the Department of Health, Education and Welfare (HEW); Service Integrated Targets of Opportunity (SITO) program;[11] Personnel Development programs funded by the Bureau of Intergovernmental Personnel Programs (BIPP) of the U.S. Civil Service Commission (CSC) under the Intergovernmental Personnel Act of 1970 (IPA); and the Department of Transportation's (DOT) Intermodel Planning Groups.[12] Several presidential-level study committees were convened in an attempt to bring together information about the faults in the grant-in-aid system and to make recommendations about what might be done to assist state and local leaders to better manage those programs. Those committees included the the President's Council on Executive Reorganizaton (1969); the President's Advisory Council on Intergovernmental Personnel Policy (1970); the President's Advisory Committee on Management Improvement (PACMI, 1973); and the OMB/NSF Interagency Study Committee on Policy Management Assistance (SCOPMA, 1974-75).[13]

Unfortunately, individual federal agency management programs were not widely supported, in part because their efforts were program specific (i.e., directed at their specific programs), and thus, they gained little general support from the public interest groups or the intended beneficiaries. The recommendations of the special study groups were ignored largely because they clashed with the jurisdictional boundaries and programmatic thrusts of the mission agencies. Each study group also recommended a federal level leadership role in intergovenrmental management, another topic that could not be resolved within the executive hierarchy. Even the General Accounting Office formulated specific recommendations in identifying the need for federal level reorientation, but no changes resulted.[14] Without a clear strategy or program related to management-development, the federal mission agencies did whatever they thought appropriate to address this problem.

Prior to 1973, the federal government had little idea of the amount of effort or funding support expended in the area of management assistance or the related area of policy planning (now called capacity-development or capacity-building). It was known that some Comprehensive Employment and Training Act (CETA), Intergovernmental Personnel Act (IPA), and HUD "701" funds were used for this purpose, i.e., for management training programs. The President's Advisory Council on Intergovernmental Personnel Policy (1970) and the President's Advisory Commission on Management Improvement (PACMI) assessed federal impacts on states and local management systems and even attempted to identify financial resources available to assist local managers in developing their management abilities. However, outside of technical and agency (or program) specific information, management skill building efforts were not coordinated, nor was state and local input solicited by any federal agency to any measurable degree.[15]

In the fall of 1973, the Office of Management and Budget began an assessment and review of the impacts on the New Federalism with the appointment of a Task Force on Technical Assistance.[16] Although the Task

Force report was never released to the public, a follow-up workshop sponsored by OMB and the General Accounting Office for interested federal agency officials and representatives of the public interest groups reaffirmed the need for more information on federal technical assistance efforts as well as other forms of federal management assistance.[17] The Task Force suggested a follow-up analysis to identify impacts of funds and regulations at the state and local levels with particular emphasis on the sources of managerial assitance available to state-local jurisdictional policy-makers. (Then) OMB Director Roy Ash authorized a one-year study of these problems and suggested formulation of a special interagency study team. The OMB/NSF Interagency Study Committee on Policy Management Assistance (SCOPMA) emerged as a compromise to the other organizational vehicles, including a Presidential Commission, which were considered.[18]

Assessment of Management Assistance

Concurrent with the formulation of SCOPMA, OMB Bulletin 75-5, entitled "Special Analysis of Federal Technical Assistance Provided to State and Local Governments," was initiated to determine federal agency funding levels as well as to identify specific management development programs available to state and local officials in this relatively undefined area.

The OMB Bulletin was developed by the Study Committee on Policy Management Assistance Co-chairperson Ann Macaluco of OMB, who also had been author of the Task Force on Technical Assistance report. The Bulletin equated management assistance with technical assistance, which was defined as an activity undertaken primarily to improve the capability of state or local government officials to manage their programs or to provide services effectively to their constituents. There was no clear definition of purpose because the framers of the Bulletin were not exactly sure of the forms or nature of this type of activity. Thus, without either a clear definition of purpose or specific guidelines on what to look for or how to ask it, the survey produced inconclusive results.[19] Agency responses tended to be incomplete, difficult to interpret, and confusing. Also, because an OMB "bulletin" does not carry the force of an OMB "circular," which is equivalent to administrative law, the federal agency respondents were not enthusiastic about compiling the detailed information called for by the Bulletin. However, the survey represented the first Executive-level effort to determine which individual agency programs provided management assistance to state and local officials, and it was the first initiative requiring them to appraise their own efforts as well.

An assessment of domestic grant-in-aid programs, administered by the 41 executive department agencies responding to OMB Bulletin 75-5 (September 1974), provided evidence that only slightly more than one percent ($512 million) of the $48.6 billion expended in Fiscal Year 1974 for domestic assistance was allocated to technical or management assistance projects at the state and local levels.[20] Overall, technical or management assistance was highly categorical, fragmented, and dominated by federal agency missions, objectives, and guidelines. The survey affirmed the fact that there was little individual agency policy direction or strategy in providing this type of assistance. There was evidence of a lack of mutual awareness of related activities and little evidence of coordinated activities on the part of the agencies. In an interview with the SCOPMA, Cincinnati City Manager William Donaldson summarized the local awareness of this problem by quipping, "When I retire, I'm going to go to Washington and spend my time introducing 'feds' to each other."

Bulletin 75-5 also affirmed that each agency had the prerogative of determing how and where its funds were to be allocated (within its Congressional mandate). The bulk of all domestic grant-in-aid funds were channeled through 12 mission agencies (Table 2) with HEW taking the lead. There was no relationship between agency funding levels and management development efforts. The agency-management-development programs were highly fragmented, multipurpose, uncoordinated, and lacked clear central policy guidance. It was evident from the response to 75-5 that agencies were having difficulty in organizing information about technical assistance as well as in managing these programs. There were few interagnecy mechanisms for assessing the impact of federal programs on state and local managers and none for coordinating these efforts. An assessment of the distribution of funding related to 80 major activities and reported by the 41 responding federal agencies indicating that:

- Of the $512 million identified as technical or managerial assistance, over 87 percent was for programmatic or functional areas related to the agency's mission, and 13 percent was for general purpose, multipurpose, or policy-associated areas (A, Figure 2).

  Of the total domestic federal grant-in-aid program ($48.6 billion in FY 1974), only 16 percent was related to the planning, control, or evaluation of the total investment (B, Figure 2).
- In the management development area, 37 activities related to the management processing were identified.
- Of those activites in the category identified as management development, 81 percent addressed some form of technical assistance, and 5 percent addressed program planning and development.
- In terms of technical assistance, almost 90 percent was for the dissemination of information, 5 percent was for training, and 5 percent for information services. Fifty to 60 percent of this amount was directed toward research and development activities.
- Approximately 40 percent of the program funds went exclusively to state governments, 7 percent to local governments, and 53 percent could be given to either; however, most of this latter percentage went to local governments (C, Figure 3).
- In terms of federal strategy, 24 percent of the grant funds had no provision for the involvement of the user government in the allocation decision. State and local governments merely

112

Table 2

Grants-in-Aid to State and Local
Governments by Federal Agencies

AGENCY	FY 1974 ACTUAL	FY 1980 ESTIMATE
Department of Agriculture	5,112	5,112
Department of Commerce	260	902
Department of Health, Education, and Welfare	19,138	33,280
Department of Housing and Urban Development	3,147	7,232
Department of the Interior	452	1,128
Department of Justice	637	470
Department of Labor	2,651	10,777
Department of Transportation	5,108	10,240
Department of the Treasury	6,302	7,559
Environmental Protection Agency	1,623	3,853
Community Services Administration	639	485
Other	522	1,450
TOTAL EXPENDITURES FOR FEDERAL GRANTS*	46,040	

*Excludes programs not directly targeted at state and local assistance.

SOURCE: Special Analyses, Budget of the United States Government, FY 1976 (Washington, D.C.: GPO, 1975); and Special Analyses, Budget of the United States Government, FY 1980 (Washington, D.C.: GPO, 1979)

Figure 2
Allocations to Management Assistance

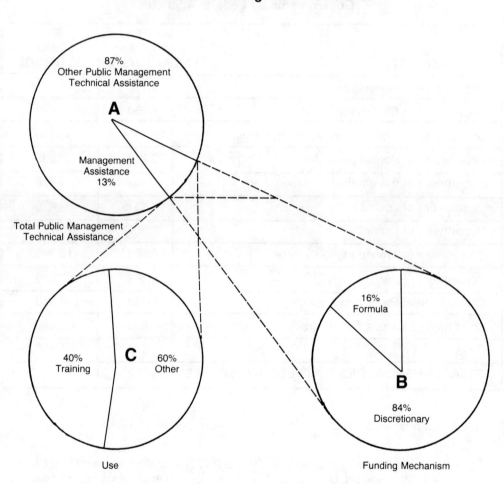

SOURCE: Preliminary Analysis of OMB Bulletin 75-5. Adapted from SCOPMA. Framework of a Strategy for Policy Management Assistance to State and Local Governments, Volume 1, OMB Internal Report (Washington, D.C.: OMB, April, 1975), Appendix 3(b), p. 10.

received funds as beneficiaries. They had some degree of involvement in planning and conducting activities related to 19 percent of the funds, but this involvement ranged from prior knowledge about the availability of funds through agency efforts at consultation about local needs, to some form of local control permitted by the funding agency. Information on the type or degree of involvement or the magnitude of this effort was not available through Bulletin 75-5.

Only 2 percent of the funds for technical assistance went to the local chief executive. Over 27 percent of these funds went to state and local agencies without requiring chief executive or legislative designation or approval. Twenty-nine percent went to agencies designated by the governor or legislature in accordance with a state plan. The remaining 42 percent went to third parties, such as special interest groups or private non-profit organizations.

It should be noted that elected officials had little control over technical assistance funds. Of the funds going to third parties, over one third went to *designated* groups. Of this amount, most went to functional area-wide agencies and a small amount (about $12 million) to universities. There was also some evidence that public interest groups were favored recipients for DOL, CSC, and HUD programs and funds.[21]

In regard to private agencies and their potential for assisting state and local managers, the information provided to OMB presented a reasonably clear picture. There was very little indication of serious concern about the management capability or about strengthening that capacity, either within or among potential "supplier" community agencies (agencies that could be used, with federal support, in assisting other agencies or units of government). Six federal agencies (HEW, HUD, DOT, NSF, CSC, and DOL) had programs to strengthen the usefulness of the universities as performers of applicable research rather than as developers of local management skills. There was little indication of consistent attitudes toward the use of public interest groups and no programmatic activity by federal agencies to strengthen the interest group roles or capabilities. There were obvious ambiguities and ambivalences within and among federal agencies about the role of state and local governments in providing technical or managerial assistance to local governments.

Actors in Management Assistance

The major federal actors, those agencies included in the OMB Bulletin review, with activities focusing on management-development areas, were HUD, HEW, DOL, the National Science Foundation's (NSF) Intergovernments Science Program and, as mentioned previously, the IPA program of the U.S. Civil Service Commission (now OPM) (Table 3). These agencies had relatively small programmatic activities directed toward the basic governmental management and decision processes at the state and local level and undoubtedly there were more related activities in these agencies. However, there was little indication that this problem had any priority within the agencies.

Table 3

Management Capacity-Building Programs
Fiscal Year 1974

Program/Agency	Federal Funding Level (Approx.)	Management Capacity-Building Program Objectives
I) HUD — Eight capacity building experiments	$1.9 Million	Funding and testing management tools and techniques to be used by state and local policy-makers in building decision-making capacity.
Section 701 Planning Assistance Grants (Housing Act of 1965)	$100 Million	Development of planning capabilities—State and area wide.
		Improvements in state and planning systems and assistance to substate regional units (including staff development administrative systems, technical assistance and monitoring and evaluation activities).
Housing and Community Development Act of 1974	Not Specifically Identified	Grants to universities to develop programs to prepare graduate students in planning, management, housing, urban affairs and improving methods of education in such professions.
		Developing policy-planning-management capacity to more effectively determine needs, set goals, and objectives, develop and evaluate programs and carry out management activities necessary for planning implementation.
		Urban Fellowship Program.
II) HEW — Capacity-Building Projects (Service Integrated Targets of Opportunity — SITO)	$5.1 Million	Experimental projects to assist state and local chief executives of general purpose governments to improve their capacities to plan and manage human service programs — also a pilot for the proposed "Allied Services Act."
Special Community Service and Continuing Education Programs (Title I of the Higher Education Act of 1965)	$4 Million	National grants for educational development projects such as urban extension programs for municipal employees
		State grants for university — government cooperation to improve community services, continuing education and community/educational programs for the elderly.
Public Service Eucation Program (Title IX of the Higher Education Act of 1965)	$4 Million	Programs to prepare graduate and professional students for public service.
		Fellowships
		Grants to assist in strengthening undergraduate programs in areas relevant to professional training for public service.
III) DOL — Comprehensive Employment and Training Act of 1974 (CETA)	Not Specifically Identified	Block grants and manpower training for 402 prime sponsors including development of job opportunities, training, education and other services to help people get jobs.
IV) NSF — Research Applied to National Needs (RANN) and Urban Technology Systems (Intergovernmental Service and Public Technology)	$5.1 Million	Research and demonstration projects linking technical assistance to state and local governmental needs.
— Research in management	$10 Million	
V) USCSC — Bureau of Intergovernmental Personnel Programs (BIPP) Intergovernmental Personnel Act of 1970 (IPA)	$15 Million	Capacity-building projects in the area of personnel systems development.

There were indications of substantial project level (as opposed to program) activities in DOT, the Law Enforcement Assistance Administration (LEAA), the Economic Development Administration (EDA), and other agencies that could be considered as major potential sources of assistance. However, neither LEAA nor DOL had major activities expressly targeted at this area. CSC was the only agency with a clearly expressed mandate (arising under the Intergovernmental Personnel Act) for this type of assistance with programs systematically implementing that mandate. NSF and the National Aeronautics and Space Administration (NASA) had no corresponding state and local counterpart agencies and so treated the entire spectrum of general purpose governments (some 40,000) rather than one segment or group as potential users of management assistance funds or services. Neither agency had a consistent awareness of similar or related assistance programs. There was also little indication of jointly-planned or jointly-funded activities between agencies.

The only grant-in-aid programs of the federal government mandated to provide management assistance to state and local governments were HUD's 701 program ($100 million primarily for substate regional planning assistance and $1.9 million in demonstration management-development grants); HEW's management-development efforts (Service Integrated Targets of Opportunity) funded at approximately $5 million; some NSF funding through the Intergovernmental Science Program; and the funding of the Bureau of Intergovernmental Personnel Program (BIPP)—U.S. Civil Service Commission ($15 million)(Table 3). Of the $79 million in grant-in-aid funding allocated for technical assistance, the IPA provided $15 million in 1974 (approximately 19 percent of the total). However, because only $63 million (81 percent of the $79 million total) was directed specifically at general management development, the IPA share became 24 percent. Because these funds were discretionary (i.e., the agencies had more flexibility in spending funds) there was little continued agency commitment to management assistance. There was a tendency for agencies to direct funding to those projects most allied with their missions. This tendency also singled out the IPA as the only significant, consistent funding source in this area.

Capacity-Building and Policy Management Assistance

OMB Bulletin 75-5 indicated considerable confusion in determining what federal agencies were doing to develop skills, capabilities, or the capacity of state and local officials to manage resources or programs (see Table 4).[22] Part of the problem was definitional. The Study Committee on Policy Management Assistance began to equate management development activities with capacity-building or development, a term that was adopted readily by the bureaucracy. Capacity-building or development eventually came to mean:

...any system, effort, or process...(for) strengthening the capability of elected chief officers, Chief Administrative Officers, Department or Agency Heads, and Program Managers...to plan, implement, manage or evaluate policies, strategies or programs designed to impact on social conditions in the community.[23]

Table 4

An Assessment of the Elements of Public Management

Public Management Function / Assessment Criteria	POLICY MANAGEMENT (PM)	RESOURCE MANAGEMENT (RM)	PROGRAM MANAGEMENT (PG)
Functional Emphasis	Strategic functions of providing guidance and leadership.	Routine support functions to ensure organizational maintenance, a capacity for adaptation and compliance with environmental constraints.	Tactical functions of executing administrative directives and policy guidance in the form of programs, activities, and services.
Purpose	To clarify and articulate community and social values and to develop priorities and establish commitments designed to meet community needs and aspirations.	To develop and maintain a human, material, financial, and informational resource base that is maximally responsive to the demands of the Policy and Program components of the organization and to ensure that all organizational elements comply with established administrative and regulatory procedures — both internal and external.	To design operating programs, services, and activities that reflect general policy guidance and are responsive to the unique and/or changing needs of clientele.
Major Concerns	What should be done and why should it be done?	How can it be done?	How to do it?
Participants and Arenas	Elected officials and their immediate staffs; dominated by "generalists."	Administrative officers; professionals specialized in budgeting, accounting, data processing, statutory and administrative law, drafting, materials procurement, personnel, recruitment and training, property management, and other similar areas. Dominated by "specialists," "generalists" are likely to be found in the staff elements devoted to legal matters or to budgeting.	Department or agency heads, their staffs, and the heads of organizational subunits. Some "generalists" though dominated by professionals specialized in some substantive aspect of a functional program area (e.g., mass transportation, health care, etc.), related methodologies (e.g., R&D, institutional development, etc.), or in resource management skills specifically required to develop, operate, and manage a major program, project, or service.

SOURCE: Executive Office of the President, *Strengthening Public Management in the Intergovernmental System* (Washington, D.C.: GPO, 1975), p. 6

This definition has been generally accepted by all federal agencies engaged in this effort and also has led to the recognition of a new area of management activities, those related to policy-making. Because this concept was even more complex than activities designed solely to build capacity or capability to manage programs or resources, the SCOPMA then concentrated its studies in the more general area and coined the phrase "policy management assistance."

Policy management was defined as:

The performance of decision-makers on an integrated, cross-cutting basis of the needs assessment, goal setting, and evaluation functions of management, the establishment of priorities and mobilization, allocation of resources; and the initiation and guidance of the planning, development, and implementation of policies, strategies, and programs that are related to sustaining or improving the physical, socio-economic, or political well-being of citizens.[24]

Policy management assistance was used synonymously with capacity-building and was viewed as a process that involved the strategic (or long term) functions of guidance and leadership with respect to a governmental jurisdiction. Capacity-building, as determined in OMB Bulletin 75-5, was concerned with efforts to strengthen the decision-making capabilties of jurisdictional managers—primarily chief elected officials serving in an administrative/management role in the three areas of policy, resource, and program management. Thus, although the OMB study effort defined capacity-building in terms of strengthening decision-making capabilities in the three functional areas, the target of the assessment was in the area of policy management.

Although a clearer picture emerges when one concentrates on the distinction between these terms, it is evident that federal level agencies themselves viewed capacity-building efforts or policy management assistance from a number of perspectives, much as the proverbial blind men felt and described the elephant: DOT equated it with technical assistance;[25] the National Training and Development Service (NTDS) saw it as training and development,[26] the Department of Labor stressed the establishment of a partnership with state and local user agencies;[27] while HEW saw a need for the "impetus to correct initiatives through administrative measures, as well as infusion of new resources."[28] Instead of the multi-faceted approach to management or capacity development which was implied, agency program officials actually lacked a clear objective upon which to concentrate resources, even if they had the desire or commitment to do so. Because of these definitional problems and the inability of agencies to assess state and local management training needs, each agency developed its own unique programs and strategies to meet the management development needs of these officials.

Problems in Assessing State and Local Management Needs

The management assistance strategies developed by federal funding agencies were based on their assessments of what these management needs were. It was not illogical that every federal agency developed its own unique strategy. The reason for this variegated approach resided in the difficulty in identifying and assessing needs.

The residue of the Great Society social programs (and the local level agencies created to administer them) and the New Federalism attempts to decentralize program administration and management left scholars and administrators with a bewildering array of assessments of state and local needs.[29] The federal government was asked to simplify grant application procedures and reduce "red tape" as well as to make programs more responsible to local needs. One means of doing so was through an analysis of state and local needs upon which to develop program strategies. However, these needs assessments provided feedback that was, at best, difficult to interpret.

The problem with assessing state and local needs was that there was too much inconsistency. Some of the problems in assessing needs were:

- there was inconsistent terminology from survey to survey;
- the responses to surveys were not necessarily what was requested; i.e., needs were listed as desires, problems, wishes, or what might be troubling the respondent at the time the question was asked;
- many persons did not understand the meaning of the terminology in assessment surveys;
- needs were often expressed in non-actionable terms; e.g., revenue needs, financial problems, etc.;
- surveys collated different forms of data and those analyzing the data tried to match them—it was like trying to add oranges and apples to obtain one total;
- each jurisdiction had unique needs which varied with such factors as size, type of government, fiscal resources, population composition, industrial and resource base, geographic location, etc.;
- the needs picture changed constantly, sometimes on a day-to-day basis; e.g., note the impacts of the energy crisis;
- priority listings did not provide a *value* weighting of individual items; i.e., the first need compared to the second and so on;
- needs listings were seldom integrated in the planning or policy-making processes of federal or even local agencies;
- city management was usually on a crisis basis; i.e., day-to-day, and also subject to political motives which might not have been logical or consistent from a program or resource management viewpoint;
- needs listings by citizens, elected officials, and professional administrators in *the same jurisdiction differed;*
- there were numerous sampling errors in need surveys;
- administrators tended to ignore needs listings in day-to-day operational decisions;
- there was seldom a validity check of needs listings, nor was there any follow-up within the same jurisdiction; and

- needs listings and priorities were used as *political* tools subject to political constraints within a community.

All of these factors created confusion among federal agency decision-makers viewing state or local needs from a top-down perspective and attempting to respond to local priorities by developing new programs. Determining how to structure management building programs created additional problems, and attempts to study needs assessments in the formulation of such programs eventually brought about the fragmented, agency-specific approach described in the response to OMB Bulletin 75-5.

From the federal perspective, programs were designed to accomplish national priorities and, therefore, tended to be too broad. They were viewed by local officials as too unresponsive to satisfy the particular needs and problems of any one jurisdiction. In trying to meet everyone's needs, these programs met almost no one's. In addition, local officials tended to be concerned with specific problems, relegating management to a category of luxury they could not afford, and it was up to the federal government to convince the user governments that better management would lead to the solution of many of the problems they identified through needs assessments. However, without Presidential leadership or the designation of some national level focal point to develop policy or guidance, the programmatic orientation of the federal mission agencies precluded this effort (with the exception of the IPA).[30] Unfortunately, the year 1974 was one of transition between administrations. The New Federalism initiatives of the Nixon bureaucracy were being replaced by the transitional policies of the new Ford Administration. State and local needs became subordinated to the efforts of a new administration to assume the leadership of the government.

Attempts to Measure Management Needs in the Final Years of the New Federalism

Studies of the last years of the Nixon Administration and the era of New Federalism revealed a litany of problems facing state and local managers. The grant-in-aid system had imposed serious stresses on these officials, and a series of uncoordinated studies were inaugurated by private and public interest groups and governmental agencies to assess various aspects of management-related problems and, tangentially, the impacts of New Federalism. The lack of centralized organization and consistency in these studies and the changing nature of the intergovernmental system in the period 1972-1975 made conclusions related to management needs difficult to formulate.

A 1973 International City Management Association (ICMA) study attempted to determine the management and staff time allocations for various management-related activities.[31] This survey was one of the first attempting to assist intergovernmental time allocations (14% of all local management activity) but it appeared to mix policy management activities (formation of goals and objectives, analysis of alternatives, and evaluation) with programmatic and resource management tasks. It reaffirmed the findings of the Study Committee on Policy Management Assistance that local managers did not differentiate between these functions. A look at critical community problems by ICMA the same year accentuated the difficulty associated with establishing needs listings and served to confirm the federal approach to solving local problems through generalized program assistance of a broad nature, i.e., DOL manpower development funding (to help meet a need identified as a "lack of jobs") or HUD community assistance grants (to meet a need identified as a "lack of housing"). The ICMA survey found that only 12 percent of the responding cities identified a lack of jobs as a *critical* need, while 22 percent noted a lack of housing as *critical*.[32] Because cities of different sizes identified different "critical" needs, the question became which need should be the federal agency's priority.

Attempting to establish programmatic priorities by reviewing a listing of federal grants obtained by smaller cities also presents a confusing picture. In the areas of jobs and housing, for example, 35 percent of the cities surveyed reported the receipt of federal assistance for jobs and 10 percent for housing. To a federal policy-maker comparing the critical needs identified by cities to actual grants received, the results are also inconsistent. In many cases cities did not request assistance in areas they identified as "critical."[33]

It is evident that federal agencies prefer the "top-down" approach to assistance programs and look toward long-term strategies. On the other hand, there is a tendency for state and local governments to prefer solutions directed at short-term problems while ignoring the possibilities of longer term solutions because the results are more readily apparent. Thus, enhancing the management ability or capacity of the decision-makers is viewed as a long-term solution.

A question that may be asked in attempting to determine management assistance policy is "how helpful has the federal government been in assisting local governments in meeting needs?" At a time when local jurisdictions were receiving approximately 25 percent of their revenues from the federal government, a 1969 ICMA survey of the perceptions of local administrators revealed that 38 percent of the respondents viewed the federal government as most helpful.[34] However, a discouraging 27 percent saw neither the federal nor state government as helpful in assisting them with local problems and implied that federal programs were not perceived as significant in helping to solve municipal problems. Nor was the state viewed by many (21 percent) as a significant helper. Thus, it it not surprising to find many municipalities relying on outside sources for such assistance—primarily consulting firms.[35]

Although some cities (state data is not available) find flexibility in federal programs, a large percentage record that programs are not responsive to local needs. Of the 868 cities participating in a 1970 ICMA survey, 28 percent felt that the federal regional offices—the key to the decentralization philosophy of New Federalism—seldom or never adjusted their programs to meet local conditions; 46 percent found "occasional" federal accomodation; 21 percent felt they could "usually" obtain adjustment; but only 5 percent noted federal responsiveness "nearly always."[36] It was evident that local officials believed that the federal grant-in-aid system was not responding adequately to locally determined priorities or problem areas and that this intergovernmental administrative opinion remained unchanged throughout this period.

The functional or programmatic orientation of federal grant programs also added to the complexity and cost of the adminstrative process for state and local officials. A sizable percentage of cities perceived interdepartmental grant-in-aid program coordination as difficult and time consuming.[37] The multitude of program areas and complex guidelines increased the expertise needed. Individual agencies sought means to simplify the process as well as to provide expertise (technical assistance) and, ultimately, resources and materials to assist state and local decision-makers in strengthening their own management capabilities.

However, the simplification thrust was uncoordinated and lacked centralized leadership from the Nixon and Ford Administrations. It was not until 1978 that the Federal Grant and Cooperative Agreement Act of 1977 finally passed and expanded the Intergovernmental Cooperation Act of 1968. This significant administrative tool provided federal agencies with authority to differentiate more clearly between award instruments—grants, cooperative agreements, and contracts (see Chapter VII). A number of other efforts in the technical assistance area were attempted by individual federal agencies, but no concerted federal strategy emerged to develop the management capabilities of state and local officials.

The lack of federal strategy to develop the management capabilities of state and local officials was no surprise. Policy development at the national level is a long-term political process, and domestic reform has always been relegated to second place following foreign affairs (except perhaps during the depression years). The problem of instituting administrative change at the national level without a national crisis, clientele group support, or a commitment by the President or Congress is formidable. Part of the problem is related to lack of integration between the political and adminstrative processes. In order to be effective, management in public agencies must integrate political and administrative processes (Figure 3). The disciplines of political science and public administration merge in public policy-making and administrative activities. Good management should lead to good program performance. In domestic affairs at the national level, public policy cannot be effective merely by promulgating rules and regulations applicable to programs actually administered by other levels of governments. Underlying this approach is an assumption that the administrators or implementors of public policy have the capability or capacity to interpret instructions and translate programs into operations (performance). Policy-makers at the national level were aware of the potential impacts of mandated administration change, which was an integral part of the devolution and decentralization strategy of the New Federalism, but they were unsure about how the impact should be measured.

The OMB/NSF Study Committee on Policy Management Assistance (SCOPMA)

In 1974, OMB created the Study Committee on Policy Management

Figure 3

Integration of Political and Administrative Processes

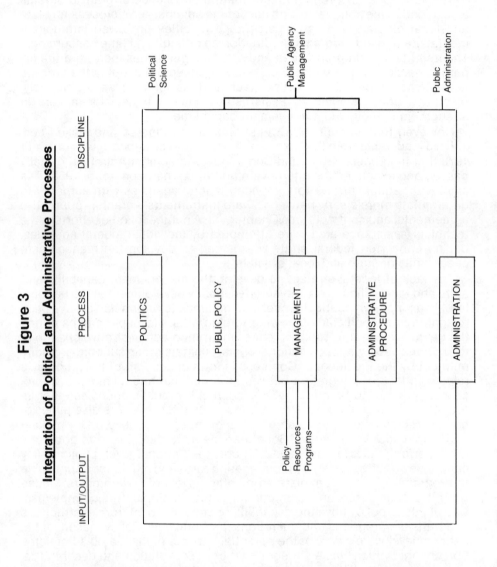

Assistance to assess the nation-wide impacts of the administrative initiatives of New Federalism on state and local level decision-makers and to determine the capacity of state and local officials to administer programs following these changes. The SCOPMA co-chairpersons, Dr. M. Frank Hersman (then Director, Intergovernmental Science and Public Technology Section, NSF) and Ann C. Macaluso (then Program Manager, OMB), attempted to accomplish this charge and at the same time overcome a lack of interest in domestic reform and the problems associated with promoting institutional change.[38] The experiences of the SCOPMA in this effort present an interesting study of the constraints in strategic planning of new programs and problems in the initiation of administrative reform at the federal level.

The variables which make needs assessment meaningful for policy development at the state and local levels are many. However, the role of the federal mission agencies in the long-term strategic planning of programs to meet the development needs of these officials also is subject to a number of intangible realities and considerations. The first constraint is the functional orientation of federal programs (i.e., they must be aligned with their own mission objectives as defined by Congress). The second constraint was indicated by the data generated through OMB Bulletin 75-5. Very few funds are available for programs in the broad area of "management capacity-building," and most of the funds that are available are discretionary in nature. Discretionary funds, by definition, may be used by the mission agencies almost as they choose (with certain legal constraints).

To overcome these two barriers to the development of programs of assistance in the area of capacity-building, the Study Committee on Policy Management Assistance analyzed the existing planning and adminstrative procedures of the mission agencies and formulated several alternatives utilizing *existing* funding levels and recognizing the *existing* administrative and political constraint system.[39]

The Study Committee on Policy Management Assistance (SCOPMA) charter was clear. The committee was

> ...to develop an inventory of federal objectives, policies and programs that directly or indirectly relate to the policy management capacity of state and local governments, and assess their impact on the policy development and service delivery capacity of state and local governments in the policy management area and assess the adequacy of the resources of the federal government that have bearing on those needs.[40]

The Committee was directed to submit a report of its findings to OMB by the spring of 1975. Its report was to reflect the realities and existing constraints within the federal system, and its recommendations were to reflect actionable items within this context.

With these limitations, the SCOPMA proposed a three part strategy for federal action:

1. Reorienting federal domestic programs in order to minimize the administrative burdens on state and local governments and the conflicts with local priorities.

125

2. Expanding and coordinating federal public management assistance specifically aimed at strengthening the overall management capacity of state and local governments that desire such assistance.
3. Improving the federal government's machinery for conducting intergovernmental business in order to bring more effective state and local participation and liaison in accomplishing the two objectives stated above.[41]

Part 1—Reorienting Federal Programs

The SCOPMA found that federal assistance efforts and programs compounded the jobs of state and local managers by sheer magnitude and numbers alone. By 1976, federal domestic assistance reached an all-time high of $55.6 billion, which was distributed through the four major block grant programs and general revenue sharing, but $42.2 billion was allocated by over 1,100 different categorical grant programs. The problem for state and local managers was not only to find the appropriate program to meet localized needs, but also to package appropriate "mixes" of programs to solve problems not matching the specific programmatic guidelines of a single federal agency. The integrated grant experiment was not widespread enough to impact on this problem and the newly passed Joint Funding Simplification Act was still sufficiently complex and unused to provide an adequate solution to this problem.

A second group of problems emerged when officials applied for assistance. Federal agency categorical assistance program rules, regulations, guidelines, and application procedures were developed by each agency to meet its own specific needs with little thought to local capabilities, staff resources, or abilities to deal with this complex system. As Governor James Holshouser noted in a videotaped interview with a SCOPMA staff member: "The best thing the federal government could do to help state and local government would be to get some of the regulations out of our hair and let us do our job." [42] The Federal Regional Councils, as key elements of the New Federalism decentralization strategy, apparently had failed to provide sufficient assistance to state and local governments, and the paperwork jungle became increasingly worse. Without top-down assistance or direction, the burden of dealing with federal grant-in-aid "red tape" remained an ever increasing headache for jurisdictional managers.

A third problem was approached through the "Planned Variations experiments of the Department of Housing and Urban Development (HUD). One of the "Variations," Chief Executive Review and Comment (CERC), was designed to alleviate the problems that developed when federal assistance was given directly to private non-profit groups or special purpose governments, bypassing general purpose governmental decision-makers having responsibility for area-wide planning development on service delivery, thus undermining their ability to control growth or respond to jurisdictional needs. For example, in FY 1970 the city of Richmond, Virginia received $18.3 million in federal assistance. In this same year, $12.3 million was allocated to non-governmental organizations in Richmond through 29 federal programs or roughly an amount equal to two-thirds of the portion of funds that were granted to the city.[43]

In an attempt to mitigate the worst portions of these three problems and to encourage partnerships between the federal, state, and local governments in the design and execution of domestic assistance programs, the SCOPMA developed five recommendations:

1. The federal government should, in its domestic assistance programs, continue moving in the direction of revenue sharing, block grant, grant consolidation, and other funding devices that allow state and local government leaders more flexibility in allocating resources and coordinating the delivery of services and benefits within the framework of more clearly stated national objectives to be accomplished by the assistance programs.
2. Federal agencies should encourage, in any performance or evaluation criteria for domestic assistance, the accomplishment of basic national legislative purposes and development or enhancement of state and local management structures necessary to carry these out, rather than creation of detailed administrative guidelines that constrain state and local flexibility.
3. Grant notification and review procedures for state and local leaders should be expanded to cover all major domestic assistance or grant activity within their jurisdictions relevant to the management of the jurisdiction, and the federal government should contribute to the cost of such review procedures.
4. Greater supervision should be exercised within federal agencies to ensure compliance with recent federal requirements for standardized and simplified grant application and administration procedures.
5. Federal agencies should more fully utilize integrated planning, awarding, and monitoring of federal grants based on the experience of the Integrated Grant Administration Program and Joint Funding Simplification Act, HUD's Planned Variations and Annual Arrangements, DOT's Unified Work Program Requirements and Intermodel Planning Groups, and other arrangements that promote state and local participation in program formulation, administration, and evaluation.[44]

Part 2—Expanding and Coordinating Federal Management Capacity Development Programs

The management capabilities of state and local elected officials have been a concern of the federal government for several reasons. First, grant recipients are implementors of federal assistance policy and the means by which services financed by the federal government are delivered to communities. Federal level policy-makers are not unaware of the casual link between agency administrative actions and the effectiveness of state and local governments. In such areas as environmental pollution, health care, welfare, and law enforcement, complex federal desires expressed in terms of guidelines and regulations attached as conditions to the receipt of federal funds must be translated into reality by recipient agency officials. If these managers are unable to implement these programs in an effective manner, the value of the funding and the program may be lost.

Second, the impacts of the program expansion resulting from the Great Society programs and the devolution and decentralization initiatives of the New Federalism require a greater sophistication and higher degree of managerial skill of state and local officials. The managers must be able to coordinate more programs and more resources and to deal with more agencies. While some jurisdictional managers have limited management development programs initiated by the state and local government, they usually cannot afford the cost or time of participating. Also, while in need of staff assistance, given the choice between line or staff (managerial) persons, few cities could afford to add the staff assistant.

As a result, most local efforts at self-improvement have been piecemeal. The increased reliance on management consultants, universities, and professional organizations offering short course organizational development, team building, or management-by-objectives workshops attests to the recognition of the problem and the search for a quick solution. While the short-term gains of this approach appear attractive, a long-term, ongoing capacity-building program for state and local officials has been lacking. The results of the survey of federal agency programs designed to measure management capacity (OMB Bulletin 75-5) indicated the lack of federal commitment and organization in this area. For example, only approximately $39 million of a total domestic allocation of $48.6 billion (less than 1/10th of 1 percent) was being spent for management capacity development activities by federal agencies in FY 1974.

While more federal agencies recognize a need for increased support in this area, established clientele groups (recipients) would not support a decrease in their allocations to shift funds to this needed area. State and local elected officials have been reluctant to request additional management development funding for fear of federal intrusion into state or local policy-making structures or prerogatives. With these constraints, the initiative rests with the federal government. The strategic requirements of such an effort of expanding existing federal mangement capacity-building programs led SCOPMA to make seven recommendations, built upon a foundation of cooperation and participation by the affected agencies, as follows:

1. The federal government should strongly reaffirm its commitment to public management assistance for state and local governments.
2. The federal government should initiate a joint effort with key state and local elected officials and their representatives to develop a policy and strategy for delivery of public management assistance embracing the three functions of policy management, resource management, and program management.
3. Public management assistance should reflect the diversity and variation of state and local governments' management needs and should be tailored to the needs of each recipient unit through the development of joint federal/recipient needs assessment processes.
4. Such assistance should also provide incentives for more intensive state government efforts to: a) strengthen, through financial and technical

assistance, local governments' management capacity, and b) remove institutional constraints (such as those on the organization, structure, finances, and personnel of local government).

5. The designers of an expanded and coordinated public management assistance effort should build on current federal strengths in technical assistance and capacity-building and should consider strengthening the capacity of user-oriented, non-federal resources such as state community development agencies, public interest groups, university public service institutes and programs, and professional associations.

6. As an interim strategy, federal agencies should substantially increase their level of investment in policy and resource management assistance relative to program management assistance, and monitor and evaluate the response of state and local elected leaders to this investment.

7. The federal government should develop a more adequate information base on agency activities relating to public management assistance that can be used for planning and evaluation of programmatic efforts, as well as for disseminating information on objective evaluations of projects and techniques that state and local officials view as successful.[45]

Part 3—Improved Federal Machinery

Complicating the development of federal administrative mechanisms or "machinery" to initiate a national effort in management capacity development are many of the constraints already discussed in this text. Internal (federal agency) factors appear just as relevant as the variables associated with determining program focus through the needs assessment process. Federal agencies are subjected to internal competition between divisions, bureaus, offices, or other organizational subunits in the continued justification of their own programs. They have little time or incentive to coordinate tangential activities. They also have their own clientele and support groups, as well as liaison linkages with the public interest groups and Congress. Again, there is little motivation to effectuate actions that may threaten or disrupt these relationships. This resistance was discovered by the Nixon Administration in promoting New Federalism devolution and decentralization initiatives.

Possible remedies to the problems that inhibit federal strategic planning efforts in developing new programs have been discussed by a number of previous intergovernmental study groups such as the Hoover Commission, Kestnbaum Commission, the President's Commission on Management Improvement, and others. The only agencies specifically tasked with an intergovenrmental mission are the Advisory Commission on Intergovernmental Relations and the General Accounting Office. These agencies, both arms of Congress and not the executive branch, have power only to investigate or study and make recommendations, not to direct. Both agencies, as well as the study groups discussed, lack enforcement or implementation powers, organizational status, or staff resources to command agency attention.

With these realities as constraints and a mission charge not to recommend the establishment of new executive agencies, the SCOPMA focused their final recommendations on the use of *existing* machinery: the Domestic Council, the Undersecretaries Group for Regional Operations, the Federal Regional Councils, and the Office of Management and Budget.[46] Four recommendations emerged from the SCOPMA:

1. A policy focal point should be designated in the Executive Office of the President, with responsibilities for overall direction, coordination, and evaluation of intergovernmental policy and programs, including capacity-building components.
2. A separate management focal point or mechanism should be provided within the Executive Office of the President to oversee the implementation of intergovernmental policies and to assure the development of effective intergovernmental processes.[47]
3. Each federal domestic agency should clearly assign functional responsibility for: obtaining state and local inputs into agency program development; integrating the planning, management, and assessment of capacity-building programs within the agency; promoting integration of and effective R&D utilization, technical assistance, and training activities in each agency; and providing a contact point for state and local officials.
4. The intergovernmental role of federal field operations should be administratively strengthened by:
   a) Increasing consultation with federal field staff in agency policy and program formulation.
   b) Further strengthening the role of the Federal Regional Councils in intergovernmental relations.[48]

The SCOPMA chose not to recommend the designation of specific responsibilities to the Domestic Council, Undersecretaries Group, or the Office of Management and Budget in order to permit a wider range of options for these agencies if President Ford chose to implement the Committee report. Unfortunately, the report was released as the Ford Administration prepared for the 1976 Presidential election campaign, and little action resulted from the SCOPMA effort at that time. However, agency awareness was heightened, the area of management capacity development was recognized at all levels of government, and the Carter Administration pledged bureaucratic reform in many areas including some of those highlighted by the SCOPMA. While it is difficult to assess the success or failure of the SCOPMA strategy in promoting institutional change in the area of capacity-building at the federal level, the issues raised by the Committee pose an agenda for the future. It is interesting to note that this same strategy appears in the recommendations of the OMB study mandated by P.L 95-224 some 5 years later (see Chapter VII).

Great Society (Creative Federalism - 1965-1968) and New Federalism (1969-1974) administrative impacts on state and local managers have been profound.[49] The assessment of these impacts may assist future federal policy-makers in avoiding the present shortcomings in enhancing state and local service delivery capabilities. The failures in the administrative mechanisms developed to implement Great Society and New Federalism programs should not be repeated by future administrations as federal officials gain a greater awareness of the complexity and balance of forces comprising the intergovernmental grant-in-aid system. The efforts of special

130

study groups such as the SCOPMA have produced long-term impacts that are just now leading to changes within the system. While the study, the reports generated, and the recommendations of the Committee are now a matter of historical record, the new awareness generated about the area of management capacity development in the intergovernmental arena has left a mark on a number of agencies. For example, the FY 1978 appropriation for the Bureau of Intergovernmental Personnel Programs, U.S. Civil Service Commission (the administrator of capacity-building projects under the Intergovernmental Personnel Act) was increased to $20 million, where it has remained to date. Also, the phrase "capacity-building" has crept into the vocabulary of many federal agency grant-in-aid project solicitation notices as a part of the project objective. Capacity-building has come to mean residual development or increased capability developed as a result of federal funding stimulation—in short, a "bonus" that is recognized as valuable by the funding agency.

The SCOPMA effort was different from those of previous intergovernmental study groups or commissions in that there was no Presidential mandate or charter, no prestigious figures, and little financial or staff support. The recommendations were aimed at an area that had little popularity or appeal to the Congress or the President. The recommendations were highly complex, but were adjusted to accommodate political reality—what was feasible instead of ultimate solutions. In spite of this, none of the recommendations were implemented, and the problems remained throughout the 1970's. However, the era of New Federalism brought some advances that have shaped the grant-in-aid system as it is today, and the study efforts of such groups as the Hoover Commissions, the Kestnbaum Commission, and the SCOPMA have brought attention and public awareness to the problems.

131

Notes

1. For background information concerning the scope of programs and their purposes, see James L. Sundquist, "Coordinating the War on Poverty," The Annals (September 1969); Advisory Commission on Intergovernmental Relations, Intergovernmental Relations in the Poverty Program (Washington, D.C.: GPO, 1966); "Special Message to the Congress Proposing a Nationwide War on the Sources of Poverty, March 16, 1964," Public Papers of the President, Lyndon B. Johnson, 1963-64 (Washington, D.C.: GPO, 1965); Joseph A. Kershaw, Government Against Poverty (Washington, D.C. The Brookings Institution, 1970); and Roger N. Davidson, "The War on Poverty: Experiment on Federalism," The Annals (September 1969). National purposes, goals, and policies of the early 1960's are discussed in William L. C. Wheaton, "Made in U.S.A.: Goals for American," Journal of the American Institute of Planners, 27 (August 1961).

2. While the causal linkage of problems of the two programs is subject to considerable debate, one common element can be identified for both programs: management capabilities of the program implementors. As one assessment noted: "It is surprising that few in the vanguard of Nixon's new American Revolution recognized that it was the lack of management capacity within local government which in part had contributed to the inability of many Great Society programs to achieve their intended results." Brian W. Rapp and Frank M. Patitucci, Managing Local Government for Improved Performance: A Practical Approach (Boulder, Colo.: Westview Press, 1977), p. 14. BOB was viewed as the main culprit and was blasted by Senator Abraham Ribicoff during Congressional hearings on the federal role in urban affairs. See Advisory Commission on Intergovernmental Relations, Improving Federal Grants Management, A-53 (Washington, D.C.: GPO, February 1977), p. 162.
   One of the few studies touching on this topic was conducted by the General Accounting Office. See Increased Intergovernmental Cooperation Needed for More Effective, Less Costly Auditing of Government Programs, B-176544 (Washington, D.C.: 1974); Fundamental Changes are Needed in Federal Assistance to State and Local Governments, GG 75-75, (Washington, D.C.: August 19, 1975).

3. For identification of frustrations see Raymond Bancroft, "America's Mayors and Councilmen: Their Problems and Frustrations," Nation's Cities (Washington, D.C.: National League of Cities, 1974), p. 60; for a listing of activities consuming management and staff time see Thomas Thorwood, "The Planning and Management Process in City Government," Municipal Yearbook (Washington, D.C.: ICMA, January 1975), p. 15. The difficulty of identifying specific management needs is outlined in an article by the author in the December, 1975 special issue of the Public Administration Review, see "Problems and Deficiencies in the Needs Assessment Process," pp. 754-758. For a study of local official attitudes and perspectives, see Ann Michel, "Intergovernmental Aid: A Local Perspective," Intergovernmental Administration: 1976 — Eleven

Academic and Practitioner Perspectives, eds. James D. Carroll and Richard W. Campbell (Syracuse, N.Y.: Maxwell School of Citizenship and Public Affairs, Syracuse, University, 1976), pp. 241-257.

4. As a percent of state and local expenditures, federal grants increased from 10.4 percent in FY 1950 to 25.2 percent in FY 1976. Office of Management and Budget, Special Analysis, Budget of the United States Government FY 1977 (Washington, D.C.: GPO, 1976), p. 264.

5. The complexity of the system to urban managers was compounded by uncoordinated programs as well as the vertical nature of the relationships that emerged. For example, 19 grant-in-aid programs established 1,800 regional districts for handling narrow functional programs. A "typical" metropolitan area is now made up of 85 units of general and special purpose local governments including the following:
    - two counties
    - 13 townships
    - 21 municipalities
    - 18 school districts
    - 31 special districts

ACIR's quest for more attention to regional coordination was largely ignored by the mission agencies. See Advisory Commission on Intergovernmental Relations, American Federalism: Into the Third Century - its Agenda, M-85 (Washington, D.C.: GPO, May 1974), pp. 10-11. A discussion on approaches in subnational coordination is contained in Harold F. Wise, Conflicts in Federal Subnational Development Programs (Washington, D.C.: Economic Development Administration, Department of Commerce, March 1976). The ACIR has published a six volume series on substate regionalism including a discussion of problems and recommendations. A recent summary of these works appeared in June 1977: Regionalism Revisited Recent Areawide and Local Responses, A-66 (Washington, D.C.: GPO).

6. See National Commission on Productivity and Work Quality, Employee Incentives to Improve State and Local Government Productivity (Washington, D.C.: GPO, March 1975). For additional information on state and local expenditures for personnel costs, etc., and a discussion of the stimulative and additive effects of federal grants, see Russell Harrison "Federal Categorical Grants and the Stimulation of State-Local Expenditures; and Laura Irwin, "Expenditure Effects of Federal Aid: Data Aggregation and the Risk of Uncertainty," Publius, 5 (Fall 1975), pp. 123-160.

7. The area of personnel management was especially hard hit. Federal impacts in the areas of the Comprehensive Employment and Training Act of 1974 (CETA), Collective Bargaining, EEO and merit systems are discussed in an article by the author, "Federal Influences in State and Local Personnel Management: The System in Transition," Public Personnel Management (Chicago: IPMA, January-February 1976).

8. For additional information on the impacts resulting from the growth of the grant-in-aid system, see David B. Walker, "How Fares Federalism in the Mid-Seventies?" The Annals (November 1974), pp. 24-5; Delphis C. Goldberg, "Intergovernmental Relations: From The Legislative Perspective," The Annals (November 1974), pp. 53-54; State and Local Fiscal Assistance Act of 1972, House Committee on Ways and Means, 92nd Congress, 2nd Session, House Report 92-1018 (Part I), April 26, 1972; "Text of President Nixon's Message on Revenue Sharing," Congressional Quarterly Almanac, Vol. 25, 91st Congress, 1st Session, 1969 (Washington, D.C.: Congressional Quarterly, Inc., 1970); and Advisory Commission on Intergovernmental Relations, The Intergovernmental Grant System as Seen by Local, State and Federal Officials, A-54 (Washington, D.C.: GPO, March 1977).

9. Executive Office of the President, Strengthening Public Management in the Intergovernmental System (Washington, D.C.: GPO, 1975).

10. HUD's capacity-building program was an 18 month demonstration involving 8 projects. Four projects involved six cities: Boston; Houston; Dayton; Cincinnati; Petersburg, Virginia; and Pritchard, Oklahoma. Four other projects assisted 83 small and medium sized cities in exploring new ways to diagnose management needs, implement change, and develop economical approaches in transferring results to other cities. See Office of Policy Development and Research, HUD, Capacity Building (pamphlet) (Washington, D.C.: GPO, undated).

11. SITO was an HEW experiment designed to test human service integration concepts in an effort to establish the feasibility of a broader block grant proposal being studied by Congress in 1972-4, the Allied Services Act of 1974. The Allied Services Act would have consolidated a number of HEW categorical grants under one heading but was not passed by Congress. A portion of the twenty-two SITO projects explored the concept of development management as a more efficient means of project guidance. See Stephen D. Mittenthan, et al., Twenty-two Allied Services (SITO) Projects Described as Human Service Systems (Wellesley, Mass.: Human Ecology Institute, April 1974). Another HEW experiment designed to assist state and local managers was Project SHARE. SHARE was developed as "...a key element of DHEW's capacity-building policy by providing state and local governments with information services to improve their capacity for planning, management and delivery of human services." SHARE functioned as an information exchange or clearinghouse for state and local governments to "share" their experiences about human service delivery systems. See "Project SHARE: A National Clearinghouse for Improving the Management of Human Services," Brochure (Rockville, MD.: DHEW Pub. No. OS-76-221, Office of Intergovernmental Systems, undated).

12. The Office of the Assistant Secretary for Systems Development and Technology, Office of R and D Policy, U.S. Department of Transportation was especially vigorous in supporting the management capacity development of state and local governments through the facilitation of

information exchange. See Support of State and Local Policy Development in General-Purpose Governments: Three Working Papers (Washington, D.C.: TST-12, April-September 1975). This document was essentially a compilation of working papers on DOT's capacity building efforts developed for the Study Committee on Policy Management Assistance. DOT information exchange also is sponsored through their TRISNET (Transportation Information System Network) and their participation in MISTIC (Model Interstate Scientific and Technical Information Clearinghouse)—an information exchange system sponsored by five Federal agencies (primarily by its National Science Foundation) and managed by the National Conference of State Legislatures to assist the 50 state legislatures in dealing with current public technology issues. See TRISNET: A Network of Transportation Information Services and Activities, Assistant Secretary for Systems Development and Technology, Office of R and D Plans and Resources (TST-20) (Washington, D.C.: June 1976); and Office of R and D Policy (TST-12), Technology Sharing: A Guide to Assistance in Obtaining and Using Research Development and Demonstration Outputs (Washington, D.C.: January 1976).

13. Each of these groups formulated recommendations addressing the same state and local problems, many of which had their roots in deficiencies created by the federal agencies in their administration and management of the grant-in-aid system. For example, see Subcommittee on Intergovernmental Relations, U.S. Senate, "More Effective Public Service: The First Report to the President and Congress by the Advisory Council on Intergovernmental Personnel Policy" (January 1973); President's Advisory Commission on Management Improvement, "Managing the New Federalism," (Washington, D.C.: President's Advisory Commission on Management Improvement January 1973): and Strengthening Public Management....In the area of improving the use of science and technology at the state and local levels in developing capacity, see National Governor's Conference, "Action Recommendations on Intergovernmental Science and Technology programs" (May 26, 1972); the proceedings of the National Action Conference on Intergovernmental Science and Technology Policy, "Action Now: Partnerships-Putting Technology to Work," Pennsylvania Office of Science and Technology (August 1972); and National Legislative Conference, "Policy Recommendations Relating to the Development of More Effective Means of Utilizing Our Nation's Scientific and Technological Resources to Meet the Needs of State Government" (August 1974).

14. See Fundamental Changes are Needed....

15. Strengthening Public Management..., p. 27 ff. A Study of the informational needs about the federal grant-in-aid systems of urban managers was conducted by the University of Oklahoma in 1972; see F. Ted Hepert and Richard D. Bingham, Personal and Environmental Influences Upon the City Manager's Knowledge and Federal Grant-in-Aid Programs (Norman: Bureau of Governmental Research).

16. See Ann C. Macaluso's "Backround and History of the Study Committee on Policy Management Assistance," in "Policy Movement Assistant—A Developing Dialogue," Public Administration Review, 35 Special Issue (December 1975), pp. 697-8.

17. See "The New Federalism—Report on Technical Assistance," OMB internal working paper never released to public (November 1973; the GAO/OMB symposium report was entitled "Summary of GAO/OMB Symposium on Technical Assistance" (April 16, 1974).

18. For a discussion on the formulation of the SCOPMA and its accomplishments, see Raymond A. Shapek, "Policy Management Assistance: Federal Efforts to Measure State and Local Management Needs," The Bureaucrat Vol. 7 (Spring 1978).

19. Partial data returns substantiating the complexity of the survey are contained in Study Committee on Policy Management Assistance, Framework of a Strategy for Policy Management Assistance to State and Local Governments, Vol. 1, Internal Report (Washington, D.C.: OMB, April 16, 1975), Appendix 3(b).

20. While OMB Bulletin 75-5 did not carry the force of an OMB circular, responses were eventually received from 41 federal departments and agencies. For a listing of respondents and the format of OMB Bulletin 75-5, see Ibid.

21. For a complete report of this very complex data, see "Mapping the Federal Assistance Effort: The Pieces of a Puzzle, But Where is the Picture?" in Policy Management Assistance....

22. Resource management refers to the development and support of administrative tools such as personnel administration, financial management, propery management, etc.; program management refers to the administrative functions required in the execution of programs including such things as planning, organizing, staffing, directing, etc. For further description of these functions, see Strengthening Public Management..., p. 5; and Phillip M. Burgess, "Capacity Building and the Elements of Public Management," in Policy Management Assistance..., pp. 705-16.

23. Strengthening Public Management..., p. 49. A subsequent study of capacity development by a Federal Region IX Task Force more selectively restricted this definition to policy development. In this sense, capacity became "...the capability of the governing board or chief executive of general purpose government to plan, implement, manage or evaluate policies, strategies or programs related to improving physical, economic or social conditions." See Task Force on Local Government Capacity-Building, Western Federal Regional Council, Federal Support for Local Decision-Making: What Works (San Francisco: Western Federal Regional Council, November 10, 1975), p. 8.

24. See Strengthening Public Management..., pp. 4-5.

25. Norman G.Paulhus and Alfonso B. Lindhares, "Policy Management Assistance in Mission Agencies," in Policy Management Assistance...,

p. 758 and also "Federal RD&D Utilization and Policy Management Assitance," in Vol. III, Report of the OMB Study Committee on Policy Management Assistance: Backround Papers and Resource Materials (Washington, D.C.: NSF, ISRU, 1975), p. 1093.

26. Fred Fisher, "The Role of Training and Development in Building the Capacity of State and Local Governments," Report of the OMB Study...., p. 657.

27. J.R. Julianelle, "Policy Management and the Intergovernmental System," Ibid., p. 1021.

28. Lois Dean, "Starting and Managing a Policy Management Assistance Effort," Ibid., p. 1029.

29. See David B. Walker, "A New Intergovernment System in 1977," Publius (Winter, 1978), pp. 105-108. Walker identified Creative Federalism initiatives as one source of today's intergovernmental relations problems.

30. See Strengthening Public Management....

31. See Thomas Thorwood, "The Planning and Management Process in City Government," Municipal Yearbook—1973 (Washington, D.C: ICMA, 1973) p. 29.

32. See International City Management Association, "Governmental Data in Municipalities 25,000 and Under," Urban Data Services Report, Vol. 7, No. 1 (Washington, D.C.: ICMA, January 1975), p. 15.

33. Ibid., p. 3.

34. International City Management Association, "Federal, State, Local Relationships," Urban Data Services Report (Washington, D.C.: ICMA 1969, p. 12.

35. International City Management Association, "Government Data in Municipalities 25,000 and Under,"....

36. See Morley Segal and A. Lee Fritchler, "Emerging Patterns of Intergovernmental Relations," Municipal Yearbook—1970 (Washington D.C.: ICMA, 1970), p. 33.

37. A study of time allocations by local government intergovernmental coordinators was conducted by ICMA in 1970. Grant writing activities alone consumed almost 30% of coordinator staff activities. See A. Lee Fritchler and Morley Segal, "Intergovernmental Relations and Contemporary Political Sciences: Developing an Integrative Typology," Publius (Winter 1972), p. 112. Previous studies have indicated that improvements to the grant-in-aid system are needed. State and local respondents to an earlier survey affirmed the need for changes at the federal level. See Replies from State and Local Governments to Questionnaire on Intergovernmental Relations, Sixth Report by the House Committee on Government Operations, Subcommittee on Intergovernmental Relations, 85th Congress, 1st Session, House Report No. 575,

June 17, 1957; Staff Report on Replies from State and Local Governments to Questionnaire on Intergovernmental Relations, Intergovernmental Relations Subcommittee of the House Government Operations
Committee, 84th Congress, 2nd Session, Committee Print, August
1956; and The Federal System as Seen by State and Local Officials, a
study prepared by the staff of the Subcommittee on Intergovernmental
Relations, Senate Committee on Government Operations 88th Congress, 1st Session, Committee Report, 1963.

38. The problem of introducing change within federal agencies has
plagued a number of national level study groups. No statisfactory solution has yet been found. See Mirra Komarovsky, ed., Sociology and
Public Policy: The Case of Presidential Commissions (New York:
Elsevier Scientific Pub. Co., Inc., 1975). Nor is the problem of promoting change the fault of the President. By 1973 despite a significant
mandate from the electorate, President Nixon could not turn his elec-
toral victory into intergovernmental policy necessary to implement his
New Federalism initiatives: See Deil S. Wright, Understanding Intergovernmental Relations (Duxbury Press, 1978), pp. 284-5; Louis
Fisher, Presidential Spending Power (Princeton, N.J.: Princeton University Press, 1975); and Improving Federal Grants Management....

39. David B. Walker discusses this constraint system in realistic terms. He
notes the nature of many aid programs include: "Poor design features,
unrealistic expectations, airy assumptions about implementation, and
a basic ignorance about the workings of intergovernmental relations
generally and of recipient jurisdictions in particular..." "A New Intergovernmental System in 1977," Publius (Winter 1978) p. 113.

40. Strengthening Public Management..., p. viii.

41. Ibid.

42. See "Intergovernmental Management: The Task Ahead," Video Tape,
available through the National Audiovisual Center. The SCOPMA inter-
viewed over 50 state and local leaders in 1974-75 to obtain a cross-
section of opinions of their views of the federal grant-in-aid system.
The interviews were edited and produced on a 30 minute videotape
which was shown to high ranking officials of the Ford Administration
in an attempt to influence federal policy related to the charge of the
Study Committee on Policy Management Assistance. In line with
Donaldson's remarks, an example of federal misunderstanding of
their own programs occurred in the Spring of 1974 with the summer
youth employment program funding. See Managing Local Government..., p. 57.

43. Strengthening Public Management..., p. IX.

44. Ibid., pp. IX-X

45. Ibid., pp. X-XI. The basic foundation of capacity-building has been to
gain public acceptance and a commitment by federal mission agencies. This philosophy was not unique to the SCOPMA. In the area of
science and technology transfer, the Committee on Intergovernmental
Science Relations of the Federal Council for Science and Technology

noted: "Technology cannot be force fed; the demand for it must be created and nurtured." See Executive Office of the President, Public Technololgy: A Tool for Solving National Problems, Report of the Committee on Intergovernmental Science Relations to the Federal Council for Science and Technology (Washington, D.C.: GPO, May 1972).

46. See Ibid., Appendix B, pp. 43-44. The SCOPMA was charged "to formulate strategic options for Federal intergovernmental policies and initiatives regarding Federal-State-local cooperation to improve the policy management capacity of all levels of government and to make recommendations for new Federal policies, procedures and programs therein." The Committee interpreted this to mean recommendations regarding the use of existing resources and agencies and not new ones.

47. The focal point issue was also significant to the Committee's recommendations. This was not the first attempt to promote the establishment of top-level coordination of intergovernmental concerns. James Sundquist, a Johnson Administration official noted:"Somewhere in the Executive Office must be centered a concern for the structure of Federalism—a responsibility for guiding the evolution of the whole system of Federal-State-local relations viewed for the first time as a single system;" in National Academy of Public Administration, The President and Executive Management: Summary of a Symposium (Washington, D.C.: October 1976), p. 42.

48. Strengthening Public Management..., pp. xi-xii.

49. For example, see Advisory Commission on Intergovernmental Relations, The Intergovernmental Grant System as Seen by Local, State and Federal Officials, A-54 (Washington, D.C.: GPO, March 1977).

CHAPTER IV SELECTED BIBLIOGRAPHY
Articles/Documents

Advisory Commission on Intergovernmental Relations. American Federalism: Into the Third Century—Its Agenda, M-95. Washington, D.C.: GPO, May 1974.

_____ . Improving Federal Grants Management, A-53. Washington, D.C.: GPO, February 1977.

_____ . Intergovernmental Relations in the Poverty Program. Washington, D.C.: GPO, 1966.

_____ . Regionalism Revisited: Recent Area-Wide and Local Responses, A-66. Washington, D.C.: GPO, June 1977.

_____ . The Intergovernmental Grant System as Seen by Local, State, and Federal Officials, A-54. Washington, D.C.: GPO, March 1977.

Bancroft, Raymond. "America's Mayors and Councilman: Their Problems and Frustrations," Nation's Cities. Washington, D.C.: National League of Cities, 1974.

Davidson, Roger N. "The War on Poverty: Experiment in Federalism," The Annals. September 1969.

Executive Office of the President. "Federal R&D Utilization and Policy Management Assistance," Report of the OMB Study Committee on Policy Management Assistance: Background Papers and Resource Materials, Vol. III. Washington, D.C.: NSF, ISRU, 1975.

_____ . Public Technology: A Tool for Solving National Problems. Report of the Committee on Intergovernmental Science Relations to the Federal Council for Science and Technology. Washington, D.C.: GPO, May 1972.

_____ . Special Analysis, Budget of the United States Government FY 1977. Washington, D.C.: GPO, 1976.

_____ . Strengthening Public Management in the Intergovernmental System. Washington, D.C.: GPO, 1975.

Fritchler, A. Lee and Morley, Segal. "Intergovernmental Relations and Contemporary Political Science: Developing an Integrative Typology," Publius. Winter 1972.

General Accounting Office. Fundamental Changes are Needed In Federal Assistance to State and Local Governments, GG75-75. Washington, D.C.: GAO, August 19, 1975.

_____ . Increased Intergovernmental Cooperation Needed for More Effective, Less Costly Auditing of Governmental Programs, B-176544. Washington, D.C.: GAO, 1974.

Goldberg, Delphis C. "Intergovernmental Relations: From the Legislative Perspective," The Annals. November 1974.

Harrison, Russell. "Federal Categorical Grants and the Stimulation of State-Local Expenditures," Publius, 5 (Fall 1975).

Hepert, F. Ted and Bingham, Richard D. Personal and Environmental

Influences Upon the City Manager's Knowledge of Federal Grant-In-Aid Programs. Norman, Oklahoma: Bureau of Governmental Research (undated).

Irwin, Laura. "Expenditure Effects of Federal Aid: Data Aggregation and the Risk of Uncertainty," Publius, 5(Fall 1975).

Macaluso, Ann C. "Backround and History of the Study Committee on Policy Management Assistance," Public Administration Review, 35. Special Issue (December 1975).

National Academy of Public Administration. The President and Executive Management: Summary of Symposium. Washington, D.C.: October 1976.

National Commission on Productivity and Work Quality. Employee Incentives to Improve State and Local Government Productivity. Washington, D.C.: GPO, March 1975.

National Governors' Conference. "Action Recommendations on Intergovernmental Science and Technology Programs." May 26, 1972.

National Legislative Conference. "Policy Recommendations Relating to the Development of More Effective Means of Utilizing Our Nation's Scientific and Technological Resources to Meet the Needs ot State Government." August 1974.

Office of Policy Development and Research, U.S. Department of Housing and Urban Development. Capacity-Building. (pamphlet) Washington, D.C.: GPO (undated).

Office of R&D Policy, U.S. Department of Transportation. Support of State and Local Policy Development in General-Purpose Governments: Three Working Papers. Washington, D.C.: TST-12, April-September 1975.

_____ . Technology Sharing: A Guide to Assistance in Obtaining and Using Research Development and Demonstration Ouputs. Washington, D.C.: TST-12, January 1976.

Pennsylvania Office of Science and Technology. "Action Now: Partnerships-Putting Technology to Work," August 1972.

President's Advisory Council on Management Improvement. "Managing the New Federalism." Washington, D.C.: GPO, 1973.

"Project SHARE: A National Clearinghouse for Improving the Management of Human Services," (Brochure) DHEW Pub. No. OS 76-221. Rockville, Maryland: Office of Intergovernmental Systems (undated).

Shapek, Raymond A. "Federal Influences in State and Local Personnel Management: The System in Transition," Public Personnel Management. January/February 1976.

_____ . "Policy Management Assistance: Federal Efforts to Measure State and Local Management Needs," The Bureaucrat, Vol. 7 (Spring 1978).

"Special Message to the Congress Proposing a Nationwide War on the Sources of Poverty," March 16, 1964, Public Papers of the President, Lyndon B. Johnson, 1963-64. Washington, D.C.: GPO, 1965.

Study Committee on Policy Management Assistance, Office of Management and Budget. Framework of a Strategy for Policy Assistance to State and Local Governments, Vol. 1 (Internal Report) Washington, D.C.: OMB, April 16, 1975.

Sundquist, James L. "Coordinating the War on Poverty," The Annals. September 1969.

Task Force on Local Government Capacity-Building, Western Federal Regional Council. Federal Support for Local Decision-Making: What Works. San Francisco: Western Federal Regional Council, November 10, 1975.

"Text of President Nixon's Message on Revenue Sharing," Congressional Quarterly Almanac, Vol. 25, 91st Cong., 1st Sess., 1969. Washington, D.C.: Congressional Quarterly, Inc., 1970.

U.S. Department of Transportation. TRISNET: A Network of Transportation Information Services and Activities. Washington, D.C.: TST-20, June 1976.

Walker, David B. "How Fares Federalism in the Mid-Seventies?," The Annals. November 1974.

Wheaton, William L.C. "Made in U.S.A.: Goals for America," Journal of the American Institute of Planners, 27 (August 1961).

Wise, Harold F. Conflicts in Federal Subnational Development Programs. Washington, D.C.: Economic Development Administration, DOC, March 1976.

Books

Carroll, James D. and Campbell, Richard W., ed. Intergovernmental Administration: 1976—Eleven Academic and Practitioner Perspectives. Syracuse, NY: Maxwell School of Citizenship and Public Affairs, Syracuse University, 1976.

Fisher, Louis. Presidential Spending Power. Princeton, NJ: Princeton University Press, 1978.

Kershaw, Joseph A. Government Against Poverty. Washington. D.C.: The Brookings Institute, 1970.

Komarovsky, Mirra, ed. Sociology and Public Policy: The Case of Presidential Commission. New York: Elsevier Scientific Publishing Co., Inc., 1975.

Mittenthan, Stephen D., et al. Twenty-Two Allied Services (SITO) Projects Described as Human Service System. Wellesley, Mass: Human Ecology Institute, April 1974.

Rapp, Brian W. and Patitucci, Frank M. Managing Local Government for Improved Performance: A Practical Approach. Boulder, Colorado: Westview Press, 1977.

Wright, Deil S. Understanding Intergovernmental Relations. New York: Duxbury Press, 1978.

Hearings

U.S. Congress, House, Committee on Government Operations, Subcommittee on Intergovernmental Relations. Replies from State and Local Governments to Questionnaire on Intergovernental Relations. Sixth Report. 85th Cong., 1st Sess. House Report No. 575, June 17, 1957.

_____ . Staff Report on Replies from State and Local Governments to Questionnaire on Intergovernmental Relations. 84th Cong., 2nd Sess., Committee Report, August 1956.

U.S. Congress, House, Committee on Ways and Means. State and Local Fiscal Assistance Act of 1974. 92nd Cong., 2nd Sess., House Report 92-1018 (Part 1), April 26, 1972.

U.S. Congress, Senate, Committee on Government Operations, Subcommittee on Intergovernmental Relations. The Federal System as Seen by State and Local Officials. 88th Cong., 1st Sess., Committee Report, 1963.

_____ . Effective Public Service: The First Report to the President and Congress by the Advisory Commission on Intergovernmental Personnel Policy. January 1973.

Chapter Five
General Revenue Sharing

Under this program, instead of spending so much time trying to please distant bureaucrats in Washington so the money will keep coming in, state and local officials can concentrate on pleasing the people, so the money can do more good.

Richard M. Nixon
1972

Revenue sharing, at best, represents a stop-gap measure which promises infinitely more than it can deliver. The nation's urban areas will be short-changed. The propriety of legislation which completely bypasses the appropriations process is questionable. The labor protections that apply to local government's share are weak and there are no labor protection provisions whatsoever in the state share. The federal civil rights guarantees are difficult if not impossible to enforce.

Arnold Cantor
AFL-CIO, 1972

Introduction

The purpose of this chapter is to explore a different type of federal funding assistance, General Revenue Sharing (GRS). GRS is different from categorical programs in that the funds are distributed to state and local governments on a relatively "string free" basis. No application is required and accountability requirements for the funds are not rigid. Finally, the funds may be used for almost anything, and the decision on how they may be spent is left to the state or local recipient government. The background of the GRS Act is important not only as a case study of compromise and executive-legislative interaction, but also because it is a new form of assistance, virtually free from federal oversight, "red tape," and control.

Perhaps equally important, GRS represents one of the successes of New Federalism. It is a form of aid that meets a wide range of needs in a broad spectrum of political situations. The consensus is that GRS, like a categorical program, is here to stay. For this reason the fiscal impacts of GRS on state and local governments and the extension of the Act in 1976 also are discussed in the chapter.

The Background of General Revenue Sharing

The debate over the concept of shared revenues between the national and state and local governments has lasted more than 10 years. Although the actors in this drama have changed from time to time and most of the issues raised have been answered or clarified and refined, several significant concerns stand out. On the positive side, the prospect of relatively "string free" funds had a strong appeal to the nation's governors and mayors, already frustrated with the burdens of grant-in-aid application and compliance requirements. On the negative side, the recipients of the services or benefits provided through the many programs of the categorical grant system viewed general revenue sharing as a subtle means of cutting categorical funds while placing the decision-making responsibility for replacement funding (by means of revenue sharing) in the hands of a political establishment hostile to their interests, especially those of minority groups. Thus, these groups, labor and minority, began a counter-campaign to ensure protection of their rights. At the same time, the smaller jurisdictions began actions to guarantee their receipt of some portion of the revenue sharing funds by means of the allocation formula. The controversy surrounding these issues, as well as others that were to emerge later, pose an interesting study of political interaction in the formulation of a law.

Historical Antecedents

The key components of President Nixon's New Federalism philosophy included the decentralization of national administrative agency decision-making to the regional level, as well as the devolution of political responsibilities to those units of government engaged in service delivery by means of special revenue sharing in the form of block grants. Also included in this strategy was an overhaul of the welfare system and reorganization of the major executive departments to coincide better with their functional responsibilities. The cornerstone of this entire effort was to be the sharing of federal revenues with state and local governments on a relatively "string free" basis. In spite of the failures of the administration to achieve major welfare reform, reorganization of the executive branch, and even meaningful decentralization, some devolution was achieved with the passage of two major block grants—the Housing and Community Development Act and the Comprehensive Employment and Training Act of 1974, both of which were signed into law by Nixon's successor, President Gerald R. Ford. However, the most controversial of the Nixon initiatives has proved to be the General Revenue Sharing (GRS) program. General revenue sharing was especially important, as one scholar noted, "...because of its uniqueness and the implications it held for federal relations in the United States, and because it would be the first major legislative test of the [Nixon] program."[1]

The concept of revenue sharing did not originate with the Nixon Administration. Federal or general revenue sharing, as we know it today, developed over a decade of study, debate, and compromise. While the phrase is relatively new in the modern context, the first proposal to share federal revenue with state governments was introduced by President Jefferson in his 1805 inaugural address. Jefferson urged that federal revenues be given to the states to meet their own objectives, such as the building of roads, canals, dredging rivers, etc.[2] However, Jefferson's request fell on deaf ears, and it was not until 1836 that Congress endorsed a form of federal revenue sharing. At that time, Andrew Jackson devised a scheme for distributing surplus federal funds to 80 state banks. Unfortunately, the participating banks viewed this largess as permanent and subsequently inflated their credit, thus contributing to the Panic of 1837.

Not all of this shared revenue was misused, however, and several worthwhile projects were recorded. Groton, Massachusetts paid off its town debt; Newburyport built a brick barn for the poor, an alms house, several schools, some highways, a fire department, a reservoir, a public park, and a pond; North Carolina used part of its funds to drain swampland; and Arkansas used the state's share to pay general governmental expenses.[3]

In the modern era, the first substantive revenue sharing proposal appeared in 1949. Representative Errett Scrwner, a Kansas Republican, introduced a proposal that called for the federal government to remit to each state one percent of federal individual and corporate taxes collected in that state. Scrwner's proposal proved unsuccessful in the House, and it was another 10 years before a serious attempt was made to have revenue sharing legislation passed.

In 1958, former Republican Congressman Melvin Laird introduced federal tax sharing legislation, which was developed as a result of his criticism of the grant-in-aid system. Some two years later, Chairman of the Council of Economic Advisors Walter Heller proposed that federal revenues be distributed to state governments with few strings attached. The Heller and Laird plans differed in that Heller felt that categorical grants-in-aid and revenue sharing should co-exist, while Laird hoped that tax sharing could eventually supplant categorical grant programs.[4]

The 1964 Presidential campaign also addressed the revenue sharing issue. The Democratic party platform urged the development of federal fiscal policies to provide some relief to hard-pressed state and local governments. Republican candidate Barry Goldwater was even more explicit in advocating the sharing of federal personal income and inheritance taxes and the replacement of the $10 billion (at the time) grant-in-aid system with tax rebates coupled with unconditional grants to "poor" localities.[5] President Lyndon Johnson also endorsed the idea of revenue sharing. Prior to the 1964 election, Johnson appointed a Task Force on Intergovernmental Fiscal Cooperation, headed by Dr. Joseph A. Pechman, to study the possibility of setting aside a fixed percentage of federal revenue each year for distribution to state and local governments. Pechman recommended that a portion of federal individual income tax revenues be shared, unconditionally, with the states. This proposal was inspired by Walter W. Heller, Chairman of the Council of Economic Advisors. The Heller initiative, introduced by Pechman's task force, resulted in a proposal which became known as the Heller-Pechman Plan. Unfortunately, this plan was never released officially, although it did receive wide circulation in government. Shortly after the 1964 election, President Johnson, plagued by the expanding war in Vietnam and faced with the opposition of the federal bureaucracy to this unconditional allocation of funds, dropped his support and the Heller-Pechman Plan died a quiet death.[6]

At this point in time, the President's retreat seemed ill-advised. The growth of the federal categorical system, in response to Johnson's Great Society initiatives, had created considerable concern among top governmental administrators. Their concerns focused on the problems of administration and manageability as the federal government became more and more involved in affecting the financial structures of state and local governments. Reflecting this view, the Advisory Commission on Intergovernmental Relations recommended broadening the mix of federal aid programs to include both revenue sharing and block grants, "...thereby gearing aid techniques to the traditional fiscal aid objectives of equalization, stimulation, demonstration, and general support."[7] The management crisis in the grant-in-aid system won other supporters, who advocated complete realignment of the categorical system with general revenue sharing or some more sensibly structured aid systems.[8] The arguments for grant reform did not prove persuasive enough to motivate Congress to seriously consider revenue sharing until local government officials and their representative lobbying groups began a persistent effort to convince Congress that only some system of direct federal assistance could reduce the fiscal pressures on these governments. A sudden outburst of proposals followed as individual congressmen sought the lead in developing an alternative that would be acceptable to the nation's mayors and governors and would not be viewed by special interest groups as a total sell-out.

During the 89th Congress, a total of 57 Democratic and Republican legislators introduced or co-sponsored five revenue sharing bills. In the 90th Congress, 55 separate bills were introduced and 100 in the 91st. Also in 1967, the National League of Cities (NLC) initiated a study of revenue sharing with the appointment of a special committee of mayors from some of the nation's largest cities. At the same time, the National Governors' Conference (now the National Governors' Association) Committee on State and Local Revenue began a cooperative study effort with the NLC group. These lobbying groups eventually recommended a revenue sharing plan that would assure a reasonable level of relatively unrestricted funds to both state and local governments.

The political forces necessary for adoption of a revenue sharing bill coalesced as the economic condition of the states and cities continued to deteriorate in the late 1960's and early 1970's. Congressional concerns began to focus on two basic goals for possible revenue sharing legislation:

- *To decentralize financial decision-making from Washington to state and local governments; and*
- *To assist state and local governments in service delivery and/ or to help relieve the fiscal pressures they were undergoing.*[9]

The goals of revenue sharing as seen by Congress coincided with President Nixon's philosophy of New Federalism and the strategy that emerged. Shortly after his inauguration in 1969, President Nixon pursued his pledge to give revenue sharing top priority by appointing an executive task force headed by the urbanologist Edward Banfield. The task force brought together representatives of the National League of Cities, U.S. Conference of Mayors (USCM), National Governors' Association (NGA), and the National Association of Counties (NACo) for a series of meetings on revenue sharing. The White House and the task force arrived at an agreement that was proposed as the Revenue Sharing Act of 1969. The political postures of the main interest groups had been stated publicly as they developed their proposals, and a commitment to the concept by all factions had been established. However, in spite of this auspicious beginning, the Administration's proposal was not enacted by the 91st Congress, and it was left to the 92nd Congress to revive the issue.

The leadership for initiating a revenue sharing proposal was assumed again by the White House when, in his January 22, 1971 State of the Union message to the nation, President Nixon proposed a $16 billion revenue transfer program. The new program called for both general and special revenue sharing. General revenue sharing was to provide $5 billion in "new money," while categorical program funding for Fiscal Year 1972 was to be maintained at Fiscal year 1971 levels. The details were clarified in a special message to Congress on February 4, 1971.[10] Nixon's proposal called for a permanent appropriation for revenue sharing based on 1.3 percent of the federal personal income tax base. The money was to be distributed on a per capita basis, adjusted for each state's tax effort. States would be permitted to negotiate a pass-through formula with local governments, but those states unable to develop an in-state agreement would work under a federally determined formula. The funds were to be distributed quarterly, without preconditions or restrictions, except for anti-discrimination requirements related to the use of the funds.

By June of 1971, both Congressman Wilbur Mills, the Chairman of the House Ways and Means Committee (who had been openly critical of the President's proposal), and Senator Edmund Muskie, Chairman of the Senate Subcommittee on Intergovernmental Relations (who was more sympathetic to the Administration's effort), announced hearings on the proposal. At the close of the hearings, eight volumes of testimony had been recorded, but no bills were proposed. Many members of Congress were opposed to the "no strings" concept. The separation of taxing and spending responsibilities emerged as the largest single issue obstructing concerted agreement on any one bill.

The states continued an extensive effort for the inclusion of a significant state role in any revenue sharing bill. Finally, near the end of November, Chairman Mills introduced the Intergovernmental Fiscal Coordination Act of 1971 (HR 11950). The bill differed from the Administration's proposal by establishing a five-year allocation of $3.5 billion per year to extend through December 31, 1976. The allocation was not fixed at a percentage of federal tax receipts, as was the Administration's plan, thus addressing the main area of concern. Further, local governments could spend their allocation in a relatively unrestricted manner, but specified high priority areas, such as public safety, environmental protection, public transporation, youth recreation programs, health, and the financial administration of government-related capital improvement programs. A state income tax incentive trust fund of $1.8 billion annually also was included in the measure.[11]

Mills stressed that his bill would avoid the basic problems of the Nixon proposal. The Mills measure did not allocate a percentage of federal revenue to state and local governments, as had the Administration's proposal, but rather provided for grants of specified amounts over the five-year period. Also, the Mills plan based the local distribution on need rather than, as in the President's plan, on the revenue raised. HR 11950 appealed to the major urban centers, and its distribution formula was centered on the central cities and poorer rural communities. The Administration's proposal eventually would have resulted in the same distribution outcome because the allocation formula was based on taxing activity which has the most impact in major urban centers. However, the end result was not as apparent to the cities as the Mills proposal; and, in the end, no compromise was agreed to and neither measure was enacted.

As 1972 began and the 92nd Congress convened, the Administration again committed $5 billion to revenue sharing in its Fiscal year 1973 budget; and by April the House Ways and Means Committee had developed a new proposal. The new House bill (HR 14370) was closer to the Administration's proposal and narrowed the list of permissible high-priority programs for local governments. The bill, bearing the title "State and Local Fiscal Assistance Act of 1972," cleared the committee on April 17. On June 22nd, the bill passed the House and began its journey through the Senate. After a number of changes, the Senate's version of HR 14370 was passed to a Conference Committee on August 15, 1972. The conference report, reflecting considerable compromise and a departure by Congress from its usual methods of providing financial assistance to stae and local governments, was accepted by the House on October 12 by a vote of 265 to 110, and by the Senate by a vote of 59 to 19 on October 13. The State and Local Fiscal Assistance Act of 1972 was signed into law by President Nixon at Independence Hall in Philadelphia on October 20, 1972. In the President's words, General Revenue Sharing was to bring "...a new sense of accountability, a new burst of energy, and a new spirit of creativity to our federal system."[12] General Revenue Sharing proved to be one of the highpoints and few successes of the New Federalism.

The 1972 Act

At the time of the signing of the Revenue Sharing Act, President Nixon noted:

> States and cities will not have to worry about filing complicated plans, filling out endless forms, meeting lots of bureaucratic controls. When we say no strings we mean no strings. This program will mean both a new source of revenue for state and local governments and a new sense of repsonsibility.

Clearly, the President and Congress intended to provide wide discretion in the use of revenue sharing funds with a minimum of checks, controls, and "strings."

The few federal "strings" that existed in the rules and regulations included:

- *Local governments may spend revenue sharing funds for all types of capital outlays or for operating and maintenance expenses in eligible categories of functions, called priority expenditures. While these categories are broad, they exclude education, case payments to welfare recipients, and general administration (activities, such as the city manager's office or voter registration, so broad in nature as not to be assignable to any of the designated functions).*
- *Recipients must not use revenue sharing directly or indirectly*

as the non-federal matching share under a federal grant (this restriction was particulary obnoxious to state and local governments).

- *Each state must maintain the amount of aid to local units at a level not less than the amount of aid given by the state in Fiscal Year 1972, except where the state strengthens the revenue raising capability of local government or assumes responsibility for local expenditures.*
- *Reports on the planned use and actual use of revenue sharing must be filed with the Office of Revenue Sharing (ORS), and published in local newspapers.*
- *Recipients must provide for the expenditures of revenue sharing funds only in accordance with the laws and procedures applicable to the expenditure of their own revenue.*
- *Recipients must not discriminate in employment and in the provision of services financed from revenue sharing funds.*
- *Recipients must require contractors or subcontractors on projects financed at least 25 percent by revenue sharing funds, to pay laborers and mechanics wage rates no less than those determined by the Secretary of Labor under the Davis-Bacon Act.*
- *Recipients must pay individuals, whose wages are paid by revenue sharing funds, wages which are not lower than the prevailing rates of pay for its other employees in similar occupational categories where 25 percent or more of the wages of all employees in the occupational categories are paid from revenue sharing funds.*
- *Recipients must use revenue sharing funds within a reasonable period of time as provided by regulation (within 24 months of the end of the entitlement period).*[13]

The policy issues integral to the formulation of rules and regulations for the implementation of the Act centered on the question of how tightly the funds should be controlled. Interest groups, such as civil rights organizations, sought strong controls to assure the nondiscriminatory use of the funds. Nonetheless, the Nixon Administration, as well as the recipient governments, sought the loosest federal control in order to encourage the greatest latitude in local decision-making. On February 22, 1973, the Office of Revenue Sharing published its proposed regulations which reflected the latter approach. However, after a series of hearings in March, the final regulations, published on April 10, 1973, incorporated suggestions contained on earlier drafts, as well as the concerns raised during the hearings. Richard Nathan summarized these changes:

- *The civil rights provisions of the regulations were expanded to clarify the nature of discriminatory actions and to define permissible sanctions to allow complete, as well as partial, entitlements to be withheld. The Secretary of the Treasury was given the responsibility of determining the remedial action most appropriate in each instance.*

- *The term "Chief Executive Officer" was defined more broadly to include "such other officials as designated by law," thus allowing governments to name their city or county managers as recipients if local laws permitted.*
- *An administrative ruling on February 15th, by the Treasury Department, that significantly limited the use of shared revenues for debt-retirement was incorporated into the final regulations, reversing an earlier position. The use of shared revenue for this purpose was restricted to cases in which debt-retirement expenditures: 1) were contracted after January 1, 1972; and, 2) were classified under one of the nine priority expenditure categories in the case of local governments.*
- *Several changes were made in audit and reporting requirements, thus simplifying record-keeping procedures.*[14]

To provide accountability, local governments were required to publish an actual use report and submit a facsimile to the audit and compliance branch of the Office of Revenue Sharing. Audits could be performed by a variety of organizations including state audit agencies, private accounting firms familiar with Office of Revenue Sharing procedures, or the Office of Revenue Sharing itself.

Perhaps the greatest procedural problem to be overcome in the drafting of the revenue sharing legislation was the specifics of the allocation formula. The legislation called for direct distribution to the states and to thousands of local governments. The problem was to decide *which* local governments or *what size* government should receive funding. The Administration's original revenue sharing measures in 1970 and 1971 proposed inclusion of all county, municipal, and township governments. The 1972 law adopted essentially this same posture, but broadened the base to include the Indian tribes and Alaskan native villages. The final distribution included the 50 states, 3,046 counties, 18,673 municipalities, 16,976 townships, and 178 Indian tribes. One-third of the annual allotment was distributed to the states and the District of Columbia, and two-thirds to the nearly 39,000 units of local government (Table 1). As finally designed, the allocation formula involved four phases of calculations: first, the aggregate sum going to the 50 states and the District of Columbia was calculated; second, this amount was split into shares for state and local governments; third, each state share was allocated among county areas; and fourth, each local jurisdiction's part of the total sum available to the county in which it was located was calculated. The last three steps were carried out in several stages because of the minimum and maximum provisions of the law (20 percent and 145 percent, respectively). These provisions meant that county areas (not county governments), townships, and municipalities were entitled to an allocation of no less than 20 percent, nor more than 145 percent of the statewide average local per capita entitlement. All but a few local governments (and those whose entitlement came to less than $200 annually) received revenue sharing funds. The provisions had the potentially adverse effect of supporting some smaller units of general purpose government that

Table 1

Types of Governments by State

State Name	Counties	Munici-palities	Townships	Indians	Total
Alabama	67	406			473
Alaska	8	119		18	145
Arizona	14	65		8	87
Arkansas	75	460			535
California	57	409		21	587
Colorado	62	258		2	322
Connecticut		34	149		183
Delaware	3	54			57
Dist. of Columbia		1			1
Florida	66	384		2	452
Georgia	158	526			684
Hawaii	3	1			4
Idaho	44	198		5	247
Illinois	102	1,270	1,436		2,808
Indiana	91	562	1,008		1,661
Iowa	99	953		1	1,053
Kansas	105	627	1,498	2	2,232
Kentucky	120	397			517
Louisiana	62	295		1	358
Maine	16	22	474	2	514
Maryland	23	151			174
Massachusetts	12	39	312		363
Michigan	83	531	1,247	5	1,866
Minnesota	87	854	1,800	7	2,748
Mississippi	82	277		1	360
Missouri	114	906	343		1,363
Montana	56	126		6	188
Nebraska	93	534	479	3	1,109
Nevada	16	17		11	44
New Hampshire	10	13	222		245
New Jersey	21	335	232		588
New Mexico	32	91		8	131
New York	57	619	930	7	1,613
North Carolina	100	456		1	557
North Dakota	53	359	1,368	5	1,785
Ohio	88	935	1,320		2,343
Oklahoma	77	561		15	653
Oregon	36	235		4	275
Pennsylvania	66	1,013	1,550	1	2,630
Rhode Island		8	31		39
South Carolina	46	262			308
South Dakota	67	309	1,031	9	1,416
Tennessee	94	320			414
Texas	254	1,022		2	1,278
Utah	29	215		4	248
Vermont	14	60	237		311
Virginia	95	232		1	328
Washington	39	266	39	16	360
West Virginia	55	227			282
Wisconsin	72	572	1,270	9	1,923
Wyoming	23	87		1	111
TOTALS	3,046	18,673	16,976	178	38,873

Source: Office of Revenue Sharing "Statement of Graham W. Watt, before the Intergovernmental Relations Subcommittee of the Senate Committee on Government Operations," *Department of Treasury News* (Washington, D.C.: June 4, 1974), p. 11.

otherwise might have given way to a larger or more effective unit.

The minimum allocation provision also slanted the distribution of funds to favor the suburbs. Every major city lost part of its allocation in order that the suburbs might be brought up to the 20 percent floor. To raise the entitlements of these and other smaller units of government to 20 percent of the statewide local per capita average, revenue sharing allocations had to be reduced for other governments, even if the residents of that government unit with a lower per capital income paid higher taxes. This result was one of the unfair effects of the distributional formula. The formula was not optimal but proved workable. As one member of the Ways and Means Committee noted: "We finally quit [attempting to develop a formula acceptable to everyone], not because we hit on a rational formula, but because we were exhausted."[15]

Political and Distributional Effects

State and local governments took considerable satisfaction in the signing of the Act and the first checks were received by December 11, 1972. The distribution formula finally developed by the Conference Committee appeared straightforward, but it pleased no one entirely. The payments for the second half of 1972 were distributed on January 8, 1973, at approximately the same time that the Administration's Fiscal Year 1974 budget was sent to Congress.

The budget appeared to refute the President's promise that revenue sharing would be "new money" and reflected strong cuts in a number of categorical grants to state and local governments. State and local political leaders, especially representatives of the clientele groups whose categorical programs were being threatened, were stunned. Georgia's Governor Jimmy Carter previously had received the personal assurance of the President "...that no other existing categorical grant program would be robbed to finance revenue sharing grants."[16] Increasing charges of double-dealing were hurled at the Administration.

Kenneth R. Cole, Jr., Director of the Domestic Council, responded to these charges of bad faith by maintaining that general revenue sharing was not intended to replace existing federal aids, but rather that special revenue sharing was intended for this purpose.[17] Categorical programs were not meant to be cut, merely consolidated. However, the reality of decreasing programs made attempts to defend the cuts increasingly hypocritical. This debate continued throughout the first year, but gradually was lost in the next few years as the categorical grant-in-aid system continued to grow, off-setting the impact of the initial cuts.

The debate over revenue sharing continued throughout 1973. The arguments lost considerable intensity as Congress reversed the Administration in its proposed Fiscal Year 1974 appropriations and as the courts reversed President Nixon's attempts to impound (not spend) funds already appropriated by Congress. The original projected 1974 budget had allocated $44.8 billion in grants to state and local governments. Through increased congressional appropriations the actual figures reached $48.3 billion. The reasons why the Administration chose a strategy of give and take, which served to alienate a huge segment of the population and jeopardized congressional support for other New Federalism initiatives, have never been fully explained.

Revenue sharing provided for the distribution of $30.2 billion to approximately 39,000 state and local jurisdictions (Table 2) over a five-year period.[18] The complex allocation process reflected the final Senate/House compromise. For example, in the fourth entitlement period (FY 1976), funds were allocated primarily as follows:

1. The $6.5 billion was allocated among the states according to a Senate formula based on population, tax effort, and income, and a five factor House formula (population, urban population, per capita income, state income tax collections, and tax effort). The higher of the two sums represented the amount released for each state.

2. Within each state, one-third of the allocation was paid to the state government and two-thirds to local governments. The local allocation was determined on a per capita basis. The local government amount was distributed to *county areas* (not governments) based upon a ratio of each individual county *area* in relation to all county areas within the state according to the formula: population—tax effort—relative income.

3. If this last calculation produced a figure which exceeded 145 percent of the per capita entitlement of the local unit of government involved, its payment was reduced to the 145 percent level and the excess shared by the remaining county areas of the state. Similarly, if any county area was allocated less than 20 percent on a per capita basis, its allocation was increased to that level.[19]

This third provision, more than any other portion of the general revenue sharing allocation formula, has proved contentious and has been subject to debate.

Fiscal Impacts on State and Local Governments

The enactment of the State and Local Federal Assistance Act of 1972 was hailed by many as the best measure ever passed by Congress. It also has been described as "...an usurpation of state rights, a threat to freedom and part of a master plot to socialize America."[20] Certainly, the impact of the Act has been substantial, and it has raised a number of controversies. The main area of impact and controversy (following the initial debates on categorical cuts, distributional and allocational formulas, and permissible expenditure areas) has been related to the fiscal impacts on state and local governments.

A General Accounting Office study of the use of revenue sharing funds found that "...restrictions on the direct use of funds and...the reduction or possibility of reductions in funding received under other federal aid programs appeared to influence some governments' direct use of funds."[21] For the most part, state and local officials enjoyed great latitude within the broad priority areas established by the Act. Over one-third of all revenue sharing expenditures as of June 30, 1973 were in the areas of education, health, social services for the poor and aged, and public transportation (Table 3).[22] The funds were expended with relative ease in locally determined

Table 2

Distribution Schedule of
General Revenue Sharing Funds

ENTITLEMENT PERIOD	AMOUNT (BILLIONS)	WHEN PAID
January - June '72	$ 2.65	12/7/72
July - December '72	2.65	1/5/73
January - June '73	2.99	4/6/73—7/6/73
July '73 - June '74	$ 6.05	Quarterly: Oct '73, Jan, Apr, July '74
July '74 - June '75	$ 6.20	Quarterly: Oct '74, Jan, Apr, July '75
July '75 - June '76	$ 6.35	Quarterly: Oct '75, Jan, Apr, July '76
July '76 - December '76	$ 3.33	Oct '76, Jan '77

Private organizations and agencies or special-purpose governmental units (such as fire districts) may request and receive shared revenues from states and/or local governments if the governments' own laws permit such transfers of their own funds.

Source: Office of Revenue Sharing, "General Revenue Sharing Fact Sheet," *Department of Treasury News* (undated).

Table 3

Reported Use of General Revenue Sharing
Through June 30, 1973*

PURPOSE	STATE GOV'TS	LOCAL GOV'TS	ALL GOV'TS
Education	$ 664.03	$ 22.9	$ 687.2
Public Safety	20.0	635.2	655.2
Public Transportation	55.6	361.3	416.9
Environmental Production/Conservation	7.4	180.4	187.8
Multi-Purpose/General Government	5.9	177.8	183.7
Other	151.9	25.7	177.6
Health	30.7	135.1	165.8
Recreation/Culture	3.7	113.0	116.7
Social Services for the Poor or Aged	61.2	26.9	88.1
Financial Administration	18.5	51.4	69.9
Housing/Community Development	1.1	24.9	26.0
Libraries	-0-	18.5	18.5
Social Development	-0-	12.9	12.9
Economic Development	2.2	9.4	11.6
TOTALS	$1,022.5	$1,795.4	$2,817.9

*As of June 30, 1973, governments had spent 42.5% of the funds they had received, for the purposes shown.

Source: Office of Revenue Sharing, "Statement of Graham W. Watt before the Intergovernmental Relations Subcommittee of the Senate Committee on Government Operations," *Department of the Treasury News* (Washington, D.C.; June 4, 1974), p. 12.

priority areas. The ease of expenditure was due largely to the budgetary discretion permitted at the state and local levels, and the fact that the Act's drafters did not require revenue sharing monies to be distinguished or kept separate from state or local funds once the revenue sharing dollars had been transferred out of the required trust fund. There was also evidence that anticipated revenue sharing funds had relieved the pressures on the taxing needs of general purpose units of governments.

In all, public officials generally were satisfied with the final form of the program. In a 1974 survey of the impact of revenue sharing funds in cities of over 50,000 population, David Caputo and Richard Cole found that 90 percent of all respondents indicated they were either somewhat or very satisfied with the program, while only 6 percent indicated dissatisfaction.[23]

The actual financial impacts of revenue sharing funds have been assessed in terms of how the revenue sharing funds actually were used and what were the *related* effects upon state and local finances.[24] Richard Nathan, in his landmark assessment of the first revenue sharing act, measured these impacts in two primary categories, new spending and substitutions.[25] As of July 1, 1973, eligible governments had received two semi-annual payments and one quarterly payment. Aggregate dollar expenditures for state and local governments to this date indicated that 25.5 percent of the funds could be classified as "new spending." This category included new capital purchases (20.6 percent), new or expended operating and maintenance expenditures (3.7 percent), and increased pay and other benefits for public employees (.9 percent).

The category of substitutions included the restoration or replacement of programs funded through other federal aid sources (.9 percent) because of the Administration's Fiscal Year 1974 budget which had proposed sharp reductions in categorical grants to state and local governments. It also included tax reductions in which revenue sharing funds were used to finance programs, to reduce the necessity for contributions from a jurisdiction's own sources of revenue, or to permit a reduction in the level of taxes (15.2 percent). A third substitution included tax stabilization, or cases in which revenue sharing funds were allocated to ongoing programs that otherwise would have been funded through a tax increase (14.3 percent). Another substitution was through program maintenance where reductions in existing programs could be avoided by using revenue sharing funds (14.9 percent). A similar substitute was the avoidance of borrowing, that is borrowing which without revenue sharing otherwise would have been undertaken (6.7 percent). Finally, substitutions included accumulating increases in fund balances, such as the development of budgetary reserves or levels beyond those that existed before the receipt of revenue sharing funds (8.6 percent).[26]

Based on Nathan's field research, the fiscal effects of revenue sharing may be summarized as follows:

- *The rate of revenue sharing fund allocation was found to be high.*
- *A high degree of substitution usage was found. In the aggregate, local governments (in the sample) allocated approx-*

imately two-thirds of their revenue sharing funds for substitution purposes; more than one-half of the replacements took the place of taxes and borrowing; 12 percent was used to fund existing programs and thus budget cuts were avoided.

- Most of the new spending was for capital improvement projects. The average local government surveyed applied 60 percent of its funding to new spending. Over three-fourths of this total was for capital purposes and the remainder for new or expanded programs.
- State governments utilized one-fifth of their revenue sharing allocations for new spending. Comparatively, state governments allocated significantly less to new spending than local governments.
- Finally, both state and local governments showed negligible use of revenue sharing funds to restore federal aid reductions or losses in employee pay and benefit levels, or to increase them.[27]

A U.S. News and World Report of February 1974 generally affirmed the Nathan study results and also reported the following additional "results" of the program:

- The added funds available for public education have helped to improve school systems.
- Increased funding for public safety has helped to bolster and modernize police forces and fire departments.
- Some antipoverty programs have been saved from extinction; others have been enlarged. Some new programs, designed to benefit the old and poor in housing, health, and recreation, have been funded.
- Public transportation systems in many cities have received needed funds, and
- New construction projects resulting from revenue sharing have provided thousands of jobs.

Other studies of the effects of general revenue sharing included significant efforts by the National Science Foundation (NSF) and the Advisory Commission on Intergovernmental Relations (ACIR). The NSF funded a number of research projects in 1974-75, exploring such areas as the distribution formula (9 projects), civil rights (9 projects), fiscal impacts, inflationary effects, public views of GRS, citizen participation and the program's impacts on state and local decision-making. A synthesis of these studies presented the findings of this $3 million research effort.[28] The findings of this effort affirmed other studies. In general, while proportionately small when compared to other sources of state and local income, GRS was significant, perhaps because the funds were "new" money and were attained without the political compromises and consequences that normally accompany movements to increase taxes or generate additional increased sources of revenue.

An equally comprehensive assessment of the effects of GRS was performed by the ACIR. Perhaps reflecting a more federally-oriented perspective than the NSF studies, the Commission reported 16 general findings:

1. *Despite the presence of conditions on the use of GRS funds, state and local policy-makers employed wide discretion in the use of the funds.*
2. *GRS tends to equalize fiscal capacities of rich and poor states.*
3. *GRS provides for more financial aid to the nation's major central cities than to the rich suburban communities.*
4. *The equalizing thrust of the GRS allocation formula is blunted by the 20 percent/145 percent entitlement provisions.*
5. *GRS is gradually being eroded by inflation.*
6. *GRS appears to be gaining public support.*
7. *Since the enactment of GRS, total federal aid outlays have continued to increase in absolute terms but have declined somewhat in relation to total state and local expenditures.*
8. *While there is no legal mandate calling for citizen participation in the decisions on the use of revenue sharing funds, publicity about the program and the requirement that recipients publish Planned and Actual Use Reports has stimulated some additional citizen participation in determining local budget priorities.*
9. *Because revenue sharing dollars can be substituted for equal amounts of state and local revenue from their own sources, many of the conditions on the use of revenue sharing funds are largely cosmetic in character, and the required reports are of little value for analysis of the ultimate impact of the program.*
10. *At this time [the ACIR study was conducted in October 1974], it is virtually impossible to determine on an aggregate basis how revenue sharing funds have been spent.*
11. *Although revenue sharing has come under fire for short-changing the poor, there is no way to prove or disprove this allegation.*
12. *The use of federal general revenue sharing to stabilize or to reduce state and local taxes precipitated a debate at the beginning of the program over the propriety of tax stabilization actions, but now that the adjustments have been made, this issue has become moot.*
13. *Revenue sharing tends to prop up certain duplicative, obsolete, and/or defunct units of local government.*
14. *The "no string" idea of GRS conflicts with federal enforcement of the antidiscrimination provisions of the law. Thus, the inclusion of this provision has extended the ability of the federal government to combat discrimination at the state and local levels, but the Office of Revenue Sharing does not possess sufficient staff to launch a vigorous affirmative action program.*

15. *The long lead time required to update local population and per capita money income data delayed realization of the Congressional intent to distribute funds to local governments on the basis of current need and effort.*
16. *The incentives for greater state use of the personal income tax have not proved strong enough to accomplish their objective.*[29]

An analysis of these evaluations leads one to conclude that GRS had a significant nationwide impact and, indeed, more than any other New Federalism initiative, served to promote a movement toward greater state and local autonomy. However, compared to the over $80 billion total of federal assistance going to state and local governments and the reality that GRS funds comprised only a small percentage of state and local governments' own source revenues, the overall significance of the program and its effects is blunted.

Revenue Sharing Extension in 1976

For the most part, initial Congressional comments following the passage of the State and Local Fiscal Assistance Act of 1972 were unfavorable. Negative comments were heard from such Congressional leaders as Representative Wilbur D. Mills, Chairman of the House Committee on Ways and Means. Not entirely satisfied with the final version of the legislation and the subsequent actions by the Administration, Mills suggested in an address before the Arkansas Legislature that he "...hoped that the program would not last beyond its alloted five years."[30] Senator Majority Leader Mike Mansfield felt that the program could not succeed.[31] Senator Adlai E. Stevenson warned the cities and states to avoid becoming too dependent on the federal government.[32]

The recommended cuts in many categorical programs in President Nixon's Fiscal Year 1974 budget added fuel to the voices of dissent. Walter W. Heller, Chairman of the Council of Economic Advisors in 1964 and a leading proponent of the initial measure, stated that "...the birth of general revenue sharing is being used to justify the homicide of selected social programs."[33]

Alarmed by the increasing volume of dissent, supporters of revenue sharing began to publicize the program's successes. A survey conducted by the Advisory Commission on Intergovernmental Relations released in June 1973 indicated strong approval of general revenue sharing by the American public.[34] Major public interest groups also significantly increased their activities on behalf of the program.[35]

It was in this atmosphere of controversy that legislation related to the extension of revenue sharing was introduced in the 93rd Congress. However, while several proposals were introduced, the issue never received significant debate in that session of Congress.

The same was not true of the 94th Congress, which convened on January 14, 1975. With the strong support of President Gerald Ford, and a more liberal flavor in the composition of reform-minded representatives in the new Congress, the atmosphere shifted not only to extension of the measure, but also to needed reform in some of the areas which were targets of the major criticism. The *Revenue Sharing Bulletin* predicted that of the provisions under discussion, besides the funding level and allocation formula, "...stronger civil rights enforcement, [and] broader citizen participation...will receive greater attention and support."[36] The prediction proved to be accurate.

After a number of changes in both houses of Congress, a Conference Committee compromise reported a measure which included a number of significant changes. A funding level of $6.85 billion for three and three-quarter years was adopted. The priority expenditures categories of the 1972 Act were dropped, and the prohibition against using revenue sharing funds to match other federal grants—a sore point with the cities—also was eliminated.[37]

On the issue of civil rights, the Conference Committee incorporated the House language against discrimination in all programs and activities of a recipient government related to the *direct* use of shared revenue. This wording meant that the nondiscrimination provisions do not apply to other programs or activities of that government, even when they may be indirectly affected, as when revenue funds are substituted for funds that otherwise would have been used in that program.[38]

Concerning public participation, the Committee report specified the necessity for two hearings, one on the proposed use of the funds by the state or local government, and a second on the budget. The hearings requirement could be waived by the Secretary of the Treasury in cases where such hearings would prove—"unreasonably burdensome,"[39] or, in the case of the budget hearing requirement, in instances where a government *already* provides for citizen participation in the budgeting process and a portion of that process includes a hearing requirement on the proposed use of revenue sharing funds.[40] The hearing requirement also included the publication of a planned use report and procedures for making a summary of the adopted budget and proposed use of revenue sharing funds available for public inspection. Accounting and auditing changes to the extended Act included a requirement that an "independent" financial and compliance audit be performed at least every three years for governments receiving at least $25,000 a year in revenue sharing funds, except when the recipient governments "are audited pursuant to generally applicable state or local audit requirement."[41]

President Ford signed the 1976 extension (P.L. 95-488) on October 13, 1976. Ford noted that "...with revenue sharing, we have begun to restore local control over local concerns."[42] With the new Act, some $25.6 billion was appropriated to the nation's state, county, township, and municipal governments.

The extension reserved the previous formula for distribution, as well as the two-thirds share for local governments and one-third share for the states. Both state and local governments are required to report to the Secretary of the Treasury the actual use of the funds and their relationship to the local budget. They also must report the planned use of funds. A notice of the proposed use must be published in the local newspaper prior to budget hearings and after the adoption of a budget. Public hearings on the proposed use are also still required.

The anti-discrimination provisions in the spending of revenue sharing funds were extended to include age, handicapped status, and religion. The law established procedures for suspension of revenue sharing funds for noncompliance and authorized the Attorney General to bring civil action in cases of alleged discrimination.

In reading Public Law 92-512 (the 1972 Act) and P.L. 94-488 (the 1976 extension), it is surprising to note that there is no statement of purpose. This omission was not an oversight by Congress, but rather the inability of Congress to agree on a single rationale. The reason was related to the broad base of support the concept received. House Speaker Carl Albert acknowledged this reality during the renewal debates by noting that the bill "...is not a Republican or a Democratic bill, neither is it a conservative nor a liberal bill."[43]Revenue sharing had something for the cities and the suburbs. It had something for the poor and also financed better public services. It has helped to ease the fiscal crunch on cities and states and has served to stabilize property taxes. GRS also has served as a substitute for categorical grants and has helped to avoid some of the negative features of the categorical system. It has produced some stability in state and local budgeting, decreased administrative costs (especially at the federal level), provided some continuity in state and local planning, and helped to revive the authority of the local chief executive by giving him/her more control of funds.

The extension of the Revenue Sharing Act, like the original Act, was a product of compromise. While civil rights leaders remained unhappy with the enforcement powers granted to the Office of Revenue Sharing and others felt that the reform efforts had not gone far enough, state and local government leaders generally were satisfied. The uncertainty, related to the flow of funds in the first years of the program, has given way to a confidence that revenue sharing is here to stay. As with categorical programs, once the flow of funds had been established, controversy shifted to the amount of funds allocated and to minor administrative problems, but not to the issue of continuation of the program.

In looking at the future, while the extension of GRS provided a slight increase over the 1976 allocation, inflation has eroded the dollar value of the program to state and local governments, and the fiscal impact of revenue sharing has lessened each year. Cities that utilize revenue sharing funds to hold down tax increases or to maintain programs will find it impossible to sustain the benefits initially derived from the program. New programs funded by revenue sharing will have to be supplemented by other funds, reduced, or eliminated. The question of the significance of the fiscal impacts of the Act continued to be of concern only to academics, and not to state and local officials faced with day-to-day problems of soaring costs and demands, and taxpayer resistance to tax increases.[44] The program will be (relatively) taken for granted until it again comes up for renewal. As Edward Bedore, Budget Director of the City of Chicago noted in field hearings on GRS held by the ACIR, "With all its faults, we love it still."[45]

Notes

1. David A. Caputo, "General Revenue Sharing and American Federalism: Towards the Year 2000," The Annals, 419 (May 1975), p. 131.
2. Sylvia V. Hewitt, "A History of Revenue Sharing," State Government XLVI (Winter 1973), p. 37. For historicial information on other shared revenue efforts by Congress, see Edward G. Bourne, The History of the Surplus Revenue of 1837 (New York: Burt Franklin, Repr., 1968; originally published in 1885).
3. Ibid.
4. Will S. Meyers, "A Legislative History of Revenue Sharing," The Annals, 419 (May 1975), pp. 2-3. See also Walter W. Heller, New Dimensions of Political Economy (Cambridge, Mass.: Harvard University Press, 1966); for Laird's views, see U.S. Congress, Congressional Record 13, pt. 3; 3446.
5. Richard E. Thompson, A New Era in Federalism? (Washington, D.C., Revenue Sharing Advisory Service; November, 1973), p. 56.
6. Ibid., p. 57. See also James A. Maxwell and J. Richard Aronson, Financing State and Local Governments, 3rd ed. (Washington, D.C.: The Brookings Institute, 1977), pp. 71-74.
7. Advisory Commission on Intergovernmental Relations, Fiscal Balance in the American Federal System (Washington, D.C.: GPO, 1967), p. 5.
8. "A Legislative History of Revenue Sharing...," p. 3.
9. An open-minded questionnaire about revenue sharing was circulated among Congressional representatives in an attempt to identify progam objectives. The results indicated these two themes as well as others that were related. See U.S. Congress, House Intergovernmental Relations Subcommittee, House Committee on Government Operations, Replies by Members of Congress to a Questionnaire on General Revenue Sharing (Washington, D.C.: GPO, 1974).
10. "Revenue Sharing," Weekly Compilation of Presidential Documents 7, No. 6 (February 8, 1971), pp. 163-173; also, Richard P. Nathan, Allen D. Manuel, Susannah E. Calkins, Monitoring Revenue Sharing (Washington, D.C.: The Brookings Institute, 1975), pp. 14-16.
11. "A Legislative History of Revenue Sharing...," pp. 5-6.
12. Remarks made at the signing of P.L. 92-512, October 20, 1972, by President Richard M. Nixon, Weekly Compilation of Presidential Documents.
13. Advisory Commission on Intergovernmental Relations, General Revenue Sharing: An ACIR Re-Evaluation, A-48 (Washington, D.C.: GPO, October 1974), p. 2; also see Office of Revenue Sharing "General Revenue Sharing Fact Sheet," Department of the Treasury News (undated).
14. Nathan, p. 26.
15. Congressional Record, Vol. 118, 92nd Cong., 2d Sess. (1972), p. 22046. Speech of Representative James C. Corman, California.

16. Governor Jimmy Carter, Remarks in The New Federalism: Possibilities and Problems in Restructuring American Government (Proceedings, Conference sponsored by the Woodrow Wilson International Center for Scholars, July 1973), p. 44.

17. Congressional Quarterly, March 3, 1973, p. 472. See also "Revenue Sharing: Reports from the Grass Roots," Carnegie Quarterly, Vol 24. (Winter, 1976); and Arnold Cantor "Revenue Sharing: The New States Rights," AFL-CIO American Federationist, July 1973, for additional discussion concerning mistrust of the administrator's intentions concerning revenue sharing.

18. 31 U.S.C. Supp. II, 1224 (a).

19. For further explanation of the allocation process refer to Office of Revenue Sharing, What is General Revenue Sharing? (Washington, D.C.: U.S. Department of Treasury, August 1973).

20. "Revenue Sharing: The New...," p. 16.

21. General Accounting Office, Comptroller General of the United States, Revenue Sharing: Its use by and Impact on Local Government, April 1974, p. 29.

22. For example, during the period 1972-75, the City of Kent, Ohio allocated $1,247,656.95 as follows:

Public safety	$ 77,606
Public transportation	$151,704
Environmental protection	$158,000
Public health	$ 34,800
Recreation	$ 20,925.70
Water treatment plant	$470,000
Land acquisition	$ 86,300
Equipment	$ 96,062.08
Government operation	$118,866.86
Sewer lines	$ 33,392.31

See Department of Finance, City of Kent, Ohio, The Citizens Report—Federal Expenditures, City of Kent, Ohio, 1972-1975, pamphlet, undated.

23. David A. Caputo and Richard L. Cole, "General Revenue Sharing Expenditure Decision in Cities Over 50,000," Public Administration Review, 35 (March/April 1975), p. 140. For a more complete summary of this research, see David A. Caputo and Richard L. Cole, Urban Politics and Decentralization: The Case of General Revenue Sharing (Lexington, Mass.: D.C. Health/Lexington, 1974).

24. See Allen D. Manvel, "The Fiscal Impact of Revenue Sharing," The Annals, 419 (May 1975).

25. The basis for the sample, the survey results and participants, assumptions and conclusion are contained in Monitoring Revenue Sharing..., pp. 192-223.

26. Ibid., pp. 231 ff.

27. Ibid., pp. 231-233. For an assessment of revenue sharing impacts on the states. see Deil S. Wright, et al., Assessing the Impact of General Revenue Sharing in the Fifty States: A Survey of State Administrators (Chapel Hill, N.C.: Institute for Research in Social Science, University of North Carolina, 1972). For an excellent discussion of the limitations and restrictions related to gathering empirical evidence on the fiscal impacts of revenue sharing see David A. Caputo, "General Revenue Sharing...," pp. 130-142; also, "The Fiscal Impact of Revenue Sharing...."

28. National Science Foundation, General Revenue Sharing Research Utilization Project, Vol.4, Synthesis of Impact and Process Research (Washington, D.C.: GPO, December 1975).

29. Advisory Commission on Intergovernment Relations, General Revenue Sharing..., pp. 2-17.

30. Revenue Sharing Bulletin, February 1973, p. 2

31. New York Times, February 27, 1973.

32. Congressional Record, January 31, 1973, p. 1693.

33. Revenue Sharing Bulletin, June 1973, p. 2.

34. Advisory Commission on Intergovernment Relations, Changing Public Attitudes on Government and Taxes, June 1974.

35. The major public interest groups include the National League of Cities, U.S. Conference of Mayors, National Association of Counties, National Governor's Association, the International City Management Association, the Council of State Governments, and the National Conference of State Legislators.

36. Revenue Sharing Bulletin, November 1974, p. 8.

37. For a review of the debates over revenue sharing see General Revenue Sharing, Hearings before the Subcommittee on Revenue Sharing of the Senate Committee on Finance, 94:1 (Washington, D.C.: GPO, 1975); Extending and Amending the State and Local Fiscal Assistance Act of 1972, Rept. 94-1207, 94:2 (Washington, D.C.: GPO, 1976), and Revenue Sharing Bulletin, September 1976.

38. See Conference Report to Accompany H.R. 13367, The State and Local Fiscal Assistance Act Amendments of 1976, H. Rept. 94-1720, 94:2 (Washington, D.C.: GPO, 1976).

39. "Unreasonably burdensome" was defined to mean cost in excess of 15 percent of the annual revenue sharing entitlement of a jurisdiction.

40. Conference Report..., p.8.

41. Ibid., p. 39.

42. Press release, The White House, October 13, 1976.

43. Quoted in Samuel H. Beer, "The Adoption of General Revenue Sharing: A Case Study in Public Sector Politics," Public Policy, Spring 1976, p. 193.

44. Again, a landmark study of the fiscal effects of the extended Revenue Sharing Act was compiled by Richard P. Nathan (and Charles F.

Adams, Jr., and Associates). See Revenue Sharing: The Second Round (Washington, D.C.: The Brookings Institute, 1977).

45. Quoted in, Advisory Commission on Intergovernmental Relations, General Revenue Sharing..., p. 62.

CHAPTER V SELECTED BIBLIOGRAPHY
Articles/Documents

Advisory Commission on Intergovernmental Relations. American Federalism: Into the Third Century—Its Agenda, M-85. Washington, D.C.: GPO, May 1974.

_____. Changing Public Attitudes on Government and Taxes. Washington, D.C.: GPO, 1974.

_____. Fiscal Balance in the American Federal System. Washington, D.C.: GPO, 1967.

_____. General Revenue Sharing: An ACIR Re-Evaluation, A-48. Washington, D.C.: GPO, October 1974.

_____. Improving Federal Grants Management, A-53. Washington, D.C.: GPO, February 1977.

_____. The Intergovernmental Grant System as Seen by Local, State, and Federal Officials, A-54. Washington, D.C.: GPO, March 1977.

Bancroft, Raymond. "America's Mayors and Councilmen: Their Problems and Frustrations," Nation's Cities. Washington, D.C.: National League of Cities, 1974.

Beer, Samuel H. "The Adoption of General Revenue Sharing: A Case Study in Public Sector Politics," Public Policy. Spring 1976.

Cantor, Arnold. "Revenue Sharing: The New States Rights," AFL—CIO American Federationist. July, 1973.

Caputo, David A. "General Revenue Sharing and American Federalism: Toward the Year 2000," The Annals, 419 (May 1975).

Caputo, David A. and Cole, Richard L. "General Revenue Sharing Expenditure Decisions in Cities Over 50,000," Public Administration Review, 35 (March/April 1975).

Department of Finance, City of Kent, Ohio. The Citizens Report—Federal Revenue Expenditures, City of Kent, Ohio, 1972-75. (undated).

Executive Office of the President. Public Technology: A Tool for Solving National Problems. Report of the Committee on Intergovernmental Science Relations to the Federal Council for Science and Technology. Washington, D.C.: GPO, May 1972.

_____. Strengthening Public Management in the Intergovernmental System. Washington, D.C.: GPO, March 1977.

General Accounting Office. Fundamental Changes Are Needed in Federal Assistance to State and Local Governments, GG 75-75. Washington, D.C.: GAO, August 19, 1975.

_____. Increased Intergovernmental Cooperation Needed for More Effective, Less Costly Auditing of Governmental Programs, B-176544. Washington, D.C.: GAO, 1974.

_____. Revenue Sharing: Its Use and Impact on Local Government. Washington, D.C.: GAO, April 1974.

Hepert, Ted and Bingham, Richard D. Personal and Environmental Influences Upon the City Manager's Knowledge of Federal Grant-In-Aid Programs. Norman, Oklahoma: Bureau of Governmental Research, 1975.

Hewitt, Sylvia V. "A History of Revenue Sharing," State Government, XLVI (Winter 1973).

Irwin, Laura. "Expenditure Effects of Federal Aid: Data Aggregation and Risk of Uncertainty," Publius, 5 (Fall 1975).

Manuel, Allen D. "The Fiscal Impact of Revenue Sharing," The Annals, 419 (May 1975).

Meyers, Will S. "A Legislative History of Revenue Sharing," The Annals, 419 (May 1975).

National Commission on Productivity and Work Quality. Employee Incentives to Improve State and Local Government Productivity. Washington, D.C.: GPO, March 1975.

National Science Foundation. General Revenue Sharing Research Utilization Project, Vol. 4. Synthesis of Impact and Process Research. Washington, D.C.: GPO, December 1975.

Office of Revenue Sharing, U.S. Department of Treasury. "General Revenue Sharing Fact Sheet," Department of Treasury News. (undated).

_____ . What is General Revenue Sharing? Washington, D.C.: Department of Treasury, August 1973.

"Revenue Sharing: Report from the Grass Roots," Carnegie Quarterly, Vol. 24 (Winter 1976).

"Text of President Nixon's Message on Revenue Sharing," Congressional Quarterly Almanac, Vol. 25. 91st Cong., 1st Sess., 1969. Washington, D.C.: Congressional Quarterly, Inc., 1970.

The New Federalism: Possibilities and Problems on Restructuring American Government. Proceedings of Conference. Woodrow Wilson International Center for Scholars, July 1973.

Thompson, Richard E. A New Era in Federalism. Washington, D.C.: Revenue Sharing Advisory Service, U.S. Department of Treasury, November 1973.

U.S. President. "Revenue Sharing," Weekly Compilation of Presidential Documents, No. 6 (February 8, 1971).

_____ . "Special Message to the Congress Proposing a Nationwide War on Sources of Poverty," March 16, 1974, Public Papers of the President, Lyndon B. Johnson, 1963-64. Washington, D.C.: GPO, 1965.

_____ . Weekly Compilation of Presidential Documents. October 20, 1972.

Walker, David B. "How Fares Federalism in the Mid-Seventies?," The Annals. November 1974.

Wheaton, William L.C. "Made in the U.S.A.: Goals for America," Journal of the American Institute of Planners, 27 (August 1961).

Wise, Harold F. Conflicts in Federal Subnational Development Programs. Washington, D.C.: Economic Development Administration, Department of Commerce, March 1976.

Books

Bourne, Edward G. The History of the Surplus Revenue of 1837. New York: Burt Franklin, Reprint, 1968.

Fisher, Louis. Presidential Spending Power. Princeton, NJ: Princeton University Press, 1975.

Caputo, David H. and Cole, Richard L. Urban Politics and Decentralization: The Case of General Revenue Sharing. Lexington, Mass: D.C. Health and Company, 1974.

Maxwell, James A. and Aronson, J. Richard. Financing State and Local Governments. 3rd ed. Washington, D.C.: The Brookings Institute, 1977.

Nathan, Richard P., Manuel, Allen D. and Calkins, Susannah E. Monitoring Revenue Sharing. Washington D.C.: The Brookings Institute, 1975.

_____, Adams, Charles F. and Assoc. Revenue Sharing: The Second Round; Washington, D.C.: The Brookings Institute, 1977.

Rapp, Brian W. and Patitucci, Frank M. Managing Local Government for Improved Performance: A Practical Approach. Boulder, Colorado: Westview Press, 1977.

Wright, Deil S., et al. Assessing the Impacts of General Revenue Sharing in the Fifty States: A Summary of State Administrators. Chapel Hill, NC: Institute for Research in Social Science, University of North Carolina, 1975.

_____ . Understanding Intergovernmental Relations. New York: Duxbury Press, 1978.

Hearings

Corman, James G. (Speech) Congressional Record, Vol. 118. 92nd Cong., 2nd Sess., 1972.

U.S. Congress, House, Committee on Government Operations, Intergovernmental Relations Subcommittee. Replies by Members of Congress to a Questionnaire on General Revenue Sharing. Washington, D.C.: GPO, 1974.

_____ . Replies from State and Local Governments to Questionnaire on Intergovernmental Relations, Sixth Report by the House Committee on Government Operations. 85th Cong., 1st Sess., House Report No. 575. June 17, 1957.

Chapter Six
Grant Consolidation:
History and Perspectives

In one sense, today's intergovernmental relations are merely a logical, almost inevitable outgrowth of President Johnson's Creative Federalism when the seeds of the present system were sown. The expansive redefinition of the partnership principle, the emphasis on the direct federal ties with local governments, the growing urban and people focus in aid programs, the move into servicing areas formerly deemed to be the responsibility of states or localities or even the private sector, and especially the tendency to enunciate highly ambitious national policy goals while relying on grants to a range of subnational units to implement them—all these traits of the current intergovernmental relations were present in the Creative Federalism efforts to the mid-sixties. The present, in this sense, is clearly linked with the past and especially the Johnson period.

Another set of contemporary tendencies clearly traces their origins to the Nixon-Ford era.

A third body of opinion acknowledges the contributions of the New Federalism and of Creative Federalism. But those in this group concentrate heavily on the actions of Congress in 1976 and 1977 and of President Carter in 1977 to fashion a cluster of aid programs that would help bolster the national economy as well as the operations of state and local governments.

David B. Walker
1979

Introduction

By the late 1970's, it was apparent that the host of categorical grant-in-aid programs that had been developed in the 1960's as a product of the "War on Poverty" and the Great Society had developed a life and supporting clientele groups to assure their perpetuation. By this time, too, former President Nixon's New Federalism attempts to devolve and decentralize programs and responsibilities to the state and local levels were fading into the past, and the efforts became submerged to new priorities and imperatives. The same can be said about the Nixon effort to consolidate categorical programs under the heading of "block" grants in the guise of special revenue sharing. On the surface, it appears logical to group similar grant-in-aid programs under one heading with one set of rules, regulations, and application procedures (as opposed to a separate process for each program). However, the fears of diminished funding, loss of control, and other variables have led to Congressional resistance to such a method. There is no rational answer to opponents of grant consolidation, nor any logical reasons why subsequent administrations or Congress have failed to pursue grant-in-aid administrative reform along these lines, but there is a logic based on the historical evaluation of the major block grant programs that have evolved.

Despite the ostensible illogic of Congressional resistance to block grants, there are historical reasons for the development of Congress's antipathy to the idea. The experiments of the early 1970's in grant consolidation represented by four major block grant programs did not provide definitive arguments regarding assistance reform for either proponents or detractors of the principle of consolidation.

The purpose of this chapter is to appraise block grants, not only for their historical significance, but also for their impacts in shaping the federal assistance effort and redefining the federal system. The unique evolution of each program, the basis for its development, the political compromise that led to its final form, and the characteristics of the block grant itself all provide lessons on the workings of our intergovernmental system. Of special note is the interaction between the executive agencies and the Congress in the development of each program. The block grants are an important and viable part of the federal effort to provide assistance to state and local governments. They represent a form of assistance reform as well as experiments with new concepts and tools. They are also characteristic of a representation of an era—a program management thrust that has had mixed success. Unfortunately, this form of assistance has proved to be confusing to the general public and the Congress. The confusion is due, in part, to conceptual and operational differences. As a result, too many block grants have become associated with interrelated or ill-defined goals and objectives and political expediency. This chapter is concerned with exploring and clarifying these problems as they relate to federal assistance program administration.

Forms of Federal Assistance

There are three major types of grants within the federal system: categorical, general revenue sharing, and block grants. The most numerous, and those which represent the largest portion of federal grant-in-aid dollars, are the categorical grants. There are approximately 400 categorical type programs (Table 1).

Categorical Grants

The categorical grants are those designated by Congress for use in a specific program for which funding assistance is available. These awards are usually limited to narrowly defined activities such as fellowship or training programs, waste treatment facility construction, crime prevention, or some service-oriented function. Besides having a functional identification, the funds are awarded by means of some form of allocation mechanism. These mechanisms define the types of categorical grants available. There are basically four types of categorical grants; formula-based, project, formula-project, and full reimbursement.

Formula-based grants are those that have been allocated among recipients according to eligibility factors, ratios, or formulas which have been specified in the authorizing legislation or adminstrative rules and regulations related to that program. Awards for library acquisitions authorized for institutions of higher eduction under the Higher Education Act of 1965 are examples. In this cae, each eligible college or university library is given a predetermined (by formula) amount of funds for this purpose, upon completion of an application for this assistance. The formula may be based on

Table 1

Number and Estimated Dollar Volume of Categorical Grants, By Type, FY 1975

| | NUMBER | PERCENT | ESTIMATED OUTLAYS (BILLIONS) | |
			AMOUNT	PERCENT
Formula-based grants	146	33.0%	$25.8	69.0%
Allotted formula	(97)	(21.9)	(8.6)	(23.0)
Project grants subject to formula distribution	(35)	(7.9)	(2.8)	(7.4)
Open-end reimbursement	(14)	(3.2)	(14.4)	(38.6)
Project grants	296	67.0	11.6	31.0
TOTAL	442	100.0%	$37.4	100.0%

SOURCE: Advisory Commission on Intergovernmental Relations, *Categorical Grants: Their Role and Design,* A-52 (Washington, D.C.: GOP, May, 1977), p. 92.

population served by the recipient, size, fiscal effort, or any number of factors and usually is based on a Congressional determination of equity.

Project grants are those for which potential applicants submit specific, individual applications in the format and at the times indicated by the grantor agency. A proposal to develop a management training program for urban officials would be one of the projects HUD or even the Department of Labor might fund. Project grants constitute the largest number of grant programs, but provide fewer dollars than formula-based categorical programs (Table 2).

The third category is actually a combination of the first two. A formula-project grant is one for which a statutorily based formula is used to determine the amount available to a recipient. The distribution of this award usually occurs by a state, which considers applications from eligible recipients after receiving an allocation from a federal agency. The Intergovernmental Personnel Act (IPA) is an example of this type of assistance procedure. Under the IPA, states receive 80 percent of the total fiscal year IPA appropriation. Each state receives an allocation calculated on the basis of its population and the number of government workers employed in that state. The state must then allot at least 50 percent of its allocation to benefit local governments, some of which submit project proposals and applications to the state. Project proposals must be within the federal statutory guidelines indicated by the authorizing legislation (the public law). In this ex-

Table 2

Categorical Grants and Estimated Outlays (Fiscal Year 1975)

	Number and Estimated Dollar Volume of Categorical Grants, By Type		Estimated Outlays (Billons)	
	NUMBER	PERCENT	AMOUNT	PERCENT
Formula-based	146	33.0%	$25.8	69.1%
Allotted formula	(97)	(21.9)	(8.6)	(23.1)
Project grants subject to formula distribution	(35)	(7.9)	(2.8)	(7.4)
Open-end reimbursement	(14)	(3.2)	(14.4)	(38.6)
Project	296	67.0	11.6	30.9
TOTAL	442	100.0%	$37.4	100.0%

SOURCE: Advisory Commission on Intergovernmental Relations, *Summary and Concluding Observations: The Intergovernmental Grant System: An Assessment and Proposed Policies,* A-62 (Washington, D.C.: GPO, June, 1978), p. 4.

ample, the relationship between the formula allocation and the total project funding available in any one state is very clear.

For a full or open-ended reimbursement grant, also a type of formula grant, the federal government will reimburse a specified portion of state-local program costs. Thus, competition for funds is eliminated, and the grantee is assured a fixed percentage of allowable (total) project costs. In this instance the grantee shares the costs of the project with the federal funding agency. An example of this type of categorical program would be inter-state highway funding in which the state assumes 10 percent and the federal government 90 percent of the project costs.

Cost-Sharing and Matching

Most federal programs were developed with the belief that the recipient, the primary beneficiary, should share in the costs of the project. Thus, cost-sharing or matching requirements were built into the statutes. In cost-sharing, as the term implies, the grantee pays for a portion of the costs of a given project. Matching funds refers to the dollar amount paid by the grantee to "match" the amount paid by the funding agency. The match differs from cost-sharing in that matching requirements usually specify a fixed percentage, i.e., 50-50. 75-27, 90-10, etc. The percentage, ratio, or amount the grantee is to share or match is dictated by the regulations of that specific program. Some programs require no recipient contribution, while others are based on specific ratios or percentages (Table 3). In the table, low match programs are those requiring less than 50 percent from the recipient, while high match programs require an amount greater than 50 percent. Variable match programs may specify some formula or conditions by which the matching requirement changes. There is little explanation for the considerable diversity in these requirements which exists among programs.

Table 3

**Matching Requirements and Grant Recipients;
Grants to State and Local Governments, FY 1975**

	NO MATCH	COST-SHARED	LOW MATCH	50 PERCENT	HIGH MATCH	VARIABLE MATCH	UN-CLASSIFIED	TOTAL
State	52	2	59	41	1	6	1[a]	162
State-substate	20	7	21	10	0	0	3	61
Local	18	0	1	1	0	0	0	20
Mixed public-private higher education	80	33	64	7	0	2	13[b]	199
TOTAL	170	42	145	59	1	8	17	442

[a]Includes one supplemental grant unclassified as to match.

[b]Includes two supplemental grants not classified as to match and six grants with declining federal shares.

SOURCE: Advisory Commission on Intergovernmental Relations, *Categorical Grants: Their Role and Design*, A-52 (Washington, D.C.: GPO, May, 1977), p. 169.

Cost-sharing may be required in actual dollars or in equivalent expenditures such as personnel costs or services, which are called "in-kind" matching. These services, as with cash, must represent actual expenditures by the grantee agency and are subject to audit.

Revenue Sharing and Block Grants

Revenue sharing or general revenue sharing (GRS) represents a formula-based allocation to state and local governments without cost sharing requirements. It is somewhat programmatic, in that some areas of expenditure are encouraged and others prohibited by the authorizing legislation (refer to Chapter V). GRS also represents a fixed allocation. Thus, it shares the characteristics of a formula grant, but allocations are made directly to the recipient from the Department of the Treasury rather than through some intermediate agency.

The final major categorization of assistance award is the block grant. Block grants are designed primarily for general purpose governments and are based on a statutory formula for use in a number of activities within some broad programmatic or functional area. The purpose of the block grant concept is to consolidate a number of categorical programs under a generic heading to permit more grantee discretion in the use of the funds, as well as to reduce application requirements and paperwork. The range of permissible activities is greater than under categorical programs, and there are fewer conditions restricting the grantee's use of the funds. Surprisingly, while block grants are hailed as a means of reducing the proliferation of categorical programs and their concommitant paperwork, they have not been especially well received by the general public and are not well regarded by the Congress. There are a number of reasons for this anomaly which will be discussed later.

Basic Characteristics of Block Grants

The Advisory Commission on Intergovernmental Relations (ACIR) has identified five basic design characteristics that are common to the four primary block grants (Table 4).[1] These traits provide a basis for differentiating this form of grant-in-aid assistance from others:

1. Federal aid is authorized for a wide range of activities within broadly defined functional areas.
2. Recipients have substantial discretion in identifying problems and designing programs and allocating resources to deal with them.
3. Administrative, fiscal reporting, planning, and other federally imposed requirements are kept to the minimum amount necessary to ensure that national goals are being accomplished.
4. Federal aid is distributed on the basis of a statutory formula, which results in narrowing federal administrator's discretion and providing a sense of fiscal certainty to recipients.
5. Eligibility provisions are statutorily specified and favor general purpose governmental units as recipients and elected officials and administrative generalists as decision-makers.[2]

Table 4

Structural and Fiscal Characteristics of

Contemporary Block Grant Programs, 1977

PROGRAM	YEAR OF ENACTMENT	NUMBER OF CATEGORICAL PROGRAMS CONSOLIDATED	FY 1976 ACTUAL OUTLAY (IN MILLIONS)[a]	DISTRIBUTION FORMULA	PRIMARY RECIPIENT	MATCHING REQUIREMENTS	MAINTENANCE OF EFFORT REQUIREMENTS
Partnership for Health	1966	9	$90	population	states	none	no
Omnibus Crime Control and Safe Streets	1968	0	405	population	states	90-10 (planning) 50-50 (construction) 90-10 (other "action" Programs)	yes
Comprehensive Employment and Training[c]	1973	17	1,358	unemployment, previous year funding level low income	general purpose local units and states	none	no
Housing and Community Development[d]	1974	6[e]	750	population, housing overcrowding, poverty	general purpose local units	none	yes

[a]Executive Office of the President, Office of Management and Budget, Special Analyses: Budget of the United States Government Fiscal Year 78, Washington, D.C. U.S. Government Printing Office, 1977.

[b]Excludes part C discretionary grants and part E (corrections) formula and discretionary grants.

[c]Excludes public service and emergency employment programs.

[d]Excludes outlays for urban renewal and the phase out of other categorical programs replaced by the block grant.

[e]A seventh program - Section 312 Housing Rehabilitation Loans - was also initially proposed for consolidation.

SOURCE: Advisory Commission on Intergovernmental Relations, Block Grants: A Comparative Analysis, A-60 (Washington, D.C., October, 1977), p. 7.

ACIR's definition of a block grant, based on a combination of these characteristics is: "...a program by which funds are provided chiefly to general purpose governmental units in accordance with a statutory formula for use in a broad functional area, largely at the recipients' discretions."[3]

Block grants generally result from the consolidation of a number of categorical programs, represent a fairly substantial dollar outlay, are formula-based in allocation, and pay most, if not all, of the costs of the program. Maintenance of effort (a requirement that a recipient jurisdiction continue to expand its own funds at the same level as the year prior to enactment of the program) also may be part of the block grant requirements.

Block Grants vs Categorical Grants

Categorical grants have been established to respond to particular needs or problems that were of national interest. Federal funds were used to provide incentives for other units of government to undertake activities in these areas, as well as to support or maintain the activity already started. The four existing block grants share both of these purposes, stimulation and support, but the mixture varies from grant to grant.

Many categorical programs were originated to meet common needs of state and local governments. ACIR cites 23 grants in the area of pollution control and abatement, 36 for social services, and 78 in the area of education.[4] In the area of transportation safety, for example, nine categorical programs were developed: one for basic highway safety; three for formula grants involving railroad crossings, railroad obstacles, and high locations; three project grant programs subject to a state allocational restriction associated with seatbelt law incentives, reduced traffic fatalities, and special bridge replacement; and two project grants for railroad safety and motor vehicle diagnostic inspection.[5] Although some difficulties occur because of program overlap and confusion concerning rules and regulations related to each program, these are not the major problems which block grants are intended to eliminate.

The major problems with categorical grants are the specificity and narrowness with which they attempt to address a problem. For example, a community may be ineligible for assistance if its needs or proposed program does not coincide exactly with the description or purpose of the grant program. The community also may be ineligible if the program includes certain income restrictions, cost-sharing, or other requirements that may not apply to the program or circumstances of the community or that they may impose conditions which that community may be unable to meet.

This narrowness causes administrative problems for grantor agencies as well as for potential grantees. The dilemma is how to address a specific area of need as a national interest while permitting the recipient government to utilize those funds in the best manner according to its unique problems and circumstances. One solution to this dichotomy is to bring together, or consolidate, similar programs with similar purposes under one broadened legislative authority. Although this concept is relatively new, programs which laid the foundations for our current block grants appeared in the 19th century when the federal government made direct cash grants to state and local governments in general areas such as banking, education, agriculture, defense, and internal improvements.[6] A more recent expression of the rationale for grant consolidation for programmatic purposes was by the first Hoover Commission in 1949 which suggested that "...a system of grants be established based upon broad categories— such as highways, education, public assistance, and public health—as contrasted with the present system of extensive fragmentation."[7] This suggestion was followed in the 1950's by proposed legislation to establish block grants by consolidating programs in the areas of public health, agriculture, and vocational rehabilitation.

These efforts proved unsuccessful largely because of Congressional disinterest, and they led one observer to conclude that "...the assumptions on which the block grant proposal rest are not valid in all instances or, at least, run counter often to other objectives which are more compelling."[8] This logic appeared to prevail in the mid-1960's, when hundreds of new categorical programs were enacted and the amount of federal aid to state and local governments increased fivefold. However, there was little Congressional effort to develop broader based legislation. Congressional reluctance to overhaul the categorical system can be attributed to several factors; the traditional difficulty of Congress to agree on broad program objectives; the desires of individual members to protect certain programs; the fragmented nature of Congressional committee jurisdiction over functional programs; pressures from interest and recipient groups as well as the federal bureaucracy; failures to guarantee to recipient groups or clientele that the funding levels would not be reduced; and the low priority accorded to grant-in-aid reform as a public issue.[9]

At first seeming to threaten the categorical system, block grants now augment it and indeed have become somewhat "categorical" in character through the amendment process. Each grant program developed is a product of its history, the programs from which it evolved, the social and political conditions predominant at the time of its passage, and the character of the President and his administration. Each block grant program is discussed in this context to afford the reader a brief look at significant developmental variables as well as the uniqueness of each program.

Evolution of the Block Grant Concept

The impetus for major change to the categorical system came as a result of programmatic fragmentation in the health area which began with the passage of the Social Security Act of 1935. The Social Security Act authorized a small program of federal formula grants in support of health services. During the following years, categorical health programs proliferated in a number of areas, causing the Hoover Commission to comment that because of this proliferation, local health officers would find it difficult to develop balanced health programs adopted to meet local needs.[10] The Commission went on to advocate not only simplification and decentralization of federal health grants, but also creation of a generalized health grant system. The federal administration of this health system was to be minimal. As with many reform proposals which lack public attention or support, there was no serious Congressional action on the Commission's recommendations, although bills to create a block grant for health programs were submitted in the 80th and 81st Congresses.[11]

The categorical approach to health assistance received another critical review several years later by the U.S. Commission on Intergovernmental Relations. This Commission, known as the Kestnbaum Commission, was also a temporary study group created by statute to examine the role of state and local governments in the grant-in-aid system. Its report was submitted to the President in 1955 and contained a careful assessment of the federal intergovernmental system in a number of functional areas including health. While generally laudatory of the federal role in the health area and of the categorical approach in general, the Commission expressed concern over the indefinite tenure of these grants once they had served their purpose. The Commission argued that since the primary purpose of a categorical grant was to adopt measures for controlling disease and developing new public health precedures, the need for categorical incentive funding disappeared at some point in time and the federal responsibility ended.[12] Further, the restrictive nature of categorical grants constrained the development of programs in this area and became an obstacle to local initiatives and development. The prevailing system of individualized program grants, with their separate reporting and accounting requirements, posed excessive administration problems for grant recipients. The Commission recommendation was to allocate all federal health grants to the states "...on the basis of a uniform formula susceptible of flexible administration."[13] The arguments were the same as those of the Hoover Commission and the results identical. Again, while the report received widespread attention and led to some substantive changes to the intergovernmental grant-in-aid structure, no substantive change occured in the health area.

Emergence of a Block Grant in Health

While Congressional action in response to the recommendations for health grant reform lagged, action by the Administration was more positive. The proposal to simplify grant administration by consolidating similar programs was adopted by the newly formed Department of Health, Education, and Welfare (HEW). The Eisenhower Administration subsequently proposed legislation to consolidate all eight of the Public Health Service grants into two. One was to be a formula grant for basic support and service improvement, and the other a project grant for health related experimentation. The Administration's proposal was introduced in the House of Representatives (83rd Cong., 2nd Sess.), but the counterpart measure was never reported out of the Senate Committee on Labor and Public Welfare.[14] For all practical purposes, further action toward grants consolidation ceased for almost 15 years.

The federal grant system was reviewed again as part of a two year effort by the Intergovernmental Relations Subcommittee of the House. The Subcommittee report, released in 1958, was critical of the system and suggested that some problems could be solved by shifting funds between programs, but there was no recommendation for programmatic consolidation. A report of the Joint Federal-State Action Committee, which had been formed by the National Governors' Conference at the suggestion of President Eisenhower, addressed these same concerns at approximately the same time. The Joint Committee went one step further than the Intergovernmental Subcommmmittee and endorsed the concept of a single block grant in the public health area, in principle but not in substance, recognizing that "...past Congressional opposition made a block grant proposal unrealistic..."[15] Once more, meaningful reform in the health area through consolidation was delayed, largely because of unarticulated opposition to a concept that had never been tested.

The topic of grant reform through consolidation remained unresolved until the newly formed Advisory Commission in Intergovernmental Relations (ACIR) addressed the issue in 1961. The ACIR studied the arguments pro and con consolidation, and, like the Joint Federal-State Action Committee, concluded that "...the variety and force of these arguments make unrealistic the adoption at this time of the block grant approach...."[16] It recommended, instead, the transfer of funds among and between the various programs authorized under the Public Health Service Act, the same approach advocated by the House Intergovernmental Relations Subcommittee some three years earlier. In this manner the ACIR hoped to promote the flexibilty of the block grant approach while avoiding the potential problems and the Congressional antipathy associated with the concept.

During this era, Congressional attitudes concerning the block grant concept were hostile for a number of reasons. The assumptions underlying this rationale included:

- *the primary purpose of federal aid is to provide states with financial support to carry out a program's purpose;*
- *the alignments and pressures of political action are different at the national level from those at the state and local levels;*
- *federal controls (e.g., standards, audits, and other reviews) would be substantially reduced if the purpose of the program were broadened); and*
- *more effective and efficient use of public funds will result if states have wider latitude in directing expenditures.*[17]

These were the more public pronouncements. The real heart of the resistance was the fear of changing relationships between constituent or recipient groups and of reducing funding levels. No promises by the Administration could alleviate these apprehensions.

Criticism of the nation's health programs continued in the early 1960's with the appointment of the National Commission on Community Health Services. This four-year effort was under the sponsorship of the American Public Health Association and the National Health Council. The study explored not only the topic of health care, but also the planning, organization, financing, and delivery of health services at all levels of government. The Commission found so many substantial problems with the existing patchwork of grant programs that they strongly advocated a comprehensive approach to health program delivery as a means of correcting the excessive fragmentation and over-specialization that had developed.[18] While the Commission's report was not published until 1967, its recommendations received widespread attention. They helped focus the direction of other efforts to reform the nation's health care system and were a vital consideration in the movement to extend the legislative authority of a number of public health formula grant programs.

A comprehensive grant approach as a cure to the fragmentation of the national health grant program structure emerged from the 1965 White House Conference on Health. The results of the Conference, along with the work of the National Commission on Community Health Services and an extensive HEW study effort conducted in 1965, appeared to influence the Administration's attitude toward the health grant system. President Johnson's health message to the Congress in early 1965 lauded the many legislative advances made in the health area, but noted the need for further improvements.[19]

The President's special message set forth the Administration's proposed health program for the year, but more important, it endorsed a broader view, promoting better service delivery. President Johnson recommended "...a program of grants to enable states and communities to plan the better use of manpower, facilities, and financial resources for comprehensive health services."[20] The growing number of categorical programs and the piecemeal approach they represented were criticized and a comprehensive public health service program (a block grant) was recommended to begin in FY 1968. Thus, the Administration advocated a multifaceted attack based on a foundation of programmatic consolidation, the first strong endorsement of the concept.[21] The thrust of the proposal was a new partnership among all levels of government and the private sector.

On the following day, the Administration's proposal, the Comprehensive Health Planning and Public Health Services Amendments of 1966 (P.L. 89-749), was introduced in the Senate.[22] Following hearings on September 29, the Bill was reported out, largely unchanged from the Administration's version. The House introduced a more limited version of the Senate Bill (H.R. 18231). The Senate accepted the House amendments to this Bill, and the Bill was sent to and signed by the President on November 3.[23] The funding level of the Act was modest (Table 5).

The new block grant incorporated all nine categorical formula grants for health service programs under the administration of the Public Health Service. This new consolidated single grant, which now was known as the Partnership for Health Act, was considerably broader in scope than the categorical programs it replaced and led to a number of actions unifying state level health efforts (Figure 1). Key provisions of the Act included:

- *Administrative responsiblity was assigned to the state health and mental health departments.*
- *A single state health plan, which was to be approved by HEW, was required (Section 314(a)).*

- *The funding level of the block grant was slightly higher than the total of the categorical programs.*
- *The Act contained a 15 percent "set-aside" for state mental health authorities, thus preserving a categorical component (Section 314(e)).*

Table 5

Federal Outlays for GRS Block Grants
and Other Assistance to State and Local Governments
(Dollar Amounts in Millions)

GRANT	1972	% TOTAL	1976	% TOTAL	1978	% TOTAL	EST. 1980	% TOTAL
GENERAL REVENUE SHARING[1]			6243	10.6%	6823	8.8%	6863	8.3%
Comprehensive Health Grants	90		128		88		45	
Criminal Justice Administration	281		519		346		223	
Employment and Training	——		1698		1992		1948	
Community Development Block Grants	——		983		2464		3272	
Social Services	1930		2251		2809		3020	
Subtotal[2]	2301	6.6%	5579	9.4%	7699	9.9%	8508	10.3%
Other Grants	30953	90%	45807	77.5%	56824	73%	64780	78.1%
Total Grants to State & Local Government	34372		50094		77889		82937	

[1]Excluded are other general purpose fiscal assistance and TVA.
[2]Excluded are school aid in federally affected areas and local public works.

SOURCE: Office of Management and Budget, *Special Analysis: Budget of The United States, Fiscal Year 1980* (Washington, D.C.: GPO 1979).

On the negative side, the Act contained no pass-through provisions for local governments; there was no resolution of conflicting federal-state-local priorities; and there was no provision to require use of the funds in strict accordance with the comprehensive health planning called for by the Act. The only provision by which the program could be evaluated was the provision that funds be spent according to health plans developed by the state.[24]

Amending the Act

The Partnership for Health Act was reviewed again by the House Committee on Interstate and Foreign Commerce less than one year later and prior to its implementation. The House hearings led to several major changes in the original legislation. The first change was related to funding. The Administration argued that the modest increases authorized were far less than the amount needed to assist in the improvement of state health departments and were inadequate for exercising the flexibility in the use of the funds promised by the Act.[25] As a result of this criticism, a modest increase each year for the next four years was approved. A second area of concern was the distribution of funds between state and local recipients. As in the original Administration proposal, a 70 percent allocation was proposed under Section 314(d) of the Act to be used by the states for providing services to com-

Figure 1

Partnership for Health Act Results

SECTION	RESULTS
1) 314(a) Grants to States for Comprehensive State Health Planning.	The creation of State level health planning agencies.
2) 314(b) Project Grants for Areawide Health Planning.	The creation of areawide health planning agencies within the State.
3) 314(d) Grants for Comprehensive Public Health Services	Combination of health grants with increased State discretion in the expenditure of funds in the areas of general health, tuberculosis, cancer, mental health, heart disease, chronic illnesses, home health services, and radiological health.
4) 314(e) Project Grants for Health Services Development.	Combination into one program of several others with increased discretion in the expenditure of funds in community health, tuberculosis, cancer, mental health, mental retardation, venereal disease and neurological and sensory diseases.

munities. This "70 percent" provision was accepted and incorporated in the amendments. Finally, the Secretary of HEW was authorized to use up to one percent of the funds provided under four sections of the Act for evaluation of these programs. The Senate hearings on the amendments were not substantial, and the amendments became public law on December 5, 1966 (P.L. 90-171).

The Act was amended once again in 1970. For the first time federal priorities were specified, and authority for the block grant was extended for three years, through FY 1973. However, even with modest increases in the funding authorizations (to $130 million in FY 1971, $145 million in FY 1972, and $165 million in FY 1973), the program was not, as anticipated, the primary source of federal support of state and local health efforts. Following the initial 1966 consolidation, Congress passed a number of new categorical programs, several of which logically should have been included in the Partnership for Health block grant.

The Act was not reviewed again until 1974. In this third review of the Act, the stress shifted to accountability. To that date, little information was available on program expenditures by the states, and the House Committee on Interstate and Foreign Commerce called for a significantly increased effort to gather data and evaluate the results of the program.[26] The Senate made several minor changes and passed a limited extension of the Act as it debated alternatives to the block grant mechanism. The final version was passed and forwarded to President Ford, who pocket vetoed the bill, noting budgetary problems.[27]

An identical bill, the Revenue Sharing and Health Services Act of 1975, was introduced in the House in the following year. The only controversy the measure encountered came from Secretary of HEW Casper Weinberger. Weinberger's primary objections were to the limited management features in the Bill and the use of the term "health revenue sharing." Weinburger argued that detailed descriptions of the programs in the Bill limited its flexibility and that the revenue sharing label was inaccurate.[28] In spite of these objections, a revised version was passed by both the House and Senate, but again vetoed by President Ford in July. This time, however, the veto was overridden by strong margins in both Houses and became law on July 29, 1975 (P.L. 94-92).

Thus, the first experiment in categorical program consolidation was greeted by some controversy and less than widespread enthusiasm. There were specific reasons for this less than enthusiastic response. Some of these reasons are related to the unique development and history of this particular block grant, while others may be generalized to the block grant concept in toto.

The Advisory Commission on Intergovernmental Relations provides an interesting assessment in this regard. ACIR measured both Congressional "intent" associated with this legislation and the attitudes of the Administration. ACIR noted several predominating Congressional purposes or concerns that give some indication of the role of block grants in the categorical system.[29]

First, the purpose of categorical program consolidation was to reduce paperwork and the administrative burden of complying with the requirements of a number of related programs. This reduction has proved to be one of the primary incentives in providing a block grant approach. An affiliated purpose was to provide programmatic flexibility to state health agencies in the use of federal funds. The wording of the Act was intended to assist the states in establishing and *maintaining* health service programs unrestricted by burdensome administrative requirements. ACIR points out that other interpretations would shift the stress from state health program maintenance to promoting innovation, experimentation, and reform, two clearly different purposes.[30] Under the first interpretation, the stress is on a perennial federal *support* role; under the second, the emphasis is on short term projects The first approach is long term, the second year-by-year.

The key to the actual intent of the Act appears related to the basis of most federal grant-in-aid programs; the program was designed to promote national "goals" by increasing the capacity of state and local assistance recipients to strengthen their own programs. The block grant approach stressed comprehensive health planning in the state, and thus states were directed to work together with local governments in order to develop program and spending priorities. Pursuit of national "goals" or priorities, another central concern of the Partnership for Health Act, was the greatest source of ambiguity in the Act and its most controversial feature.[31]

Congress is forced to make a basic decision in the formulation of any grant-in-aid program. The decision must be on how to support national priority areas and encourage state and local recipients to adopt these same goals and apply them to their own situation. Thus, the funds become a "carrot" incentive and the governing rules and regulations the "stick" to ensure compliance in return for the use of the funds. This issue of incentive funding and regulatory enforcement goes to the heart of federal provision of grant-in-aid assistance and still lacks resolution. On the one hand, Congress wishes the state and local governments to pursue goals that they have deemed to be of national concern. On the other hand, they feel compelled to keep conditions upon such assistance that appear to imply a level of distrust. Any attempt to generalize from the experiences or assessment of this one program would be oversimplification, but the "carrot-stick" approach is the foundation of the grant-in-aid system and readily apparent in the Partnership Act.

The same confusion over motivations is visible, but to a lesser degree, in an assessment of an administration's intent or purposes in developing a grant-in-aid program to present for Congressional action. As indicated previously, the position of an administration is largely a reflection of Presidential philosophy. Presidents, such as Eisenhower, Nixon, and Ford, promoted and encouraged programmatic decentralization or laissez faire, a "loose" philosophy. associated with the Republican (presidential) party; while Democratic Presidents, such as Kennedy and Johnson, but not Carter, have reflected a controlled expansionist philosophy—or more programs for more people, but with more controls (sticks). In the case of the Partnership for Health block grant program, the Administration's position (to promote unrestricted state flexibility in the use of the funds) was diametrically opposed to Congressional attempts to enforce accountability and responsiveness to national health priorities. This motivational dichotomy was not resolved in the second major block grant program which emerged several years later.

The Omnibus Crime Control and Safe Streets Act of 1968

The Partnership for Health Act represented a consolidation of a number of categorical assistance programs into one broad, comprehensive health grant program. In contrast, the Safe Streets Act was the first federal program specifically designed from the outset as a block grant. The grant was born in an era of intense civil unrest, assassinations of key political figures, racial disorder, and campus disturbances that set the tone of the presidential election of 1964. It was conceived to address a national problem of high priority in the minds of most Americans. Unlike the Partnership Act, Congressional intent was clearly to assign a major share of not only the planning, but also the funding allocation and the administration of the program directly to the states (Table 6).

Table 6

Principal Recipient and Federal Agency Roles in Contemporary Block Grant Administration
1977

| | ACTIONS BY RECIPIENT | | | ACTIONS BY FEDERAL AGENCY | | | |
PROGRAM	Plan Submission	Application Submission	Detailed Reporting	Plan Review & Approval For Substantive Content	Application Approval	Monitoring Evaluation, Auditing	Discretionary Grant Awards
Partnership for Health		X [a]			X [b]		
Omnibus Crime Control and Safe Streets	X	X	X	X	X	X	X
Comprehensive Employment and Training Act	X	X	X	X	X	X	X
Housing and Community Development	X	X		X	X	X	X

[a] Since 1970, preprinted assurances are filed indicating that all statutory planning and other program requirements are met.

[b] Contents are reviewed to ensure that statutorily specified procedures have been followed.

SOURCE: ACIR, Block grants: A Comparative Analysis, A-60 (Washington, D.C.: GPO, October, 1977), p. 9.

The reasons for this philosophical shift are not related to the experiences of the Partnership Act nor to the debates that surrounded the amendments of the Act, but rather to a clearly discerned national problem of high public interest and concern. After addressing the crime issue in the 1964 Presidential campaign, President Johnson delivered the first presidential message devoted exclusively to crime on March 8, 1965. In essence the President declared that crime was no longer a local problem, but a national concern which should be attacked by a "War on Crime" at all levels of government.[32] According to the message, the federal government would take a meaningful leadership role in assisting state and local authorities to deal with the problem of crime. The President went on to call for the establishment of a Commission on Law Enforcement and Administration of Justice to investigate the basic causes of crime and to make recommendations for its control and prevention.

As a follow-up to the message some six months later, President Johnson submitted a plan to Congress calling for a pilot program "to provide assistance in training state and local enforcement officers and other personnel, and in improving the capabilities, techniques, and practices in state and local law enforcement and prevention and control of crime."[33] The pro-

prosed Law Enforcement Assistance Act was the first block grant program designed exclusively to assist state and local governments in reducing crime, a goal that previously had been considered a state and local concern.[34]

The Act cleared the House and Senate with little opposition, partly because of the small appropriation involved, a mere $7 million, and partly because, as with health, no one wanted to be on record as opposed to a measure designed to address a volatile national concern. The Act also proposed creating the Office of Law Enforcement Assistance (OLEA) to promote innovation in the prevention of crime, training in crime prevention techniques, and assessment of the causes of crime and crime control. The low funding level of the Act was intended to stimulate local efforts at crime prevention but not be a major means of support. Thus, federal incentive funding opened the door to a legitimate federal role in local criminal justice affairs.

The next major advance was brought about with the creation of the President's Commission on Law Enforcement and Administration of Justice, headed by Attorney General Nicholas Katzenbach. The Commission was created by Executive Order on July 23, 1965. After 18 months of rigorous study, the Commission's 1967 report, *The Challenge of Crime in a Free Society,* called for increased federal support for all sectors of the criminal justice system, but warned that the federal government must avoid the impression of control or interference in local affairs in this effort.

The report was issued at a significant time. By 1967, crime rates had risen sharply and were being viewed with growing concern at all levels of government. These views were reinforced by reports issued by the National Advisory Commission on Civil Disorder at this same time. The issue was clearly a national one demanding a national solution.

In a February 6, 1967 message to Congress on "Crime in America," President Johnson proposed a massive categorical assistance program to local governments for law enforcement. The President proposed by-passing state governments, as he had with many other Great Society programs, to provide direct aid to localities. His rationale was simple: law enforcement was a local function and responsibility. The Administration's position was summarized by Attorney General Ramsey Clark during the Congressional hearings on crime which were held in April 1976 "...the state doesn't have the experience, it doesn't have the people, it doesn't make the investment in law enforcement and police that local governments make."[35] The primary concern during the hearings was over the "big brother" image of the federal government and fears of a national police force that would interfere in or dominate local operations. The question of whether the program might more properly be a block grant as opposed to a categorical grant received scant attention.

Passage of an Original Block Grant

Stimulated by the memory of the recent civil riots in Detroit and Washington, D.C., Congressional action was swift. The most notable addition to the bill before the Senate was by Senate Minority Leader Everett M. Dirkson, who introduced an amendment proposing a block rather than a categorical approach. The rationale was that crime reduction would occur only when there was a unified effort based on state planning and supervision.[36] Congressional debate over the measure ended on June 6, 1968, following the assassination of Senator Robert F. Kennedy. The Omnibus Crime Control and Safe Streets Act of 1968 was signed into law by President Johnson on June 19 and became the first major grant mechanism designed as a block grant from the outset.

The Act contained five significant provisions:

- It established a Law Enforcement Assistance Administration (LEAA) to carry out the functions and provisions of the Act.
- It provided for grants of up to 90 percent of the costs of development and operation of state planning agencies. Forty percent of the planning funds available to the state were to be made available to local governments.
- It authorized action block grants for the states. Eighty-five percent of these funds were to be allocated to the states based on population Of this amount, 75 percent must be passed to local governments.
- Grants of 100 percent were authorized for research, demonstration, and training to be administered by the National Institute of Law Enforcement and Criminal Justice. Criminal justice educational assistance loans and grants were also authorized.
- The FY 1969 appropriation authorization was $100 million. Of this amount, $25 million ws for planning grants, $50 million for law enforcement action grants, and $25 million for training, education, and research. The FY 1970 authorization increased this amount threefold—to $300 million.

The LEAA block grant program, as the Omnibus Crime Control and Safe Streets Act became known, apportioned federal funds on a per capita basis among the states to be utilized for any purpose associated with an attempt to reduce crime. Funds were allocated in two parts: first, to support the operations of state planning agencies (SPA's); and second, to assist local governments. Action grants were for the purpose of strengthening the capacities and capabilities of all state criminal justice agencies.

States were required to establish a planning agency in order to qualify for funds (refer to Table 6). This agency was to be supervised by a gubernatorially appointed board of public officials and citizens. The purpose of the state agency was to develop a comprehensive criminal justice plan and to fund projects submitted by local law enforcement agencies. Planning grants were given automatically to qualified states, but action grants were given only after state plans were approved by the LEAA.

The Safe Streets Act was born in a period of considerable social unrest and civil disorder resulting in significant pressures on the Administration and Congress to "do something." These pressures led to the formulation of program goals that were unrealistic and unattainable—creating a frustration and discontent with the LEAA that became increasingly apparent with each passing year.[37] Perhaps the greatest difference between the two block grant programs is related to their funding levels (refer to Table 5). Unlike the Partnership for Health Act which was never generaously funded (indeed many observers have felt that it never had a chance to demonstrate its full potential in the health care field for this reason), substantial sums have been allocated for the Safe Streets Act (literally billions) without significant, at least measurable, results in reduced crime.

The Safe Streets Act was not fully without strings as a purist of the block grant concept might demand. The crime control portion of the block grant is state oriented, but it contains statutory restrictions on the state's use of funds. A 1971 amendment added a program of financial aid for correctional institutions, and in 1974 the Congress passed the Juvenile Justice and Delinquency Prevention Act. In 1976, a fund set-aside was established for neighborhood crime prevention and for juvenile justice programs. Each change reflected a reassessment and adjustment by Congress to respond to the pressures of the times. In 1971, correction was a public issue; in 1973, it was crime control; and in 1974, juvenile justice was a significant public issue. The state planning agencies required under the Act were to establish judicial planning committees. These committees were directed to prepare annual plans which were to be approved by LEAA. Also, state courts were allocated a portion of the state block grant. Other "strings" included various matching requirements at varying rates and the restriction that the amount of funding which could be applied to salaries was limited to one-third of the costs of that particular project.

Through the years, restrictions on the use of funds, creation of new programs, confusing matching requirements, and "earmarking" have changed the nature of the original Act. This same parallel occurred with the Partnership for Health Act. While some of these changes were born of necessity, others were a product of the initial confusion in program goals and objectives. In either case, the experience of the Safe Streets Act suggests that our intergovernmental system is too complex to permit a pure block grant approach. Each attempt to formulate this type of comprehensive, all encompassing program has been met by restrictions that are expedient, politically motivated, necessary, or a requirement generated by social pressures or conditions.

Because the goals of the Safe Streets Act were broad and unrealistic from the start and because adequate evaluation requirements were not incorporated in the Act, its success cannot be determined objectively. The over $7 billion that has been provided in funding has not resulted in a significant decrease in crime in the United States; however, some observers claim that this amount has not been enough, given the magnitude of the problem. Perhaps the best summary of the Act appeared in the 1972 Congressional report on the block grant programs of the LEAA:

> *In some respects the block grant programs have resulted in better coordination of criminal justice agencies and improvements in criminal justice services, but regretably it must be said that they have achieved far less than the Congress and the public rightfully expected considering the vast amounts of public funds which the taxpayer has provided.*[38]

The Comprehensive Employment and Training Act of 1973 (CETA)

The evolution of the Comprehensive Employment and Training Act of 1973 (CETA) reflects its own unique history and little of the block grant experience of the Partnership for Health or Safe Streets programs. If anything, CETA represents a new approach—localization of decisional authority and a broader range of flexibility and local discretion than the previous block grant programs. Seventeen categorical programs were incorporated into Title I of CETA, but they represented only a fraction of the total programs and funds available for federal manpower development. Forty-seven programs, administered by 10 separate federal agencies, currently exist for this purpose. Also, Title I accounts for less than one-fourth of the total federal outlays for manpower and approximately two-fifths of the total CETA appropriation. In short, the federal manpower program effort still is dominated by categorical funding and programs.

In part, the reason for this disparity is, like the Safe Streets program, a reaction to the times at its passage, to its historical evolution, and to the compromises that accompanied its development. The decentralization provisions of the Act were a direct outgrowth of the New Federalism initiatives of the Nixon Administration of the late 1960's and early 1970's. The intent of these initiatives was to move decisional authority away from Washington and the federal bureaucracy and into the hands of the users of these services and programs, while retaining some overview responsibility to ensure that the Congressional intent of the authorizing legislation was fulfilled. The second influence of the times was the national concern about excessively high unemployment that, in some areas such as Detroit, was reaching proportions last seen during the Great Depression of the 1930's. Thus, the Act reflected a mixture of presidential politics, public pressures, and historical precedent.

Heritage of the Manpower Program

Federal involvement in manpower programs goes back almost 60 years, to the Vocational Rehabilitation Administration that grew out of World War I. The heritage of those categorical programs that were aimed at unemployment, and especially at minorities and the disadvantaged in terms of skills, education, or training, is in the programs that emerged from the New Frontier and Great Society programs of the 1960's.[39] Among the major programs that emerged during this decade were vocational education under the Area Redevelopment Act of 1961 (ARA), skills training activities authorized by the Manpower Development and Training Act of 1962 (MDTA), and the antipoverty and work experience programs of the Economic Opportunity Act of 1964 (EOA). Each Act laid a foundation that contributed to the development of CETA.

The ARA reflected national interests in preparing individuals for private sector employment with vocational rehabilitation. It characterized President Kennedy's goal of full employment and was designed primarily to stimulate economic growth in high unemployment areas by authorizing loans to private companies willing either to relocate or expand facilities in economically depressed areas. Participating private firms were authorized worker subsistence and training allowances to help develop a skilled labor market. Local governments were eligible for financial assistance for improvements to public facilities in support of commercial development..

One year after ARA's passage, President Kennedy submitted to Congress an even more comprehensive manpower development program, which ultimately resulted in the Manpower Development and Training Act. The new Act had four main purposes: 1) to meet labor shortage needs, 2) to provide employment opportunities, 3) to provide skills training, and 4) to assist the unemployable and those in the poverty category to become employed.[40] The emphasis was on retraining already skilled workers who had been displaced by the rapid technological advances that followed World War II and the Korean conflict. The eligibility criteria restricted recipients to heads of households with at least three years of job experience. Applied classroom and on-the-job training was emphasized. The classroom training aspect was administered by the Departments of Labor and Health, Education, and Welfare in conjunction with each State Employment Service (SES). On-the-job training programs were administered solely by the DOL.

After a short time, it became evident that the primary beneficiaries of the MDTA training programs were those already well qualified and that minority and the least skilled or hard core unemployed participants were receiving little assistance. This discovery led to changes in the program in 1963 which expanded coverage to include youthful, minority, and poverty level participants and which emphasized job placement for the less qualified. The net effect on employment of these disadvantaged groups and on unemployment in the nation was negligible.[41]

The manpower programs derived from the Great Society movement in this same period moved away from the goal of reducing unemployment for society as a whole to a focus on the problems of poverty and discrimination. The shift was apparent in Congressional amendments to the MDTA which stressed providing tools to the disadvantaged so that they could develop their own ability to escape from poverty. The most significant tools for this attack were provided through the Economic Opportunity Act of 1964 and its 1967 amendments. This arsenal included the Job Corps, the Neighborhood Youth Corps, the Work Experience Program, Community Action Programs, Operation Mainstream, the Concentrated Employment Program, Special Impact, the Service Careers and New Careers Program, and Adult Basic Education Programs.[42] While the programs had different target groups and purposes, their basic thrust was to assist the hard core unemployed. Another feature of these programs was a tendency to bypass state and local governments and to deal directly with nonprofit organizations and community groups on the assumption that state and local governments would not channel the funds to the target groups.

The precedent of bypassing state and local governments and dealing directly with local organizations, and even creating these organizations, was established primarily by the Office of Economic Opportunity (OEO). In short order, this precedent led to a proliferation of duplicative and often ineffective community-based organizations which frequently worked at cross purposes with each other (refer to Chapter II). The coordination problems caused by uncontrolled programs and organizational proliferation became a serious concern. The response to this concern was the creation of an equally confusing host of federal coordinating agencies.

In 1967, the Concentrated Employment Program (CEP) was created to bring the EOA and MDTA programs under a single local sponsor. In 1968, the Cooperative Area Management Planning System (CAMPS) was established by Executive Order to bring together intergovernmental manpower planning and resource allocation. Federal planning grants were awarded to state and local governments to establish CAMPS committees and staffs. The CAMPS committees were to develop local and regional plans to be integrated into state plans for approval by the federal agencies concerned with particular programs.

The CAMPS committees proved relatively ineffective. They encountered a number of obstacles that were beyond their capabilities to overcome. The numerous manpower development programs and agencies that had been created to coordinate this system were just too many to contend with. Many agencies felt that their programs were their own domain and resented outside interference. The CAMPS staffs were not uniformly effective; the quality of state and local plans were often poor; some federal agencies resisted the efforts of the CAMPS; and the planning efforts often became embroiled in state and local political disputes.

The CAMPS effort did establish, however, several precedents that later were to influence the formation of CETA. It established the groundwork for regularized communication and coordination efforts between federal agencies. The funding of state and local CAMPS planning staffs established a cadre of professional planners, and the involvement of the recipient groups in the planning and resource allocation process established a precedent of recipient input.[43] Many planning personnel later were absorbed in the CETA effort, and the participation of the citizen groups was incorporated in the prime sponsor resource allocation process of CETA.

Manpower Revenue Sharing

As part of its New Federalism initiatives, the Administration proposed six "special revenue sharing" proposals in 1971.[44] These proposals were designed to consolidate a number of existing categorical programs into block grants in an effort to reduce "strings" and increase recipient discretion and flexibility in the use of the funds.[45] One of these initiatives was labeled "Manpower Revenue Sharing."

The Manpower Revenue Sharing proposal reflected much of the philosophy and experience gained through the previous manpower programs, especially the decentralization provisions of the Manpower Training Act of 1969 (MTA), a measure that had been vetoed by the President.[46] However this proposal went much further than its predecessors and passed complete decision-making responsibility for resource allocations directly to state and local governmental recipients. In essence, it called for the revamping of the entire manpower grant-in-aid system. The Congressional response was to reject this proposal in favor of a new categorical manpower program, the Emergency Employment Act of 1969 (EEA).

Passage of the EEA represented a setback in the move to consolidate the growing assortment of manpower programs under the block grant authority. In response to Congressional indifference and even hostility to the Administration's six special revenue sharing proposals, President Nixon claimed that he possessed sufficient authority to consolidate manpower programs under provisions of the Economic Opportunity Act.[47] Watergate interfered with his testing of this authority.

Considerable Congressional debate ensued over the issues of decentralization, (local) control over social programs, and the appropriate role and responsibilities of the various agencies. One student of manpower legislation has characterized the key issue as:

...not decentralization and decategorization.... Rather,...the definition of the relationship between federal ,state, and local levels of government and between governments and community action groups in a decentralized , decategorized manpower system.[48]

After over five years of manpower reform efforts by the President and Congress, the signing of the Comprehensive Employment and Training Act by President Nixon on December 28, 1973 was almost anticlimactic. While the Act stressed decentralized control, it also provided a middle ground between recipient discretion and centralized control. Block grants would be provided directly to 500 local and state "prime sponsors" to plan and operate local manpower programs. The Secretary of Labor was made responsible for ensuring that these sponsors complied with the law.

The Comprehensive Employment and Training Act of 1973 contained seven major titles, but Title I was the largest in terms of dollars and scope of services available. Title I replaced several categorical manpower programs, including on-the-job institutional skill training under the MDTA and the work experience programs authorized by the Neighborhood Youth Corps, Operational Mainstream, and others. State and local governments were given authority to devise their own manpower programs and allocate funds accordingly. Funds could be used for the following purposes:

- *Recruitment, orientation, counseling, testing, placement, and follow-up services.*
- *Classroom instruction in organizational skills and other job-related training.*
- *Subsidized on-the-job training by public and private employers.*
- *Allowances for persons in training.*
- *Supportive services such as needed medical care, child care, and assistance in obtaining bonding if needed for employment.*
- *Transitional public employment programs.*[49]

Prime sponsors (eligible governmental units with a population of 100,000 or more) or combinations of local governments could be recipients of the funding and could establish authorized programs. To obtain funding, a prime sponsor had to submit a comprehensive manpower plan to the Secretary of Labor and to appoint staff and a planning council with representation from the client community, local organizations, the employment service, education and training agencies, business, labor, and others.

Two titles of CETA of 1973 provided for public service employment. Title II provided funds for full-time public service jobs. Its original purpose was to provide "transitional" employment in public service areas. This training was supposed to lead to permanent employment in the private or public sector. However, as the recession in 1973-74 deepened, the Department of Labor relaxed its enforcement of this standard. Eligibility for Title II assistance was limited to areas having an unemployment rate of at least 6½ percent. On the other hand, Title VI funds were available regardless of the local unemployment rate; the more severe the unemployment, the greater the amount of funding that could be obtained. Unlike Title II, which stressed longer term impacts, Title VI's purpose was to provide temporary jobs to help solve the immediate unemployment crisis. Both titles gave special consideration to persons who had been unemployed for the longest time.

Title III was a "catch-all" provision of the Act, which permitted grants for manpower services to special groups of persons whose employment needs were not met by other provisions of the Act. For example, programs were available for native Americans, youth, those with limited capability to speak English, ex-offenders, the elderly, and others who were disadvantaged in the labor market.

Title IV consisted of provisions for a "Job Corps" which was transferred to CETA from the Economic Opportunity Act. The Job Corps established training centers to provide remedial academic and skill training for the nation's economically deprived youth.

Finally, Title V established a National Commission for Manpower Policy. The Commission was made up of the heads of several federal agencies, state and local elected officials, persons served by manpower programs, and representatives of other concerned groups. Its task was to identify the nation's manpower needs and goals, conduct research, evaluate the effectiveness of federally assisted manpower programs, and issue an annual report to Congress on its findings. Also, as mentioned previously, Title VI contained provisions for funding temporary jobs during times of special economic stress.

The CETA progrm was renewed in 1975, but expired on June 30, 1976. H.R. 12987, the Emergency Jobs Programs Extension Act of 1976, extended the CETA authorization for FY 1976-77. This Bill (now P.L. 94-444) provided for an increase in the number of persons who could be employed and for a rehiring of current CETA employees. The Emergency Supplemental Appropriations Act of 1976 (P.L. 94-266) also contained funds for CETA-type jobs for disadvantaged youth and for summer recreation employment programs. The CETA program has been renewed annually and is likely to be continued. As one source noted, "...the expiration of the popular CETA program would play havoc with local employment and would add substantially to the nation's unemployment rolls."[50]

ACIR has characterized CETA as a hybrid block grant.[51] Elements of the general revenue sharing concept (decentralization) and the manpower categorical programs (local discretion) were incorporated in the Act. The Act strives for a balance between recipient flexibility and accountability. Its major feature is its reliance on local prime sponsors (as recipients) to determine their own needs and priorities and to develop their own programs. This reliance has led to a number of problems because local officials who were generally unfamiliar with manpower programs "interpreted" the Act more liberally than it was intended and created a number of "negotiation" situations when DOL was forced to compromise rather than to require those jurisdictions to repay funds.[52]

There are also a number of lessons that have been gained from the CETA experience. The first lesson is that change takes time. Previous recipients of categorical programs which may be included under a block grant require a period of adjustment to assimilate new rules, regulations, or procedures. Organizational changes must precede procedural changes. Once the organizational machinery is in place, other changes will flow relatively smoothly. Also, what occurred indirectly in this case was the development at the local level of managerial capacity that will have long term payoffs in increased local capablities to administer more effectively all federal programs. A second lesson is related to the state-local roles. Under CETA, the state is expected to serve as the program manager, an expectation which local recipients view as a needless intrusion in local affairs. Experience indicates that the state's positive role in providing guidance and assistance should be stressed to avoid friction and reduce antipathy. Finally, the block grant concept is not the same as that associated with general revenue sharing. Decentralization does not require or dictate a "hands-off" federal role. The responsible federal agency must ensure accountability to Congress and provide leadership and direction while it allows recipient discretion. The CETA block grant does not negate federal responsibility; it simply changes the nature of recipient involvement in program development and implementation within the broad structure and confines of the authorizing legislation.[53] The federal role is not to be a participant in this process in the sense of a policeman, but rather as a concerned partner. The most important contribution by CETA to the block grant concept has been the development of the concerned partner relationship.

The Housing and Community Development Act of 1974

The Housing and Community Development Act of 1974 (HCDA) was developed through a process of compromise between the Administration's policy goals and the demands of recipient groups which were nurtured by long standing categorical programs. The issues between the Congressional groups debating the measure were embedded so firmly that up to the final day of the conference sessions between the House and the Senate, there was a clear danger of a breakdown that would result in no legislation whatsoever.[54] In the end, the Conference Committee adopted a compromise which established a middle road between Congressional penchants for a strong federal regulatory role and President Nixon's New Federalism emphasis of shifting decisional responsiblity to local governments. While sharing many of the characteristics of the precedent block grant programs, the HCDA reflects its own unique heritage and affords its own contribution to the evolution of the block grant approach.

Legislative Background

Presidential and Congressional concern over the state of housing, particularly in urban areas, has been especially acute following major economic upheavals and wars. Urban blight and the needs of returning veterans have prompted consideration, if not passage, of numerous programs designed to address at least one facet of the problems presented. However, prior to passage of the HCDA, no one program attempted to address the wide range of issues or to provide a level of support designed to have a long term and lasting impact in addressing the problems of urban areas. The HCDA (1974) resulted, in large part, because of an attempt to establish this goal.

After World War II, Congress stated for the first time a national housing goal that was not restrictive or linked to some other policy objective. In the Housing Act of 1949, this goal was clearly stated:

The Congress hereby declares that the general welfare and security of the nation and the health and living standards of its people require housing production and related community development sufficient to remedy the serious housing shortage, the elimination of substandard and other inadequate housing in blighted areas, and the realization as soon as feasible of the goal of a decent house and suitable living environment for every American family, thus contributing to the development and redevelopment of communities and to the advancement of the growth, wealth and security of the nation.[55]

The goal of a "decent house and suitable living environment for every American family" was difficult to define. The 1949 Act interpreted housing broadly; the concept of community development was applied more narrowly. Housing, as applied to community development, referred to land acquisition, slum clearance, and rehabilitation of undesirable land for subsequent resale.

In 1953, President Eisenhower appointed the President's Advisory Committee on Government Housing Policy and Programs to study and recommend changes to the nation's existing housing policy. The Committee's report recommended expansion of the 1949 Act and a shift in urban renewal policy from a piecemeal or block-by-block approach to comprehensive planning to deal with the needs of broader areas within the cities.[56] Each community was to develop a program to attack its urban decay problems. This approach also established a precedent for local participation and involvement that later appeared in the 1974 HCDA.

The Committee's report led to the passage of the Housing Act of 1954 (P.L. 560, 83rd Cong.). The two most significant features of this Act were a change in the concept of urban renewal to urban redevelopment and an introduction to urban planning. The first change meant that rehabilitation could be applied to the repair and restoration of houses, rather than to slum clearance alone, as used in the former sense. The second change meant that all grants would be given to official planning agencies responsible for the urban development planning functions. A number of Acts further expanding the federal interest in urban development policy were passed by Congress in the next few years: Title VIII of the Housing Act of 1961, which provided for the preservation of open space, urban beautification, and historical preservation; Title VII of the Housing Act of 1965, which established grants for water and sewers and neighborhood and land acquisition; and Title I of the Demonstration Cities and Metropolitan Act of 1966, which provided grants for the Model Cities Program.[57] This series of categorical program adjustments created an increasingly confusing system of aid for community development and increased the complexity and difficulty of obtaining assistance.

The Housing Act of 1968 included the creation of Neighborhood Development Programs (NDP's). These programs permitted communities to receive financial assistance for planning and conducting urban renewal projects on a more timely basis than under previous legislation.

By President Nixon's first term, the need for community development program consolidation was becoming apparent even to those who previously had opposed the concept. President Nixon's 1971 State of the Union address was both a culmination of a series of events and a recognition of the need to revise the federal aid system. The first area of reform came in community development. A second program, which provided administrative assistance to local governments, was Planned Variations (refer to Chapter III)). Planned Variations was an experiment that permitted cities participating in the Model Cities Program to reduce some of the paperwork and coordination problems that were part of the original progam. It also later permitted selected cities to utilize additional resources in addressing projects developed in the first phase of the program.

In the following three years, a number of measures were proposed. The Administration advocated the New Federalism philosophy of no federal restrictions on local use of funds, while Congress insisted on sufficient federal control to ensure accountability and the achievement of national objectives. Both Congress and the Administration introduced a long and complex series of proposals, none of which resulted in legislation (see Table 7).

Of the six special revenue sharing proposals pushed by the Administration, the main effort centered on the Better Communities Act (BCA).[58] The goals of the BCA were to distribute funds on the basis of need, to reduce federal regulation, to strengthen local decision-making, and to increase flexibility in the use of the funds. An assessment of the BCA's possible consequences revealed that it might, in effect, lead to less funding for the cities and fewer incentives for elected officials to address the problems of "poverty, discrimination and the inequities in access to decent housing, education, and urban services."[59] For this reason, more than others, the BCA was not well received by Congress.

It was no surprise that the BCA died in Congress, much to the irritation of the Administration. The battle resumed when the Administration

Table 7

Chronology of Measures Leading to The HCDA

March 19, 1970 —	The Housing Consolidation and Simplification Act of 1970.
April 22, 1971 —	The Urban Community Development Special Revenue Sharing Act of 1971.
June 10, 1971 —	The Housing Consolidation and Simplification Act of 1971.
July 8, 1971 —	The Housing and Urban Development Act of 1971 (HR9688).
July 22, 1971 —	The Community Development Act of 1971 (S2333).
December 10, 1971 —	The Brooke-Mondale Housing Reform Amendments of 1971 (Amendments to S2333).
March 2, 1972 —	Senate passes the Housing and Urban Development Act of 1972 (S3248).
April 19, 1973 —	Better Communities Act (HR7277, S1743).
May 9, 1973 —	Community Development Assistance Act of 1973.
July 14, 1973 —	Housing Act of 1973 (S2182)
September 5, 1973 —	Barrett-Ashley Housing and Community Development Act of 1973 (HR10036).
March 11, 1974 —	Housing and Community Development Act of 1974 (S3066).
June 20, 1974 —	Housing and Community Development Act of 1974 (HR15361).
August 22, 1974 —	The Housing and Community Development Act of 1974 signed into law (Public Law 93-383).

resubmitted the BCA later in the year. The Senate and House provided their own measures—the Community Development Assistance Act of 1973 (S. 1744) and the Housing and Community Development Act of 1973 (H.R. 10063). Each Bill was also a resubmittal of previously proposed legislation. This time the Administration and Congress were willing to compromise and a measure finally was proposed that was accepted. After considerable debate and the breaking of new ground in a number of areas, President Gerald R. Ford signed the resulting Housing and Community Development Act of 1974 (P.L. 93-383).

The final Act was a massive eight-title comprehensive bill. It encouraged programs ranging from comprehensive county development and major reforms in federally-assisted housing and planning to new standards for mobile home construction and flexibility in housing credit funding. The funding authorization, the highest to any single programmatic measure in history, was $11.9 billion (refer to Table 5).

The Community Development Block Grant (CDBG) that emerged from this long struggle was a hybrid from the start. It contained a mix of funding mechanisms and program operational devises. While still in the basic form of a decentralized block grant, it included administrative controls to ensure accountability and yet it afforded local discretion. The CDBG represented a combination of past programs in community development. It authorized funds and programs for metropolitan as well as for non-metropolitan areas and attempted to link housing and community development activities. While broadly stating programmatic objectives, the Act was nevertheless restrictive in carefully listing and defining eligible activities. It also permitted a mix of funding mechanisms not characteristic of block grants, such as formula entitlement, discretionary, and hold harmless (assurance that previous recipient funding levels would be maintaned) provisions. However, as opponents feared, the funding mix served to reduce entitlements in some areas.

The various titles of the HCDA were relatively clear-cut in purpose. Title I established authorization for the program, Title II extended and reformed the public housing program, Title III provided mortgage credit assistance, Title IV extended and reformed the comprehensive planning assistance program, Title V extended and reformed the rural housing programs, Title VI dealt with mobile home construction and safety standards, Title VII addressed consumer home mortgage assistance, and Title VIII authorized a number of miscellaneous programs and activities, including amendment of the national housing goal to include more emphasis on preserving existing housing.[60] The Act was broad in scope and ambitious in perspective. In subsequent hearings over amendment of the HCDA, its broad purpose was aptly stated by Senator William Proxmire, Chairman of the Committee on Banking, Housing and Urban Affairs:

The new law was designed to make our cities viable human communities by stimulating housing construction rehabilitation by fostering the elimination and prevention of

*slums and blight, and by achieving other objectives impor-
tant to community life.*[61]

Initial assessment of the Act produced a series of complaints. Detractors noted that it provided no encouragement to local governments for addressing human needs directly; it represented a piecemeal and unbalanced attack on the nation's housing problems; there was no common standard for developing state community affairs agencies; there was no active role for states in the program; funding was insufficient; the distribution of Title I block grants was inequitable; and, finally, the Act's housing titles "show quite clearly the total lack of national commitment."[62] According to the *Washington Post,* "The new Act does not embody any fresh, coherent, comprehensive federal housing policy. Instead it offers the kinds of tinkering and testing which often signify general frustration in a lowering of sights."[63]

A more objective assessment of first-year effects of the Act produced more moderate comments—some positive. Richard Nathan, in a Brookings Institute study, concluded that the basic idea appeared to be working. The HCDA attempted to combine capital expenditure for recipient government use of the funds. Nathan noted that capital spending had clearly dominated first-year allocations and many jurisdictions had used block grant funds as leverage in securing additional private and public capital. Local jurisdictions had exercised greater flexibility in the use of the funds, and local elected officials had been more predominant because their roles became more important under the block grant program than under the previous categoricals.[64]

However, the clear winners and losers were the cities. Because of the distribution in funding provided by the Act, those cities that previously had invested heavily in such programs as urban renewal, the Neighborhood Development Program, and Model Cities were penalized while those that had invested in open space and water and sewer facilities gained. The losing cities were those seeking federal assistance for basic physical and social problems; those that benefited were cities using federal aid for environmental matters and major facilities construction.[65] In relative terms smaller jurisdictions and the suburbs gained at the expense of the older, larger, central cities.

The HCDA of 1977

The Congressional debates over renewal of the Act centered around the issue of who would get the greatest share of the HCDA "pie." The Housing and Community Development Act of 1977, which was signed into law by President Carter on October 17, 1977, contained many modifications to the objectives and character of the basic block grant program.

The most controversial issue raised by the various Congressional committees debating the HCDA concerned the allocation formula. It was resolved by adopting three formula choices from which a jurisdiction could select the option that provides the largest amount of funding. In the three options, the original distribution formula based on population, extent of poverty, and housing overcrowding was retained. For metropolitan

200

cities and urban counties, an allocation formula option was calculated on: 1) the extent of growth lag in the city or county (counted once); 2) the extent of poverty (counted one and one-half times); and 3) the age of the housing in the city or county (counted two and one-half times). For states and non-metropolitan areas, the formula alternative was based upon: 1) the age of housing (counted two and one-half times); 2) the extent of poverty (counted one and one-half times); and 3) population (counted once). These alternatives were designed to produce greater assistance for older central cities with declining populations Also, a part of the 1977 Law included instructions to utilize the funds to meet the needs of low-income and moderate-income families.

The final major addition to the law was a new block grant program for Urban Development Action Grants (UDAG), a pet project of Patricia Harris, who was Secretary of HUD at the time the Act was being considered by Congress. The UDAG authorized a multiyear commitment of funds for the revitalization of distressed neighborhoods.[66]

These modifications quieted some discontent, but they did not solve all the problems. A considerable number of block grant funds still are distributed to the cities that need them least. There is also a bias toward individualized urban problems rather than mutual concerns affecting regions or areas. The 1977 amendments were a decided shift away from a pure block grant concept and nearer to the categorical approach from which the HCDA originated. However, the Act still retains more recipient flexibility than its categorical forerunners and requires less detailed review of proposals while maintaining reasonable federal oversight. The final concern is whether local level officials can resist the temptation to use their new prerogatives for political purposes.

The HCDA in Perspective

The HCDA attacked two perplexing problems inherent in block grant programs: how to allocate funds to best address specific problems and how to maintain a balance between federal oversight and recipient flexibility. The more basic issues are related to purpose—who is to be served, what type of progams should be funded, and what are the program priorities. These decisions have been left to each administration.[67] As a block grant, the HCDA has three distinguishing features: fewer strings are attached; funding allocations are by formula, and federal funding may cover 100 percent of project costs. The only prior submissions required are an application, a three year community development plan, and a plan for meeting housing needs, especially those of low-income families (refer to Table 6). Other features include a "hold harmless" provision (assuring funding for counties at the same level as the year prior to passage of the HCDA) and a set-aside to be used at the discretion of the Secretary of HUD. Of the four block grants reviewed, the HCDA most nearly approaches the model of an ideal block grant as developed by the ACIR.

Block Grants in The Intergovernmental System

The four block grants examined in this Chapter provide a developmental view of the historical or antecedent growth, political compromise, and imaginative formulation of different programs for different purposes. The developmental aspects of each block grant highlight the conceptual and operational trade-offs made to guarantee the survival and longevity of these programs. Block grants mean different things to different people. Charles Schultze, President Johnson's Budget Director and President Carter's Chief Economic Advisor, has called them a "cop out."[68] Enthusiasm has been constrained, and the general response from recipients is one of cautious praise with reservations.[69] Block grants have resulted in reduced paperwork, but primarily at the federal level. Congressional debates continue to be concerned with distribution and allocation questions more than with the appropriateness of the instrument. Block grants are not yet funded at a level that make them more significant than the categorical approach, but they have an impact that is greater than their size in the overall scheme of federal assistance.

One of the benefits of the block grant approach has been the capacity-building potential and the effects of decentralized decision-making. While this learning process has taken time and resulted in costly errors, it will have long term returns in better management and an increased sense of community responsibility.

In addition to managerial development, new systems and organizational expertise have come about, which should assist local governments in dealing more effectively with federal counterparts in the future. One author has even suggested that local program administrators will accrue the same programmatic values as their federal counterparts as a result of this process.[70] Once the local counterpart shares the perspective of the federal program official, policy choices also will be consistent, and the local agency will reflect the same goals and objectives as the federal agency without the necessity for elaborate procedural regulations. While there is no empirical evidence to substantiate this phenomenon, consistency in program administration is a first step toward greater efficiency.

On the negative side, external influence over local decision-making often is construed as one more step toward undue federal influence and interference. There is some evidence of this trend in categorical programs, but none seems to have resulted from block grant programs as, for example, was feared in the Safe Streets Act.[71]

The block grant is basically a formula-based grant with entitlement predetermined by the authorizing legislation. The formula established by Congress determines who the recipients will be and what amounts they will receive, rather than determination by some competitive process which characterizes the categorical approach. The formula usually assures a steady amount of funds that can be incorporated in multi-year planning, thus lending a measure of stability to local budgeting processes. The determination of eligibility and formula have become the critical elements in program allocation. In block grants, more than categorical programs, Congress is influenced in these decisions by organized interests and voting blocks. The losers, without a champion, become the minority groups and those with low-incomes. The winners are usually the more affluent, better educated, organized, and more consistent voters. Thus, the suburbs and counties have gained at the expense of the older, central cities if the experiences with the crime-control, manpower and community development block grants are valid indicators. The cost of political compromise in block grants is high and may be disadvantageous to the groups at which these programs, in categorical form, were targeted.

The greatest advantage of block grants is the flexibility they permit in recipient use of the funds. Recipient flexibility has been variable among the four block grants examined in this Chapter. In the case of Safe Streets and CETA, federal agencies have been accused of being intrusive. Intrusion has not been viewed as a problem with the Partnership for Health or HCDA programs.

The development of a partnership relationship among levels of government has been slow. Local officials sometimes view the state as another layer of bureaucracy between the source of funds and the problems. However, if a state is highly competent and is capable of providing assistance, it can facilitate coordination and can resolve problems or provide technical advice when needed. In this case, state participation may be more welcome. On the other hand, if the state can do no more than add to the paperwork burden, there will be growing resentment against a more activist state role. This area is another case where roles and expectations in block grants should be defined carefully by the authorizing legislation.

There is no doubt that block grants are here to stay. However, for a variety of reasons no new block grants have been enacted into law since 1974, although several consolidation proposals have been introduced. The primary reason for the lack of a movement toward more block grants is the strong resistance to changing categorical programs by the recipient groups which is a "back-lash" to the New Federalism concept that is associated with the Nixon Administration. This resistance was especially apparent in the recent efforts of the Environmental Protection Agency to have an integrated grant program introduced in Congress.[72]

Another reason for the lack of further action on block grants is that they originally were conceived as a grant-in-aid reform mechanism. Although the need for intergovernmental financial aid reform has been apparent for years, Congress has been reluctant to undertake reform of this nature. The reluctance is due, in part, to the low political gains associated with this type of action and, in part, to the number of persons whose interests would be affected did not wish to change the status quo. Given these considerations, members of Congress feel they would lose more than they would gain.

Intergovernmental reform efforts have centered around such changes as the creation of a special office in the Executive Office of the President (a focal point of responsibility) to coordinate and integrate grant-in-aid administration and management (refer to Chapter VII). Another reform thrust has been omnibus in scope and directed at adjustment of administrative procedures. This effort would have all federal grant-in-aid programs administered by uniform, generally applicable federal assistance requirements[73].

Block grants represent a unique chapter in our intergovernmental history. Each block grant program has added to the store of knowledge and experience of the Congress, federal administering agencies, and state and local governments. New coordinative linkages have merged, planning capabilities and managerial capacity have been developed, and increased efficiency in service delivery has resulted. Perhaps the greatest gain has been in the new partnerships that have been developed between the intergovernmental actors. Change takes time, and the experience of the block grant concept is still too new to determine the permanent changes that will result. As yet, there has been no quantitative evaluation of enhanced service delivery or better attainment of national goals as a result of block grants, as opposed to categorical programs, but the prognosis is encouraging.

Notes

1. Title XX of the Social Security Act replaced Titles IV-A and VI of the Social Security Act of 1975. The current funding of Title XX is $2.7 billion. The funds are allocated to the states on the basis of state population. States must develop an annual plan which is submitted to the HEW regional office. As a formula grant of considerable magnitude, Title XX is considered by some to be a fifth block grant; however, because it does not share a history of development nor characteristics similar to the other major block grant programs discussed in this chapter, it has been excluded. Also, as with the Safe Streets Act, Title XX was not the result of categorical program consolidation, but unlike Safe Streets, it was not a New Federalism or Great Society initiative.

2. Advisory Commission on Intergovernmental Relations, Block Grants: A Comparative Analysis, A-60 (Washington, D.C.: GPO, October 1977), p. 6. See also Restructuring Federal Assistance: The Consolidation Approach, Bulletin No. 79-6 (Washington, D.C.: ACIR, October 1979).

3. Ibid.

4. Advisory Commission on Intergovernmental Relations, The Intergovernmental Grant System: An Assessment and Proposed Policies, B1 (Washington, D.C.: GPO, undated), p. 15.

5. Ibid.

6. For discussions of the purposes and origins of federal assistance, see Daniel J. Elazar, The American Partnership: Intergovernmental Cooperation in the Nineteenth Century United States (Chicago: University of Chicago Press, 1962); and W. Brooke Graves, American Intergovernmental Relations: Their Origins, Historical Development and Current Status (New York: Charles Scribner's Sons, 1964).

7. Commission on Organization of the Executive Branch of the Government, Overseas Administration, Federal-State Relations, Federal Research, Report to Congress, March 1949, p. 36.

8. Selma J. Mushkin, "Barriers to a System of Federal Grants-in-Aid," National Tax Journal, XIII, No. 3 (September 1960), p. 198.

9. Carl W. Stenberg and David B. Walker, "The Block Grant: Lessons from Two Early Experiments." Publius, Spring 1977, p. 32.

10. Commission on Organization of the Executive Branch of the Government, Committee on Federal Medical Services, Task Force Report on Federal Medical Services, Appendix O of the Commission Report, January 15, 1949, pp. 64-5.

11. Selma J. Mushkin and John F. Cotton, Sharing Federal Funds for State and Local Needs, Praeger Special Studies in U.S. Economic and Social Development (New York: Praeger Pub., 1969), p. 113.

12. U.S. Commission on Intergovernmental Relations, A Report to the President for Transmittal to Congress, June 1955, pp. 25-52. See also the Commission's Report, Study Committee Report on Federal Aid to Public Health, June 1955. For background information on the development of public programs, see John J. Hanlor, Principles of Public Health Administration, 4th ed. (St. Louis: The C.V. Mosby Co., 1964).

13. Ibid., p. 252.

14. Advisory Commission on Intergovernmental Relations, Modification of Federal Grants-In-Aid for Public Health Services (Washington, D.C.: GPO, January 1961), p. 4.

15. See U.S. Congress, House, Committee on Government Operations, Subcommittee on Intergovernmental Relations, Thirteenth Report: Federal-State-Local Relations, Federal Grants-In-Aid, 85th Cong., 2nd Sess., August 8, 1958, p. 7; and Joint Federal-State Action Committee, Final Report to the President of the United States and to the Chairman of the Governors' Conference (Washington, D.C.: GPO, February 1960), for committee views and attitudes on grant consolidation in this period.

16. Advisory Commission on Intergovernmental Relations, Modification of Federal Grants-In-Aid..., p. 21.

17. Selma J. Mushkin and John F. Cotton, Functional Federalism: Grant-In-Aid and PPB Systems (Washington, D.C.: The George Washington University, 1968), pp. 114 and 189; as quoted in Advisory Commission on Intergovernmental Relations, Block Grants: A Comparative Analysis, A-60 (Washington, D.C.: GPO, October 1977), p. 4; also, Leonard Robins, "The Impact of Converting Categorical into Block Grants: The Lessons from the 314(d) Block Grant in the Partnership for Health Act," Publius, Winter 1976.

18. National Commission on Public Health Services, "Health is a Community Affair," a prepublication of the Report of the National Commission on Community Health Services (Cambridge, Mass: Harvard University Press, 1966).

19. President Johnson, "Advancing the Nation's Health," Special Message to Congress, January 7, 1965, Public Papers of the President, 1965, Vol. 1 (Washington, D.C.: GPO 1966), p. 20.

20. Ibid.

21. See Daniel Elazar, American Federalism: A View From the States, 2nd ed. (New York: Thomas Y. Crowell Co., 1972); and Michael Regan, The New Federalism (New York: Oxford University Press, 1972).

22. U.S. Congress, Senate, Comprehensive Health Planning and Public Health Services Amendments of 1966, S.3008, 89th Cong., 2nd Sess., 1966.

23. For a review of the amendments considered during the congressional hearings, refer to U.S. Congress, Senate, Committee on Labor and Public Welfare, Comprehensive Health Planning and Public Health Services Amendments of 1966, S. Rept. 1965 to Accompany S.3008, 89th Cong., 2nd Sess., 1966; and House Committee on Interstate and Foreign Commerce, Comprehensive Health Planning and Public Services Amendments of 1966, Hearings.

24. Advisory Commission on Intergovernmental Relations, The Partnership for Health Act: Lessons From a Pioneering Block Grant, A-56 (Washington, D.C.: GPO, January, 1977).

25. U.S. Congress, House, Committee on Interstate and Foreign Commerce, Partnership for Health Amendments of 1967, Hearings before the House Committee on Interstate and Foreign Commerce on H.R. 6418, 90th Cong., 1st Sess., 1967.

26. U.S. Congress, House, Committee on Interstate and Foreign Commerce, Health Revenue Sharing and Health Services Act of 1974, Report Together with Minority and Additional Views, 93rd Cong., 2nd Sess., 1974 (House Report No. 93-1161).

27. President Ford, Memorandum of Disapproval, Disapproval of the Health Revenue Sharing and Health Services Act of 1974, December 23, 1974.

28. U.S. Congress, House, Committee on Interstate and Foreign Commerce, Health Services Programs, Hearings Before the Subcommittee on Health and the Environment on H.R. 2954 and H.R. 2955, 94th Cong., 1st Sess., February 19, 1975.

29. Refer to Advisory Commission on Intergovernmental Relations, The Partnership for Health Act: Lessons..., pp. 21-23.

30. Ibid., p. 21.

31. National goals generally are described as those which would benefit all segments of society. Thus, the Partnership for Health Act also attempted to address problems that went beyond the borders of any one jurisdiction. For one view of the purpose of federal goals, see G. Gregory Raab, "Comprehensive Health Care: The Role of Government in Planning and Regulations," Newsletter, Vol. 52, No. 5 (Charlottesville, Virginia: University of Virginia, January 1976).

32. President Johnson, Message to Congress, "Crime, Its Prevalence and Measures of Prevention," March 8, 1965.

33. Law Enforcement Assistance Act of 1965, P.L. 89-197 (September 22, 1965).

34. Advisory Commission on Intergovernmental Relations, Making the Safe Streets Act Work: An Intergovernmental Challenge (Washington, D.C.: GPO, 1970), p. 8.

35. U.S. Congress, House, Committee on the Judiciary, Subcommittee No. 5, Anti-Crime Hearings, 90th Cong., 1st Sess., 19067, p. 65. See also U.S. Congress, Senate, "General Minority Views." The Omnibus Crime Control and Safe Streets Act of 1967, 90th Cong., 2nd Sess. 1968.

36. Advisory Commission on Intergovernmental Relations, Safe Streets Reconsidered: The Block Grant Experience 1968-1975, A-55 (Washington, D.C.: GPO, January 1977), p. 14. See also Carl W. Stenberg and David B. Walker, "The Block Grant: Lessons from Two Early Experiments," Publius, Spring 1977.

37. See, for example, "Bell Proposes LEAA Demise," County News, December 19, 1977. For a discussion on the purposes of block grants comparing each of the programs, see Advisory Commission on Intergovernmental Relations, Block Grants: A Roundtable Discussion, A-51 (Washington, D.C.: GPO, October 1976); and for state and local perspectives, see Morris Ploscowe, "Federal, State, and Local Responsibility in Connection with Crime Control," Tax Policy, Vol 35, Nos. 7-8 (July-August 1968).

38. U.S. Congress, House, Committee on Government Operations, Block Grant Programs of the Law Enforcement Assistance Administration, p. 6, quoted in ACIR, Safe Streets Reconsidered:..., p. 28.

39. For a detailed history of federal manpower programs, see Garth L. Mangum, The Emergence of Manpower Policy (New York: Holt, Rinehart, and Winston, Inc., 1969).

40. See Garth L. Mangum and John Walsh, A Decade of Manpower Develop-

ment and Training (Salt Lake City, Utah: Olympus Pub. Co., 1973).

41. Evan Clague and Leo Kramer, Manpower Policies and Programs: A Review, 1935-75 (Kalamazoo, Mich.: The W.E. Upjohn Insititute for Employment Research 1975), pp. 10-16.

42. For complete descriptions of these programs, see, U.S. Department of Labor, Employment and Training Report of the President (Washington, DC.: GPO, 1976).

43. Advisory Commission on Intergovernmental Relations, The Comprehensive Employment and Training Act: Early Readings from a Hybrid Block Grant, A-58 (Washington, D.C: GPO, June 1977), pp. 5-6.

44. In his January 22, 1971 State of the Union Address, President Nixon proposed the consolidation of 130 categorical programs into six special revenue sharing packages: education, law enforcement, manpower training, rural community development, urban community development, and transportation.

45. For a complete discussion of the special revenue sharing initiatives, see Advisory Commission on Intergovernmental Relations, An Analysis of the Administration's Grant Consolidation Proposals, M-70 (Washington, D.C.: GPO, 1971).

46. The proposed bill contained provisions for decentralization and the creation of a federal job program that proved obnoxious to the Administration.

47. See U.S. Department of Labor, Manpower Report of the President, 1973 (Washington, D.C.: GPO, 1973).

48. Robert Guttman, "Intergovernmental Relations Under the New Manpower Act," Monthly Labor Review, June 1974) p. 11.

49. U.S. Department of Labor, Manpower Administration, "The New Manpower Act—A Summary," reprinted from Manpower Magazine, March, 1974. The provision for transitional public employment has led to a number of problems. Some cities have utilized Title I funds to relieve public employees laid-off as a result of the recession. This has led to disputes with DOL which maintains that the intent of Congress was Title I funds to be spent for training the hard-core unemployed. See Andrij Bilyk, "CETA Title I: A Case of Priorities," Nation's Cities, February 1976, pp. 14-15.

50. Quoted in Marvis Mann Reeves and Parris N. Glendening, "Federal Actions Affecting Counties," The County Year Book, 1977 (Washington, D.C.: National Association of Counties, 1977), p. 43.

51. See Advisory Commission on Intergovernmental Relations, The Comprehensive Employment and Training Act: Early Readings....

52. See, for example, Andrij Bilyk, "CETA Title I...."

53. Advisory Commission on Intergovernmental Relations, The Comprehensive Employment and Training Act: Early Readings from a Hybrid Block Grant, A-58., pp. 60-61. Other excellent sources of information about CETA, its evaluation, formulation, and interpretation can be found in the following: The Grantsmanship Center News (May-July 1976); Center for Law and Social Policy, How to Monitor

Federally-Funded Public Service Employment Programs (Washington, D.C.); General Accounting Office, Programs and Problems in Allocating Funds Under Titles I and II—CETA (Washington, D.C.: GPO); National Urban Coalition, Community Manpower Workbook (Washington, D.C.: National Urban Coalition, 1974); and the Center for Community Change, Federal Programs Monitor, a bimonthly newsletter (Washington, D.C.: Center for Community Change).

54. Mary K. Nenno, "The Housing and Community Development Act of 1974: An Interpretation; Its History," Journal of Housing (August 1974), p. 345.

55. Sec. 2, "Declaration of National Housing Policy," Housing Act of 1949, underlining Added.

56. The President's Advisory Committee on Government Housing Policies and Programs, Government Policy and Programs: A Report (Washington, D.C.: GPO, 1953), p. 1.

57. Advisory Commission on Intergovernmental Relations, Community Development: The Workings of a Federal-Local Block Grant, A-57 (Washington, D.C.: GPO, March 1977), p. 4 ff.

58. H.R. 7277, 93rd Cong., 1st Sess., 1973; S. 1742, 93rd Cong., 1st Sess., 1973.

59. Richard T. LeGates and Mary C. Morgan, "The Perils of Special Revenue Sharing for Community Development," AIP Journal, July 1973, p.254. For an assessment of the impacts, see J. Burby, "Revenue Sharing: Democrats Seek Alternatives to Neutralize Sharing as a Political Issue," National Journal, April 3, 1971, pp. 719-730; Office of Evaluation, Community Development and Planning, HUD, Community Development Block Grant Program—Urban Counties: The First Year Experience (Washington, D.C.: GPO, June 1977).

60. For a detailed discussion of the Act and its various titles, see Mary K. Nenno, pp.345-363; and David Garrison, "Community Development Block Grants: A Whole New Ball Game for City Hall," Nation's Cities, November 1974, pp. 49-58.

61. U.S. Senate, Committee on Banking, Housing and Urban Affairs, Hearings Before the Committee on Banking, Housing, and Urban Affairs, 94th Cong., 2nd Sess., (Washington, D.C.: GPO, August 23-26, 1976), p. 1.

62. Albert L. Hydeman, Jr., and Eugene R. Eisman, "Community Development and the States," Planning, January 1976, p. 14. For additional complaints about the HCDA, see Mary K. Nenno, "First Year Community Development Grant Experience: What Does It Mean?," Journal of Housing, April 1976; and Karen Kerns, "Community Development Block Grants: The First Year," Nation's Cities, July 1975.

63. Quoted in Arthur J. Magida, "Housing Report/Major Programs's Revised to Stress Community Control," National Journal, September 14, 1974, p. 1376.

64. Richard P. Nathan, et.al., "Monitoring the Block Grant Program for

Community Development," <u>Political Science Quarterly</u>, Vol. 92, No.2 (Summer 1977), pp. 221-2.

65. Richard Delson and Richard LeGates, <u>Redistribution Effects of Special Revenue Sharing for Community Development</u>, Working Paper #17 (Berkeley, Calif.: Institute of Government Studies, 1976), p. 22; also Richard P. Nathan, et.al., <u>Block Grants for Community Development</u>, U.S. Department of Housing and Urban Development (Washington, D.C.: GPO, January 1977).

66. See M. Carter McFarland, <u>Federal Goverment and Urban Problems: HUD Successes, Failures, and the Fate of Our Cities</u> (Boulder Colo.: Westview Press, 1978); "House Boosts Aid Share for Older Cities," <u>Congressional Quarterly</u>, May 14, 1977; "Administration Targets Aid to Aging Cities," <u>Congressional Quarterly</u>, March 5, 1977; and Rochelle L. Stanfield, "Civil War Over Cities' Aid—The Battle No One Expected." <u>National Journal</u>, August 6, 1977.

67. Bernard J. Frieder and Marshall Kaplan, "Urban Aid Comes Full Cycle," <u>Civil Rights Digest</u>, Spring 1977, pp. 12-23. See also John D. Szabd, "Urban Report/Community Development Progam Shows Signs of Progress," <u>National Journal</u>, November 29, 1975; and Rochelle L. Stanfield, "Government Seeks the Right Formula for Community Development Funds," <u>National Journal</u>, February 12, 1977.

68. From a speech delivered at the first National Conference on Congregate Housing for Older People, Washington, D.C., November 1975.

69. See, for example, M. Carter McFarland, <u>Federal Government...</u>, and Advisory Commission on Intergovernmental Relations, <u>Block Grants: A Comparative Analysis,....</u>

70. Edward J. Clynch, "The Nationalization of Block Grant Spending: An Initial Determination," <u>Publius</u>, Winter 1976.

71. <u>Ibid.</u>

72. The measure was finally introduced when the title of the Act (as well a other amendments) was changed from the Consolidated Environmental Assistance Act to the Integrated Environmental Assistance Act of 1979 (H.R. 4213 and S. 1136).

73. One such recent proposal is the Federal Assistance Reform Act of 1979 (S-878). This approach establishes generally applicable requests and authorizes the President to designate a single rule-making agency to establish standard rules and regulations in each area.

CHAPTER VI SELECTED BIBLIOGRAPHY
Articles/Documents

"Administration Targets Aid to Aging Cities," Congressional Quarterly. March 5, 1977.

Advisory Commission on Intergovernmental Relations. An Analysis of the Administration's Grant Consolidation Proposals, M-70. Washington, D.C.: GPO, 1971.

_____. Block Grants: A Comparative Analysis, A-60. Washington, D.C.: GPO, October 1976.

_____. Block Grants: A Roundtable Discussion, A-51. Washington, D.C.: GPO, October 1976.

_____. Community Development: The Workings of a Federal-Local Block Grant, A-57. Washington, D.C.: GPO, March 1977.

_____. Making the Safe Streets Act Work: An Intergovernmental Challenge. Washington, D.C.: GPO, 1970.

_____. Modification of Federal Grants-In-Aid for Public Health Services. Washington, D.C.: GPO, January 1961.

_____. Safe Streets Reconsidered: The Block Grant Experience 1968-1975, A-55. Washington, D.C.: GPO, January 1977.

_____. The Partnership for Health Act: Lessons From a Pioneering Block Grant, A-56. Washington, D.C.: GPO, January 1977.

_____. The Comprehensive Employment and Training Act: Early Readings From a Hybrid Block Grant, A-58. Washington, D.C.: GPO, June 1977.

_____. The Intergovernmental Grant System: An Assessment and Proposed Policies, B1. Washington, D.C.: GPO (undated).

"Bell Proposes LEAA Demise," County News. December 19, 1977.

Bilyk, Andrij. "CETA Title I: A Case of Priorities," Nation's Cities. February 1976.

Burby, J. "Revenue Sharing: Democrats Seek Alternatives to Neutralize Sharing as a Political Issue," National Journal. April 3, 1971.

Center for Community Change. Federal Programs Monitor (A Bimonthly Newsletter). Washington, D.C.: Center for Community Change.

Center for Law and Social Policy. How to Monitor Federally-Funded Public Service Employment Programs. Washington, D.C.: Center for Law and Social Policy, 1976.

Clynch, Edward J. "The Nationalization of Block Grants Spending: An Initial Determination," Publius. Winter 1976.

Commission on Organization of the Executive Branch of the Government, Committee on Federal Medical Services. Task Force Report on Federal Medical Services. Appendix O of the Commission Report, January 15, 1949.

Commission on Organization of the Executive Branch of the Government. Overseas Administration, Federal-Site Relations, Federal Research. Report to Congress, March 1949.

Delson, Richard and LeGates, Richard. Redistribution Effects of Special Revenue Sharing for Community Development, Working Paper #17. Berkeley, Cal.: Institute of Governmental Studies, 1976.

Frieder, Bernard J. and Kapan, Marshall. "Urban Aid Comes Full Cycle," Civil Rights Digest. Spring 1977.

Garrison, David."Community Development Block Grants: A Whole New Ball Game for City Hall," Nation's Cities. November 1974.

Guttman, Robert. "Intergovernmental Relations Under the New Manpower Act," Monthly Labor Review. June 1974.

"House Boosts Aid Share for Older Cities." Congressional Quarterly. May 14, 1977.

Hydeman, Albert L. Jr. and Eismann, Eugene R. "Community Development and the States," Planning. January 1976.

Joint Federal-State Action Committee. Final Report to the President of the United States and to the Chairman of the Governors' Conference. Washington, D.C.: GPO, February 1960.

Kerns, Karen. "Community Development Block Grant: The First Year," Nation's Cities. July 1975.

LeGates, Richard T. and Morgan, Mary C. "The Perils of Special Revenue Sharing for Community Development," AIP Journal. July 1973.

Magida, Arthur J. "Housing Report/Major Programs Revised to Stress Community Control," National Journal. September 14, 1974.

Muskin, Selma J. "Barriers to a System of Federal Grant-In-Aid," National Tax Journal. Vol XIII, No. 3 (September 1960).

_____ and Cotton, John F. Functional Federalism: Grant-In-Aid and PPB Systems. Washington, D.C.: The George Washington University, 1968.

Nathan, Richard P. "Monitoring the Block Grant Program for Community Development," Political Science Quarterly, Vol. 92, No. 2 (Summer 1977).

_____., et al. Block Grants for Community Development. U.S. Department of Housing and Urban Development. Washington, D.C.: GPO, January 1977.

National Urban Coalition. Community Manpower Workbook. Washington, D.C.: National Urban Coalition, 1974.

Nenno, Mary K. "First Year Community Development Grant Experience: What Does It Mean?," Journal of Housing. April 1976.

_____. "The Housing and Community Development Act of 1974: An Interpretation; Its History," Journal of Housing. August 1974.

Office of Evaluation, Community Development and Planning, HUD. Community Development Block Grant Program—Urban Counties: The First Year Experience. Washington, D.C.: GPO, June 1977.

Plowcowe, Morris, "Federal, State, and Local Responsibility in Connection with Crime Control," Tax Policy, Vol. 35, Nos. 7-8 (July-August 1968).

President Ford.Memorandum of Disapproval. Disapproval of the Health Revenue Sharing and Health Services Act of 1974. December 23, 1974.

Raab, G. Gregory. "Comprehensive Health Care: The Role of Government in Planning and Regulations," Newsletter. Vol. 52, No. 5. Charlottesville, Virginia: University of Virginia, January 1976.

Robins, Leonard. "The Impact of Converting Categorical into Block Grants: The Lessons From the 314(d) Block Grant in the Partnership for Health Act," Publius. Winter 1976.

Stanfield, Rochelle L. "Civil War Over Cities' Aid—The Battle No One Expected," National Journal. August 6, 1977.

_____ . "Government Seeks the Right Formula for Community Development Funds," National Journal. February 12, 1977.

Stenberg, Carl W. and Walker, David B. "The Block Grant: Lessons From Two Early Experiments," Publius. Spring 1977.

Szabd, John C. "Urban Report/Community Development Program Shows Signs of Progress," National Journal. November 29, 1975.

The Grantsmanship Center News. May-June 1976.

The President's Advisory Committee on Governmental Housing Policies and Programs. Government Policies and Programs: A Report. Washington, D.C.: GPO, 1953.

U.S. Commission on Intergovernmental Relation. A Report to the President for Transmittal to Congress. June 1955.

U.S. Congress, House, Committee on Government Operations. Block Grant Programs of the Law Enforcement Assistance Administration. Quoted in Advisory Commission on Intergovernmental Relations. Safe Streets Reconsidered: The Block Grant Experience 1968-1975, A-55. Washington, D.C.: GPO, January 1977.

U.S. Congress, House, Committee on Government Operation Subcommittee on Intergovernmental Relation. Thirteenth Report: Federal-State-Local Relations. Federal Grants-In-Aid. 85th Cong. 2nd Sess., 1974.

U.S. Congress, House, Committee on Interstate and Foreign Commerce. Health Revenue Sharing and Health Services Act of 1974, Report Together with Minority and Additional Views. 93rd Cong., 2nd Sess., 1966.

U.S. Congress, Senate, Committee on Labor and Public Welfare. Comprehensive Health Planning and Public Health Services Amendments of 1966, Senate Report 1965 to Accompanying S. 3008. 89th Cong., 2nd Sess., 1966.

U.S. Department of Labor. Employment and Training Report of the President. Washington, D.C.: GPO, 1976.

_____ . Manpower Report of the President, 1973. Washington, D.C.: GPO, 1973.

_____ . Manpower Administration. "The New Manpower Act—A Summary," Reprinted from Manpower Magazine. March 1974.

Books

Clague, Evan and Kramer, Leo. Manpower Policies and Programs: A Review

1935-75. Kalamazoo, Michigan: The W.E. Upjohn Institute for Employment Research, 1975.

Elazar, Daniel H. American Federalism: A View From the States. 2nd ed. New York: Thomas Y. Crowell Co., 1972.

_____ . The American Partnership: Intergovernmental Cooperation in the Nineteenth Century United States. Chicago: University of Chicago Press, 1962.

Graves, Brooke W. American Intergovernmental Relations: Their Origins, Historical Development and Current Status. New York: Charles Scribner & Sons, 1964.

Hanlor, John J. Principles of Public Health Administration. 4th ed. St. Louis: The C.V. Mosby Co. 1964.

Mangum. Garth L. The Emergence of Manpower Policy. New York: Holt, Rinehart, and Winston, Inc., 1969.

_____ . and Walsh, John. A Decade of Manpower Development and Training. Salt Lake City, Utah: Olympus Publishing Co., 1973.

McFarland, M. Carter. Federal Government and Urban Problems: HUD Successes, Failures, and the Fate of Our Cities. Boulder, Colorado: Westview Press, 1978.

Muskin, Selma J. and Cotton, John F. Sharing Federal Funds for State and Local Needs. Praeger Special Studies in U.S. Economic and Social Development. New York: Praeger Publishing, 1969.

National Commission on Public Health Services. "Health Is a Community Affair," a prepublication of the Report of the National Commission on Community Health Services. Cambridge, Mass: Harvard University Press, 1966.

Reagan, Michael. The New Federalism. New York: Oxford University Press, 1972.

Hearings

U.S. Congress, House, Committee on Interstate and Foreign Commerce. Comprehensive Health Planning and Public Services Amendments of 1966, Hearings.

_____ . Health Services Programs, Hearings Before the Subcommittee on Health and the Environment on H.R. 2954 and H.R. 2955. 94th Cong., 1st Sess., February 19, 1975.

_____ . Partnership for Health Amendments of 1967, Hearings Before the House Committee on Interstate and Foreign Commerce on H.R. 6418. 90th Cong., 1st Sess., 1967.

U.S. Congress, House Committee on the Judiciary, Subcommittee No. 5. Anti-Crime Hearings. 90th Cong, 1st Sess., 1967.

U.S. Congress, Senate. "General Minority Views," The Omnibus Crime Control and Safe Streets Act of 1967. 90th Cong., 2nd Sess., 1968.

_____ . Committee on Banking, Housing and Urban Affairs. Hearings Before the Committee on Banking, Housing and Urban Affairs. 94th Cong., 2nd Sess. Washington, D.C.: GPO, August 23-26, 1976.

Chapter Seven
Managing Federalism

Collectively, the federal assistance system is an array of often conflicting activities and initiatives which defy understanding to all but the most serious students of this system. All programs have commendable objectives, but the growth has had detrimental side effects on the intergovernmental management system.[1]

Elmer B Staats
Comptroller General
of the United States
1979

Introduction

Significant changes have occurred in the federal grant-in-aid system during the past decade. Grants to state and local governments have increased by over 400 percent and in Fiscal Year 1982 are estimated to exceed $84 billion. Today, the federal grant-in-aid system is equivalent to a major industry which has substantial impact on our national economy as well as on the financial stability of state and local government.

The purpose of this chapter is to discuss and explore the impacts of these changes and the administrative and management adjustments that have occurred in the period following the era of New Federalism. President Carter initiated a series of administrative changes to the grant-in-aid system upon assuming office in 1977. These changes were more in terms of the enforcement of existing policies rather than new initiatives. However, these adjustments appeared to have greater impacts than reform measures that had been attempted by previous administrations.

Two reform trends have become evident from an assessment of intergovernmental events of the 70's. The first trend indicates a more activist role for state governments in the intergovernmental partnership. The second is a movement toward long-needed reform of the federal grant-in-aid system. This chapter focuses on this trend, which is highlighted by the comprehensive study of the federal assistance system that was mandated by the Federal Grant and Cooperative Agreement Act of 1977 (P.L. 95-224). The reform efforts of the Carter Administration and the final results of this study effort are indicators of the emergence of a new era in federal-state-local relationships, an era where government is becoming proactive rather than just reactive.

Even more significant than the growth in federal funding have been the changes in administrative rules and regulations associated with the grant-in-aid system. As the aggregate level of federal funding has grown, federal agencies have increased their efforts to ensure compliance with the terms, conditions, and purposes of intergovernmental program legislation. The mandated OMB study indicated that there are now 59 cross-cutting, generally applicable requirements of this nature, and the number continues to grow. All of these requirements add to the costs of the administrative overhead for assistance recipients as well as for the federal agencies involved. They demand staff time and resources that decrease the ability of program officials to carry out the very programs they are responsible for implementing.

Intergovernmental Reform
Under the Carter Administration

In his campaign for the Presidency in 1975, one of candidate Carter's themes was a promise of governmental reorganization to promote efficiency and effectiveness. This promise by a presidential candidate was hardly a new one, but it was one that President Carter took seriously upon assuming office in 1977. The thrust of the effort was a series of administrative reform action coupled with support in the development of Congressional initiatives aimed at longer term, broader, more comprehensive change. However, unlike previous reform intitiatives by an administration, the President's directives were initiated by Presidential memoranda or executive order and reached to the heart of the problems. Some problems were alleviated, some paperwork was reduced or eliminated and some measure of order as instituted in the system. This piecemeal approach to intergovernmental reform is palatable to the general public, the interest groups, Congress, and the bureaucrats alike. More drastic reform usually is not. The result of these efforts to date has been some improvement, but the basic problems still exist. The federal assistance system still requires major substantive reform.

The Carter Administration and the 95th Congress have made a number of attempts to improve and simplify the grant-in-aid system, now more accurately called the federal assistance system. Among the more significant efforts have been the following:

1. July 19, 1977—Review of all federal planning requirements which are part of federal assistance programs.

    An OMB study group, convened for this purpose, identified over 4,000 planning requests attached to 162 federal assistance programs administered by 17 federal agencies. Following the OMB study group's report in early June 1978, President Carter directed the heads of executive departments to "eliminate, correct and rewrite the identified planning requirements." This resulted in an OMB directive to this effect, which was issued on August 14, 1978.[2]

2. September 9, 1977— White House memoranda "Cutting Federal Red Tape for State and Local Grant Recipients"and "Sharing Federal Audit Plans."

    In an effort to "simplify and streamline" the federal aid system, President Carter initiated a series of White House memoranda to the heads of executive departments and agencies. The first contained 12 steps designed to simplify the grants process in three areas: application and reporting, regulation revision, and grants payments. Agencies were directed to comply with these directives.[3]

    The second memorandum had the same purpose as the first, but also was designed to enhance federal-state-local cooperative efforts as well as to develop a better federal image. In the directive

"Sharing Federal Audit Plans," President Carter instructed agencies to make plans for auditing state and local government recipients available to those agencies so that federal audits could be coordinated with other audit requirements.[4]

3. March 23, 1978—White House memorandum and Executive Order 102044.

   A third White House memorandum related to federal assistance reform resulted in an executive order to promote and encourage state and local participation in the development of federal regulations. The order was designed to make state and local governments, as well as public interest groups, more active partners in the intergovernmental process. It also resulted in the recision of OMB Circular A-85, which was the same as the White House order but did not fulfill its objectives (see Chapter I).

4. March 27, 1978—Creation of the Interagency Coordinating Council (IACC).

   As part of the Administration's efforts to improve its urban policy and programs, President Carter created the IACC. The IACC was comprised of high-level federal agency officials representing agencies with urban programs. These officials were brought together to discuss needed improvements, to examine local development plans, and to resolve interagency conflicts. The IACC was chaired by the President's Cabinet Secretary and Assistant for Intergovernmental Affairs, Jack H. Watson, Jr. The IACC, which replaced the Domestic Council, continues to coordinate the development of domestic policy.

THE WIZARD OF ID by permission of Johnny Hart and Field Enterprises, Inc.

Of these initiatives, the one having the most significant impact was the September 9, 1977 White House memorandum "Cutting Red Tape for State and Local Government Recipients." The September statement indicated reform measures in five areas of grants management in an effort to "...prevent the waste of tax dollars...(and) ensure that the money which is spent produces superior results."[5] The first reform was to simplify and reduce federal agency application, reporting, and planning requirements. Second, administrative reforms were initiated related to federal financial management practices. Third, federal audit processes were simplified. Fourth, agencies were directed to assess requirements related to cross-cutting regulations designed to achieve national goals; and fifth, steps were suggested to improve the process by which federal regulations are developed and issued. A subsequent White House release indicated a partial listing of 20 actions taken by 12 federal agencies to reduce significantly "bureaucratic red tape" in response to this directive.

Federal agency heads were directed to take immediate steps to implement the memoranda and deadlines were established. The first follow-up came on March 13, 1978, when Jack Watson initiated a memorandum to all federal agency intergovernmental coordinators (positions that had been created by the September 7 action) "for consulting with state and local leaders and for ensuring that their views are reflected in the development of departmental policy."[6] Watson was asked to perform the initial follow-up to assess agency progress in responding to the President's directive. Watson's review indicated that federal agencies had indeed taken the Presidential memoranda seriously and had initiated a number of actions in compliance with both the letter and "spirit" of the directive.

The response to the President's suggestions to cut red tape was considerable. A sampling of paperwork reduction efforts by executive agencies revealed that genuine savings were possible and indeed had been initiated. In the area of grant application requirements, the Environmental Protection Agency reduced their requirements by 25 percent; the Urban Mass Transit Administration reduced theirs by 50 percent. Other agencies reported similar savings.[7] While this reduction may not appear significant, some grant applications run hundreds of pages in length, and the cost-savings in paper, staff time, and postage add up to staggering sums.

A second area of response was that of initiating grants payments through letters of credit as opposed to checks. Checks, which take more time to process, often are difficult to associate with a specific grant program. The Department of Health, Education, and Welfare converted 196 grant recipients to letters of credit, and all of the Departments of Energy and Interior active grants were converted. In total, 4,725 new letters of credit were added to the existing 17,120, which brought the dollar outlay for these letters in FY 1978 to $84.7 billion. Also, a number of agencies converted to the electronic fund transfer system; almost every federal agency adopted the recommended check labeling system; six programs were brought under the advance funding system; and OMB began a review of federal cash management practices to investigate all possible avenues for savings and elimination of unnecessary federal costs in all areas of government activity.[8]

The third area, and perhaps the one creating the most friction with state and local recipients of federal assistance, was in the development of regulations. In his March 23 implementing memorandum to Executive Order 12044, the President instructed agencies to ensure that their regulations reflected consultation with state and local officials, that they contained "grandfather" clauses (so that changed regulations would not affect grantees in the middle of a project year), and that they were simplified and in plain English. In response, the Department of Energy, the Department of Labor, the Department of Housing and Urban Development, the Department of Transportation, the Department of Agriculture, the Environmental Protection Agency, the Department of Justice, the Department of Commerce, the Department of Treasury, and the Department of Health, Education, and Welfare all took steps to ensure public comment on proposed rule changes, as well as on procedures to permit grantees to complete the grant year before implementing rule changes. The greatest number of agency actions occured in the area of regulation review and simplification.[9] One of the most significant and far-reaching actions was that taken by HEW.

Then Secretary of HEW Joseph A Califano, Jr. served as the Cabinet leader in initiating changes representative of Administration policy. As leader of the largest federal domestic funding agency and the one alleged to have the most complicated administrative problems, Secretary Califano's actions also had the most impact. Augmenting the impact of size is the fact that in most areas of the country, HEW functions as the "cognizant" (or responsible) audit agency in administering audit requirements for all federal programs. Thus, HEW actions represented the Administration's position and attitude more clearly than those of any other agency. In a September 19, 1977 memorandum, Secretary Califano announced Operation Common Sense, "a comprehensive effort to review, simplify, and whenever possible, abbreviate HEW's massive program and administrative regulations."[10] The Secretary announced a "top-to-bottom" overhaul of HEW's methods for developing regulations so that new regulations would reflect the President's standards, which called for "necessity, simplicity, timeliness, and clarity."[11] A parallel action was initiated by HUD with the establishment of a Grant Review Task Force on June 23, 1978.

Perhaps more significant to the assistance recipient community were Califano's earlier actions in grant and contract management. In early 1977, before the President's announced reform measures and virtually ignored by the press, Secretary Califano instituted a far-reaching series of administrative actions, which were not designed to ease the burden on state and local assistance recipients, but rather to enforce *existing* policy and to tighten controls over federal program officials. The directive applied to all HEW Assistant Secretaries and major department heads responsible for HEW's $7 billion grant and procurement systems. The strategy obviously was based on a "trickle down" theory which assumes that high level enforcement and control will impact on each succeeding lower level.

The Califano memorandum called for enforcement of grant and contract policies on six points: failure to schedule procurement and grant awards properly (dispursing too many funds at the end of the fiscal year, rather than throughout the year); failure to protect the government's interests in competitive procurement (not ensuring adequate competition for contracts); failure to limit noncompetitive procurement (not using existing procurement procedures); failure to ensure that contracts and grants were performed properly; failure to comply with established award procedures (presence of favoritism, conflicts of interest and subjectivity in the award of discretionary grants); and inadequate price and cost analysis (inadequate cost advisory analysis procedures).[12]

The effects of this memorandum were immediately apparent throughout HEW and caused a shock wave, especially in the academic community. On August 24, 1977, the Committee on Governmental Relations of the National Association of College and University Business Officers initiated a letter to all members warning colleges and universities to pay special heed to the Califano memorandum. They pointed out the effect of an HEW suspension of a letter of credit for a major university because it failed to submit its quarterly financial report, one of the points of the Califano memorandum.[13] Clearly, the President, through HEW, signaled that not only should the system be simplified to relieve grantee burdens but also that existing management procedures should be enforced. This action was especially surprising to officials of colleges and universities, who felt that non-compliance threats from federal agencies could be ignored as they had in the past.[14] Secretary Califano continued this new "tough" enforcement policy with a February 16, 1978 release directed at assuring that colleges and universities and other recipients of grants and contracts should maintain accounting and other support systems which would control and protect the use of federal monies.[15].

Planning and Regional Review

President Carter's management initiatives also were aimed at eliminating problems in the areas of planning and regional review. In the case of planning, one of the most persistent and vexing complaints by state and local officials concerned the multiple planning requirements attached to grant programs. These requirements were designed to promote the development of long-term goals and objectives and to force state or local level coordination of activities. The officials did not debate whether forced planning and the development of planning agencies were good or bad. They were concerned about the attachment of specific planning requirements enacted with each federal program as a condition of aid and subject to approval by the funding agency (sometimes prior to the award of assistance). To them many of these planning requirements appeared duplicative, unnecessary, and often at odds with each other. In the aggregate, because these requirements were not coordinated, they had become an unreasonable burden.

One of the Carter Administration's early reform initiatives directed the heads of executive departments and agencies to review planning requirements with a view toward elimination of unnecessary ones and simplification of others where possible. Agencies were directed to provide a progress report by January 1979 and a final report by July 1979.[16] The Director of OMB was directed to monitor this reform effort. The President's June memorandum was followed by a memorandum on the same subject on August 14, 1978.

James T. McIntyre, Jr., Director of OMB, instructed federal agency heads to implement planning requirement reform proposals that had been submitted ot OMB several months earlier. He also convened an interagency task force on planning requirements to exchange information and make suggestions on program direction.[17] Agency actions in response to this effort included the elimination or simplification of nearly 1400 planning requirements by HEW, consolidation or simplification of 165 planning requirements by EPA, and the elimination of 50 requirements by the Law Enforcement Assistance Administration program.

The area of regional review was also a concern of the Carter administration. Past attempts at improvements and reform had been only partially successful. The Intergovernmental Cooperation Act of 1968 had established a national policy promoting intergovernmental coordination and cooperation (refer to Chapter II). The OMB implemented the Act, first through Circular A-82 and later through Circular A-95, which established procedures for the coordination of federally assisted programs at the state and local levels. Coordination of proposals under A-95 is brought about through the review of applications for assistance by state and areawide planning agencies sharing common boundaries (for federally assisted planning activities) at the substate level. Nealy 250 federally assisted programs must be reviewed through this process prior to submission of an application for funding assistance to the concerned agency.

OMB reassessment of the effectiveness of the A-95 procedure indicated a number of problems, none of which came as a surprise.[18] There was evidence to confirm the lack of federal compliance in a number of areas, and there were comments about time delays in processing applications and about the general value of the clearinghouses. OMB's first recommendation was to enforce federal compliance as a means of making A-95 work. A second recommendation was more difficult to implement. It required an annual assessment of the system, conducted in a manner that would not increase further the reporting burden of participating governments. Other recommendations addressed more complex issues involving the federal influence in substate districts and urban and policy decisions. Vincent Puritano, (then) Associate Deputy Directory of OMB's Office of Intergovernmental Affairs, summarized the study effort by noting:

> We will want to trim and firm the A-95 system to serve as a tool in intergovernmental cooperation.... Our options will be aimed at strengthening the hand of the chief elected officials at all levels of government in havng their views and priorities known on proposed federal projects and in nationalizing planning at the various levels of government.[19]

However, no final action resulted from OMB's A-95 reevaluation, and in early 1977 attention shifted to OMB's efforts to review the effectiveness of the Federal Regional Councils to link federal decision-making authority in the field or region nearest to the source of the problems (refer to Chapter II).

In August of 1977, the OMB began an initial assessment of the Federal Regional Council (FRC) system and process, which was followed by a broader-based assessment begun after several meetings of the Undersectretaries Group, the policy board governing the FRC's, and a memorandum from Jack H. Watson, Jr.[20] In the April 24, 1977 memorandum, Federal

Regional Council chairmen, governors, and state and local interest groups were requested to comment on an option paper concerning the future of the FRC's which had been developed by OMB. Although noting some areas of FRC successes, the option paper indicated the Council's failures to resolve policy conflicts among member agencies; their inability to represent the individual concerns of state and local governments in the formulation of national policy; the lack of member support by the parent federal agencies; the lack of White House, OMB, and executive agency level support of the FRC's; diffuse objectives and membership; staff and funding limitations; a lack of authority of the FRC Chairman and staff; and a lack of (program) agency involvement in FRC initiatives. In short, the FRC system was not being supported by the agencies and the Councils were unable to operate as originally planned.[21]

The result of the Watson memorandum and OMB assessment was in effect a holding action. The FRC's continued in operation, but the FRC system was to be evaluated further as part of the President's Reorganization Project. OMB was directed to prepare an option report for the President to determine the future of the FRC's.[22] The OMB assessment was completed in late August 1979.

The President's decision, based on this report, was to maintain a federal presence in the regions through the FRC's. The solution was a "nonsolution" in the sense that the fate of the FRC's remains undecided. The gist of the decision was that a linkage between the executive office and the regions was needed and that it was better to sustain the FRC presence then to dissolve it and attempt to recreate it when needed at some future date. This "decision" is analogous to that of sustaining the federal draft board machinery in case it is needed.

Many of Carter's reform efforts were reported at the face value of the White House press releases. Reports of accomplishments in 1977 and 1978 were often misleading and federal agencies "stretched" the facts in order to assure the President that they were complying. The changes the President desired indeed may bear fruit in the 1980's, but final judgement of the reality of these accomplishments cannot be made at this time.

The Federal Grant and Cooperative Agreement Act of 1977

Perhaps the most significant intergovernmental action to occur in the late 1970's was the passage of the Federal Grant and Cooperative Agreement Act of 1977. Passage of the Act (P.L. 95-224) was the culmination of a reform action that was little heralded by the press, but which represented a combined 5-year effort by administrative officials and Congressional representatives. Because of the potential long-term impacts of this Act and the studies it mandated, it may emerge as equivalent to the Intergovernmental Cooperation Act of 1968 — a major change agent in facilitating assistance reform.

By the early 1970's federal agencies and state and local governments had developed relationships (ways of doing business) that facilitated the cash transfer process and satisfied the nation's law-makers that national purposes were being served. However, with the Arab oil embargo and the subsequent energy "crunch," inflation became a greater concern than ever before.

Government agencies were asked to reduce waste, increase productivity, and generally to do more at less cost. One result of this "belt-tightening" movement was a demand by the public for increased efficiency and effectiveness in government. The governmental response, in part, was a review of the way business was being done. As a result of these investigations, scandals surfaced in such things as: "kickback" schemes, government waste, mismanagement, and fraud. Whistle blowing became a popular release for frustrated bureaucrats, but it further added to the image of a corrupt, or at least incompetent, bureaucracy.[23] In the midst of this movement toward reform, the climate was ripe to promote an issue that was misunderstood by most congressmen and of little interest to the general public, but the essence of the effort was broad-based federal assistance reform.

The Federal Grant and Cooperative Agreement Act grew out of recommendations by the Commission on Government Procurement that had conducted a two year review of federal spending practices. The Commission was created in November 1969 by P.L. 91-129 to study and recommend to Congress methods "to promote the economy, efficiency, and effectiveness" of procurement actions by the executive branch of government.[24] While the Commission was to study procurement (i.e., contract actions), their analysis revealed an overlap and confusion between procurement and grant-type activities. Procurement actions are used to purchase a good or service, while grants are intended to provide "assistance." The Commission found many instances where grants were used in lieu of procurement actions, primarily because procurement actions require competitive bidding, are more difficult to develop than the award of a grant, and take considerably more time to process than a grant. The Commission's recommendations included a call for legislation clarifying the use of assistance and procurement and for making a distinction between grants and a form of assistance that falls between a grant and a procurement action: a cooperative agreement.

After the Commission's report was transmitted to Congress, separate interagency task forces were convened by the executive branch to review the Commission's recommendations. The task group reports were issued in September 1973, and following a two year review process, formal acceptance followed on June 23, 1975. Bills were subsequently introduced by both Houses in the 93rd and 94th Congresses , but it was not until the 95th Congress that a measure was reported out of committee.

There was no question of the need for special legislation in the grant and cooperative agreement area. Federal spending through grants and contracts comprises almost one-third of the national budget. In spite of the magnitude of this effort, there had been no statutory guidance to inform the executive branch agencies about Congressional intent in the use of grant, contract, or cooperative agreement award instruments. The Federal Grant and Cooperative Agreement Act was designed to express this intent, and perhaps more importantly, to make the federal assistance system more "rational."[25] The Act not only was a needed reform measure, but one which addressed issues that had been long standing.

Grants vs. Contracts

One concern of federal managers was whether the use of the wrong award instrument would stifle competition. For example, competition could be restricted by the use of a grant or cooperative agreement instead of a contract. In many instances, profit-making organizations are not competitive with non-profit organizations when grants are utilized in "contract or procurement type" activities, such as in research programs.

There is much temptation to bypass the procurement system by using a grant. Federal agency experience has demonstrated situations in which grants are used in lieu of contracts to avoid the more detailed and complex procedures related to processing contracts. In these situations, their use effectively, although inadvertently, eliminates profit-making institutions because grant instruments do not permit the inclusion of a management fee and require cost-sharing. Therefore, in these situations, most private consulting firms cannot compete with non-profit institutions such as universities. When the procurement system is bypassed by using a grant, the effects of this strategy is readily apparent to the private sector competing for federal funds.

Under the provisions of the Federal Grant and Cooperative Agreement Act, contracts are restricted to procurement relationships and grants, and cooperative agreements are restricted to assistance relationships. Section 4 of the Act stipulates that:

> Each executive agency shall use a type of procurements contract as the legal instrument... whenever the principal purpose of the instrument is the acquisition, by purchase, lease, or barter, of property or services for the direct benefit or use of the Federal Government....

Grants vs. Cooperative Agreements: Substantial Involvement

An even more complex but related concern at the base of P.L. 95-224 is the use of cooperative agreements instead of grants. Both legal instruments are assistance awards which establish a relationship between the federal government and a recipient. The difference between a cooperative agreement and grant is the *level of involvement* of the funding agency in the project. In addition to addressing the distinction between assistance and procurement (grants versus contracts), P.L. 95-224 also tried to clarify the intent of grants versus cooperative agreements as:

> *Grant:* A grant is appropriate whenever the purpose is to transfer money, property, services or anything of value to a recipient to accomplish a purpose of support or stimulation authorized by statute, rather then acquisition of property or service for the direct benefit or use of the federal government; and no substantial involvement between the funding agency and the recipient during the performance of the activity is contemplated.

> *Cooperative Agreement:* A cooperative agreement is appropriate when the purpose is to transfer money, property, services, or anything of value to a recipient to accomplish a public purpose of support or stimulation authorized by statute, rather than acquisition of property or services for the direct benefit or use of the federal government; and substantial involvement is

anticipated beween the executive agency and the recipient during the perfomance of the activity.

The difference between the two assistance award instruments is plainly "substantial involvment." OMB attempted to clarify this relative distinction as follows:

When the terms of an assistance instrument indicate the recipient can expect to run the project without agency collaboration, participation, or intervention as long as it is run in accordance with the terms of the assistance instrument, substantial involvement is not anticipted.

A) Substantial involvement does not include:
1. Agency approval of recipient plans *prior* to award.
2. Normal exercise of federal stewardship responsibilities during the project period such as site visits, performance reporting, financial reporting, and audit to ensure that the objectives, terms, and conditions of the award are accomplished.
3. Unanticipated agency involvement to correct deficiencies in project or financial performance from the terms of the assistance instrument.
4. General statuatory requirements understood in advance of the award such as civil rights, environmental protection, and provision for the handicapped.
5 Agency review of performance *after* completion.
6. General administrative requirements, such as those included in OMB Circulars A-21, A-95, A-102, A-110, and FMC 74-4.

B) Conversely, anticipated involvement during performance would exist and, depending on the circumstances, could be substantial where the relationship includes:
1. Agency power to immediately halt an activity if detailed performance specifications (e.g., construction specifications) are not met. These would be provisions that go beyond the suspension remedies of the federal government for nonperformance as in OMB Circulars A-102 and A-110.
2. Agency review and approval of one stage before work can begin on a subsequent stage during the period covered by the assistance instrument.
3. Agency review and approval of substantive provisions of proposed subgrants or contracts. These would be provisions that go beyond existing policies on federal review of grantee procurement standards and sole source procurement.
4. Agency involvement in the selection of key recipient personnel. (This does not include assistance instrument provisions for the participation of a named principal investigator for research projects.)
5. Agency and recipient collaboration or joint participation.
6. Agency monitoring to permit specified kinds of direction or redirection of the work because of interrelationships with other projects.

7. Substantial direct agency operational involvement or participation during the assisted activity is anticipated prior to award to insure compliance with such statutory requirements as civil rights, environmental protection, and provision for the handicapped. Such participation would exceed that normally anticipated under (4) above.

8. Highly prescriptive agency requirements prior to award limiting recipient discretion with respect to scope of services offered, organizational structure, staffing, mode of operation, and other management processes, coupled with close agency monitoring or operational involvement during performance over and above the normal exercise of federal stewardship responsibilities to ensure compliance with these requirements.[26] (See Figure 1)

Obviously, the meaning of "'substantial involvement" is subject to considerable interpretation, and OMB has continued to attempt to provide clear guidance to federal agencies with little success. Research and development agencies, such as the National Science Foundation (NSF) and the Environmental Protection Agency, have not yet solved this new problem.[27] While grants are the preferred assistance vehicle, the greater involvement required by cooperative agreements is attractive to federal program managers who are also scientists and would prefer more active participation in the research effort.

The Federal Grant and Cooperative Agreement Act was also significant because it mandated a study of federal assistance programs (Section 8 of the Act.) The objectives of this required study are "to develop a better understanding of alternative means of implementing federal assistance programs and to determine the feasibility of developing a comprehensive system of guidance...." OMB was assigned to conduct this study and to report to the Congress no later than February 3, 1980, two years from the signing of the Act into law.[28] The results of the study, which were formally reported to Congress on March 1, 1980, may provide the framework for major legislative change. The recommendations of this study will be discussed in a later section of this chapter.

Congressional Actions in Assistance Reform

Congress and the Executive Branch have worked together throughout the 1970's to resolve the administrative and management problems of the assistance system. One significant step forward was the appointment of the Commission on Federal Paperwork in 1974 (P.L. 93-556). The Commission made 520 recommendations for the reduction of paperwork, 151 of which were implemented by the Executive Branch.[29] OMB noted that these efforts alone resulted in a 9.4 percent reduction in reporting hours in agencies subject to OMB control under the Federal Reports Act.[30] Other Congressional efforts, while not resulting in legislative reform, were the first steps in establishing a base for such major reform.

By the summer of 1978, Congressional strategies to simplify the grant process were evident in a number of hearings concerning proposed legislation. Among the more serious efforts were "The Federal Assistance Reform Act"

Figure 1

Degree of Substantial Involvement
(Federal Management Actions
Over Supported Work Activity)

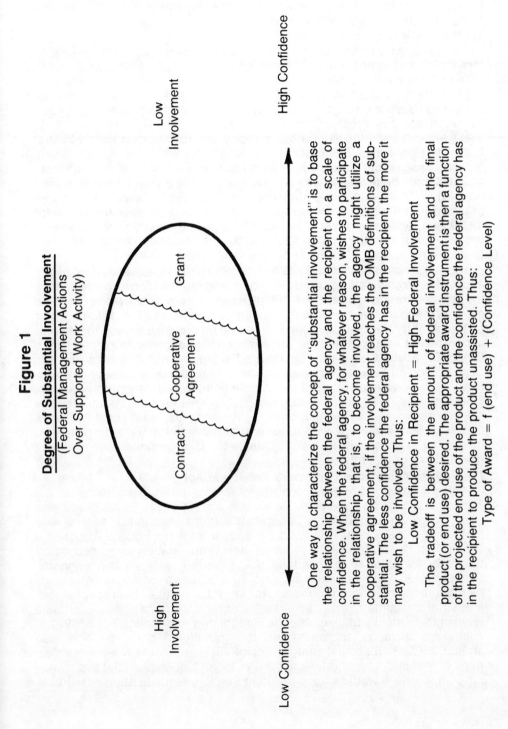

One way to characterize the concept of "substantial involvement" is to base the relationship between the federal agency and the recipient on a scale of confidence. When the federal agency, for whatever reason, wishes to participate in the relationship, that is, to become involved, the agency might utilize a cooperative agreement, if the involvement reaches the OMB definitions of substantial. The less confidence the federal agency has in the recipient, the more it may wish to be involved. Thus:

Low Confidence in Recipient = High Federal Involvement

The tradeoff is between the amount of federal involvement and the final product (or end use) desired. The appropriate award instrument is then a function of the projected end use of the product and the confidence the federal agency has in the recipient to produce the product unassisted. Thus:

Type of Award = f (end use) + (Confidence Level)

(S. 3266); "The Federal Assistance Paperwork Reduction Act" (S. 3267); and "The Hidden Tax Reduction Act" (S. 3144).

The Federal Assistance Reform Act

The purpose of the Federal Assistance Reform Act of 1978 was to streamline and simplify the generally applicable requirements attached to federal assistance and their implementation, to provide for multi-year funding of certain grant programs, to expedite the processing of applications for federal assistance involving more than one grant, and to extend and amend the law relating to intergovernmental cooperation. The key factor of S. 3266 was a recommendation to create an Office of Intergovernmental Administration in the Executive Office of the President. The Office would coordinate federal assistance programs, maintain liaison with state and local officials, provide technical assistance, and provide management oversight and review. State incentive grants also were included in the proposal. These grants were intended to encourage states to change their policies toward distressed local governments in order to promote solutions to urban problems. A total appropriation of $350,000,000 was proposed for the incentive grant program. Unfortunately, it died in Committee.

The Act was reintroduced in 1979 and 1980 with an adjusted purpose to encourage simplification, standardization, and more uniform compliance in the administration of national policy requirements which have become generally applicable to federal assistance programs. The reform effort shifted slightly from the previous theme that employed a federal focal point of control (for example, see the same recommendations in the report of the OMB/NSF Study Committee on Policy Management Assistance and the Commission on Federal Paperwork) to an overall attack on rules and regulations themselves in an attempt to promote uniformity. Interestingly enough, Title II of the new proposal authorized the President to submit federal assistance program consolidation plans to Congress, "when he determines that such consolidations will utilize one or more of the Bill's purposes," a theme not popular with the 96th Congress. This proposal also was not reported out of committee.

The Federal Assistance Paperwork Reduction Act

A second major Congressional grant reform initiative in 1978 was the Federal Assistance Paperwork Reduction Act (S. 3267). S. 3267 was proposed to reduce unnecessary paperwork burdens imposed on federal aids recipients. In particular, Title I of the proposal, as in the Federal Assistance Reform Act, was intended "...to encourage simplification and standardization in the administration of national policy requirements which are generally applicable to federal assistance, to strengthen the supervision and implementation of such requirements, and to reduce their overall administrative burden and adverse economic impact on assistance recipients." Title II would amend the 'Budget and Accounting Act of 1921 to encourage advance appropriations for grant-in-aid programs and also amend the Congressional Budget Act of 1974 to provide five-year projections of new budget authority and outlays for all federal financial assistance programs. Title III would amend the Joint Funding Simplification Act of 1974 to provide stronger incentive for federal agencies to develop joint funding projects and to utilize joint management funds in financing such projects.

Like the second Federal Assistance Reform Act, the Federal Assistance Paperwork Reduction Act attempted to deal with the administration of generally applicable federal assistance requirements in two areas: those designated in a single Act specifying broad coverage and those consistently placed into Acts authorizing or reauthorizing individual grant programs. These requirements generally are referred to as cross-cutting. Examples of the former include environmental protection and uniform relocation assistance. The latter requirements would include civil service merit sytems, public participation, and minimum wage standards. The problem was that these requirements are not administered uniformly from agency to agency. This Act would designate a single agency to estabish standard rules and regulations to monitor program implementation by federal funding agencies. Title I of the Act also would have permitted greater standardization and streamlining of other across-the-board federal rules and regulations.

The Federal Assistance Paperwork Reduction Act was also an omnibus reform move containing many of the provisions called for by the White House, OMB, ACIR, GAO, and the public interest groups. Although omnibus, it was still incremental and it fell short of more drastic reform measures such as program consolidations or wholesale terminations and reauthorizations. This proposal, too, was never reported out of committee.

Hidden Tax Reduction Act

A third reform measure proposal introduced before Congress on May 25, 1978 contained the misleading title of "The Hidden Tax Reduction Act" (S. 3144). This proposal was based on the assistance reform recommendations of the Commission on Federal Paperwork. The Commission recommendations incorporated in the measure included placement of paperwork and information management under the control of one agency, commitment by national leaders to paperwork control, and implementation of a policy called "Service Management" to deliver services to the public at the least cost. The proposal provided for a broad based "re-evaluation and restructuring of the methods and procedures utilized by the federal government for the management, collection, dissemination, and control of governmental paperwork and information gathering."[31] The Act noted that unnecessary paperwork and red tape hindered the effectiveness of federal programs, imposed tremendous cost while reducing productivity, and generated mistrust and anger in the federal system. To address this problem, the measure proposed elimination of unnecessary reports to Congress, paperwork impact assessments of proposed legislation, and assignment of central management and control responsibility for federal paperwork reduction efforts (in effect, the same administrative adjustments which were called for by the 1977 White House memoranda).

Title VI of the proposed Act was designed to provide relief to state and local governments. Under Title VI comprehensive reform would be initiated:

(A)to operate federal programs in a manner which reflects respect for and trust in the capabilities of state and local governments;

(B)to provide high-level officers in the Executive Office of the President and the agencies for state and local officials to contact to resolve issues resulting from legislation, regulations, program procedures, and program reviews;
(C)to simplify, wherever possible, federal requirements of state and local governments through the development of standard requirements and procedures, such as standard planning requirements;
(D)to coordinate state and local governmental activities and related federal activities;
(E)to permit the acceptance of state statutes, regulations, and procedures where state action wil accomplish the policies and objectives of applicable federal law; and
(F)to undertake continuing research into administrative problems in federal, state, and local relationships, and to seek prompt reform.

The intent of this measure was to simplify planning, application, reporting, and other requirements imposed on state and local governments. In particular, subsection (E) would provide for federal acceptance of state procedures for meeting cross-cutting national policy requirements.

As with most other Congressional attempts at assistance reform, this proposal was never reported out of committee. However, each proposal moves Congress closer to an omnibus reform measure, and the climate is ripe for the initiation and passage of a major reform bill in the next few years. The similarity between these proposals and the administrative reform efforts of the Carter Administration indicate a coordinated effort. For this reason, a more careful look at the procedural thrust of the Administration's effort in at least one area is warranted.

Presidential Initiatives in the Area of Cross-Cutting Federal Requirements

The Carter Administration has undertaken a series of initiatives in promoting substantial procedural reform without the necessity of legislative action or authorization. These actions were initiated by President Carter in his September 9, 1977 memoranda and executive orders providing guidance to heads of executive departments and agencies which were discussed earlier. The impact of these initatives is just now being assessed.

In his September initiative (cited earlier), President Carter stated:

The federal grants-in-aid system has developed because of the importance...of dealing decisively with national problems in a way that preserves and encourages innovative participation by state and local governments....Unfortunately,...as grants have proliferated, it has grown increasingly irrational, inefficient, and insensitive to the various local needs and idiosyncracies it was originally designed to accomodate.

...Intelligent reform of this system will not only prevent the waste of tax dollars, it will ensure that the money which is spent produces superior results. Therefore, my administration is working to improve the management of federal aid and improve the part-

nership with state and local governments....[32]

One of the major thrusts of this effort was to deal with the problems associated with national goals imposed on assistance recipients. These requirements cut across all programs and increased the administrative and actual costs of the assistance effort. The problem was addressed procedurally in the following manner:

Problem. One of the paperwork burdens associated with the flow of federal funds to state and local governments is that of the large number of assurances that the grant applicant is meeting national goals,...the intra-agency requirements ought to be more nearly standarized to the point where a single set of assurances could be kept in a central information file, thus eliminating the need for multiple requests for demonstration of compliance with the same or comparable requirements. At the same time, agencies should move to adopt common sets of assurances where possible.

Procedural Action. All agencies were directed to re-examine their requirements for separate sets of assurances of grantee compliance with "national goal" requirements for each grant and to consolidate them into a single agency set of assurances where practicable and where not expressly prohibited by statutes.[33]

A compendium of federal agency implementing actions in this area indicated the following actions had been taken with respect to cross-cutting requirements:

Certain cross-cutting requirements (such as those dealing with citizen participation, environmental impact, and equal employment opportunity) were identified as priorities for simplification. The Council on Environmental Quality attempted to develop a single framework for all environmental impact requirements imposed by a federal agency. Draft regulations resulting from this effort are now being reviewed, following extensive state, local, and agency consultation.

A single handbook cataloging all citizen participation requirements imposed as a condition of the receipt of federal funds was prepared by the Community Services Administration.

A Presidential announcement to restructure and strengthen the Equal Opportunity Commission gave the EOC the authority to pursue the simplification of government grant regulations prohibiting discrimination in hiring by state and local governments.[34]

Cross-cutting requirements attached to federal assistance also were studied extensively by ACIR as part of its massive, 14-volume study of the intergovernmental grant sytem. In a summary volume published in June 1978, ACIR noted:

This Commission does not question these goals or their desirability. But, we do question the manner of their administra-

tion, their multiple cumulative impact, and the long term implications of using federal aid devices for various regulatory purposes. These are the questions, then, that force a separate consideration of these new-type conditions.

In response to them, the Commission urges that Congress and the President reassess all such requirements with a view toward consolidating those that are partially or wholly duplicative of one another and eliminating those that have been found to be incapable of implementation or inordinately burdensome (which is to say counter-productive), fiscally or managerially.

For each of those requirements that emerges from this process, the cost of implementation to federal agencies or recipient governments should be recognized and provided for by law. Moreover, for each, a single unit within the Executive Branch should be given clear authority for achieving standardized guidelines and simplified administration. In this effort, the estimated costs of compliance should be considered and "certification acceptance" procedures permitted, wherever appropriate.

In advancing these proposals, the Commission strikes a balance between recognizing the merit of most of the goals embodied in these cross-cutting requirements and narrowing the gap between promise and performance that overlap, poor administration, and nonattention to costs and manpower have produced.[35]

One of the key elements in ACIR's five-point strategy for implementing its study was "sensible conditioning," based on:

...careful assessment, both before and after their enactment, of the impact of generally applicable intergovernmental regulatory standards and procedures, including the federal capacity to enforce them fairly and uniformly; the costs as well as prospective benefits of their achievement; the suitablity and necessity of the use of intergovernmental aid programs as a major instrument for pursuing these national objectives; the clarity and precision of the objectives and principles to be applied in their executive and judicial interpretations; and the relationships and possible contradictions between and among these various national policy objectives. The Commission emphasizes that these are the minimum steps necessary to bring some semblance of order to an area wherein regulations have run riot.[36]

In its study, the ACIR also raised the question of the utility of the cross-cutting requirements. Everyone seems to agree that the objectives or legislative intent of cross-cutting requirements is laudable and in many instances necesary; however, no one has stopped to assess the costs and impacts compared to the benefits.

The costs and impacts of the administrative requirements associated with the grant-in-aid system are not measurable, but they are recognized by state and local officials as a significant burden. Several efforts were initiated in the 1970's to ease the effect of this burden. One effort was to stimulate the improvement of state and local productivity; another was to develop a coherent national urban policy to promote uniform assistance to the nation's cities.

Productivity Improvement

The National Center for Productivity and Qualtiy of Working Life was created in 1975 as an outgrowth of the National Commission on Productivity by P.L. 94-136, "in an attempt to reverse the slow growth trend in productivity improvement...." rather than specifically as an assistance reform strategy. However, the Center's tasks also included an assignment to "identify, study, and review existing government statutes, regulations and fiscal policies which adversely affect productivity growth...."[37] The recognition that federal programs affected the nation's productive effort was not new. Federal impacts could be seen in the following policy areas:

Pricing policies in regulated industries, such as transportation, power, and communications.

Fiscal and monetary policies that alter demand, supply, investment, and income distribution.

Tax laws which affect investments.

Standards establishing the quality of output (e.g., food, drugs, and environmental pollution).

Regulating quality and quantity of input (e.g., through equal opportunity laws or occupational safety and health laws.[38]

The grant-in-aid system has been recognized as an important factor affecting state and local productivity.[39] Even though it permits service to be delivered, this impact is negative because of the costs associated with compliance requirements imposed by the grants system. A GAO study of state and local government productivity found that the federal grant system seldom rewards grantees for efficient and effective performance. In some cases, the report noted, "insufficient federal program concern for performance and inadequate grantee incentives may cause program performance to suffer in comparison with other state-funded programs."[40]

Surprisingly, the linkage between the assistance reform efforts of the Carter Administration and the productivity improvement movement did not occur. The President did not renew the authorization for the National Center. which gave way at the end of Fiscal Year 1978 to the National Productivity Council, which the President did not choose to appoint. Thus ended a promising effort at developing institutional capacity to produce reform rather than through procedural mandate—the usual federal approach. Federal abandonment of this approach appeared to signal total federal assumption of responsibility for solving the nation's problems, something that became evident in the development of national urban policy.

A National Urban Policy

The heart of productivity improvement and federal assistance reform lies not only in federal administrative efforts to reduce encumbrances or "red tape," but also in the means by which the assistance effort is structured. It has been long recognized that the federal government alone cannot solve all of the problems of the grant-in-aid system or all of the problems of the nation. The answer and the foundation of the capacity-building efforts of the federal government has been to provide the tools which are intended to facilitate the roles of the nation's recipient governments in helping themselves as well as to pursue broader ranged national objectives. A failure of this philosophy was the short-lived effort of the productivity improvement programs. Another such failure was the attempt to develop and impose a national urban policy from the top down. This effort began with an attempt to define a "national" urban policy and ended with the new perspectives and realizations that followed passage of Proposition 13 in California.

Cities historically have been the direct providers of services and centers for jobs, learning, recreation, and culture. Today, cities are finding it more and more difficult to fulfill their historic roles. Faced with rapidly rising costs and increasing taxpayer resistance to higher taxes, many cities, especially older ones, are finding it difficult, if not impossible, to maintain existing services, much less afford new ones. Cities today represent poverty, pollution, high crime rates, poor school systems, high taxes, physical blight, and overcrowding. Population has been shifting steadily from the central cities to the suburbs and from the cities and suburbs in the Northeast and Mid-West to the South and West. Private industry representing jobs and the tax base has followed this trend, leaving the poor, less educated, and elderly behind. The nature of this shift has created a growing disparity between the needs of increasing numbers of impoverished residents and the services available to them.[41]

Federal attempts to alleviate this situation have been piecemeal. By 1977, it was obvious that a coordinated federal effort would be necessary to provide any discernible impact in addressing the plight of the cities. In April 1977, President Carter created a Cabinet-level Urban and Regional Policy Group (URPG) chaired by Patricia R. Harris, then Secretary of the Department of Housing and Urban Development (Harris was replaced by former Mayor of New Orleans Moon Landrau in the fall of 1979). Members of this group included representatives of the Office of the Vice President, the Departments of Labor, Commerce, Housing and Urban Development, Transportation, Treasury, Interior, and Health, Education, and Welfare; the Environmental Protection Agency; and the Community Service Administration. The mission of the URPG was to prepare administrative and legislative recommendations as a first step in the development of a national urban policy. The problems, as seen by the URPG, were many:

Nearly 160 million people, three-fourths of the population of the United States, live in urban areas.

Almost half of the cities with populations over 500,000 and one-fourth with population of over 50,000, are experiencing economic distress.

Fifteen of the largest cities, mostly those in the Northeast and Mid-West, have been steadily losing population.

234

The colder, "snow-belt" cities of the North have been losing employment to the South and West.

One-third of all metropolitan housing and nearly half of all inadequate housing is located in central cities.

Families leaving cities have greater incomes than those moving in.

Tax revenues are not keeping pace with rising costs.

The image of cities as dwelling places has been tarnished. Only 10 percent of those responding to a federal survey indicated the city was the best place to live.[42]

With these consideratoins, the URPG developed a national urban policy based on four broad-ranged goals:

1. *To preserve the heritage and value of our older cities;*
2. *To maintain the investment in our older cities and their neighborhoods;*
3. *To assist newer cities in confronting the challenges of growth and pockets of poverty in a fair, efficient, an equitable manner; and*
4. *To provide improved housing, job opportunities, and community services to the urban poor, minorities, and women.[43]*

To implement these goals, the URPG developed a 10-part strategy that was translated into a national urban policy.[44] More significant, however, was the program proposed to support this policy. On March 27, 1978, President Carter unveiled a multi-faceted plan designed to provide $8.3 billion in aid to assist cities in combating problems ranging from urban decay to uncontrolled growth. The proposal, as outlined in his message to Congress, included a major overhauling of existing programs as well as initiation of new ones. In his address, the President noted, "The deterioration of urban life in the United States is one of the most complex and deeply rooted problems we face....The federal government has the clear duty to lead the effort to reverse this deterioration."[45]

The Administration's proposal included at least 16 major thrusts, ranging from tax credits and loan guarantees to a "Livable Cities" program for community arts development. Perhaps the most important of the thrusts were long-range plans for revamping existing federal assistance programs. A task force, headed by HUD Secretary Harris, developed 160 assistance reform proposals affecting 40 federal programs that could be implemented by executive order. Unfortunately, this first effort at defining and developing a national urban policy was not received well by Congress or by the cities.

The primary complaint about Carter's urban plan was that it was not sufficiently funded. Dr. Philip M. Hauser, a sociologist, noted, "Generally, I feel the President's program goes in the right direction, but the plan is probably underfunded for its objectives."[46] Other comments were more terse and one Washington columnist was totally negative:

None of the 160 recommendations call for eliminating any single existing federal program—despite the almost universal acknowledgement that some of them are real losers. Instead, the recommendations would guarantee more bureaucracy, regulations, and frustrations for local officials.[47]

The Carter plan in the views of many local elected leaders "...showed no evidence of understanding the heavy involvement of the nation's counties on the life of their residents whether they are in or outside of cities and villages."[48] The less than enthusiastic support for the nation's first urban policy is characterized in the response of the National Association of Counties, "...we welcome the President's new initiatives in urban areas. But they are a tiny drop in the great sea of Congressionally approved programs that together become a total urban policy.[49]

In attempting to implement its national urban policy, the Administration became embroiled in economic issues, special interest group concerns, and Congressional indifference. After one year, the Administration could claim only a partial victory. While several major provisions of the policy were not enacted by Congress, 13 lesser ones were. Many of these steps were considered highly significant, but the overall results of this effort are not yet apparent. As ACIR noted, "It may take years to fully assess the impact of the changes."[50] While representative of a major reform effort, the national urban initiatives have done little to alleviate the adminsitrative burden associated with federal assistance. The attempt to develop a substantial urban policy did not forestall the revolt of California taxpayers reacting to the increasing costs of government. This reaction also has significant implications for the future of the federal assistance system.

Proposition 13

The groundswell of taxpayer discontentment with rising taxes, inadequate services, and perennial allegations of bureaucratic ineptitude, whether true or not, reached a peak on June 6, 1978, when Californians voted overwhelmingly for a state constitutional amendment to place extensive limits on state and local taxing powers. Proposition 13 on the California ballot restricted realty taxes to one percent of the market value of property after July 1, 1978. Further, assessment increases were limited to a maximum of two percent annually. Current property values on assessment must be based on assessments in effect on March 1, 1975. Additionally, future state tax increases must be approved by a two-thirds vote of the State Legislature and new local taxes by a two-thirds vote of qualified voters. The impact of the Law was to decrease local government revenues in California by $7 billion annually.

Passage of Proposition 13 led to dire predictions of massive program cuts and public employment lay-offs, most of which did not occur as other sources of funds and spending cuts allowed jurisdictions to maintain the status quo.[51] The California educational system was not so fortunate. Proposition 13 "meant fewer courses, smaller enrollments, no pay raises, and pessimism about the future," for California educators.[52]

The passage of Proposition 13 had a psychological effect on the nation. The vote was construed as a warning to the nation's elected leaders that government had expanded as far as, or further than, the citizens would tolerate and that there was a dire need for belt-tightening and administrative reform.[53]

Proposition 13 also had both revenue and outlay implications for the federal government. The greatest impact was in the area of matching and maintenance of effort requirements of federal assistance programs. As indicated earlier, matching requirements refer to the maximum percentage of assistance the federal government will pay and the minimum grantee share. Maintenance of effort stipulations require that the grantee maintain a specified level of fiscal effort to be eligible for federal funding. Both areas would reflect a lessened local capability to meet the federal share.

The second outlay area impacted was in federal compensation programs. Under these programs, the federal government reimburses state and local governments for revenues lost because federal landholdings are exempt from state and local taxation. The federal government pays a rate equivalent to the local burden. If the local share is decreased, as it was after passage of Proposition 13, so is the federal share.

The third area affected was federal formula grants. Some formulas use grantee expenditures or tax effort as a factor in determining the allocation of federal funds. California's reduced tax effort raised questions about how much more the state would lose as a result of this mandated adjustment.

The General Accounting Office indicated that more time would be needed to assess long term effects of Proposition 13 for a number of reasons. Much of the impact would be determined by local efforts to offset the reduced revenues as well as by state infusion of emergency funds; matching requirements would be mitigated by the use of in-kind resources as opposed to hard cash; 15 programs permitted the federal agency to authorize discretionary waivers of maintenance of effort requirements; only a small number, three of 17 possible compensation programs, could be affected by Proposition 13; and of the 93 federal programs which distribute funds by formula, only 32 had tax effort as a factor. Of these, state and local efforts would largely determine the resulting impact.[54] Proposition 13 and the GAO assessment highlighted the complex interrelationship and intergovernmental dependency inherent in the federal assistance system.

The passage of Proposition 13 also was the introduction to the new era of federal, state, and local intergovernmental relations—one characterized by a recognition of the need for more federal attention to state and local input in federal program development and planning, more careful direction and management of assistance programs, and fewer frills. This era is a transitory period which emphasizes administration and management and is characterized by more complex and interwoven intergovernmental relationships. The trends that are being predicted for the future lend credence to the thesis that the federal system is in a state of transition.

Trends in Federalism for the Future

A trend is no more than an evolutionary projection based on observation and the gathering of facts that become indicators when appropriately assembled. In the past 10 years, there has been a significant number of data indicators that may be used to form a basis for describing trends in the federal assistance system. A few of the more significant trends are:

The broader eligibility and entitlement provisions of general revenue sharing, the Housing and Community Development Act, the Comprehensive Employment and Training Act, and the President's National Urban Policy have expanded the number of actors intergovernmental system to include all levels and types of governments, special districts, citizen groups, and non-profit service agencies.

The role and positions of the various actors is becoming increasingly blurred. While the federal government is still the senior partner, direct aid to localities and the impossibility of policing the federal aid system has forced an increase in local spending discretion and autonomy. In addition, states have begun to attack this pass-through trend, and there is now movement to require all federal funds entering the state to be reallocated by the state legislature as a means of financial control.

Congressionally mandated formula funding has increased in the past 10 years. General revenue sharing, the block grants, formula and open-ended categorical programs are all in this grouping. The result of this trend may be seen in stronger efforts by public and recipient interest groups to influence the allocation formula of programs as well as to call for public support for identified needs.

Recipient discretion is generally greater today than 10 years ago. Revenue sharing and block grants promote more recipient discretion than categorical programs. The added mix of assistance packages permits greater choice and discretion in compiling an assistance package at the state or local level.

In spite of the administration's concerns in this area, more "strings" or conditions are being attached as a requirement for federal assistance. An array of common purpose requirements is now an integral part of all assistance packages. These "cross-cutting" requirements include those related to ensuring equal rights for all citizens, employment of the handicapped, environmental and historic preservation, and occupational health and safety; and they all add to the procedural and paperwork burden and costs associated with federal assistance.[55]

These five trends focus directly on the recent evolution and development of the federal assistance effort. Two of these trends merit closer examination because federal impacts in these areas may have long term implications for change on the intergovernmental system and may dictate the nature of the emerging realigned federal-state-local partnership. One change, that of increasing programmatic centralization, runs counter to the repeated efforts of the past three administrations to decentralize decision-making authority to lower levels of government. The second change, federal level management reform, will have longer term effects on the grant-in-aid system and the supporting intergovernmental structure.

It is apparent that the 1980's will find a grant-in-aid structure based on greater centralized management and control. This control will take place at two levels—by the state and by the federal government. The most signficant indicator of the federal role is yet to be determined. The federal role is bound to be influenced by actions taken in response to the federal assistance study mandated by the Federal Grant and Cooperative Agreement Act. However, as with other factors described in this chapter, it is important to remember that the degree of interaction, impact, or influence of one intergovernmental actor on another varies for each entity, area, and state or local government.

Factors Leading to an Increased State Role

The probability of more active state participation in the fiscal affairs of local governments, which is related to assistance effort, takes at least three forms: 1) the impacts of state funding on local decision-making; 2) the effect of federal funds passed through the state for distribution to local units of government; and 3) federal financing of state programs. Movements within each of these areas indicate a trend toward a stronger state role for the 1980's.

1. As with federal funding, there is little doubt that state funding of local programs affects the decisional or resource allocation process. State grants to local units of government take two forms: general support and categorical support. General support grants are given without direction or specification on how they may be used. Categorical grants include formula (entitlement is determined by some formula) and project grants. (given in response to specific applications by local governments for state funding assistance). In an ACIR survey of state aid to cities and counties, 38.6 percent of the state aid received was for general support and 61.4 percent was for categorical programs. For counties, the percentage of general support received was even higher—53.5 percent with 46.5 percent for categorical grants.[56] State distributive payments to local governments amounted to 34.5 percent of all receipts in FY 1976 and represented 36.9 percent of state general expenditures.[57] The largest category of assistance was in education, followed by welfare. Surprisingly, state aid to local governments for general support was third.

The impact of this large amount of state funding assistance on local decision-making has increased as the percentage of state aid has increased over the past 10 years. As with federal impacts and the resultant influence on local decisions, state influences determine not only allocation decisions, but also local spending priorities, especially in counties.[58] The effect of state expenditures is felt most strongly in the area of highways and roads, but local spending is stimulated most by state grants in the areas of law, justice and legal services, and recreation. Over one-half of city and three-fourths of county officials responding to an ACIR survey indicated that they would make different allocation decisions if the state permitted. The state grants indeed affected local budget priorities.[59]

Today, the states are in a much more powerful position politically and legally than 10 years ago. The reapportionment decisions of the 1960's (Baker vs. Carr and Reynolds vs. Simms) have strengthened the two party system in many states and have led to more activism by interest groups. State executive branches also have been strengthened noticeably in the last decade. Governors have been granted greater powers to staff and reorganize and to develop budgets and control a greater portion of state funds. In short, state institutions are more effective and more able to exert a greater influence over local government policy than ever before. Whether they choose to utilize this power is a question yet to be resolved.

2. The second indicator of the increasingly important role of the state in the intergovernmental system is the influence of the state on federal funds distributed by the state to local units of government. A recent survey of federal pass-through funding indicated that 41 percent of the federal funds received by the state were channeled to local government. The greatest concentrations of this funding were in the areas of public welfare (57 percent of the total passed to local government) and education (56 percent).[60]

Federal conditions attached to the funds sometimes circumscribe state policy in relation to local governments.[61] However, states also may impose additional conditions in order to carry out plans and policies as long as these conditions are consistent with the federal purpose. State conditions attached to pass-through grants, which are generally procedural rather than performance-oriented, have had little impact on local policies and allocation decision. This is not to say that the lack of impact will persist in the 1980's; and, indeed, indications are that it will not as the states strive for greater fiscal control.

Federal grants constitute approximately one-fourth of total state revenue receipts and thus have a substantial influence on state policy. State discretionary control of these funds is minimal. In one survey, state budget officers estimated that 83 percent of the funds received were passed-through according to federal requirements, 8 percent by state law and only 10 percent by state administrative discretion.[62] State governors generally exercise more control over federal funds than state legislatures, but only slightly more than 10 percent of all states require some form of legislative approval in determining how discretionary funds are passed-through to local governments. Thus, while the level of federal funding to the state is significant, states have not chosen to exercise significant control over the bulk of funds funneling through them, probably because of the difficulty in intervening between the federal funding agency and the intended recipient.

There has been a movement to gain some measure of control over these funds; and in several states, most notably Pennsylvania, the legislature calculates federal funds entering the state in their budgeting process and reappropriates the monies to local units of government. There has been some effort by other states to move in this direction. Needless to say, this effort is not popular at the local level, but it has received some national support. The ACIR recently issued an information bulletin on this subject to state executive and legislative officers recommending that they adopt legislation to "include all federal aid in (state) appropriation bills; prohibit spending of federal funds over the amount appropriated by the (state) legislature; and set specific spending priorities by establishing sub-program allocations."[63] As federal outlays increase and continue to form a larger portion of state and local budgets, state re-appropriation is a single and logical option for gaining fiscal control over state programs.

3. The third indicator of a change in the state role in the intergovernmental system is evident in the effects of federal funding of state programs. This impact has been one of the most significant factors in altering state-local relationships over the past decade. The federal government relies on the state to distribute 70 percent of the total grant funds destined for state-local programs. In most cases, the substate allocation, as well as conditions attached to the allocations, is left to the states, most of which have chosen not to exercise this opportunity to attach state policy objectives to this assistance.

Over 40 percent of all federal funds received by the state in this category have been passed-through to local units of government(Table 1). Most of this amount went to counties in the form of public welfare assistance. The second highest category was for education, followed by manpower programs. The second largest dollar amount received by the state, however, was for highways, but states pass-through very little of this amount. The preferred method of allocation of these funds was by formula rather than by project grant.

Federal aid to states has had significant impacts in the functional areas of welfare, education, public health, highways, and criminal justice programs. It was also the multitude of planning requirements and other strings attached to federal grants that has led, in large part, to the proliferation of substate single purpose and multi-jurisdictional districts (almost 1800). In this sense, grants promote fragmentation.

State aid to education stands out as one of the biggest issues of the 1970's. More than half of the states have changed their funding programs for public education in the last decade. During this period, state financing of education rose from 39 percent to over 50 percent of total allocations.[64] This incease also was marked by attempts to reduce state outlays by legislating budget restrictions, instituting educational controls, and imposing tax limitations on school districts. Proposition 13 also was a response to this trend.

Unfortunately, the trend also has been toward greater state assumption of what were previously local functions. A 1976 ACIR survey found increased state assumption of local programs in the areas of public health and welfare, municipal courts, pollution control, property tax assessment standards, building codes, land use regulation, and others.[65] These shifts were usually the result of local requests or were accompanied by local support for the assumption.

Federal policy has had a confusing effect on state-local relationships. The federal government has instituted a growing number of programs which bypassed the state and provided aid directly to urban areas. The

241

Table 1

State Pass-Through of Federal Grant Funds to Local Recipients in Selected States,[1] by Function (amounts in 000s): FY 1974 (est.)

FUNCTION	NUMBER OF STATES	FEDERAL GRANTS RECEIVED	RETAINED BY STATE GOVERNMENT		PASSED THROUGH TO LOCAL RECIPIENTS	
			AMOUNT	PERCENT	AMOUNT	PERCENT
Education	26[2]	$2,746,177	$1,189,181	43%	$1,556,996	57%
Public welfare	27	7,266,942	3,429,903	47	3,837,039	53
Highways	25[3]	2,214,514	1,893,806	86	320,708	14
Health and hospitals	27	456,382	304,648	67	151,734	33
Criminal justice	27	367,545	125,198	34	242,347	66
Housing and community development	26[2]	20,319	10,438	51	9,881	49
Manpower	25[4]	1,475,089	1,234,300	84	240,789	16
All other	24[5]	945,445	465,025	49	480,420	51
Total for States	22[6]	$14,134,352	$8,287,582	59%	$5,846,770	41%

[1]As many as 27 states: Alaska, Arizona, California, Colorado, Connecticut, Delaware, Georgia, Hawaii, Idaho, Illinois, Iowa, Maryland, Michigan, Minnesota, Missouri, Montana, Nevada, North Carolina, North Dakota, Oregon, Pennsylvania, Rhode Island, South Carolina, South Dakota, Vermont, Virginia, and Wisconsin.
[2]All states in footnote 1 except South Dakota.
[3]All states in footnote 1 except Georgia and South Dakota.
[4]All states in footnote 1 except North Carolina and North Dakota.
[5]All states in footnote 1 except North Carolina, South Dakota, and Rhode Island.
[6]All states in footnote 1 except Georgia, North Carolina, North Dakota, Rhode Island, and South Dakota.

SOURCE: Advisory Commission on Intergovernmental Relations, *The Intergovernmental Grant System as Seen by Local, State, and Federal Officials,* A-54 (Washington, D.C.: GPO, March, 1977), p. 88.

National Urban Policy was an example of an attempt to achieve national goals by relying on subnational units to implement them. There also has been an expansion of federal assumption of state and even local responsibilities. Programs such as general revenue sharing and block grants characterize this effort because they all have strings and allocation formulas that have intruded on state prerogatives.

Finally, in the past few years, federal policy has been dictated, in large part, by the threats of recession. A series of counter cyclical assistance programs, such as the Local Public Works Program, the Anti-Recession Fiscal Assistance Program, and the expansion of the Public Service Employment Programs (of the Comprehensive Employment and Training Act of 1973) have had significant impacts on state governments, largely because of the substantial numbers of dollars involved (13.9 billion in 1976-77). Most of this sum bypassed the state and was added to local revenues. The focus of this shifting policy is difficult to discern, in part because it represented not only a response by the President to economic imperatives, but also counter-recession reactions by the Congress.

During this period the states too have grown in viability. State executive agencies have become more sophisticated, state governors have been granted greater control over monies, personnel systems have been strengthened, and state legislatures have removed some of the budgeting and spending limitations imposed by archaic constitutional provisions when the states were formed. In short, state institutional capacity has improved. In spite of this growing capability to manage internal affairs, state governments continue to rely heavily on federal initiatives, especially in the area of education. Former Secretary of HEW, Joseph Califano, recently sounded a warning about the nature of this uneasy partnership. The "partnership," he noted, "between education and the federal government is fraught with dangers of federal intrusion and-domination."[66] Federal action too often follows state or local inaction.

It is evident that the state has the capacity to strengthen its role in this partnership so long as it does not become complacent. Given these factors (the effects of state funding on local decision-making and the movement to attain a greater state role in controlling pass-through funding), the next decade should witness increasingly activist state governments and more resistance to federal intrusion in state or local affairs. Califano's warning may be an indicator of greater state resistance to federal intervention. This factor, in turn, will require an adjustment in federal attitudes about the thrust of the grant-in-aid effort to achieve national goals, a trend that is evident in the increasing requirements for public participation and recipient input to federal program development.[67]

Federal Management Reform

Management improvement requires a commitment and the ability to make needed changes. Efficiency and the improvement of productivity are basic management concerns. While the federal government cannot mandate changes on state and local officials, it should avoid placing barriers in the path of reform efforts by these governments, respond positively to state and local self-development initiatives, and have its own house in order to facilitate the process of change. Most federal program officials are aware of this dilemma, but lacking Presidential commitment to these objectives they have failed to act. The brightest star of the late 1970's was the initiation of efforts to bring together and develop management capacity in the federal bureaucratic establishment.

President Carter attempted to initiate management control of the federal establishment through structural reorganization rather than management through the budgeting process. During his 1976 campaign, candidate Carter announced at the New Hampshire primary, "Don't vote for me unless you want to see the executive branch of government completely reorganized."[68] The emphasis of this reform, as it subsequently emerged following his election, was in three areas: federal agency reorganization, conversion of executive budgeting to a zero-based format (a move toward greater efficiency on budgeting and inter/intra agency management control), and civil service reform.

Following a history of reform through structural reorganization as Governor of the State of Georgia, President Carter attacked the image of governmental agencies in an effort to make them not only more comprehensible, but also more responsive to the average citizen. Using the authority granted to him by the Reorganization Act of 1977, the President hoped to institute organizational reform without the Congressional pressures and long consultation processes that traditionally have accompanied major executive reform efforts. Under the 1977 Act, reorganization plans may be submitted to Congress by the President and become effective within 60 days unless vetoed by either House.

The primary means to develop these reorganization initiatives was the President's Reorganization Project (PRP). The PRP was created by OMB to represent federal interests, to improve coordination with concerned public and citizen groups, and to develop programs and proposals for reorganizing the federal establishment.[69] During its two years of existence, the PRP developed six reorganization plans, all of which were implemented, but none of which was especially significant in scope. In short, the PRP effort did not fulfill Carter's promises to overhaul the federal establishment. Other Carter initiatives have had more apparent success.

Carter's second reform effort was more dynamic than the PRP Program. On February 14, 1977, President Carter instructed agency heads to "...develop a zero-based system within your agency in accordance with the instructions to be issued by the Office of Management and Budget...."[70] Those instructions were issued on June 29, 1977, in OMB Circular A-11. Briefly, zero-based budgeting (ZBB) requires each agency to rejustify each budget item, starting from a zero base, and to establish priorities based on requested dollar levels. The system forces intragency bargaining as priorities are established and allows OMB budget examiners to weigh priorities between agencies.

Unlike many other Presidential reform initiatives, zero-based budgeting has been accepted and has taken hold in the federal bureaucracy. However, it has had little impact on the size of the federal budget. The lack of impact is evident in comparing the FY 1978 budget (the first prepared according to ZBB) to its predecessor. This budget and the FY 1978 budget are virtually identical although ZBB impacts can be seen in the FY 1981 budget.[71]

Although the impact on the size of the budget may not seem significant (75 percent of the federal budget is obligated and thus uncontrollable), zero-base budgeting has brought line manager involvement to the budgeting process, forced agencies to establish program objectives, and generated innumerable agency assessments of the consequences of various priorities and funding levels. Perhaps, too, the logic and justification required in a ZBB exercise, in the long run, will force more management control and rationality in the budgeting process. A significant portion of federal agency time and resource is being devoted to this effort.

One of the PRP recommendations that may have been the hallmark of that program and one that is labeled as one of the most significant Carter reform effort, is the reorganization of the civil service system. The civil service reform package was sent to Congress in March 1978, and approved in October. The five features of the effort include changes in the organization of the U.S. Civil Service Commission, modification of employee appeals processes, creation of a Senior Executive Service (SES), merit pay incentives for members of the SES, and codification of the labor rights of federal employees. The most controversial of these reforms, and perhaps the one promising the greatest long-term impact in the bureaucracy, was the creation of the Senior Executive Service.[72] Under the SES, senior career executives, (under the old system general schedule grades of GS 16-18) could elect to give up some of the guarantees related to pay inceases and tenure. They would then enter a competitive system where greater pay increases could be achieved and career progression accelerated. Most former "supergrades" elected to enter this new system.

While some critics of the plan felt that the reform effort did not go far enough, there is general agreement that the effect of these changes will instill federal bureaucrats with a greater consciousness and concern about performance and productivity.[73] In time, this reform effort may stand out as the most important domestic achievement of the Carter Administration.[74]

Federalism in Transition

The trends toward greater centralization at the state level and the long-term downward flow impacts of federal management reform efforts indicate increasing cohesion in the grant-in-aid system. The growth of federal aid, the increasing impacts of cross-cuttng federal regulations, and the use of "strings" to promote national goals and purposes suggest the emergence of a new era in the growth of American federalism. However, while the glimmers of an emphasis on administration and management activities may justify this area as a designation or caveat for the new era, the signals are mixed enough to command caution. With a lack of clear indicators, the late 70's can best be labeled only as a period of transition without positive identification.

Certainly, the reform initiatives of the Carter Administration are a step in the right direction and they represent an improvement over previous federal assistance reform efforts which have been spawned by special studies or commissions or through key management activities. While these actions have led to improvements in the administration of federal assistance programs, they have not been completely successful.

On the legislative side, Congressional actions seem to indicate an increasing pressure for reform. The Federal System Reform Act of 1978 (S. 3266), the Hidden Tax Reduction (S. 3144), and the Paperwork Reduction Act (S. 3267) represent several of the many recent measures which were brought before Congress only to die a quick death. However, the possibility of Congressional action continues with the introduction of additional reform proposals each year.

If reform is on the agenda for the 1980's, a question may be raised in two parts. First, how can significant federal assistance reform be brought about, and which areas would have the most impact and importance in improving the administration and management of the intergovernmental system?

The answer to the first part of this question is not clear. The recent administrative reform efforts, the bills proposed by Congress, the innumerable study reports dating back to the Hoover and Kestnbaum Commissions, and, more recently, the Study Committee on Policy Management Assistance, the Commission on Federal Paperwork, and the laborious ACIR grant-in-aid system study, all have resulted in recommendations ranging from piecemeal to comprehensive reform or change. However, the problems have proven to be too complex and the variables too numerous to provide an easy solution. No one solution has been able to command a consensus.

The federal government has not readily accepted management improvement or change nor, to any great extent, have state and local governments. Federal programs can be used by state and local managers to strengthen their own capacity to govern their own resources; but there is little indication that this has occurred or that federal program managers have recognized this importance of the state and local role in the efficient control and management of federal dollars in the (more) effective delivery of services. Federal reform has focused on extensive procedural controls rather than on fostering the atmosphere of trust in which state and local governments voluntarily comply with the terms of assistance agreements. The recent abuses noted in the welfare program have fed fuel to this fire, and there is a tendency by the federal agencies and the Congress to generalize the lessons learned from one progrm to all others. Before meaningful reform can be promulgated, the stereotyping must be overcome.

On the average, almost one-fourth of state and local expenditures are federal funds. When matching funds are included, over one-third of state and local budgets are linked directly to federal programs. In the absence of a clear federal management strategy and in view of inconsistent funding, changing priorities, and increasing paperwork, the federal assistance system will remain a maze through which only the more sophisticted state and local governments may pass. The costs of maintaining this sophistication will continue to rise and to impose an increasingly disproportionate burden on those who can ill afford the price.

Standardizing federal administrative procedures can lead to pro forma compliance on the part of assistance recipients, but the question is, "to what end?" The lack of incentives and the unwillingness to stimulate change have led to programmatic stagnation and encouraged an arena of crisis management, instead of long-term improvement based on a spirit of cooperation.

Prognosis For The Future

The President and the Congress will continue to change federal agency administrative structures and procedures, thus, seeking an easy route to reform where none eists. Many past efforts have been reactions to the perception that OMB is unwilling or unable to control the responses and actions of the federal agencies. Every study of federal assistance has called for the establishment of a national focal point to coordinate the assistance effort. While OMB is a natural location for such an enterprise, it is evident that OMB has not sought vigorously this responsibility. The Congress, state and local leaders, and the public interest groups, all have been critical of OMB's lack of responsiveness.[75] It is only through the implementation of the recommendations of the P.L. 95-224 study that there may be a more activist OMB. (See Appendix D for draft recommendations.)

The President's recent attempts at administrative reform are in areas already covered by OMB directives. The most recent efforts are similar to those of previous administrations. These efforts are a response to legitimate state and local complaints about the inequities of the system, and yet meaningful reform has not occurred. Until domestic policy commands presidential attention in the same manner as foreign policy, presidents will continue to ignore the complex problems of the intergovernmental system.

Congressional efforts to simplify the administration of grants have been more meaningful than the piecemeal executive initiatives promulgated thus far. Passage of the Federal Grant and Cooperative Agreement Act of 1977 was a giant step in the right direction. For the first time, a clear distinction between the various assistance vehicles has been made and the involvement of federal agencies and the grantee community has been established. Perhaps even more important will be the federal assistance study mandated by the Act.

The first drafts and requests for review of the 2000 page OMB study effort were released in September 1979. Following comment and external review, the final report was forwarded to the Congress in March 1980. OMB has attempted to maintain a close liaison with the Congress in this effort and the results promise to be the linking equation needed for substantial federal reform.

The study itself opened vistas never before attempted by study groups. The fact that the study was mandated by the Congress was not lost on OMB. The questions they raised went beyond assistance reform to the very heart of federal assistance policy:

1. *Should the status quo be adjusted by providing a more central system for guiding federal assistance?*
2. *Over what guidance subjects might a comprehensive system of guidance have jurisdiction?*
3. *How much authority should any central agency have?*
4. *Should the guidance responsibilities be assigned to one agency for all subjects, or should different agencies have responsibility for different subjects?*
5. *Should the authority to issue central guidance be established by statute? Should a central agency be established by statute? Should the guidance function be seen as political or non-political?*
6. *How should the accountability of assistance recipients to the government be determined or classified?*
7. *Should distinctions in the degree of federal supervision be made among recipients based on their type, competence, prior performance, or the type of activity assisted?*
8. *How important is the development of clear definitions and usages of common assistance terms to improving assistance management?*[76]

The draft of the Executive Summary of the OMB report responds to these questions and has been included as an appendix to this text. The report may set the stage for massive, substantive reform should Congress choose to act. The question of presidential politics in 1980 may affect action one way or the other. At this point, it is too early to say more than that the stage is set. Congressional legislative efforts to standardize and simplify the system are evident in the proposals introduced before Congress, and it is only a matter of time before an omnibus reform measure will be passed. Perhaps the OMB study will provide that moving force.

The federal system has experienced a number of structural changes in the past decade. It is not clear which direction future changes will take, but for the present (as in the past), domestic reform will not be of high priority, nor is it likely to promote widespread change. It is evident, however, that intergovernmental relationships are becoming more formalized and structured. Conflict is inevitable as governments compete more strongly for limited assistance dollars. Strict rules are one means to ensure equity. The debates over the distribution formulas of these dollars are bound to increase and, at least for the present, the larger, older cities of the Northeast and Mid-West will continue to receive the largest share of the federal "pie."[77]

The federal government is attempting to promulgate requirements to represent one standard, not the same principle interpreted by many different federal agencies. Such requirements already are evident in the audit provision of the General Revenue Sharing Act and new consolidated audit policies issued in 1979 by OMB for grants-in-aid.[78] A single audit standard represents a large step forward when one considers the fact that 80 federal audit guides have been issued by 14 agencies. However, even if a single audit standard applicable to all federally assisted programs is promulgated, there is no assurance that it will include requirements that state and local accounts be maintained and financial statements be prepared according to generally accepted accounting principles. Coordinated financial management will require active participation in the development of these standards by federal aid recipient governments and clearer directions, but these roles are yet to be clarified.

The President's study of federal planning requirements should produce more order to the system as the federal government attempts to link planning requirements to operating funds. Legislation introduced in 1978 was designed to strengthen areawide planning by requiring a single, overall areawide development plan. Its implementation may serve to eliminate many duplicate program planning needs.

The pressure to economize in the aftermath of Proposition 13 also has affected the future of the federal assistance effort. Programs of the mid-1970's, which stressed innovation, demonstration, or technology transfer, have given way to general governmental support to meet citizen demands for more services but no more taxes. The new types of federal assistance—general revenue sharing, the block grants, and more generally directed formula-based grants—also have changed the nature of intergovernmental relations. More money is being sent directly to local governments and is being used for general purpose expenditures. While labeled as temporary, these programs are likely to be around for some time and to represent a subsidy upon which local governments have developed a dependency that will not be severed readily.

Finally, several external forces are exerting an influence on the shape of the intergovernmental system. The effects of the energy crisis are just now becoming a way-of-life reality. Another significant factor is the size, composition, and nature of the public sector work force. Increasing technology complexity, the requirements for more sophisticated operations, and the public employee response to these demands (i.e., greater management capability as well as a larger work force) will have a significant impact on the federal system. As ACIR has noted:

These trends indicate the emergence of a new American federal system with a transformed and incredibly complex network of intergovernmental relations. And, although the changes have been piecemeal and apparently discontinuous, the system is substantially different from its predecessor only one decade ago.[79]

Change is apparent, but the nature of this change is contingent upon a significant number of variables. The 1980's should afford a clearer view of where the federal system is going and what it has become. The era of New Federalism is clearly at an end. The federal management initiatives of the late seventies ushered in a new era that is characterized by a receptivity to large scale reform of the grant-in-aid system. However, the Reagan Administration is committed to a political philosophy drastically different than what emerged as a domestic policy in the last years of the 1970's. Administrative and management reform during this period required not only enforcement of existing regulations but the creation of new ones. The Reagan Administration appears committed to a reversal of this approach, but it is yet too early to predict a distinct direction. The next few years may set the tone for the decade and afford a clearer view of where the federal system is going and what it has or will become. In any case a new era is in the offing, with the new label or caveat describing our intergovernmental or federal system yet to be determined. Until then the appropriate descriptor in this transitory period is "Managing Federalism."

Notes

1. Elmer B. Staats, "The New Mix of Federal Assistance: Categorical Grants, Block Grants, and General Revenue Sharing," American Federalism: Toward a More Effective Partnership, report and papers from the National Conference of American Federalism in Action, Washington, D.C., Feburary 20-22, 1975 (Washington, D.C.: ACIR, undated), p. 59.
2. General Accounting Office, Perspectives on Intergovernmental Policy and Fiscal Relations, GGD-79-62 (Washington, D.C.: GPO, June 28, 1979), p.5.
3. Federal Aid Simplification, White House Status Report (Washington D.C.: The White House, September, 1978), unnumbered pages. The complete text of the Presidential memoranda contained in this report.
4. Ibid.
5. President Carter, The White House, "Statement by the President" September 9, 1977.
6. Jack H. Watson, Jr., The White House,"Federal and Reform Follow-up," memorandum, March 13, 1978.
7. Federal Aid Simplification,..., pp. 32-36.
8. Ibid., p. 40.
9. Ibid., pp. 40-50.
10. Secretary Califano, Department of Health, Education, and Welfare, memorandum, September 19, 1977.
11. Ibid.
12. Secretary Califano, Department of Health, Education and Welfare, "Actions Required to Correct Major Deficiencies in the Contracting and Grants Processes," May 18, 1977; also "Califano Seeks Curb on Abuse in Grant Contract Procedures," Higher Education and National Affairs, May 20, 1977, pp. 4-5; and U.S. Congress, House, Committee on Government Operation, "Lack of Guidelines for Federal Contract and Grant Data," 45th Cong., 2d Sess., Committee print (Washington,D.C.:GPO,September 29, 1978).
13. Committee on Governmental Relations,National Association of College and University Business Officers, "Suspension of HEW Letter of Credit and Withholding of Payments," August 24, 1977.
14. See also James L. Rowe, Jr., "U.S. Agencies Fail to Heed Auditor's Findings," The Washington Post, October 22, 1978, p. 17.
15. U.S. Department of Health, Education, and Welfare, news release, HEW News, February 16, 1978; and Committee on Governmental Relations, National Association of College and University Business Officers, "DHEW Audit Resolution Policies," February 21, 1978.
16. See President Carter, The White House, "Implementation of Federal Planning Requirements and Reform Proposals for Domestic Assistance Grants", June 21, 1978.
17. Director McIntyre, OMB,"Implementation of Federal Planning Requirement Reforms," memorandum,August 14, 1978. As an attachment, the OMB memorandum included a copy of the June 5, 1978 OMB memorandum to the President indicating agency actions in compliance with the

Presidential directive. See Director, OMB, "Report on Review of Federal Planning Requirements and Plan for Implementation of Reforms," June 5, 1978.

18. See General Accounting Office, Improved Cooperation and Coordination Needed Among All Levels of Government—Office of Management and Budget Circular, A-95, GGD-75-52 (Washington, D.C.: GPO, February 11, 1975); and General Accounting Office, Federally Assisted Areawide Planning: Need to Simplify Policies and Practices, GGD-77-24 (Washington, D.C.: GPO, March 28, 1977).

19. Vincent Puritano, "Regionalism and Reorganization," County News, January 9, 1978, p. 4a.

20. Jack H. Watson, Jr., The White House, "Federal Regional Council Assessment," April 24, 1977.

21. Office of Management and Budget, memorandum "Assessment of the Federal Regional Council System." undated.

22. Vincent Puritano, "Regionalism...," p. 4a.

23. See, for example, "Uncle Sam's Fraud Hot Line: A Hit with Angry Taxpayers," U.S. News and World Report, August 20, 1978, p. 38; also, Timothy B. Clark, "Making Government Workers Toe the Performance Line," National Journal (July 14, 1979), and Richard D. Lyons, "Carter Plans Proposed to Protect Whistle-Blowers in Goverment," The New York Times, February 16, 1978, p. A18.

24. Quoted in U.S. Senate, Committee on Governmental Affairs, Federal Grant and Cooperative Agreement Act of 1977, S. 431, 95th Cong., 1st Sess. (Washington, D.C.: GPO, September 22, 1977), p. 3.

25. Ibid., p. 6

26. Office of Management and Budget, "Implementation of Federal Grant and Cooperative Agreement Act of 1977 (P.L. 95-224)," Part III, Federal Register, May 19, 1978.

27. An early discussion of this problem is contained in Robert D. Newton, "Administrative Federalism," Public Administration Review, Vol. 38, No. 3 (May/June 1978), pp. 252-255.

28. Office of Management and Budget, "Plan for the Study of Federal Assistance Programs," Federal Register, Part V, January 8, 1979,

29. See Commission on Federal Paperwork, A Report of the Commission on Federal Paperwork: Federal/State/Local Cooperation," (Washington, D.C.: GPO, July 15, 1977).

30. Office of Management and Budget, Paperwork and Red Tape—New Perspectives—New Directions (Washington, D.C.: Office of Management and Budget, June, 1978), p. 33.

31. U.S. Senate, Congressional Record (May 25, 1978), pp. S8339-S8346.

32. President Carter, Statement by the President, quoted in Federal Aid Simplification, White House Status Report, September 1978, p.9.

33. Ibid., p. 71.

34. Ibid., p. 55.

35. Advisory Commission on Intergovernmental Relations, Summary and

Concluding Observation, A-62, June 1978, p. 75.

36. Ibid., p. 78.

37. See General Accounting Office, The Federal Role in Improving Productivity—Is The National Center for Productivity and Quality of Working Life the Proper Mechanism?, FGMSD-78-26 (Washington, D.C.: GPO, May 23, 1978). The first Congressional effort for productivity improvement occurred with the establishment of the National Commission on Productivity in 1970.

38. Ibid., p 22. See also Larry Froelich, "Government Rules Hurt Investment," Akron Beacon Journal, March 9, 1977, p. B7.

39. General Accounting Office, State and Local Government Productivity Improvement: What is the Federal Role?, GGD-78-104 (Washington, D.C.: December 6, 1978). p. iii.

40. Ibid., p. 46. For some of the positive incentive features of the grant system, see National Commission on Productivity and Work Quality, Employee Incentives to Improve State and Local Government Productivity, CP75015 (Washington, D.C.: GPO, March 1957). For other potential federal roles in improving productivity, see Committee for Economic Development, Improving Federal Program Performance (N.Y.: C.E.D., September 1975); and C.E.D., Improving Productivity in State and Local Government (N.Y.: C.E.D., March 1976).

41. A New Partnership to Conserve America's Communities (Washington, D.C.: The President's Urban and Regional Policy Group Report, March 1978, p. 2.

42. "Will More Billions Save Our Cities?," U.S. News and World Report, April 10, 1978, p. 21.

43. A New Partnership to Conserve..., pp. 111-112.

44. For the full text of this policy notice, refer to Ibid., pp. 11-13 ff.

45. Quoted in Grayson Mitchell, "Carter Unveils Urban Plan of $8.3 Billion," Los Angeles Times, March 28, 1978, p. 1.

46. Quoted in Michael· Hirsley and Ed McManns, "Carter Plan Funding Leaves Experts Cold," Chicago Tribune, March 29, 1978, pp. 11-12.

47. David S. Broder, "Urban Policy: A House of Cards," Los Angeles Times, March 28, 1978, p. 7.

48. Quoted in "Urban Caucus Set," County News, April 10, 1978, p. 1.

49. Quoted in Bernard F. Hillenbrand, "Urban Policy Misses Mark," County News, April 10, 1978, p. 7.

50. Quoted in "New Partnership Draws Mixed Reviews in First Year," Public Administration Times, July 1, 1979, p. 4. For the full ACIR evaluation, refer to ACIR, Information Bulletin No. 79-4, The National Urban Policy: One Year Later.

51. State Bailout Saves Prop 13 Job Cuts," Public Administration Times, July 1978, p. 1.

52. Beverly T. Watkins, "Proposition 13 and Higher Education, 12 Months Later," The Chronicle of Higher Education, May 29, 1979, p. 29.

53. Timothy B. Clark, "Making Government Workers Toe the Performance

Line," National Journal, July 14, 1979, pp. 1162 ff.

54. General Accounting Office, Will Federal Assistance to California Be Affected by Proposition 13?, GGS-78-100 (Washington, D.C.: GPO, August 10, 1978).

55. David B. Walker, "A New Intergovernmental System in 1977," Publius, Winter 1978, pp. 101-115.

56. Advisory Commission on Intergovernmental Relations, The Intergovernmental Grant System as Seen by Local, State, and Federal Officials, A-54 (Washington, D.C.: GPO, March 1977), p. 57.

57. Council of State Governments, The Book of The States: 1978-1979, Vol. 22 (Lexington, Ky:Council of State Governments, 1978), p. 602.

58. Advisory Commission on Intergovernmental Relations, The Intergovernmental Grant System..., p. 60.

59. Ibid., p. 63.

60. Advisory Commission on Intergovernmental Relations, The States and Intergovernmental Aids, A-59 (Washington, D.C.: GPO, February 1977), p. 23.

61. David B. Walker and Albert J. Richter,"States and the Impact of Federal Grants," State Government, Spring 1977, p. 86.

62. Ibid.

63. Quoted in "Federal Commission Touts State Legislative Control Over Federal Grant Funds," National Association of State Universities and Land-Grant Colleges, Circular Letter No., 11, May 12, 1977, p. 1.

64. David B. Walker, "The Localities Under the New Intergovernmental System: Will More Aid Assist, Atrophy, or Asphyxiate America's Counties, Cities, and Towns?," paper presented at a seminar on "A Federal Response to the Fiscal Crisis in American Cities," June 15, 1978, p. 8.

65. Ibid.

66. Quoted from a speech reprinted in National Association of State Univesities and Land-Grant Colleges, "Fight for Federal Dollars But Against Federal Domination," Circular Letter No. 16, October 12, 1978, p. 7.

67. For an excellent discussion of this effort, see Pablo Eisenberg, "Monitoring Government: Issues/Challenges/Approaches," Foundation News, Vol. 20, No. 2 (March/April 1979), pp. 43-7.

68. Quoted in Elizabeth Drew, American Journal: The Events of 1976 (New York: Random House, 1976), p. 40.

69. For a complete description of the PRP, see John R. Dempsey, "Carter Reorganization: A Midterm Appraisal," Public Administration Review, Vol. 39, No. 1 (January/February 1979), pp. 74-78.

70. Quoted in Donald Haider, "Zero-Base: Federal Style," Public Administration Review, Vol. 37, No. 4 (July/August 1977), pp. 400-407.

71. John R. Dempsey, "Carter Reorganization...," p. 76.

72. For a full discussion of these reform measures, refer to the following: Alan K. Campbell, "Civil Service Reform: A New Commitment," Public Admini-

stration Review, Vol. 38, No. 2 (March/April 1978), pp. 99-103; Timothy B. Clark, "Making Government Workers Toe the Performance Line." National Journal, July 14, 1979, pp. 1162-1166; and Timothy B. Clark, "Senior Executive Service—Reform From the Top," National Journal, September 30, 1978, pp. 1542-1546.

73. See articles by Bernard Rosen, Lawrence C. Howard, and Frederick C. Thayer in Public Administration Review, Vol. 38, No. 4 (July/August 1978) pp. 301-314.

74. John R. Dempsey, "Carter Reorganization...," p. 77.

75. General Accounting Office, Perspectives on Intergovernmental Policy..., p. 39.

76. See Office Management and Budget, Managing Federal Assistance in the 1980's: A Study of Federal Assistance Pursuant to the Federal Grant and Cooperative Agreement Act of 1977 P.L. 95-224): Study Overview (Washington, D.C.: OMB, August 27, 1979); also, A-7 Description of Existing Guidance: Summary Analysis; A-8 Description of Existing Guidance: Inventory of National Policy Requirements; B-1 Alternatives for a Comprehensive System of Guidance: Basic Concepts; B-2 Alternatives for a Comprehensive System of Guidance: System Models; C. Alternative Means of Implementing Federal Assistance; D. Evaluation of P.L. 95-224; E. Equity, Fairness, and Competition, F. Research and Development; G. Recipient Related Issues; H. Environment of Federal Assistance.

77. For an assessment of federal aid trends, see General Accounting Office, Changing Patterns of Federal Aid to State and Local Governments, 1969-75, PAD-78-15 (Washington, D.C.: GPO, December 20, 1977).

78. See T. Jack Gary, Jr., "A Single Audit of Federally Assisted Programs?," Public Administration Review, Vol. 39, No. 4 (July/August 1979), pp. 389-394.

79. Advisory Commission on Intergovernmental Relations, The Intergovernmental Grant System: An Assessment and Proposed Policies, B1 (Washington, D.C.: GPO, undated), p. 27.

CHAPTER VII SELECTED BIBLIOGRAPHY

Articles/Documents

Advisory Commission on Intergovernmental Relations. The National Urban Policy: One Year Later. Information Bulletin No. 79-4.

_____ . Summary and Concluding Observation, A-62. Washington, D.C.: GPO, June 1978.

_____ . The Intergovernmental Grant System: An Assessment and Proposed Policies, B1. Washington, D.C.: GPO (undated).

_____ . The Intergovernmental Grant System as Seen by Local, State, and Federal Officials, A-54. Washington, D.C.: GPO, March 1977.

_____ . The States and Intergovernmental Aids, A-59. Washington, D.C.: GPO, February 1977.

American Society for Public Administration. News and Views. October 26, 1976.

A New Partnership to Conserve America's Communities. Washington, D.C.: The President's Urban and Regional Policy Group Report, March 1978.

Broder, David S. "Urban Policy: A House of Cards," Los Angeles Times. March 28, 1978.

"Califano Seeks Curb on Abuse in Grant Contract Procedures," Higher Education and National Affairs. May 20, 1977.

Campbell, Alan K. "Civil Service Reform: A New Commitment," Public Administration Review, Vol. 38, No. 2 (March/April 1978).

Clark, Timothy B. "Making Government Workers Toe the Performance Line," National Journal. July 14, 1979.

_____ . "Senior Executive Service—Reform From the Top," National Journal. September 30, 1978.

Commission on Federal Paperwork. A Report of the Commission on Federal Paperwork: Federal/State/Local Cooperation. Washington, D.C.: GPO, July 15, 1977.

Committee for Economic Development. Improving Federal Program Performance. New York: Committee for Economic Development, September 1975.

_____ . Improving Productivity in State and Local Government. New York: Committee for Economic Development, March 1976.

Committee on Governmental Relations, National Association of College University Business Officers. "Suspension of HEW Letter of Credit and Withholding of Payments." August 24, 1977.

Dempsey, John R. "Carter Reorganization: A Midterm Appraisal," Public Administration Review, Vol. 39, No.1 (January/February 1979).

Director, OMB. "Implementation of Federal Planning Requirement Reforms," Memorandum. August 14, 1978.

_____ . "Report on Review of Federal Planning Requirements and Plan for Implementation of Reforms." June 5, 1978.

Eisenberg, Pablo. "Monitoring Government: Issues/Challenges/Approaches," Foundation News, Vol. 20, No. 2 (March/April 1979).

Federal Aid Simplification. White House Status Report. Washington, D.C.: The White House, September 1978.

"Federal Commission Touts State Legislative Control Over Federal Grant Funds." National Association of State University and Land-Grant Colleges. Circular Letter No. 11, May 12, 1977.

Froelich, Larry. "Government Rules Hurt Investment," Akron Beacon Journal. March 9, 1977.

Gary, T. Jack, Jr. "A Single Audit of Federally Assisted Programs?," Public Administration Review, Vol. 39, No. 4 (July/August 1979)

General Accounting Office. Changing Patterns of Federal Aid to State and Local Governments, 1969-75, PAD 78-15. Washington, D.C.: GPO, December 20, 1977.

_____ . Federally Assisted Areawide Planning: Need to Simplify Policies and Practices, GGD 77-24. Washington, D.C.: GPO, March 28, 1977.

_____ . Improved Cooperation and Coordination Needed Among All Levels of Government—Office of Management and Budget Circular, A-95. GGD 75-52. Washington, D.C.: GPO, February 11, 1975.

_____ . Perspectives on Intergovernmental Policy and Fiscal Relations, GGD 79-62. Washington, D.C.: GPO, June 28, 1979.

_____ . State and Local Government Productivity Improvement: What Is The Federal Role?, GGD 78-104. Washington, D.C.: GPO, December 6, 1978.

_____ . The Federal Role in Improving Productivity—Is the National Center for Productivity and Quality of Working Life the Proper Mechanism?, FGMSD 78-26. Washington, D.C.: GPO, May 23, 1978.

_____ . Will Federal Assistance to California Be Affected by Proposition 13?, GGD 78-100. Washington, D.C.: GPO, August 10, 1978.

Haider, Donald. "Presidential Management Initiatives: A Ford Legacy to Executive Management Improvement," Public Administration Review, Vol. 39, No. 3 (May/June 1979).

_____ . "Zero-Based: Federal Style," Public Administration Review, Vol. 37, No. 4 (July/August 1977).

Hillenbrand, Bernard F. "Urban Policy Misses Mark," County News. April 10, 1978.

Hirsley, Michael and McManns, Ed. "Carter Plan Funding Leaves Experts Cold," Chicago Tribune. March 29, 1978.

Lyons, Richard D. "Carter Plans Proposed to Protect Whistle-Blowers in Government," The New York Times. February 16, 1978.

"Memoranda from OMB Director James T. Lynn to the twenty department and agency heads participating in PMI." July 27, 1976.

Mitchell, Grayson. "Carter Unveils Urban Plan of $8.3 Billion," Los Angeles Times. March 28, 1978.

National Association of State Universities and Land-Grant Colleges. "Fight for Federal Dollars But Against Federal Domination," Circular Letter No. 16. October 12, 1978.

National Commission on Productivity and Work Quality. Employee Incentives to Improve State and Local Government Productivity. CP75015. Washington, D.C.: GPO, March 1975.

"New Partnership Draws Mixed Reviews in First year," Public Administration Times. July 1, 1979.

Newton, Robert D. "Administrative Federalism," Public Administration View, Vol. 38, No. 3 (May/June 1978).

Office of Management and Budget. "Assessment of the Federal Regional Council System," Memorandum (undated).

_____ . A-7 Description of Existing Guidance: Summary Analysis.

_____ . A-8 Description of Existing Guidance: Inventory of National Policy Requirements.

_____ . B-1 Alternatives for a Comprehensive System of Guidance: Basic Concepts.

_____ . B-2 Alternatives for a Comprehensive System of Guidance: System Models.

_____ . C. Alternative Means of Implementing Federal Assistance.

_____ . D. Evaluation of Public Law 95-224.

_____ . E. Equity, Fairness, and Competition.

_____ . F. Research and Development.

_____ . G. Recipient Related Issues.

_____ . H. Environment of Federal Assistance.

_____ . "Implementation of Federal Grant and Cooperative Agreement Act of 1977 (P.L. 95-224)." Part III. Federal Register. May 19, 1978.

_____ . Managing Federal Assistance in the 1980's' A Study of Federal Assistance Pursuant to the Federal Grant and Cooperative Agreement Act of 1977 (P.L. 95-224): Study Overview. Washington, D.C.: OMB, August 27, 1979.

_____ . Paperwork and Red Tape—New Perspectives—New Directions. Washington, D.C.: OMB, June 1978.

_____ . "Plan for the Study of Federal Assistance Programs," Federal Register. Part V. January 8, 1979.

President Carter, The White House: "Implementation of Federal Planning Requirements and Reform Proposals for Domestic Assistance Grants." June 21, 1978.

Puritano, Vincent. "Regionalism and Reorganization," County News. January 9, 1978.

Rosen, Bernard; Howard, Lawrence C. and Thayer, Frederick C. Public Administration Review, Vol. 38, No. 4 (July/August 1978).

Rowe, James L., Jr. "U.S. Agencies Fail to Heed Auditor's Findings," The Washington Post. October 22, 1978.

Secretary, Health, Education, and Welfare. "Actions Required to Correct Major Deficiencies in the Contracting and Grants Processes." May 18, 1977.

_____ . Memorandum. September 19, 1977.

Staats, Elmer B. "The New Mix of Federal Assistance: Categorical Grants Block Grants, and General Revenue Sharing," American Federalism:

Toward a More Effective Partnership. Washington D.C.: Advisory Council on Intergovernmental Relations (undated).

"State Bailout Saves Prop. 13 Job Cuts," Public Administration Times. July 1978.

"Uncle Sam's Fraud Hot Line: A Hit with Angry Taxpayers," U.S. News and World Report. August 20, 1978.

"Urban Caucus Set," County News. April 10, 1978.

U.S. Congress, House, Committee on Government Operations. Lack of Guidelines for Federal Contract and Grant Data.45th Cong., 2nd Sess., Washington, D.C.: GPO, September 29, 1978.

U.S. Departement of Health, Education, and Welfare. "News Release," HEW News. February 16, 1978.

U.S. President. Statement by the President quoted in Federal Aid Simplification: White House Statement of New Perspectives—New Directions. Washington, D.C.: OMB, June 1978.

Walker, David B. "A New Intergovernmental System in 1977," Publius. Winter 1978.

_____. "The Localities Under the New Intergovernmental System: Will More Aid Assist, Atrophy, Or Asphyxiate America's Counties, Cities, and Towns?" Paper presented at a seminar on "A Federal Response to the Fiscal Crisis in American Cities," June 15, 1978.

_____ and Richter, Albert J. "States and the Impact of Federal Grants," State Government. Spring 1977.

Watkins, Beverly T. "Proposition 13 and Higher Education, 12 Months Later," The Chronicle of Higher Education. May 29, 1979.

Watson, Jack H., Jr.The White House,"Federal and Reform Follow-up." Memorandum. March 13, 1978.

_____. "Federal Regional Council Assessment," April 24, 1977.

"Will More Billions Save Our Cities?" U.S. News and World Report. April 10, 1978.

Books
Council of State Governments. The Book of the States: 1978-1979, Vol. 22. Lexington, Kentucky: Council of State Governments, 1978.

Drew, Elizabeth. American Journal: The Events of 1976. New York: The Random House, 1976.

Rose, Richard. Managing Presidential Objectives. New York: The Free Press, 1976.

Hearings
U.S. Congress, House. "Reorganization Plan No. 2 of 1970." Hearings before a subcommittee of the Committee on Government Operations, 91st Cong., 2nd Sess., 1970.

U.S. Congress, Senate, Committee on Governmental Affairs. Federal Grant and Cooperative Agreement Act of 1977. S. 431, 95th Cong., 1st Sess., Washington, DC.: GPO, September 22, 1977.

APPENDICES

APPENDIX A

A GUIDE TO COMMONLY USED TERMS, ABBREVIATIONS, AND ACRONYMS

ACIR: Advisory Commission on Intergovernmental Relations. A permanent commission established by Congress (PL-380) in 1959 "to give continuing attention to intergovernmental problems." ACIR's mandate includes bringing together participants from federal, state, and local governments to consider common problems, to provide a forum for addressing issues related to the administration of assistance programs, to provide technical assistance to the executive and legislative branches of the federal government in the review and assessment of proposed legislation and its overall effect on the federal system, to encourage study of emerging problems that may require intergovernmental cooperation, and to develop appropriate recommendations pursuant to its statutory responsibilities.

*ALLOCATION FORMULA: The quantitative formula by which grant funds are distributed to eligible recipients. Usually it is specified in legislation, but sometimes is provided by regulations.

ANNUAL ARRANGEMENTS: A program to facilitate coordination among grant programs and to increase the city's capacity to set priorities. Involves negotiations between HUD field offices and cities aimed at packaging categorical programs into community development activities (See also HUD, Planned Variations, HCDA).

ARC: Appalachian Regional Commission. Grants of the ARC, a Federal-Interstate Compact, are directed in multi-county areas to help develop assistance. The eligible units of government are the Appalachian states and through them, multi-county organizations (local development districts) certified by the states. Funding for FY-74 was $3.45 million.

APPLICANT: Includes one or more state or local governments or other public or private agencies acting separately or together in seeking assistance with respect to a single project.

ASPA: American Society for Public Administration. A non-profit professional association of practitioners, teachers, researchers, and students of public administration.

---

* NOTE: The asterisked definitions were taken from Advisory Commission on Intergovernmental Relations. Summary and Concluding Observations — The Intergovernmental Grant System: An Assessment and Proposed Policies, A-62 (Washington, D.C.: GPO, June 1978), Glossary, pp. 79-82. The remaining definitions were developed in whole or in part by Raymond A. Shapek as a staff member of the OMB/NSF Study Committee on Policy Management Assistance. See Executive Office of the President, Strengthening Public Management in the Intergovernmental System (Washington, D.C.: GPO, 1975), Glossary

BLOCK GRANT: A consolidation of functional programs into one grant in which grantees are eligible through a formula or very broad application process. (See LEAA, CETA,HCDA)

CAPACITY BUILDING: A term used to refer to any system, effort, or process—including a federal grant or contract—which includes among its major objectives strengthening the capability of elected Chief Executive Officers, Chief Administrative Officers, department and agency heads, and program managers in general purpose governments to plan, implement, manage, or evaluate policies, strategies, or programs designed to impact on social conditions in the community.

Capacity Building is used as a generic term to refer to programs, projects, services, or activities designed to strengthen the capabilities of general purpose governments—national, state, regional, or local—to perform the functions associated with Policy Management (PM), Resource Management (RM), or Program/Operations Management (OM), (See also Elected Official, Policy Management, Resource Management, Program Management, Technical Assistance, Federal Assistance Programs).

CATALOGUE OF FEDERAL DOMESTIC ASSISTANCE: A compilation of federal programs of assistance available to states, localities, and other recipients, prepared annually by the Office of Management and Budget and updated semiannually.

CATEGORICAL GRANTS: A grant-in-aid offering limited use for a specific objective, requiring the recipient to match a fraction of the grant. (Also a conditional grant).

CED: Committee for Economic Development. The CED, founded in 1942, is comprised of 200 trustees (it is not a membership organization) drawn from the business and academic communities who conduct research and formulate policy recommendations on major economic issues. Areas of research have included education, national economic policy, government management, and urban and area studies. CED conducts local and regional policy forums for discussion, research, and economic policy recommendation.

CERC: Chief Executive Review and Comment. A process which allows local elected officials to review and comment on local grant applications. A city strategy statement of community development goals, objectives, problems, and solutions is formulated by a committee made up of the major HUD grant recipients involved. After negotiation between the local chief executive and the HUD area office director, a memorandum of understanding is drafted. This process enables city executives to improve their coordination of HUD-funded programs and to increase their abilities to set local priorities as well as to receive reasonable assurance the funds will be provided during the year. Over 200 cities have participated in this program since it was initiated in December of 1970.

CIVIL SERVICE COMMISSION: Now OPM (Office of Personnel Management), (See IPA, F.E.I.).

CLOSED-END: A legislative appropriation with a limit, i.e., an "end". Contrasted with open-end.

CETA: The Comprehensive Employment and Training Act of 1973. Establishes a broad-based block grant program of manpower and manpower-related activities including recruiting, training, and other manpower services. Chief executives or "prime sponsor" designees must appoint and staff a planning council with advisory and evaluative responsibilities which is responsible for developing a comprehensive manpower plan.

CRP: Community Renewal Program. HUD's Community Renewal Program was among the earliest to provide comprehensive planning assistance to local governments. CRP was superceded by the Comprehensive Planning and Management Assistance Program, i.e., HUD "701." (See also HUD 701).

COMPREHENSIVE PLANNING ASSISTANCE (701): A categorical grant program based on Section 701 of the Housing Act of 1965. Grants are given to support a broad range of planning and management activities by HUD, including comprehensive planning, development, and improvement of management capacity for plan implementation and development. All recipients must produce a plan with both a housing and land use element.

*CONDITIONAL GRANT: A grant that is awarded with limitations (conditions) attached to use of the funds. Both categorical and block grants are conditional, although the categorical grant generally has a greater number and severity of conditions.

*COST-SHARING: The provisions by which the costs of assisted programs are shared between the grantor and the recipient (and sometimes by third parties).

COG'S: Council of Governments. COG's represents multi-jurisdictional cooperative arrangements to permit a comprehensive approach to planning, development, transportation, environment, and similar problems that affect the region as a whole. They are comprised of designated policymaking representatives from each participating government within the region. COG's are substate regional planning agencies established by states and are responsible for areawide review of projects applying for federal funds (A-95 Project Notification and Review) and for development of regional plans and other areawide special purpose arrangements.

COUNCIL OF STATE GOVERNMENTS: The CSG is a joint agency of all state governments—created, supported, and directed by them. Its purpose is to strengthen all branches of state government and preserve the state governmental role in the American federal system through catalyzing the expression of states' view of major issues; conducting research on state programs and problems; assisting in federal-state liaison and state-regional-local cooperation; offering training, reference and consultation services to state agencies, officials, and legislators; and serving as a broad instrument for bringing together all elements of state government.

*DISCRETIONARY GRANT: A grant awarded at the discretion of a federal administrator, subject to conditions specified by legislation. Generally use interchangeably with project grant.

DOL: The Department of Labor (See also CETA)

DOT: The Department of Transportation.

ECONOMIC DEVELOPMENT ADMINISTRATION (EDA): Department of Commerce. An FY 1974 obligation of $7,700,000 (requested $900,000 in FY 1975) was used in the development of multi-county district (and redevelopment areas) planning capabilities with an emphasis on the creation of jobs for the unemployed and underemployed (Federal Catalog Code 11.302).

ELECTED OFFICIAL: A term used to refer to elected and/or appointed officials who typically and on a continuing basis exercise policy-making and/or strategic (or policy) management functions. Accordingly, the term "elected officials" includes Chief Executive Officers (CEO) or Chief Adminisrative Officers (CAO)—e.g., city managers, appointed officials whose principal tasks are to assist the CEO or CAO in the policy-making process, and legislators—including councilmen and commissioners of general purpose governments.

ELIGIBILITY: Refers to legislative and administrative criteria for determining which units of government (or other potential beneficiaries—e.g., Indian Tribes, non-profits, universities, individuals, etc.) are entitled to be recipients of federal assistance programs. Federal entitlement procedures distinguish applicant beneficiaries from recipient beneficiaries, for they are sometimes different. (See also Federal Assistance Programs, Categorical Grants, Revenue Sharing, Block Grants).

EXECUTIVE ORDER (E.O.): Executive Order of the President. Most federal efforts to come to grips with the management problems resulting from the proliferation of federal categorical programs are a consequence of administrative rather than legislative initiatives. The administrative initiatives are typically in the form of E.O.'s or of OMB Circulars (e.g., A-95). Congressional action establishing ACIR and the emerging role of Congress' General Accounting Office (GAO) are notable exceptions.

EPA: The Environmental Protection Agency.

FEDERAL ASSISTANCE PROGRAMS: A term used to refer to the variety of federal programs available to state and local governments (including counties, cities, metropolitan, and regional governments), schools, colleges, and universities, health institutions, non-profit and profit organizations, and individuals and families. Current federal assistance programs are listed in the annual Catalogue of Federal Domestic Assistance. Federal assistance programs provide assistance through grant or contractual arrangements and include technical assistance programs or programs providing assistance in the form of loans.

FEDERAL ASSISTANCE REVIEW (FAR): A three-year federal effort initiated in the late 1960's, conducted by OMB and agencies represented on the Domestic Council, for the purpose of decentralizing, standardizing, and simplifying the federal grant system.

FEI: The Federal Executive Institute. FEI was established in 1966 to provide opportunities for developing management skills among supergrade officials in the federal service.

FEDERAL GRANT AND COOPERATIVE AGREEMENT ACT of 1977: (P.L. 95-224) An Act which was passed to clarify the meaning of the assistance award instruments in grants and cooperative agreements. Cooperative agreements are differentiated from grants by requiring the "substantial involvement" of the funding agency in the assistance relationship. Perhaps more important is the study mandated by the Act. OMB is tasked to perform a substantive evaluation of the federal assistance system and report its findings to Congress in the first such authorization ever passed by Congress.

FEDERAL LIAISON OFFICES (FLO): Federal Liaison Offices are maintained in Washington, D.C. by many state and local governments to facilitate relationships with federal agencies and federal program administrators. FLO's are a product of the proliferation of federal assistance programs and the complex and non-uniform set of federal practices that range from the application through the reporting and auditing process.

*FEDERAL PROGRAM INFORMATION ACT OF 1977: Legislation providing for the continuation and improvement of a central source of information about federal assistance programs, including continual revision and making the information accessible to potential assistance recipients through the use of modern computer technology.

*FMC CIRCULAR 73-2: A federal management circular establishing the principles for audit of federal operations and programs by Executive Branch agencies. (Now A-73)

*FMC CIRCULAR 74-4: A federal management circular establishing cost principles applicable to grants and contracts with state and local governments. (Now A-87)

*FMC CIRCULAR 74-7: See OMB Circular A-102 below.

*FORMULA-BASED CATEGORICAL: A categorical grant under which funds are allocated among recipients according to factors specified in legislation or in administrative regulations.

FORMULA GRANT: Grant allocations based on specified formulas incorporated in the outlying statutes. (See Grant-In-Aid).

*FORMULA-PROJECT CATEGORICAL: A project for which a formula specified in statutes or regulations is used to determine the amount available for a state area, and then funds are distributed at the discretion of the administrator in response to project applications submitted by substate entities.

FRC: The Federal Regional Councils. (See also FAR). Established under E.O. 11647 in February 1972, they are comprised of the chief regional offices of DOL. HEW, DOT, OEO, EPA, LEAA, DOA, and DOI serving the ten standard federal regions. Their primary charge is to develop clearer working relations between federal grant-making agencies and state and local governments and to improve coordination in the categorical grant-in-aid system.

*FUNGIBILITY: A grant is "fungible" when the recipient is able to use the grant moneys for purposes other than those specified in the grant authorization.

GAO: The General Accounting Office. GAO is an arm of the Legislative Branch whose charge includes an evaluation function vis-a-vis federal policies and programs. GAO efforts have included some attention to the intergovernmental relations process.

*GENERAL APPLICABLE REQUIREMENTS: Performance requirements that Congress attaches more or less across the board to all grant programs. They are usually imposed to achieve certain national policy objectives, such as uniform relocation benefits, equal employment opportunities, and environmental protection. Also called cross-cutting requirements.

GENERAL REVENUE SHARING (GRS): A block grant program which authorizes expenditures to be allocated as determined by recipient governments, for example: public safety, environmental protection, public transportation, health, recreation, libraries, social services for the poor and aged, financial administration.

GRANT-IN-AID: Federal transfers of payments to states or federal or state transfers to local governments for specified purposes usually subject to a measure of supervision and review by the granting government or agency in accordance with prescribed standards and requirements.

GRANTS-IN-KIND: Donations of federal surplus property or commodities to state and local governments.

GSA: General Services Administration.

*HOLD HARMLESS: A grant provision that guarantees recipient grants equal to at least some percentage—often 100%—of a previous year's grant. It is designed to protect the recipient from sharp decreases in grant revenue due to fluctuations in the formula's factors or the changes in the formula itself. Often used only for temporary transition periods, staged at decreasing percentages for successive years.

HCDA: The Housing and Community Development Act (See also Revenue Sharing Block Grants).

HEW: The Department of Health, Education, and Welfare (See also SITO, FAR).

HUD: The Department of Housing and Urban Development. HUD efforts, measured by dollars invested, constitute major elements of current federal capacity-building programs. In addition, HUD "701" (the Comprehensive Planning Assistance Program) is one of the few existing sources of federal support to state and local governments for developing Policy Management Capacity. (See also Policy Management).

HUD "701": Refers to Section 701 of the Housing Act of 1954 (and subsequent amendments) which provides for grants to strengthen the "planning and decision-making capabilities of chief executives of state, area-wide, and local agencies to promote more effective use of the nation's physical, economic, and human resources." (See Comprehensive Planning Assistance).

*IN-KIND MATCH: A recipient's fulfilling of its cost-sharing obligation by a contribution other than cash, such as the rental of space or equipment or staff services. Sometimes called "soft-match."

266

ICA: The Intergovernmental Cooperation Act (1969). In past, this Act (1) provided for supplying grant information to governors and legislatures regarding federal grant program activities within their states, and (2) modified the "single state agency" requirement in any federal grant statutes.

INTERGOVERNMENTAL COOPERATION ACT OF 1968: The first successful multifaceted legislative effort by the federal government specifically aimed at improving the administration of federal grant-in-aid programs. It addresses such issues as better information for governors and state legislators regarding grants coming into their states, the waiver of the single state agency requirement, and better coordination of federal programs having areawide and intergovernmental significance.

INTERGOVERNMENTAL COORDINATING MECHANISMS: Methods of necessary information and resource flows among different levels of government. (See A-95).

*INTERGOVERNMENTAL PERSONNEL ACT OF 1970: Another landmark intergovernmental statute, with the purpose of strengthening state and local personnel administration, training, developing state and local employees, and encouraging the temporary exchange of personnel between the federal government and state and local governments.

ICMA: The International City Management Association. The ICMA is the professional society for the appointed Chief Executive Officers in cities, counties, towns, councils of governments, and other local general purpose governments. Its primary objectives include strengthening the quality of urban government through professional management and developing and disseminating new concepts and approaches to management through training programs, information services, and publications. (See PIG's).

IGA: Integrated Grants Administration. A process of consolidating individual grant applications and administrative procedures into a single application and process. There are presently 26 FRC administered pilot projects which allow applicants of multiple related grants to submit a single application with a single set of financial control, record keeping and auditing requirements. (See FAR).

IPG: Intermodal Planning Groups. Intermodal Planning Groups are bodies composed of DOT field personnel and representatives of other federal mission agencies charged with promoting integrated planning, policy, and program development for highways, urban mass transit, airways, railways, etc., at the state, regional, and local level. Unified Work Programs are documents required by the DOT of planning grant recipients, which integrate the urban, airways, and highway planning processes into a coordinated total transportation planning effort.

IPA: The Intergovernmental Personnel Act (See also Capacity Building, Mobility Programs). Administered by the Bureau of Intergovernmental Personnel Programs of the Office of Personnel Management, IPA grants are for a broad range of personnel administration improvement activities, training of expert employees, government mobility assignments, and technical assistance. Ten percent of the total allocation is discretionary and 80% is based on a population/public employment formula. (See OPM)

JOINT FUNDING SIMPLIFICATION ACT: The Joint Funding Simplification Act of 1974 (P.L. 93-510) was signed into law on December 5, 1974. The purpose of this Act is to enable state, local governments, and other public or private organizations and agencies to use federal assistance more effectively by drawing upon resources from more than one federal agency, program, or appropriation. The Act encourages federal resources in support of projects of common interest. It is administered through OMB Circular A-111.

LEAA: Law Enforcement Assistance Administration. LEA Planning Grants (block) are used to set up a state law enforcement planing agency and assist them to develop, implement, and monitor a statewide comprehensive plan. At least 40% of the funds must be passed through to local governments. LEAA was established under the CETA Block Grant.

*****MAINTENANCE OF EFFORT:** A requirement that the recipient maintain the level of program expenditures financed from his own resources prior to receipt of a grant and use the grant funds to supplement state-local expenditures for the aided activities.

*****MATCHING SHARE:** The contribution that recipients are required to make to supplement the grantor's grant moneys.

MISSION AGENCY: Any federal department or agency whose legislation gives it responsibility for promotion of some cause or operation of some system as its primary reason for existence (mission) and which is appropriated funds for the conduct of this mission.

MOBILITY PROGRAM: A type of executive development activity in which an employee of one government unit is temporarily assigned to another governmental unit, either within or outside his own agency, to develop management skills or perception of problems facing the other unit. The technique is also used, albeit rarely, to develop liaison between various governmental entities. Also used to provide technical assistance and training on a short term basis. (See Title IV of the Intergovernmental Personnel Act of 1970).

MODEL CITIES: Shorthand for the Demonstration Cities and Metropolitan Development Act (1966). The "Model Cities Act" provided the basis for (1) integrating the planning function with general policy-making for disadvantaged neighborhoods in those cities which were funded, and (2) for the recognition of metropolitan area-wide planning agencies. The Model Cities Program had a major impact on increasing local government's capacity to engage in more comprehensive planning activity. (See also Planned Variations, CERC).

NACo: National Association of Counties. NACo's membership includes 21,000 elected or appointed county governing officials and other management and policy officials. The association provides a research and reference service for county officials. Committees include roads and highways, national resources, county planning, education, etc. (See Public Interest Groups).

NASPAA: National Association of Schools of Public Affairs and Administration. NASPAA, an affiliate of the American Society for Public Administration, is a national professional education association representing almost 300 university programs, with a stated objective of advancing education and training in public affairs and public administration. It serves as a national center for information on programs and developments in this field and represents the concerns and interest of member institutions in the formulation and support of national policies for education in public affairs and public administration.

NCSL: National Council of State Legislators. In January 1975, the NCSL formally came into existence, replacing three previously-existing organizations (National Legislative Conference, National Conference of State Legislative Leaders, National Society of State Legislators). The NCSL is the only nationwide organization representing all state legislators (7,600) and their staffs (approximately 10,000) and seeks to advance the effectiveness, independence and integration of the state legislature as an equal coordinated branch of government. It also fosters interstate cooperation and represents states and their legislatures with Congress and federal agencies.

NGC: National Governors' Conference. Founded in 1958, the National Governors' Conference is a membership organization that includes governors of the states, territories, and Puerto Rico. The NGC seeks to improve state government, addresses problems requiring interstate cooperation, and endeavors to facilitate intergovernmental relations at the federal/state and state/local levels. Now called the National Governors' Association.

NLC: National League of Cities. The NLC is a federation of 50 state leagues of municipalities as well as individual cities with populations over 30,000, state capitals, and the ten largest cities in each state. The NLC seeks to develop and effect a National Municipal Policy, a statement of major municipal goals in the United States, in order to help cities solve critical problems they share in common. The NLC represents municipalities with Congress and federal agencies and maintains information and consulation services. (See Public Interest Groups.).

NTDS: National Training and Development Service. NTDS is a non-profit organization that fosters new personnel training and development techniques for public service employees at every level of government and seeks to enhance the training capacity within government agencies. Its governing board is comprised of representatives from six major public interest groups.

OMB: The Office of Management and Budget in the Executive Office of the President. A number of efforts to rationalize, streamline, or otherwise improve the process of intergovernmental relations have OMB administrative directives as their source—e.g., A-95. (See also Executive Order).

*OMB CIRCULAR A-85: A management circular which prescibes a procedure for federal agency consultation with chief executives of state and local general purpose governments in advance of the issuance of new regulations that have an intergovernmental effect. Sponsored by Executive Order in 1977.

*OMB CIRCULAR A-95: A management circular establishing a four-part procedure by which state and local governments and certain others are involved in the evaluation, review, and coordination of federal and federally assisted programs and projects before they are approved.

*OMB CIRCULAR A-102: A management circular establishing uniform administrative requirements for grants-in-aid to state and local governments. Formerly known as FMC 74-7.

*OMB CIRCULAR A-111: A management circular establishing a procedure permitting and encouraging state and local grant recipients to obtain funds from multiple federal sources through the submission of a single application, a single audit, and negotiation with a single point of federal contact. Superseded the procedure initially established by the IGA. (See Joint Funding Simplification Act.)

*OPEN-END REIMBURSEMENT GRANT: Often regarded as a formula grant, but characterized by an arrangement wherein the federal government commits itself to reimbursing a specified portion of state-local program expenditures with no limit on the amount of such expenditures.

OPM: Office of Personnel Management. (Formerly the U.S. Civil Service Commission).

*PASS-THROUGH: A process by which a state government receives federal grants and passes the money through to substate jurisdictions. Such action may be mandated by the grant statute or result from a state decision.

PACMI REPORT: The Report of the President's Advisory Committee on Management Improvements (1973). The PACMI Report included a recommendation to establish in the Executive Branch "a permanent center for overall attention of the problems of interlevel relationships."

PLANNED VARIATIONS: Refers to an experimental effort within the context of the Model Cities Program to extend the program planning effort beyond the (disadvantaged) neighborhoods originally targeted by the Model Cities Program to the entire city and to provide chief executives with review and comment authority over all federal programs in order to increase local policy management capacity. (See also CERC, Model Cities, HUD).

POLICY MANAGEMENT (PM): A term used to refer to the capacity of elected officials to perform, on an integrated, cross-cutting basis, the needs assessment, goal setting, and evaluation functions of management; to mobilize and allocate resources; and to initiate and guide the planning, development, and implementation of policies, strategies, and programs that are related to sustaining or improving the physical, socioeconomic, or political conditions that have a bearing on the quality of life in a community.

Thus, Policy Management is a process that involves the strategic functions of guidance and leadership from a jurisdictional or territorial perspective and the exercise of strategic management functions, including the capacity to relate these functions to other participants or entities whose policies or activities affect the performance of these functions. Accordingly, Policy Management capacity includes as well the ability to build or strengthen governmental institutions and area or "place" oriented structures that address and respond to community policy and program development issues and the ability to improve governmental systems—including intergovernmental processes for integrated needs assessment, goal-setting management, and evaluation. (See also Program Management; Resource Management; Capacity Building; Elected Official; Policy Management Assistance).

POLICY MANAGEMENT ASSISTANCE (PMA): Policy Management Assistance is a term used to refer to any system, effort, or process—including a federal grant or contract—which has among its major objectives strengthening the capability of elected officals to exercise the strategic needs assessment, goal-setting, and evaluation functions of management on a jurisdictional or territorial basis. (See also Policy Management, Program Management, Elected Officials, Capacity Building).

PROGRAM BUDGETING: A technique of budgeting by discrete objectives and tasks to be performed; premise of the technique is output (performance). Contrasts with line-item budgeting.

PROGRAM MANAGEMENT: A term used to refer to the adminsitrative and operational functions and tactical requirements of executing policy by undertaking programs, activities, or services—i.e., the requirements of planning, organizing and staffing, directing and controlling, budgeting, and reviewing and reporting. Program Management is related to policies, programs, and strategies designed to sustain or improve the administrative conditions that have a bearing on the capacity of the organization or an organizational unit to perform its prescribed operating tasks. (See also Policy Management, Capacity Building, Technical Assistance).

*PROJECT CATEGORICAL: Nonformula categorical grants awarded on a competitive basis to recipients who submit specific, individual applications in the form and at the times indicated by the grantor agency.

PROJECT GRANT: Grants made to governments for specific purposes or projects only, which may range from 100 percent financing to partial support on a formula basis. (See also Grant-In-Aid).

PUBLIC INTEREST GROUPS (PIGS): Refers to a national network of quasi-public voluntary associatons. The so-called Big Six include the Council of State Governments (CSG), the National Governors' Association (NGA), the National League of Cities (NLC), United States Conference of Mayors (USCM), and the International City Management Association (ICMA), and the National Association of Counties (NACo). In addition to NGA, the CSG has several relegated affiliate organizations, the Nationa Legislative Conference and conferences or associations of Attorney Generals, Lieutenant Governors, State Budget Officers, State Purchasing Officials, and State Planning Agencies. The state leagues of municipalities are constituent bodies of the NLC. In addition, the American Society for Public Administration (ASPA), the National Academy of Public Administration (NAPA), and the National Association of Schools of Public Affairs and Administration (NASPAA) are the principal general public administration organizations which make important inputs into the network. More specialized are the associations of planning, personnel, and finance officials.

RANN: Research Applied to National Needs. Since its inception in 1971, this program of the National Science Foundation has sought to focus United States scientific and technological resources on selected problems of national importance, with the objective to contribute to their practical solution. Though its initial and primary emphasis had been in the areas of energy, environment, and productivity, its programs include important pilot projects and demonstrations in intergovernmental relations and urban technology utilization. Now called the Directorate for Applied Research and Research Applications (ARRP).

REGIS: A federal management information subsystem which focused on regional offices and helped to underscore the need for a better system of tracking grant applications.

RESEARCH & DEVELOPMENT: That process which includes the discovery and application of new scientific knowledge, including the design, testing, and evaluation of new materials, processes, products, and systems, whether physical, biological, or organizational.

RESOURCE MANAGEMENT (RM): A term used to refer to the cross-cutting administrative and organizational support functions and their management. Resource Management includes personnel administration; property management—including facilities, equipment, and materials and supplies; information management; and financial management—including capital budgeting and insurance. Resource Management is related to the core tools and support functions of management and the routine requirements of organizational maintenance. Thus, Resource Management is concerned with policies, programs, and strategies designed to sustain or improve the administrative support systems that have a bearing on the capacity of the entire organizational entity and its counstituent parts (a) to perform prescribed tasks and (b) to adapt to a changing management environment—changes resulting from events of situations internal (e.g., new priorities or budget mismanagement) or external (e.g., revenue short falls or new regulations) to the organization.

Thus, Resource Management is to be distinguished from Policy Management (concerned with the strategic functions of guidance and leadership) and Program Management (concerned with the tactical functions of executing policies in the form of concrete programs). Assessments of state and local government capacity continue to surface major deficiencies with respect to achieving adequate Resource Management capacity. Moreover, the extremely small federal Technical Assistance investment which is not targeted on strengthening Program Management capacity is largely targeted on Resource Management (e.g., the HUD municipal management information demonstration). Almost no Technical Assistance is allocated to Policy Management. (See also Capacity Building, Technical Assistance).

REVENUE SHARING: See General Revenue Sharing (GRS).

*RMIS: The Regional Management Information System made available to FRC's as new tools for their task of interagency and intergovernmental coordination in the field.

*SECTION 204, DEMONSTRATION CITIES AND METROPOLITAN DEVELOPMENT ACT OF 1966: The first federal legislative provision requiring applications for an array of urban assistance programs to be refer to a metropolitan planning body and general purpose local governments in its area for comment as to their consistency with comprehensive planning. It also required areawide planning bodies to be composed of or responsible to elected officials of an areawide governmental unit or constituent general purpose local governments.

STATE: Means one of the several states of the United States, the District of Columbia, the Commonwealth of Puerto Rico, Guam, the Virgin Islands, and American Samoa.

*STATE MUNICIPAL LEAGUE: State associations of municipalities which offer a broad range of services to their constituents

*STIMULATIVE: A grant is stimulative when it increases the expenditures of the grantee for the specified activities over and above what they would have been in the absence of the grant.

*SUPPORTIVE: A grant is supportive when a reduction or withdrawal of the grant is unlikely to weaken support for the aided activity from the recipient's own resources.

*TARGETED: A grant is considered targeted when its eligibility and allocation provisions are drawn tightly so that only the most "needy" cases are assisted, and the amounts of aid are directly proportional to program needs.

TECHNICAL ASSISTANCE (TA): A term used to refer to the programs, activities, and services provided by the federal government, a Public Interest Group, or another Third Party to strengthen the capacity or recipients to improve their performance with respect to an inherent or assigned function. The delivery of Technical Assistance requires serving one or more of three functions: (1) transferring information, (2) developing skills, and (3) developing and transferring products. The tools of Technical Assistance include counseling, training, statistical and other expert information, process innovations (e.g., new budgeting methods), equipment or facilities, goods or services—including advisory services.

A review of current federal TA programs indicated that the overwhelming majority (over 95% measured by federal dollar investments) are contained within functional program categories administered on an agency basis and are designed almost exclusively to strengthen the capacity of state and local governments to manage federal categorical programs. A partial exception is HUD 701 and a few other programs scattered among NSF, LEAA, HEW, and elsewhere. (See also Policy Management, Program Management, Resource Management, Capacity Building, HUD 701, HNSF).

THIRD PARTIES: A term used to refer to recipients of federal Technical

Assistance (TA) dollars who are charged with delivering TA to state and local governments. Typical "third party" recipients include Public Interest Groups—for example, the National Training and Development Service (NTDS) and universities who, in turn, develop training programs, information clearinghouses, and other services designed to strengthen one or more of the management capacity elements of general purpose governments.

TITLE V REGIONAL ECONOMIC DEVELOPMENT PLANS: Are the objective of grants to multistate commissions under Title V of the Public Works and Economic Development Act of 1965 (Department of Commerce). Grantees under Title V are the Regional Commissions—Coastal Plains, Four Corners, New England, Ozarks, Upper Great Lakes, Old West, and Pacific Northwest.

*TREASURY CIRCULAR (TC) 1082: The Treasury Circular requiring federal grantor agencies to inform states of grant awards made within their jurisdictions.

UNDER SECRETARIES GROUP (USG): The Under Secretaries Group is a committee composed of the Under and Deputy Secretaries of the agencies represented on the Federal Regional Councils which serves as a steering group for the FRC's. It is also supported by working group of representatives designed by the member agencies. The Under Secretaries Group was established in 1979 and replaced by an Interagency Coordinating Committee.

UNITED STATES CONFERENCE OF MAYORS (USCM): Members of this organization are mayors of cities with a population exceeding 30,000. The Conference promotes improved municipal government by cooperation among cities as well as with state and federal government. The USCM provides research, information, counseling, and legislative reference services to cities, and maintains a specialized library. (See Public Interest Groups).

APPENDIX B

FEDERAL REGISTER, VOL. 43, NO. 98—FRIDAY, MAY 19, 1978

[3110-01]

OFFICE OF MANAGEMENT AND BUDGET

IMPLEMENTATION OF FEDERAL GRANT AND COOPERATIVE AGREEMENT ACT OF 1977 (PUB. L. 95-224)

Proposed OMB Guidance

AGENCY: Office of Management and Budget.

ACTION: Notice of proposed OMB guidance for Federal agency use in implementing the Federal Grant and Cooperative Agreement Act of 1977.

SUMMARY: The Federal Grant and Cooperation Agreement Act distinguishes between procurement and assistance relationships and mandates that Federal agencies use contracts for procurement transactions:

Sec. 4. Each executive agency shall use a type of procurement contract as the legal instrument reflecting a relationship between the Federal Government and a State or local government or other recipient: (1) whenever the principal purpose of the instrument is the acquisition, by purchase, lease, or barter, of property or services for the direct benefit or use of the Federal Government; or (2) whenever an executive agency determines in a specific instance that the use of a type of procurement contract is appropriate.

and grants or cooperative agreements for assistance transactions:

Sec. 5. Each executive agency shall use a type of grant agreement as the legal instrument reflecting a relationship between the Federal Government and a State or local government or other recipient whenever: (1) The principal purpose of the relationship is the transfer of money, property, services, or anything of value to the State or local government or other recipient in order to accomplish a public purpose of support or stimulation authorized by Federal statute, rather than acquisition, by purchase, lease, or barter, of property or services for the direct benefit or use of the Federal Government; and (2) no substantial involvement is anticipated between the executive agency, acting for Federal Government, and the State or local government or other recipient during performance of the contemplated activity.

Sec. 6. Each executive agency shall use a type of cooperative agreement as the legal instrument reflecting a relationship between the Federal Government and a State or local government or other recipient whenever: (1) The principal purpose of the relationship is the transfer of money, property, services, or anything of value to the State or local government or other recipient to accomplish a public purpose of support or stimulation authorized by Federal statute, rather than acquisition, by purchase, lease, or barter, of property or services for the direct benefit or use of the Federal Government; and (2) substantial involvement is anticipated between the executive agency, acting for Federal Government, and the State or local government or other recipient during performance of the contemplated activity.

Federal agencies must implement sections 4, 5, and 6 by February 3, 1979. OMB's intent in issuing guidance is to promote consistent implementation of the Act. Release of final guidance is anticipated by July 1978.

Comments in response to this notice may lead to extensive revisions of the guidance. If it is not possible to obtain consensus on the best manner to treat a specific issue in the time available, the issue will be removed from the guidance and included in the 2-year study of Federal assistance relationships mandated in section 8 of the Act.

The study of Federal assistance relationships will focus on developing a better understanding of alternative means for implementing Federal assistance programs and on determining the feasibility of developing a comprehensive system of guidance for Federal assistance programs. In undertaking the study, OMB is required by the Act to consult and, to the extent practicable, involve representatives of the executive agencies, Congress, General Accounting Office, State and local governments, other recipients, and interested members of the public. To meet the intent of the Act, OMB will publish the draft study plan for comment in the FEDERAL REGISTER in late May-early June 1978.

DATES: Written comments on the proposed guidance must be received on or before June 20, 1978.

ADDRESS: Comments should be sent in duplicate to Vincent Puritano, Deputy Associate Director for Intergovernmental Affairs, Office of Management and Budget, Room 9025 NEOB, Washington, D.C. 20503.

FOR FURTHER INFORMATION CONTACT:

Thomas L. Hadd, Intergovernmental Affairs Division, Office of Management and Budget, Room 9026 NEOB, Washington, D.C. 20503, telephone 202-395-5156.

Draft, OMB Guidance to Agencies for Implementing the Federal Grant and Cooperative Agreement Act, Pub. L. 95-224

Introduction. The Federal Grant and Cooperative Agreement Act of 1977 (Pub. L. 95-224), signed February 3, 1978, requires executive agencies to distinguish procurement relationships from assistance relationships. A major objective of the Act is to achieve consistency in the use of legal instruments by agencies for procurement and assistance transactions. This is a preliminary step toward a broad review of the administration of Federal assistance programs and the relationships created by the terms and conditions of legal assistance instruments. Section 4 of the Act requires the use of procurement contracts for all acquistion activity. Sections 5 and 6 require the use of grants or cooperative agreements for specified types of assistance relationships. Section 9 authorizes the Director of the Office of Management and Budget to issue supplementary interpretative guidelines to promote consistent and efficient implementation of sections 4, 5, and 6. Subsection 10(d) authorizes the Director to except individual transactions or programs from the Act's provisions.

In addition, Section 8 of the Act requires OMB to conduct a study of Federal assistance relationships and submit a report to Congress in 2 years. The guidelines that follow are based on OMB authorizations under sections 8, 9, and 10(d).

CONTENTS

A. OMB interpretation of the Act.
B. Distinguishing between procurement and assistance.
C. Characterization of grants and cooperative agreements.
D. Agency decision structure for selection of instruments.
E. Administrative requirements for grants and cooperative agreements.
F. Specific guidelines for grants.
G. Specific guidelines for cooperative agreements.
H. Assistance transactions involving only nonmonetary transfer.
I. OMB exception policy.
J. OMB exception procedures.
K. Joint funding under grants and cooperative agreements.
L. Agency records.
M. OMB reporting requirements.

GUIDANCE

A. OMB INTERPRETATION OF THE ACT

1. *General purposes of the Act.* OMB views the Federal Grant and Cooperative Agreement Act as an important opportunity to review, improve, and simplify the broad array of Federal assistance relationships. It sees the Act's objective of Federal consistency for various types of relationships coinciding with the President's goal of making Federal program actions more understandable and predictable. Agencies should give serious consideration to the policy implications of the Act's provisions, particularly sections 4, 5, and 6, pertaining to the use of contracts, grants, and cooperative agreements as these involve the essence of the way agencies perform fundamental functions.

2. *Orderly implementation of sections 4, 5, and 6.* These sections of the Act require agencies to use contracts for all procurement actions, and grants or cooperative agreements to transfer money, property, services, or anything of value to recipients to accomplish a Federal purpose of stimulation or support authorized by statute. Subsection 10(b) says: "Nothing in this Act shall be construed to render void or voidable any existing contract, grant, or cooperative agreement or other contract, grant, or cooperative agreement entered into up to 1 year after the date of enactment of this Act." The legislative history clearly indicates that Congress intended this provision to provide 1 year for orderly implementation of sections 4, 5, and 6. The Act was signed February 3, 1978. Agencies have until February 3, 1979, to implement these sections in accordance with the OMB guidelines.

3. *Interpretation of specific provisions of the Act.* To promote consistency, agencies should interpret subsections 4(2), 7(a), and 7(b) of the Act as follows:

a. Subsection 4(2) allows the use of contracts "whenever an executive agency determines in a specific instance that the use of a type of procurement contract is appropriate." This is not a negation of section 5 or 6. Two examples of its use might be:

(1) Where an agency is involved in a two-step situation in which it may "procure" medicines which it in turn "grants" to non-Federal hospitals.

(2) Where an agency procures by contract from a supplier, goods or services to be delivered directly to an assistance recipient. Federal procurement of technical assistance to be rendered to a State or local government would come under this subsection of the Act.

This subsection does not authorize the use of a procurement contract with an assistance recipient as the instrument for providing the assistance. Until the Federal Acquisition Regulation is published, the Federal Procurement Regulation and the Armed Services Procurement Regulation govern policy and procedures regarding procurement contracts awarded under the authority of this sub-section.

b. Subsection 7(a) says: "Notwithstanding any other provision of the law, each executive agency authorized by law to enter into contracts, grant or cooperative agreements, or similar arrangements is authorized and directed to enter into and use types of contracts, grant agreements, or cooperative agreements as required by this Act."

If an agency is presently authorized to use contracts, grants, or cooperative agreements under existing statutes, this provision enables it to enter into any of the three types of arrangements, subject to the criteria set forth in sections 4, 5, and 6. If, however, an agency is prohibited from using one of these types of instruments, this subsection would not affect that prohibition.

c. Subsection 7(b) says: "The authority to make contracts, grants, and cooperative agreements for the conduct of basic or applied research at nonprofit institutions of higher education, or at nonprofit organizations whose primary purpose is the conduct of scientific research shall include discretionary authority, when it is deemed by the head of the executive agency to be in furtherance of the objectives of the agency, to vest in such institutions or organizations, without further obligation to the Government, or on such other terms and conditions as deemed appropriate, title to equipment or other tangible property purchased with such funds."

The Act repeals the Grants Act, Pub. L. 85-934, which authorized the use of grants for scientific research. This provision continues the authority in the Grants Act to vest title to equipment purchased with Federal funds in a nonprofit research organization and expands this authority to other classes of property.

The principal effect of this will be on agencies that fund research as a procurement under section 4. It allows continuation of existing practices of transferring equipment even though the research is done under a procurement contract.

B. DISTINGUISHING BETWEEN PROCUREMENT AND ASSISTANCE

1. *Basic determinations.* While one of the objectives of the Act is to distinguish between procurement and assistance relationships, neither term is specifically defined. Section 4 requires use of a procurement contract when the principal purpose is acquisition, by purchase, lease, or barter, of property or services for the direct benefit or use of the Federal Government. Sections 5 and 6 require the use of grants or cooperative agreements when the principal purpose is the transfer of money, property, services, or anything of value to accomplish a public purpose of support or stimulation authorized by Federal statute, rather than acquisition, by purchase, lease, or barter, of property or services for the direct benefit or use by the Federal Government.

Agencies should interpret the language of Section 5 and 6 which call for the use of grants or cooperative agreements to "accom-plish a public purpose of support or stimulation authorized by Federal statute" as including but not restricted to traditional assistance transactions. Thus, for example, when an agency authorized to support or stimulate basic research decides to fund a basic research project that does not fit the Section 4 language of "acquisition for the direct benefit or use of the Federal Government," it is authorized to use a grant or cooperative agreement. Conversely, agencies not authorized to accomplish a public purpose of support or stimulation are not authorized to use grants or cooperative agreements. Until the Federal Acquisition Regulation is published, the Federal Procurement Regulation and the Armed Services Procurement Regulation govern policy and procedures regarding procurement contracts.

2. *When to decide on the use of procurement or assistance instruments.* Any public notice, solicitation, or request for applications or proposals should indicate whether the intended relationship will be a procurement contract, or whether a grant and/or cooperative agreement will be used. The decision on whether a procurement or assistance relationship is intended should be made before the public announcement.

3. *What to do if the distinctions between procurement and assistance do not apply to a specific class of transactions.* Agencies should make every effort to ensure their relationships conform with those specified in the Act. If, however, there are individual transactions or programs that are important to an agency which cannot be characterized as principally procurement or assistance, an OMB exception should be requested. Sections I and J deal with OMB exceptions.

C. CHARACTERIZATION OF GRANTS AND COOPERATIVE AGREEMENTS

1. *Anticipated substantial involvement during performance.* The basic statutory criterion for distinguishing between grants and cooperative agreements is that for the latter, "*substantial* involvement is *anticipated* between the executive agency and the recipient *during performance* of the contemplated activity" (emphasis added). To ensure consistent determinations, all agencies should use only this criterion when deciding to use either a grant or a cooperative agreement.

a. As a guide to assist in making these determinations, anticipated substantial involvement during performance does not include:

(1) Agency approval of recipient plans prior to award.

(2) Normal exercise of Federal stewardship responsibilities during the project period such as site visits, performance reporting, financial reporting, and audit to ensure that the objectives, terms, and conditions of the award are accomplished.

(3) Unanticipated agency involvement to correct project deficiencies in project or financial performance from the terms of the assistance instrument.

(4) General statutory requirements understood in advance of the award such as civil

rights, environmental protection, and provision for the handicapped. 000

(5) Agency review of performance *after* completion.

(6) General administrative requirements such as those included in OMB Circulars A-95, A-102, and A-110.

b. Conversely, anticipated substantial involvement during performance would exist where the assistance instrument includes provisions such as:

(1) Agency halt to activity if detailed performance specifications (e.g., construction specifications) are not met.

(2) Agency review and approval of one stage before work can begin on a subsequent stage during the period covered by the assistance instrument.

(3) Agency review and approval of proposed subgrants or contracts, or agency participation or approval in the selection or award of subgrants or contracts let under the assistance instrument, if required by statute or authorized by OMB waiver.

(4) Agency involvement in the selection of key recipient personnel. (This does not include assistance instrument provisions for the participation of a named principal investigator for research projects.)

(5) Agency and recipient collaboration where novelty or complexity are involved.

(6) Agency monitoring to permit specified kinds of direction or redirection of the work because of interrelationships with other projects.

(7) Direct agency operational involvement or participation to ensure compliance with such general statutory requirements as civil rights, environmental protection, and provision for the handicapped.

c. Anticipated Federal involvement is a relative rather than an absolute concept. The examples provided are not meant to be a checklist. Rather, they are illustrations of the basic point that:

(1) When the recipient can expect to run the project without agency intervention as long as it is run in accordance with the general terms of the assistance instrument, substantial involvement is not anticipated.

(2) If the recipient can expect the agency to participate in managing the project, substantial Federal involvement is anticipated.

2. *Proposed OMB policy on substantial involvement.* The proposed policy of OMB is to guide agencies to limit Federal involvement in assisted activities to the minimum consistent with program requirements. Agencies should continue to implement existing grant programs through grant instruments as defined in Section 5 of the Act to the degree possible. The choice of instrument must, however, reflect the true relationship intended.

3. *How technical assistance and guidance relate to substantial involvement.* The practice of some agencies of providing technical assistance or guidance to recipients of financial assistance does not constitute substantial involvement if either:

a. The recipients are not required to follow it, or;

b. The recipients are required to follow it but it is provided prior to the start of the assisted activity and the recipient understood this prior to the financial assistance award.

4. *What to do if grants or cooperative agreements do not fit program requirements.* There may be a few cases of assistance programs where neither a grant nor a cooperative agreement is suitable. In such cases, an OMB exception should be requested in accordance with Sections I and J below.

D. *Agency decision structure for selection of instruments.* The determinations of whether a program is principally one of procurement or assistance, and whether substantial Federal involvement in performance will normally occur are basic agency policy decisions. Agency heads should ensure that these general decisions for each program are either made or reviewed at a policy level.

Congress intended the act to allow agencies flexibility to select the assistance instrument that best suits the anticipated degree of involvement for each transaction. Thus agencies should provide their program managers with criteria for selecting the appropriate instrument, consistent with general program policy decisions.

E. *Administrative requirements for grants and cooperative agreements.*

Present administrative requirements such as OMB Circulars A-95, A-102, and A-110 apply to both grants and cooperative agreements involving the transfer of Federal funds. These administrative requirements will not apply to General Revenue Sharing or Anti-Recession Fiscal Assistance Grants administered by the Treasury Department.

F. SPECIFIC GUIDELINES FOR GRANTS

1. *Increasing Federal involvement during a grant period.* At times an agency may find it necessary to increase the involvement in a grant-funded project during the period of time covered by the grant. This could happen, for example, when standard grant reports or monitoring indicates some sort of problem. If this occurs, agencies should not view the act as restricting their authority to intervene as necessary to bring the project into conformance with original intentions. Agencies should not, however, seek to become substantially involved in a grant-funded activity without converting the grant instrument to a cooperative agreement following negotiation with the recipient.

2. *Distinction between grants and subsidies.* Section 5 of the act applies to grants but not to subsidies. For a few programs, the distinction may not be clear. Where this condition exists, the proposed OMB guidance is that for the purposes of this act:

a. The term "subsidy" does not apply to financial stimulation or support provided to units of State or local government.

b. The term "grant" does not apply to general operating support provided to commercial firms.

278

1. *Alternative uses of cooperative agreements.* In all cases, the determination of when to use cooperative agreements will be based on the need for substantial Federal involvement in the assisted activity.

a. Some programs now using grants will require the use of cooperative agreements exclusively. This determination should be based on statutory requirements or policy level determinations of substantial Federal involvement in the performance of the assisted project.

b. Other programs may use grants or cooperative agreements, depending on the nature of the project or the abilities of the recipients. For example:

(1) Some projects may start out as cooperative agreements in the first year and be converted to grants after recipient capacity has been established;

(2) Other projects, initially funded as grants, may have to be renewed as cooperative agreements if there is a need to revise the project or upgrade recipient capacity.

2. *Statement of Federal involvement.* Each cooperative agreement should include an explicit statement of the nature, character, and extent of Federal involvement that causes it to be differentiated from a grant. These statements must be developed with care to avoid unnecessarily increasing Federal liability under the assistance instrument.

H. ASSISTANCE TRANSACTIONS INVOLVING ONLY NONMONETARY TRANSFERS

1. *Types of assistance included.* Sections 5 and 6 apply to programs that transfer "property, services, or any thing of value," which would include consultation, technical services, information, and data. This section of the guidance applies to agencies and programs that provide such types of nonmonetary assistance apart from fund transfers.

2. *Applicability of administrative standards.* Section E above stated that existing administrative standards (e.g., OMB Circulars A-95, A-102, A-110) apply to grants and cooperative agreements involving the transfer of funds.

Agencies should use their judgment, however, in applying these standards to nonmonetary transfers that are presently excluded from the coverage of these circulars. For example, a donation of a substantial parcel of land to a local government is the type of Federal action covered by Part II of A-95, but other administrative standards may not apply.

3. *OMB exception for nonmonetary assistance.* OMB exempts programs providing nonmonetary assistance from the provisions of section 5 of the Act. Existing agency practices for providing nonmonetary assistance where no Federal involvement in the assisted activity is anticipated should continue. Thus a formal grant instrument is not required to provide surplus property, consultation, or data. Where Federal involvement in the assisted activity is anticipated, however, a cooperative agreement is required as indicated in section 6 of the Act. Agencies engaged in the provision of nonmonetary assistance will be asked to report on these activities under Section M below.

I. OMB EXCEPTION POLICY

1. *General.* Section 10(d) authorizes the Director of OMB to "except individual transactions or programs of any executive agency from the application of the provisions of this Act. This authority shall expire one year after receipt by the Congress of the study provided for in Section 8 of this Act." Agencies are advised that, unless otherwise indicated, OMB exceptions will run through January 1981.

2. *Exceptions provided in this guidance.* Section H3 of this guidance excepts nonmonetary grants.

3. *Other exceptions under the Act.* Agencies are expected to conform with the terms of the Act unless severe disruption to a program or serious consequences to recipients would result. OMB intends to grant additional exceptions only on the basis of agency requests that include strong justification and an indication of the harm that will result if an exception is not granted. Section J below indicates the procedures agencies should follow in requesting exceptions.

4. Waiver of administrative standards. OMB is responsible for most of the administrative standards that apply to assistance programs. Agencies should follow these standards. The circulars that establish these standards presently provide procedures for granting of waivers. If, the standards appear unsuitable to a particular situation, requests for waivers should be sent to the OMB office responsible for the circular or the responsible agency if not OMB (e.g., for GSA uniform relocation provisions). Requests for waivers to financial management circulars administered by OMB should be addressed to John Lordan, Chief, Financial Management Branch, OMB, Room 6002, NEOB, Washington, D.C. 20503.

In addition, where a specific transaction such as a cooperative agreement is being considered on an experimental basis and the anticipated relationships are so unusual that specific provisions or complete standards would not apply, the agency should submit an appropriate request for a waiver.

J. OMB EXCEPTION PROCEDURES

A request for an OMB exception under this Act should be addressed to Vincent Puritano, Deputy Associate Director for Intergovernmental Affairs, Room 9025, NEOB, Washington, D.C. 20503. It should include:

1. Whether the exception is requested for a complete program or an individual transaction.

2. An explanation of why an exception is requested, including statutory, agency policy, or other reasons.

3. A statement of what the agency will do if an exception is not granted and what the implications would be if this action were taken.

4. An indication of how the agency will handle the situation if the OMB exception expires before there are any changes to either this Act or agency statutes.

JOINT FUNDING UNDER GRANTS AND COOPERATIVE AGREEMENTS

Subsection 10(c) of the Act specifically provides for projects funded under the Joint Funding Simplification Act that include more than one type of assistance relationship. Thus a project with some components funded by grants and others by cooperative agreements is entirely permissible. Agencies should view this Act as providing the opportunity and authority to participate in joint funded projects in any number of funding relationships to serve the best interests of the participating agencies' programs.

L. AGENCY RECORDS

Both Congress and OMB view this Act as a preliminary step toward long-range overhaul of Federal assistance activities. The requirement for agencies to implement sections 4, 5, and 6 in one year is, in large part, to begin the systematic gathering of data about Federal assistance relationships. Agencies should anticipate that Congressional committees, the General Accounting Office, and OMB will be asking extensive questions about the effects of implementing these sections. While the questions may vary from agency to agency, they can reasonably be expected to deal with operating experience for a year or more after full implementation. Agencies should develop systems of records that would allow them to answer questions such as:

1. How many financial grants have been awarded in accordance with section 5 of the Act? What was the dollar volume and what classes of recipients were involved (e.g., State governments, universities, hospitals, individuals)?

2. For which programs did the agency decide to use grants exclusively?

3. How many financial assistance cooperative agreements have been awarded in accordance with section 6 of the Act? What was the dollar volume and what classes of recipients were involved?

4. For which programs did the agency decide to use cooperative agreements exclusively? What is the nature and reason for the agency involvement?

5. For which programs were both grants and cooperative agreements used? What were the criteria for determining the instrument used?

6. What types nonmonetary assistance transfers were made as grants? What types as cooperative agreements?

7. What was the agency's experience in implementing sections 4, 5, and 6? How did it contribute to improved projects, management, or intergovernmental relations? What problems has the Act presented that can be expected to continue?

M. OMB REPORTING REQUIREMENTS

The experience of the agencies in making decisions necessary to implement sections 4,

5, and 6 of the Act will be important to the study required by section 8. In addition, to the more general questions about the feasibility of a comprehensive system of guidance for assistance activities, the report to Congress must include a summary of the effects of sections 4, 5, and 6. For these reasons, agencies are to provide by March 1, 1979, a report to OMB that includes the following:

1. Distinguishing between procurement and assistance:

a. For what types of activities did the agency have trouble making the distinction between procurement and assistance?

b. On what bases were the issues resolved?

2. Use of procurement contracts:

a. What activities formerly funded through grants or other assistance instruments will now be handled with procurement contracts?

b. What is the anticipated dollar volume of these procurement contracts?

c. What is expected to be the impact of this shift on the agency?

d. Who will be the principal recipients of these contracts?

e. What is expected to be the impact on the recipients?

3. Agency decisions on when to use grants or cooperative agreements:

a. Describe the process by which the agency decided which programs would use: (1) Only grants; (2) only cooperative agreements; (3) both grants and cooperative agreements.

b. Which programs, as listed in the Catalog of Federal Domestic Assistance, will fall into each of the above three categories? For those in category 3 what is the expected mix in terms of total dollars and numbers of transactions?

c. What programs not listed in the Catalog of Federal Domestic Assistance will fall into each of the three categories? For those in category 3 what is expected mix is terms of total dollars and numbers of transactions?

d. What is the anticpated first-year dollar volume of the programs in each of the three categories?

e. What types of Federal involvement in the assisted activity led to the identification of programs that would use only cooperative agreements?

f. What are the anticipated reactions of the recipients of programs using only cooperative agreements?

g. What are the anticipated liability, accountability, and other implications for the programs using only cooperative agreements?

h. What are the agency guidelines on the selection of instruments for programs that may use either grants or cooperative agreements?

i. What is the anticipated dollar volume of grants and cooperative agreements to be awarded under these programs?

j. How will the opportunity to use either grants or cooperative agreements improve administration of these programs?

k. What negative effects are anticipated from the requirement to make a choice of instruments?

l. What programs will use assistance instruments that formerly used contracts and what is the dollar volume of these new uses of assistance instruments?

4. Nonmonetary assistance transfers:

a. What were the types and dollar value of nonmonetary transfers made by the agency using grant instruments?

b. How do these grant instruments compare with monetary grant instruments?

c. What were the types and dollar value of nonmonetary transfer made under the OMB exception that did not use grant instruments?

d. How would the agency have treated these transfers had not OMB granted the exception?

e. What were the types and dollar value of nonmonetary transfers made through cooperative agreements?

f. What was the agency's experience with this use of cooperative agreements?

5. Overall evaluation of the Act:

a. What elements of the Act are contributing to improved program performance and administration?

b. What elements of the Act are particularly troublesome?

c. What proposals would the agency make for revising the Act?

VELMA N. BALDWIN,
Assistant to the Director
for Administration.

[FR Doc. 78-13610 Filed 5-18-78; 8:45 am]

APPENDIX C

FEDERAL REGISTER, VOL. 44, NO. 5—MONDAY, JANUARY 8, 1979

[3110-01-M]

OFFICE OF MANAGEMENT AND BUDGET

PLANS FOR STUDY OF FEDERAL ASSISTANCE PROGRAMS

AGENCY: Office of Management and Budget.

ACTION: Notice of plan for the study of Federal assistance programs and practices required by the Federal Grant and Cooperative Agreement Act of 1977 (Pub. L. 95-224).

SUMMARY: The Federal Grant and Cooperative Agreement Act of 1977 requires the Director of OMB to study alternative means of implementing Federal assistance programs and to determine the feasibility of developing a comprehensive system of guidance for Federal assistance programs. A report to Congress is required not later than February 3, 1980. In conducting this study, OMB intends to consult with and, to the extent practicable, involve representatives of executive agencies, Congress, General Accounting Office, State and local governments, other recipients, and interested members of the public.

This notice is to communicate the OMB plan for conducting the study and to invite contributions and participation from interested parties. A draft plan was published in the FEDERAL REGISTER for comment on June 23, 1978. This final plan reflects many of the comments received on the earlier draft.

The Act also requires Federal agencies to take specific actions by February 3, 1979. These include use of procurement contracts for procurement transactions, and grants or cooperative agreements for certain types of assistance transactions. OMB published guidance to the Federal agencies for implementing the Act in the FEDERAL REGISTER on August 18, 1978.

FOR FURTHER INFORMATION CONTACT:

Thomas L. Hadd, Intergovernmental Affairs Division, Office of Management and Budget, Room 5217, NEOB, Washington, D.C. 20503, telephone 202-395-5156.

SUMMARY OF MAJOR COMMENTS ON THE PROPOSED STUDY PLAN AND THE OMB RESPONSE

On June 23, 1978, OMB published a proposed study plan in the FEDERAL REGISTER to invite general comments on its scope and solicit participation by interested parties. Numerous comments were received from Federal agencies and others. The majority of the comments endorsed particular parts of the plan, dealt with ways to improve its clarity, or suggested topics to make it more complete.

The proposed plan divided the scope of the study into three major tasks. These were:

A. Feasibility of a comprehensive system of guidance for Federal assistance programs.

B. Alternative means for implementing Federal assistance programs.

C. Study of specific issues.

Each of these tasks was further divided into a number of subtasks.

OMB accepted and tried to incorporate virtually all suggestions for improving the plan. A summary of the more important comments follows.

A. *Feasibility of a comprehensive system of guidance for Federal assistance programs.* 1. There were a number of comments agreeing with the need to study ways of consolidating the present body of assistance guidance into a single system. Some discussed the present array of guidance and its piecemeal development. Others commented on specific elements of existing guidance that might be improved through incorporation into a comprehensive system.

2. There were a few comments on the legal or regulatory aspects of a comprehensive system of guidance.

These ranged from a proposal to develop a statutory assistance code to suggestions for the study of particular steps in the assistance process. There were comments about the total impact of regulations affecting assistance programs and the relation of this impact to the accomplishment of the primary purpose of the programs.

3. Some observers concentrated on the educational potential of a comprehensive system of guidance. They pointed out that the assistance field is becoming increasingly complex. Managers and specialists need to have better information on the full range of assistance management techniques, requirements, and alternatives available to them. It was also suggested that the educational aspect should concentrate on learning more about the basic implications of assistance policies and providing a basis for training personnel.

4. There were a number of comments about studying a comprehensive system of guidance that reflected the views of various participants in the assistance field. These included:

a. How much should the system stress standardization as opposed to flexibility?

b. How might the system relate to different classes of recipients?

c. What types of resistance can be anticipated to a comprehensive system of guidance?

B. *Alternative means for implementing Federal assistance programs.* 1. Most comments on this task stressed the importance of studying cooperative agreements. These included views that:

a. Cooperative agreements may actually be a third class of Federal/recipient relationship with elements of both procurement and assistance rather than purely assistance instruments as classified in the Act.

b. Much needs to be done to clarify the distinction between various classes of cooperative agreements and grants.

c. The needs and desires of recipients should be considered more in development of cooperative agreements than grants.

2. There were also comments on the need to study and experiment with the problem of choosing a particular form of assistance transaction from the array of alternatives. This included the need for a review of characteristics, strengths, and weaknesses of the full range of techniques available for achieving national objectives.

C. *Study of specific issues.* 1. There were a number of suggestions about studying the funding of research. These stressed the importance of finding the appropriate relationship and most effective level of Federal involvement in various types of research in order to attain the research objectives.

2. There were conflicting views on the question of basic or master agreements with recipients for meeting administrative and general Federal policy requirements. Some viewed them as more work for State government or recipients, while others asserted promise in their use.

3. The question of competition for assistance awards also drew mixed comment. A general view was that the proposed plan did not stress the issue enough. A second was that increasing competition may have negative aspects. A third opinion was that the feasibility of standards for competitive selection should be considered.

4. The issue of the eligibility of for-profit organizations drew substantial comment. Some felt that assistance awards should not be made to for-profits, while others felt the study issue should emphasize their encouragement. Some basic questions were proposed for review including:

a. The constitutionality of such awards.

b. The degree of latitude agencies should have to make such awards.

c. Special provisions that might be necessary.

5. There were a few comments in specific support of studying the concept of fixed-price or lump-sum payment assistance awards.

6. The question of cost sharing drew a few comments ranging from arguments that the practice should be eliminated to the view that a government-wide policy is not feasible.

7. There were some comments that there are classes of transactions covered by the Act which cannot be classified as either assistance or procurement.

8. Additional topics suggested for study included:

a. Non-monetary transactions including personal property and land donations.

b. Development of uniform standards and criteria for selecting recipients of formula and block grants and terminating assistance transactions by either party.

c. Relationship of the Model Procurement Code to present administrative standards on procurement.

d. Consideration of various aspects of "accountability."

e. Review of various proposals for new legislation.

f. Degree to which the Federal Government can intrude into the internal affairs of State Governments.

g. Federal controls on pass-through or sub-grants.

h. Various issues related to due process.

i. Specific terms in frequent use but with unclear definitions.

j. Relationship of Federal procedural requirements and funding cycles of various levels of government.

k. Internal agency organization theory and practice for primary assistance policy and management functions.

l. Program evaluation provisions that might be general requirements.

9. Several comments suggested that the study consider whether existing guidance contained in OMB Circulars should apply to cooperative agreements as well as to grants. We concluded that it was the intent of Congress, as expressed in Senate Report No. 93-1239, that the same guidance should apply. The report said, "A determination was made that the use of 'cooperative agreements' would not establish a class of * * * transactions that would be exempt from OMB Circular A-102 or other circulars whose authority applies to assistance transactions." This is consistent with the Administration's efforts to standardize and simplify the paperwork requirements of federally assisted programs. The study, therefore, will not address this matter. It will, however, be alert for opportunities to improve and build upon existing guidance for both grants and cooperative agreements.

In addition to the above comments on the proposed study plan, two general issues were suggested for treatment in the OMB implementation guidance, but were deferred to the study. These are:

1. Distinction between grants and subsidies.

2. Identification of types of government transactions not covered by Pub. L. 95-224.

One comment recommended that the study consider the issue of categorical grant program consolidation. While this is an important issue, OMB concluded that it is beyond the scope intended by Congress and should not be included in the study.

Finally, there were many suggestions of specific actions the government might take to resolve particular problems. Those that OMB considered to be too detailed for mention in the general study plan will be considered by the appropriate task groups during the conduct of the study.

PLAN FOR STUDY OF FEDERAL ASSISTANCE PROGRAMS

I. INTRODUCTION

Section 8 of Pub. L. 95-224 requires the Director of OMB to conduct a broad study of Federal assistance programs and related administrative practices. Section 8 says:

"The Director of the Office of Management and Budget, in cooperation with the executive agencies, shall undertake a study to develop a better understanding of alternative means of implementing Federal assistance programs, and to determine the feasibility of developing a comprehensive system of guidance for Federal assistance programs. * * * The report on the study shall include (1) detailed descriptions of the alternative means of implementing Federal assistance programs and of the circumstances in which the use of each appears to be most desirable, (2) detailed descriptions of the basic characteristics and an outline of such comprehensive system of guidance for Federal assistance programs, the development of which may be determined feasible, and (3) recommendations concerning arrangements to proceed with the full development of such comprehensive system of guidance and for such administrative or statutory changes, including changes in the provisions of sections 3 through 7 of this Act, as may be deemed appropriate on the basis of the findings of the study."

During the study, the primary attention of OMB must be on analyses that will contribute to meeting these statutory requirements. In addition, there is an extensive legislative history including recommendations on the content and conduct of the study which have been taken into consideration in this plan. Where possible, prior studies by Congress, executive branch agencies, and others will be used.

The study offers an opportunity to investigate many specific issues and problems in the Federal assistance area called to OMB's attention by State and local officials, the Congress, GAO, executive agency officials and others and to review systematically the proper Federal role in assistance activities. It is consistent with the President's objective and recent actions to simplify Federal assistance programs. A significant number of issues related to the Federal assistance system and reflected in this plan are addressed by the President's September 9, 1977, memoranda on cutting red tape; ongoing Presidential reorganization activities; and recommendations of the Commission on Government Procurement. The results of these and other reform initiatives will be integrated with the study effort as it progresses. The "comprehensive system of guidance" may prove to be an effective way to consolidate the results of these and other government activities into an integrated body of policy.

The study plan includes nine major tasks:

A. Description of existing guidance documents and processes

B. Alternatives for a comprehensive system of guidance for assistance programs

C. Alternative means for implementing Federal assistance programs

D. Analysis of Pub. L. 95-224

E. Equity, fairness, and competition in assistance transactions

F. Federal relationships in research and development

G. Recipient-related issues

H. Additional issues

I. Environment of Federal assistance

Each of these tasks will be performed as separate, but simultaneous investigation and development efforts. Core task groups composed of interested representatives from executive agencies, State and local governments, other recipients, and the public will perform substantial portions of the actual research and analysis. OMB will coordinate, review, and integrate the activities of these task groups. Parties wishing to contribute to or participate in the study are invited to contact Thomas L. Hadd, Intergovernmental Affairs Division, OMB, Room 5217, NEOB, Washington, D.C. 20503, telephone 202-395-5156 and indicate the specific task or subtask of interest. All materials submitted to OMB as a contribution to the study effort will become a part of the public record.

The study is viewed as a developmental as well as an analytical effort. Thus, during the course of the study, agreement on specific issues may be achieved or specific changes in administrative practice found to be both feasible and desirable. It is anticipated in such instances that implementation would begin immediately rather than await submission of the study report. The report would include both discussions of any actions taken and analyses and recommendations for the future.

In general, it is anticipated that draft analysis papers outlining problems, findings, and alternative solutions will be completed sometime in mid-summer 1979 by each of the task groups. To the extent practicable, these papers will be made available for public review and comment. After public and agency review, these analysis papers will be put in final form as appendices to the report to Congress. The report itself will draw heavily on these papers for factual background information and concentrate on OMB's recommendations for future action as required by the Act. OMB will make final determinations on the content of issue and analysis papers to be published.

The Act requires the results of the study to be reported to Congress within two years after the date of enactment or no later than February 3, 1980. While additional follow-on study may be necessary, the two-year statutory requirement is to allow Congress to give timely attention to an executive branch progress report.

II. SCOPE OF STUDY

The various issues to be included in the study are based on the statute itself; its legislative history; the experience of agencies in implementing Sections 4, 5, and 6 of the Act; and the numerous comments received in response to the draft study plan.

The terms "program requirements," "general Federal policy requirements," and "administrative requirements" are used throughout the plan. Program requirements are the terms or conditions of an assistance instrument (such as a grant) that are designed to ensure the purposes of the specific program are achieved. Program requirements are usually based on provisions of program statutes. General Federal policy requirements are developed to implement broad national statutory goals and have cross-cutting applicability to assistance programs. Examples of general Federal policy requirements include protection of the environment, historical preservation, payment of prevailing wages, provisions for the handicapped, and care for laboratory animals. Administrative requirements deal with the normal business processes of applying for, conducting, and terminating an assisted project that are common to all or a wide range of programs. Examples of administrative requirements include standards or standard processes for coordinating proposed projects, determining costs, financial reporting, developing new forms or public reporting plans, using government statistics, audit, and uniform requirements for various aspects of managing grant programs.

The study plan concentrates on issues that apply to all or broad ranges of assistance programs, such as general Federal policy requirements and administrative requirements. Except for a few specific questions, the study will not address program requirements. Nor will it consider the structure of assistance programs or how funds are allocated to them. The entire study relates to the processes of developing and conducting assistance programs and how these processes are guided.

For convenience, the study issues have been arrayed as nine major task elements. It is planned for each of the tasks to produce an apendix to the report to Congress which will summarize the general study findings. The nine tasks follow:

A. *Description of existing guidance documents and processes.* This task is to inventory and describe the existing requirements and guidance for assistance programs.

1. What are the general components of the existing body of guidance. This will include a description of:

a. Major types of statutes that influence assistance programs;

b. Powers of the President and the Executive Branch that influence assistance programs;

c. Varying roles of guidance agencies that are responsible for administering general national policies that affect assistance programs;

d. Range of guidance materials that assistance agencies must follow including statutes of general applicability with no supplementary guidance, Executive Orders, codified regulations and circulars, court rulings, Comptroller General determinations and opinions, instructional materials developed by guidance agencies, and other forms of guidance;

e. The major premises and broad concepts which serve as the basis for the existing body of guidance;

f. Methods of assistance agencies for handling guidance including assignment of responsibilities in large and small agencies, techniques used for staying aware of current guidance, and requirements on to applicants and recipients.

2. What is the full array of administrative requirements for assistance activities? This will include:

a. Inventory of statutes containing generally applicable administrative provisions;

b. Directory of guidance agencies responsible for administering specific statutes;

c. Inventory of guidance materials other than statutes prepared by guidance agencies and others;

d. Description of methods of interpreting, administering, and enforcing guidance by both guidance agencies and assistance agencies.

3. What is the full array of general Federal policy requirements for assistance activities? This will include:

a. Inventory of statutes containing generally applicable Federal policy requirements;

b. Inventory of guidance agencies responsible for administering general Federal policy statutes;

c. Inventory of guidance materials other than statutes prepared by guidance agencies and others;

d. Description of methods of interpreting, administering, and enforcing guidance by both guidance agencies and assistance agencies;

e. Analysis of the effects of common Federal policy themes stated differently in individual program statutes.

4. What is the applicability of government-wide administrative and general Federal policy requirements to various types of assistance programs and how have they been implemented? This will include analytical matrices for a sample of administrative requirements, general Federal policy requirements, and assistance programs by:

a. Types of assistance provided;

b. Various classes of recipients;

c. Types of activities assisted.

B. *Alternatives for a comprehensive system of guidance for assistance programs.* This will concentrate on what a comprehensive system of guidance might be and how it could be developed. All of the eleven questions under this task relate to the basic question of feasibility.

1. What is meant by "a comprehensive system of guidance"?

2. What values might a comprehensive system of guidance serve as seen by Congress, the Executive Office of the President, guidance agencies, assistance agencies, State and local governments, and other recipients?

3. What is the range of major purposes a comprehensive system of guidance might serve and what, if any, conflicts among such purposes may be present?

A new guidance system could:

a. Provide for consolidation of the full range of existing and future administrative and general Federal policy guidance;

b. Codify legal elements into a Federal Assistance Code;

c. Provide educational basis for all involved in assistance activities from basic program design and development to implementation and operation;

d. Assist in the choice of appropriate Federal role for each assistance relationship;

e. Lead to the clarification of Federal and recipient roles;

f. Guide the choice of techniques and legal instruments to support the appropriate Federal role;

g. Permit participation of recipients, both public and private, in determination of roles;

h. Provide policymakers with choices for increasing or decreasing Federal involvement in managing assistance programs;

i. Help define Federal and recipient accountability;

j. Reduce paperwork, uncertainty about Federal requirements, overhead costs, time delays, and red tape.

4. What are the features that might be included in a comprehensive system of guidance? Such features might include provisions for:

a. Greater uniformity of conflict resolution procedures;

b. Improved techniques for ensuring compliance by assisting agencies and recipients;

c. Increased help by guidance agencies to assistance agencies for implementing administrative and general Federal policy requirements;

d. Adaptation of selected procurement system features that might appropriately serve assistance transactions;

e. Increased elements of flexibility, standardization, or both;

f. Capacity for policy research and evaluation.

5. What are the alternatives for administering a new guidance system that assure adequate adherence to established policies?

6. What is the range of assistance activities that should be covered by a new guidance system?

7. What are the major problems of developing a new guidance system? This would include a description of such matters as:

a. Sheer size and scope of the range of subjects to be covered;

b. Varying degrees of interest that may be present for making a new guidance system work;

c. Possible special interests that would not favor a new guidance system;

d. Cost of a new guidance system;

e. Problems arising from the basic Federal Government structure and organization of assistance agencies.

8. How might a new guidance system relate to the internal systems of State and local governments, universities, other recipients?

9. What would be the major problems of implementing a new guidance system? This would consider such issues as organizational assignment of responsibilities, policy consistency and integration, timing of conversion, and cost of conversion.

10. How might a new guidance system serve in the development of new assistance programs?

11. How might a new guidance system be affected by future congressional actions and program legislation?

C. *Alternative means for implementing Federal assistance programs.* This task will examine a number of areas for which additional guidance could be developed.

1. What additional guidance is needed for transactions covered by Sections 4, 5, and 6 of the Act or indicated by agency experience in implementing these sections? This analysis will consider:

a. Meaning of "procurement;"

b. Meaning of "assistance;"

c. Monetary grants, including the concept of a "grant," descriptions of types of grants, key features of grants, normal agency involvement in the assisted activity under grants;

d. monetary cooperative agreements including the concept of a cooperative agreement, descriptions of types or classes of cooperative agreements including financial joint ventures, and opportunities presented by cooperative agreements;

e. The concept of contracts, cooperative agreements, and grants as discrete classes of transactions related to specific purposes in contrast to the concept of a continuum that reflects varying degrees of Federal risk, accountability, and control;

f. Meaning of "substantial involvement in the assisted activity." This would include analysis of involvement in program substance, administrative involvement, general Federal policy requirements that may lead to substantial involvement, substantial involvement in relation to technical assistance, forces leading to the increase or decrease of Federal involvement, relationship of Federal involvement to recipient capacity;

g. Possible criteria for choosing cooperative agreements other than substantial involvement during performance;

h. Special issues related to non-monetary grants and cooperative agreements. This would include such topics as problems of property transfers and joint ventures and undertakings;

i. Types of transactions that have caused agencies the most difficulty in implementing Sections 4, 5, and 6;

j. Distinctions between grants and subsidies;

k. Problems that have led to OMB exceptions;

l. Issues involved in applying the Act to international assistance transactions;

m. Potential of the concept of lump-sum grants;

n. Productivity issues arising from alternative assistance relationships.

2. What additional guidance is needed for types of assistance not covered by Sections 5 and 6? This can include issues related to direct payments, loans and loan guarantees, insurance or assumptions of risk, subsidies, technical assistance.

.3. What alternatives to Federal assistance should be considered as possible ways for achieving national objectives? Such alternatives can include Federal regulation, direct Federal action, federally mandated State regulation, other techniques of Federal leadership.

D. *Analysis of Pub. L. 95-224.* Part of the report to Congress is to include recommendations for improving the Act. The questions included in this task are the ones identified thus far that relate to the Act itself. These are:

1. What were the agencies' early experiences in implementing Sections 4, 5, and 6?

a. What changes in agency practices occured?

b. What transactions previously managed as procurement contracts are now managed as assistance awards, and vice versa?

c. What program management issues arose as a result of the framework decisions required by the statutory framework?

d. How do the transactions of agencies and their programs aggregate?

e. What is the picture of Federal control and involvement shown?

2. What definitions need to be added or clarified in the Act including procurement, assistance, State and local government, others?

3. Are there classes of transactions that are neither procurement nor assistance?

4. Should "substantial involvement during performance" remain the sole criterion for selecting cooperative agreements?

5. What linkages to other statutes are created by the Act's definitions and classifications, and what are the effects of these linkages?

a. How does the term "assistance" relate to the various missions of Federal agencies;

b. How does the description of "grants" relate to general Federal policy requirements?

6. How should programs or transactions for which OMB has provided exceptions be handled over the long run?

7. What should be the future provisions for OMB's exception authority?

E. *Equity, fairness, and competition in assistance transactions.* This task will concentrate on the questions that have been raised about the equity, fairness, and competition related to assistance transactions. Many of the questions will deal with both legal and administrative procedural issues.

1. What should be the policy and practice for general public notification of the agency's intent to fund or provide assistance?

2. What policies should exist for competition, including:

a. General policy on competition,

b. Different types of competition that could be used,

c. Eligibility of different classes of recipients?

3. What purposes are served by com-

petition in the award of assistance intended to stimulate or support recipient activity? How should standards for competition in assistance and procurement activities compare?

4. What are the equity and fairness issues of recipient selection, including:

a. Different selection techniques;

b. Rights of applicants not selected?

5. What issues relate to the choice of particular assistance instruments, such as:

a. Variations of reciprocal rights by classes of relationships;

b. Problems and opportunities that arise from different relationships with recipients of the same class in a single program.

6. What should be the policies and procedures for completion and termination under different classes of assistance relationships?

7. What should be the policies for timely audit of completed transactions and resolutions of audit exceptions?

8. What should be the policies and procedures for due process, including:

a. Uniform administrative and judicial remedies for resolution of disputes at Federal, State, and local levels. Possible use of arbitration;

b. Uniform provisions for debarment and suspension?

9. What issues of equity and fairness relate to third parties?

These would include:

a. Beneficiaries of programs run by recipients;

b. Subgrantees and contractors of recipients

c. Others somehow affected by an assistance transactions but not a party to it;

d. Variations arising from different instruments or degrees of Federal involvement.

10. What equity and fairness issues are related to unanticipated costs of complying with general Federal policy requirements?

F. *Federal relationships in research and development.* The general field of expanding and applying knowledge has presented a series of important questions. These are:

1. What are the effects of using both procurement and assistance transactions to fund basic research, developmental or applied research, and demonstration of established techniques?

a. How does the choice of transaction type relate to agency mission?

b. What are the consequences for both the Federal agencies and the performers of using either a procurement

contract or an assistance instrument?

c. Do inconsistencies result from the "principal purpose of the transaction" test? If so, what is the impact?

2. What issues are present and what generalizations can be made about the use of cooperative agreements and grants for basic research, developmental or applied research, Federal commercialization and technology innovation objectives, demonstration of established techniques?

3. What issues relate to varying degrees of Federal direction and control over research and development?

a. Those related to general Federal policy and administrative requirements;

b. Those related to programmatic or substantive aspects of the work to be performed;

c. Range of views on researcher autonomy vs. Federal direction and control;

d. Cost of varying degrees of Federal direction and control in relation to accomplishment of desired ends.

4. What issues arise from research done by different classes of recipients including:

a. Process of selecting recipients;

b. Degree and form of Federal control?

5. Is there a need for additional policy guidance on the support or stimulation of:

a. Development of new knowledge;

b. Application of new knowledge?

G. *Recipient-related issues.* A number of issues have been identified that are related to particular classes of recipients or recipients in general. These are:

1. What are the particular problems or issues related to the following classes of recipients:

a. For-profit organizations, including:

General eligibility for assistance transactions

Cost sharing

Payment of fees;

b. Non-profit organizations, including:

Distinguishing characteristics

Rationale for preferred treatment;

c. Volunteer service organizations;

d. State governments;

e. Local governments;

f. Indian tribes;

g. Universities;

h. Subgrantees?

2. What can be done to improve the

participation of recipients in the design of programs that affect them? This would include:

a. Executive Order 12044 on Federal rulemaking;

b. Constraints imposed by the Federal Advisory Committee Act;

c. Existing patterns of relationships among functional personnel at different levels of government;

d. The Intergovernmental Cooperation Act and OMB Circular A-85 (consultation with heads of State and local governments in development of Federal regulations) experience.

3. Should there be standards for selecting recipients of formula and block grants?

4. What is the relationship of program procedural requirements to Federal, State, and local funding cycles?

5. What are the limits to the allowable degree of Federal intrusion in State affairs that should be established for:

a. Federal program statutes;

b. Agency authorities for developing program implementation requirements?

6. Should there be special cost provisions for research done by State governments?

7. How should Attachment "O" of OMB Circular A-102 relate to the American Bar Association Model Procurement Code?

8. How can basic agreements between a Federal agency and a recipient or master agreements between a number of agencies and a recipients simplify compliance with administrative and general Federal policy requirements?

9. What policy and operational considerations stem from varying levels of recipient management capacity?

H. *Additional issues.* The questions that follow are ones that do not fit into any of the preceding tasks.

1. Should there be a change in the cost reimbursement policies for technical assistance established by the Intergovernmental Cooperation Act?

2. What cost sharing policies should apply to assistance programs?

3. What is the relationship between a comprehensive system of guidance and the proposed Federal Assistance Paperwork Reduction Act and Small Communities Act?

4. Should there be a policy on Federal efforts to stimulate expanded use of technological innovations? What might it be for:

a. Interactions between Federal agencies,

b. Interactions between the Federal Government and other parties,

c. Identifying appropriate management methods and uses for cooperative agreements?

5. Should special preference and allocation provisions of the procurement system (e.g., small business, minority business, and Indian preference) be extended to assistance programs?

6. What are the degrees of applicability or suitability of existing administrative standards to different types of grants and cooperative agreements with different types of recipients?

I. *Environment of Federal assistance.* This task is to describe the environment in which a comprehensive system of guidance for assistance programs must operate. Its purpose is to make explicit the array of different and often competing values that are major influences in the development of Federal assistance programs and the means by which they are administered. It will serve as a supportive analysis for the other study tasks.

1. How do assistance programs come into being? This will include an analysis of:

a. Political process of program development;

b. Variations in perceptions of goals, objectives, and needs for the program;

c. Customary lack of total need analysis or total cost estimation for general policy requirements as well as substantive assistance programs;

d. Relatively narrow scope and purpose of most assistance programs;

e. Array of choices including direct Federal action, direct assistance to beneficiaries, or use of intermediaries;

f. Relationship of assistance to regulatory actions;

g. Frequent changes in concepts and perceptions over the life of a program.

2. What are the different concepts of Federal and recipient accountability, including fiscal or resource stewardship, program accountability (ends and results), process accountability (how achieved)?

3. What are other competing concepts of assistance system design? This will include an analysis of such basic values as:

a. General redistribution of resources by the Federal Government vs. the stimulation or support of specific objectives;

b. Pluralism or the strong participation of all parties as partners vs. Federal dominance;

c. Recipient operational autonomy vs. Federal accountability;

d. Emphasis on fairness for all parties vs. Federal convenience;

e. Desire for management flexibility vs. desire for uniformity and standardization;

f. Emphasis on response to recipient determined needs vs. federally specified goals, activities, and procedures.

VELMA N. BALDWIN,
Assistant to the Director for Administration, Office of Management and Budget.

[FR Doc. 79-619; Filed 1-5-79; 8:45 am]

APPENDIX D.

DRAFT EXECUTIVE SUMMARY OF THE OMB STUDY OF THE FEDERAL ASSISTANCE SYSTEM MANDATED BY P.L. 224 FEBRUARY 25, 1980.

This report on improving the management of federal assistance is the result of a two-year study by the Office of Management and Budget as required by the Federal Grant and Cooperative Agreement Act (P.L. 95-224). It describes actions the Administration is taking and includes recommendations to Congress. The findings and recommendations in the report represent a broad agreement among the federal agencies, assistance recipients, and other informed observers on important changes that are needed in federal assistance management. The actions proposed in the report complement and extend reform initiative of this Administration in a number or areas, including paperwork and red-tape reduction, financial management and regulatory reform.

Federal Assistance Programs Today

Over half the federal budget is used to fund assistance programs and activities. *Assistance takes such diverse forms as direct payment, grants, cooperative agreements, subsidies, loans, loan guarantees, insurance, services, information, and property donations. While federal assistance has been used to meet national needs for nearly two centuries, most of the growth has occurred in the last two decades. Six trends characterize the changing environment of federal assistance.

1. New programs have been developed to deal with extremely complex and interrelated problems such as saving cities, reducing unemployment and promoting economic development. The administration of each of these programs requires new and highly specialized technical knowledge. This necessary specialization, however, has made it increasingly difficult to manage program interactions, as for example, when environmental programs impact efforts under economic development and employment programs.

2. Many units of state and local government have consolidated functions into organizations such as human resource agencies and departments of economic development. These organizations, along with universities and some other recipients, now receive assistance from a number of federal sources. On the federal side, however, Congress and the agencies think and act primarily in terms of single programs with little regard for the affects of their uncoordinated actions on multi-source recipients.

3. An increasing number of national socio-economic objectives (such as preventing discrimination, protecting the environment, and providing for the handicapped) are imposed as general conditions for receiving assistance. The result is that many programs now have multiple and sometimes conflicting objectives.

---

* The F.Y. 1981 Budget shows that 58% of the Budget is used for direct benefit payments for individuals and grants to states and localities. There are also other assistance categories.

4. The number and types of assistance recipients has grown. An increasing number of small governments, non-profit organizations, and others have become participants. Grants and cooperative agreements are increasingly used to fund activities in the private sector. Many smaller units lack the resources and capacity to meet present assistance requirements and standards, while for-profit organizations are not familiar with the newer federal relationships.

5.With the increasing range of program purposes and broader variations in recipient capacities, has come an ever growing number of types of grants and other forms of assistance. Some are entitlements while others must be competed for. Some are to support the customary activities of recipients while others are to stimulate new activities. Some require federal approval of extensive plans, while others are accompanied by close, on-site monitoring. As a result, there is growing confusion over rights, responsibilities, and accountability.

6. There is an increasing frequency of assistance related disputes and a whole new body of assistance law is being developed by the courts. These disputes between federal agencies and recipients disrupt what should be close working relationships for accomplishing national objectives.

These six trends parallel and are directly related to the growing complexity in society, but they have led to an altogether higher order of complexity for assistance management by federal agencies and recipients than has ever existed before.

Individually, most assistance programs are working. Roads and homes are being built. Services are being provided and environmental progress is being made. Research is being conducted on a broad front. The basic challenge is to find better ways of managing or coping with the new complexity without disrupting the real accomplishments of federal assistance.

Study Findings

The Federal Grant and Cooperative Agreement Act required OMB to study "the feasibility of developing a comprehensive system of guidance for federal assistance programs." As a result of the study, OMB has concluded that what is needed is a more structured process for management of general assistance policies, including greater central leadership. This leadership must stress the use of talents throughout the government in a coordinative and cooperative manner. Initial efforts should be concentrated on the forms of assistance, that are the source of the greatest immediate problems. Thus, early work will deal primarily with crosscutting policies that apply to grants and cooperative agreements. They include such national policies as avoiding discrimination, protectng the environment, and providing for the handicapped. They also include administrative policies such as grant standards and financial management requirements. The study identified 59 such policies.

The principal finding of the study can be listed under three categories—organizational, process, and conflict resolution.

1. Organizational. More attention must be paid to the interaction of the requirements for assistance programs and the government-wide policies that

guide them. This will require organizational changes in the Congress, the Executive Office of the President, and the departments and other executive agencies that administer assistance programs. These changes are to provide a network for assistance policy development, implementation, evaluation, and oversight to coordinate the diffused activities of today. There has been important progress in developing administrative standards for some types of assistance and this work must continue for areas where standards are appropriate. But the new need is for more dynamic managerial interaction.

2. Process. In addition to the organizational changes, there must be new processes for anticipating the impacts of proposed policy changes, obtaining the necessary coordination of policy implementation, and detecting when improvements in policies or implementing practices need to be made. The primary responsibilities for administering assistance programs must continue to be vested in the department and other executive agencies. In addition, responsibilities for government-wide regulations and guidelines for many general assistance policies must continue to be assigned to designated guidance agencies. This is because of the highly technical nature of policies such as environmental protection assigned to CEQ and recipient personnel policies assigned to OPM. The new process must meet the needs of agencies responsible for administering assistance programs and those responsible for the crosscutting policies. There must be far more cooperation and coordination, both among the federal agencies, and between agencies and recipients, in the development and implementation of general assistance policies. Although continuing specialization is required, the current practices of independent action must be tempered by actions to reduce the level of unnecessary complexity.

3. Conflict Resolution. Techniques and processes must be developed for the fair, speedy, and economical resolution of conflicts and problems that occur over assistance policies and requirements. These processes must operate on a geographically and organizationally decentralized basis as much as possible. They must be capable of leading to the most workable solutions for unavoidable conflicts between competing but legitimate objectives and requirements. Central agency involvement in these processes should be limited to major policy conflicts.

Recommendations to Congress

Throughout this study, both the agencies and recipients have repeatedly pointed to the role of Congress in establishing both the statutory requirements for assistance programs and the general policies that guide them. The study has identified 59 general federal policy and administrative requirements that apply to assistance programs, most of which are based in statute.

These include such policies as prevention of discrimination, protection of endangered species, historic preservation, and care for animals used in research. They also include administrative requirements such as provisions for audits and recipient procurement under grants. In addition, Congress has included different provisions in numerous program statutes (as for citizen participation) which may be impossible for recipients operating under more than one of these programs to meet.

While the existing committee structure is well suited to meeting the needs of individual programs, there is no Congressional focal point for considering the complex interaction of general policies on assistance programs.

Proposed Legislative Actions

1. A major source of complexity in federal assistance management is the continuing expansion in the number of narrow, categorical assistance programs. There is a need to establish a regularized process by which the President can propose program consolidations and proceed with them unless Congress objects. The Administration has supported such legislation and strongly urges its passage.

In addition there must be processes for projecting the impacts of proposed policy changes, obtaining the necessary coordination of policy implementation, and detecting when improvement in policy or implementing practices needs to be made. As discussed below, much can be done within the Executive Branch to meet the growing need for improved assistance management. OMB is willing to undertake the work necessary, but it should have the necessary tools in the form of statutory authorities. While much of the work can be started under existing authorities, there should be clear statutory authority for OMB to:

2. Direct the executive departments and agencies to establish clear points of responsibility for coordinated implementation of assistance policy. While some departments have taken such steps, many have not, and government-wide progress toward improving assistance management is not possible without a network of officials who can speak for their departments or agencies and coordinate internal policy activities and implementing actions.

3. Establish a government-wide process for the development, implementation, and evaluation of asssistance policies. The process must involve both agencies responsible for administering assistance programs, and those with crosscutting policy responsibilities. This process, while not requiring additional resources, should greatly increase coordination and cooperation both among the agencies and with recipients. The legislation should re-emphasize the existing authority of the President to designate agencies to be responsible for development of government-wide regulations and guidelines for implementing general assistance policies. OMB should have the authority to review and approve such regulations and guidelines prior to issuance by the designated agencies.

4. Temporarily suspend the operation of regulations or guidelines for implementing a general assistance policy statute should it become evident that unless suspended, serious, unanticipated disruption will result. Any suspension actions would be reported to Congress if the conflict is a direct result of statute.

5. Issue regulations for achieving uniform implementation of the Federal Grant and Cooperative Agreement Act and continue to except programs or transactions from the Act's provisions.

Major Actions Being Taken by
the Executive Branch

The recommended congressional actions are important steps toward dealing with the complexity of modern assistance management. But there is much the Executive Branch can begin to do on its own. Some of the major actions that are being taken or are planned include:

Presidential Action

1. Designation of OMB by Presidential directive as the assistance policy focal point in the Executive Branch. This directive will instruct OMB to:

- Make formal arrangements with the agencies and recipients for consultation on assistance policy matters.
- Establish priorities for evaluation and improvement of specific assistance policies.
- Establish a new process for the development, implementation and evaluation of government-wide assistance policies.
- Establish policies and processes for the resolution of disputes among the agencies and with recipients.

In addition, it will direct all executive departments and agencies to:

- Identify an official responsible for representing the agency's position on assistance policy issues and ensuring agency compliance with approved government-wide policies.
- Participate fully in the new process for developing, implementing, and evaluating government-wide policies.
- Comply with the new policies and procedures for resolving disputes.

Actions by OMB

2. The OMB Associate Director for Management and Regulatory Policy has been designated as the policy official responsible for coordinating assistance policy among all agencies and within OMB.

3. An Assistance Policy Branch has been established to conduct policy reviews and support the Associate Director's coordinative efforts.

4. An interagency assistance policy group will be established to participate in the evaluation and improvement of assistance management policies and to suggest priority areas of activity to OMB. In addition, closer working arrangements will be established with the Advisory Commission on Intergovernmental Relations on policy evaluation and development. Improved access of all major recipient groups to the policy process will be achieved through periodic meetings convened in cooperation with ACIR. All three steps are to insure a continuing flow of advice and information on improving assistance management.

5. A policy will be developed for guiding the management of other assistance policies to:

- Specify the process for developing, implementing and evaluating government-wide assistance policies.

- Provide for OMB review and clearance of government-wide assistance policy regulations and guidelines prior to issuance on an exception basis.
- Establish assistance management performance standards for all agencies to meet in relation to the new guidance process.
- Improve analysis of impacts of proposed general assistance policies.

6. A government-wide policy will be developed to require agencies to establish fair, speedy, and economical processes for resolving recipient disputes. In addition, OMB will evaluate new processes for decentralized conflict resolution and promote system improvements as appropriate.

7. Improved guidance for implementing the Federal Grant and Cooperative Agreement Act will be developed, with particular emphasis on alternative relationships (e.g. procurement contracts, grants, and cooperative agreements) in:
- Stimulation and support of research and development.
- Provision of assistance to the general public through state or local governments and other classes of intermediary recipients.

8. Additional policies will be developed for:
- Proper uses of competition in awarding assistance that are distinct from procurement competition.
- Payment of fees and profits under grant-type assistance.
- Policies for grants and cooperative agreements with for-profit organizations.

9. Arrangements will be made to improve information on the rules and availability of assistance programs and awards.

10. Policy analyses will be conducted with particular emphasis on:
- Developing clearer understanding of different types of assistance relationships with initial concentration on the different forms of grants and cooperative agreements
- Clarifying the language used in assistance statutes and implementing guidance.
- Clarifying the different forms and degrees of recipient accountability.
- Certification of the management systems of major recipients as meeting federal policy requirements (e.g. procurement, audit, and planning).

11. Issues related to existing OMB assistance policies raised during the study will be considered in the ongoing policy evaluation process. These include:
- Federal financial management requirements for small recipients.

- Problems of recipients in receiving fair reimbursement of indirect costs.
- Multiple and cross-agency audits for recipients.
- Allowance of interest as an element of assistance cost.
- Provisions for termination, suspension, and debarment or recipients.

All of these actions will complement other ongoing OMB activities.

Actions by the Agencies

12. Work already under way by the Office of Personnel Mangement and major agencies to develop assistance personnel and materials for education and training in the area of assistance management will be continued.

13. After a priority schedule has been developed by OMB with the advice of interagency assistance policy group, the agencies will conduct joint reviews of existing assistance policies and recommend improvements.

The Anticipated Results

The actions recommended to Congress and those planned for the Executive Branch have been developed with care to protect the interests of recipients and to avoid disrupting the operation of vital assistance programs. They are designed to meet widely diverse needs of recipients and highly specialized objectives of many programs. Inherent is the recognition that hundreds of programs serving tens of thousands of recipients through hundreds of thousands of transactions lead to issues that can only be resolved on a decentralized basis. But many of these issues revolve around a relatively small number of government-wide policies.

Thus these recommendations stress processes. Some processes are to prevent or resolve conflicts at the policy level. Others are to speed resolution of unavoidable conflicts at the recipient level. Much stress is placed on improved cooperation and coordination, both among agencies and with recipients. Strong emphasis is placed on clarifying relationships and expectations.

Although closely interrelated, these actions are not presented as an ultimate solution and experience may dictate some adjustment over time. They represent, however, the best thinking of the largest number of informed participants and observers of the assistance process from around the country that have ever pooled their ideas for improving the management of federal assistance.

INDEX